OFF WHITENESS

OFF WHITENESS

Place, Blood, and Tradition
in Post-Reconstruction Southern Literature

Izabela Hopkins

The University of Tennessee Press / Knoxville

Copyright © 2020 by The University of Tennessee Press / Knoxville.
All Rights Reserved. Manufactured in the United States of America.
First Edition.

Library of Congress Cataloging-in-Publication Data

Names: Hopkins, Izabela, author.
Title: Off whiteness : place, blood, and tradition in post-reconstruction Southern literature / Izabela Hopkins.
Description: First edition. | Knoxville : The University of Tennessee Press, 2020. | Includes bibliographical references and index. | Summary: "This book examines the concept of whiteness as imagined by four Southern writers of the post-Reconstruction period: Thomas Nelson Page, Ellen Glasgow, Charles Waddell Chesnutt, and Alice Dunbar-Nelson. Izabela Hopkins argues that the unique narrative positions of these writers, offering their perspectives from both sides of the color line, allow for an objective scrutiny of the role of place and heritage in conceptions of Southern whiteness. By examining these authors, the project presents an alternate interpretation of Southern whiteness and demonstrates that reconstructions of whiteness need not be reduced to outward manifestations of color—white or black—but rather purposefully explore the ambivalence existing in the US South of the early twentieth century"—Provided by publisher.
Identifiers: LCCN 2020023685 (print) | LCCN 2020023686 (ebook) | ISBN 9781621905813 (hardcover) | ISBN 9781621905820 (pdf)
Subjects: LCSH: American literature—Southern States—History and criticism. | Whites in literature. | American literature—African American authors. | American literature—19th century—History and criticism. | Southern States—In literature. | Southern States—Intellectual life.
Classification: LCC PS261 .H675 2020 (print) | LCC PS261 (ebook) | DDC 810.9/975—dc23
LC record available at https://lccn.loc.gov/2020023685
LC ebook record available at https://lccn.loc.gov/2020023686

TO MY PARENTS

CONTENTS

Acknowledgments
ix

Introduction. In the Wilderness, or Encounters with Whiteness
1

PART ONE
PASSING PLACE—IMAGINED OR REAL

ONE
Through a Stranger's Eyes: Nature, Place, and Whiteness in Thomas Nelson Page
19

TWO
Ellen Glasgow and the Plight of Retrospection
41

THREE
The Inevitability of Passing in Charles Waddell Chesnutt and Alice Dunbar-Nelson
57

PART TWO
A TOUCH OF THE TAR BRUSH, OR THE AMBIVALENCE OF WHITENESS

FOUR
Living with Specters in Thomas Nelson Page
79

FIVE
Ellen Glasgow and the Ambivalence of Ideals
97

SIX
Debunking the Ideal in Charles Waddell Chesnutt
119

PART THREE
MONSTER MASH, OR A PALER SHADE OF WHITE

SEVEN
Thomas Nelson Page and the Burden of Heritage
137

EIGHT
Ellen Glasgow's Fictions of Verisimilitude
153

NINE
"There Ain't No Going Back":
The Work of Charles Waddell Chesnutt
177

Epilogue. Southern Heroes and Symbols
195

Notes
205

Bibliography
235

Index
253

ACKNOWLEDGMENTS

I am grateful and indebted to Professor David Roberts (Birmingham City University), who first encouraged me to publish my work, and for his invaluable support and advice over the years. I have benefited from Doctor Anthony Mellors's scholarly expertise as well as his thought-provoking conversations. My special thanks and gratitude go to my friends Dee and Brian Gough, who have been subjected to, and stoically endured, a lot of whiteness and the South.

I am especially grateful to acquisitions editor Thomas Wells for seeing merit in the project and his stalwart support throughout, and to Jon Boggs for his invaluable advice and assistance. Annalisa Zox-Weaver meticulously edited the manuscript. I feel privileged to have this work published by the University of Tennessee Press.

OFF WHITENESS

INTRODUCTION
In the Wilderness, or Encounters with Whiteness

A SOUTHERN VARIETY OF WHITENESS

Mention whiteness and the South in the same breath and the conversation inevitably veers off toward color, but what if more were at stake? What if, instead of color, we should speak of conditions of whiteness that are not skin-deep? A while ago, I was struck by the title of a recent American comedy-drama series called *Hart of Dixie* (2011–2015). "Hart," here, is immediately recognizable as a pun. It relies on the parallel between the symbolism of "heart" and the historical and regional connotations of Dixie, while promising authenticity and perhaps an insight into the essence of Southerness. Buried beneath the simple association between the common surname Hart and "heart," which suggests that the central character will indeed be central and emotionally rich, lies the heraldic figure of the white hart, a mythical symbol of sanctified beauty, purity, and innocence.[1] The show's director adopts this symbolism to build an alternative view of the South, the view that has largely remained obscured by the infamy of slavery. The story is set in the fictional town of Bluebell, Alabama, which in this narrative has come a long way since the Birmingham riot of the 1960s, and equality now reigns supreme. The town boasts a black mayor, Lavon Hayes, who lives in the grandest house, its architecture harking back to the old plantation days. Burt Reynolds, his female pet alligator, roams freely about the place, frightening the occasional visitor, while the locals have long become accustomed to the eccentricity and grown immune. Bluebell oozes quaintness and picturesqueness amply spiced up by a reverence for time-honored traditions. Baking contests and pageants galore, and the sorority of waspish belles still meets as it did in the days of yore to plot good deeds and charitable enterprises—and gossip. In this cradle of political correctness, blacks and whites rub shoulders amiably. Whatever social divisions there may be are accentuated subtly and encoded in individual occupations, behavior, and standards and, largely, left to the viewer to observe and decode.

The sun never sets on Bluebell, and the viewer gradually learns its endearing quirks, which inadvertently become symbolic of the South, along with the show's heroine, Dr. Zoe Hart, freshly arrived from New York City. The director employs the old and tested device of introducing the region from a stranger's perspective, which works as well here as it did in nineteenth-century fiction. Ambitious, driven, and erratic, Zoe is the product of a brief encounter between a successful, career-driven Northerner and a Southern gentleman doctor, who leaves Zoe a share in his practice. If this plot sounds familiar, that is because it is a modern take on a well-worn nineteenth-century literary convention. Zoe initially signs up for life in the South for a brief period, having arrived at a crossroads in her career, and she finds the place as quaint and alien as it is presented to the audience. Yet her prejudice gradually melts away, and she becomes beguiled by the sense of place. Now she is the eponymous Hart of Dixie: the South triumphs again!

The diegesis functions as a narrative of reconciliation in which a half-Northerner marries a Southerner, and they live happily ever after. Such a scenario makes it all too tempting and easy to dismiss *Hart of Dixie* as an inaccurate and utopian portrayal of the South, the result of the director's immoderation in the exercise of poetic license or an impeccably liberal and somewhat white appropriation of American history. But that would be a mistake, for in fact the show, despite all its supernumerary quaintness or because of it, typifies the ambiguity that has characterized portrayals of the South. The title itself signals this ambiguity by leaving open the question of what lies at the *heart* of Dixie. The very absence of the race question in *Hart of Dixie* marks it as an antithesis to films such as D. W. Griffith's paean to racist values, *The Birth of a Nation* (1915), or the more recent critique of race relations in the South, in *The Help* (2011). It is more akin to Hollywood's moonlight and magnolias visions of the region immortalized in Margaret Mitchell's *Gone with the Wind* or the romanticized adaptation of Joel Chandler Harris's stories in *Song of the South* (1946). These films, and many more, peddle images of the region as racist, other, exotic, comically backward, yet also a reassuring repository of solid family values based on firmly established traditions and self-reliance. The South has become the locus of a mythology with an apparently universal allure. This mythology is essentially a "white mythology," which is to say that it is born out of the unique sociocultural legacy of the South and revolves around conceptions of whiteness; of what it means to be white or off white. Both white and off white suggest an affinity; for, in terms of color, they are not polar opposites. Yet, despite their close linguistic affiliation, the term off white points to an ambivalence at the heart of whiteness, the ambivalence that can only stem from the existence of enduring criteria that reach beyond the visibility of color. Writers such as Ellen Glasgow, Charles Waddell Chesnutt, Alice Dunbar-Nelson, Thomas Nelson Page, and later William Faulkner, Robert Penn Warren, Erskine Caldwell, and Flannery O'Connor, among many notable Southern writers, typify the ambivalence of such designations by examining the allure of this legacy and its impact on the construction of Southern identity and whiteness.[2]

The question of whiteness is far from absent from *Hart of Dixie*, despite its seeming color blindness. Rather, the show offers an alternative narrative to the standard fare of binary classifications, placing the black mayor among the whitest inhabitants of the town. This counter-narrative is possible because it posits historical repeatability at the center of whiteness, which relies on the replication of social and cultural standards rather than color. Because of the blighted history of the South and its race relations, the presence of white in whiteness lends itself naturally to conflations of whiteness with the visibility of skin color, race, and white supremacy. Toni Morrison's seminal *Playing in the Dark: Whiteness and the Literary Imagination* examines how the presence of the black man underpins the construction of the hallmark American hero as white and superior. Yet, the words of Roxana, a manumitted white slave and one of the protagonists of Mark Twain's *Pudd'nhead Wilson*, point to a more elusive and illusive aspect of whiteness: "'Yah-yah-yah jes' listen to dat! If I's imitation, what is you? Bofe of us is imitation *white* —dat's what we is—en pow'full good imitation, too—Yah-yah-yah!—we don't mount to noth'n as imitation *niggers*'." Roxana separates the visibility of white from being white and identifies imitation as the *modus operandi* of whiteness.[3]

To admit that imitation sustains the propagation of whiteness is to recognize the significance of the baggage of historic consciousness that the first settlers carried, a consciousness based on the reverence for birth and rank, and which predated the establishment of chattel slavery. It was also a vision built on aspiration for social betterment which, in time, came to rely on the replication of preconceived ideals in the lifeworld. Because this alternative narrative of whiteness evolved in response to a conviction of historic legacy, it could exist independently of the visibility of blackness. What is certain about whiteness is that it plays with visibility and resists monochromic classifications. When it comes to the discourse of whiteness, to borrow from Shakespeare, "nothing is/But what is not."[4] Roxana is fully aware of this antagonism, which permits her to occupy an irreconcilably undecidable position of being, simultaneously, white and non-white—the conundrum of being what she is not. And this undecidability lies at the heart of whiteness; it forms its puzzle for which the notions of white supremacy or race cannot fully account.[5]

Yet, this ambivalence of whiteness does not disturb the ease with which black and white are yoked in a dichotomous marriage, the marriage that has led to commonplace assumptions in contemporary cultural theory that "whiteness requires blackness to define itself." The urge to explain whiteness in relation to the exploitation and subjugation of the racial other is particularly prevalent in contexts marked by Western expansionist ambitions such as that of the United States. The existence of chattel slavery was a contentious topic in nineteenth-century America, a subject heatedly debated between the North and the South, not because of its inherent iniquity and absurdity, but for different economic and political reasons aimed at promoting the interests of the two regions.[6] Indefensible and incomprehensible by modern standards, chattel slavery was defensible, though not unanimously, in nineteenth-century Southern states. It inspired impassioned declarations like that of John C. Calhoun, who, speaking for the whole region, thundered before the Senate in 1837 that "we of the South will not, cannot, surrender our institutions."[7] It was, however, the association of slavery and its ugly offspring, servitude, bondage, lack of agency and personhood, all disseminated through minstrel shows, black figure advertising, and the spectacle of lynching, that spurred on the genesis of a feeble notion of white privilege and homogeneity. Yet, these outgrowths of slavery as criteria for the conception of whiteness prove inadequate insofar as they rely on the black body, transmogrifying it into a strange fruit for consumption through disempowerment and castration, all the while dispensing with the actuality of the black body.[8]

Calhoun's impassioned defense of "our institutions" suggests that there was more to the South than chattel slavery. After all, Southerners, first and foremost, prided themselves on their aristocratic genealogy. The popularity accorded to Sir Walter Scott's heroes in the region had nothing to do with their status as slave owners, but with the values of heroic courage, chivalry, and honor they internalized—in short, the values associated with nobility pre-ordained by virtue of birth and place. To speak of white pride, however ephemeral and spurious, as a direct corollary of slavery is to overlook the troubling fact that the first settlers arrived in the New World equipped with the concept of bond servitude that had long been practiced in England and that white indenture predated and later existed alongside chattel slavery. Those subjected to bond servitude were the poor and landless, laborers and the Irish under the English occupation of their country. Immigration did not materially improve their fortunes and, in the words of Marquis de Chastellux, who visited Virginia in 1782, the poor European Americans had "little but their complexion to console them." Two centuries later, the benefits of this white privilege were still scarce in evidence, and Ellen Glasgow, reminiscing about her childhood in the South, was able to observe that "'the poor whites' had nothing but the freedom of malnutrition." Although white, as a skin color, began to symbolize privilege and freedom, it was certainly not synonymous with whiteness that plays out against social, cultural, and historical expectations and proscriptions.[9]

To lock whiteness into the black and white dichotomy reduces the complexity of the construct, or what Mike Hill terms its "epistemological stickiness and ontological wiggling." And if Benjamin Franklin's classification is to be trusted, it would also be a perilous undertaking, as one would be hard pressed to find a white person, and not only in America. Writing in 1751, Franklin declares: "All Africa is black or tawny; . . . America (exclusive of the newcomers) wholly so. And in Europe, the Spaniards, Italians, French, Russians, and Swedes are generally of what we call a swarthy complexion; as are the Germans also, the Saxons only excepted, who, with the English, make the principal body of white people on the face of the earth." With one stroke of the pen, Franklin tars most European nations with the same brush, but his classification of the Saxon and English as white foregrounds the veneration of the Anglo-Saxon heritage in the nineteenth century—the heritage that became pivotal to constructions of whiteness. If anything, Franklin's taxonomy points to a symbolic definition of whiteness that moves beyond the corporeality of the body and suggests a divide between whiteness proper and the visibility of white. Writing a century later, Herman Melville was aware of this propensity of whiteness toward the symbolic. In *Moby-Dick*, he wrestles with the proliferation of its significations that vacillate from innocence, mourning, and blankness to alterity, finally conceding that "not yet have we solved the incantation of this whiteness and learned why it appeals with such power to the soul." The success of Melville's effort, and also his failure, lies in the identification of the arbitrariness of whiteness, which forces him to leave the question unresolved.[10]

Contemporary definitions of whiteness reflect Melville's vacillations and cautiously proceed to present a case for it as a cultural construct and practice privileging those with white skin that is subject to fluctuating currents of historical, regional and political affinities, and racial politics of identity. Linking whiteness to white skin and, consequently, physical appearance, conveys a sense of corporeality that does not sit comfortably alongside designations of whiteness "as a system of privilege." On the contrary, the whiteness of Franklin's or Melville's imagining reaches beyond the immediate corporeality and into the realm of the symbolic. For this mechanism to work, the subject will have to identify himself as being present in the world in relation to others before his desire for whiteness, based on the recognition of the "system of privilege" that operates in it, can be formulated. Speaking of the formation of identity, Judith Butler concludes that it depends on the focus of the subject's desire. This formulation makes possible the equation of the desire for whiteness with a desire for privilege. Divorcing whiteness from the corporeality of white as an identity leaves intact its socio-cultural and historical constructedness, but disrupts the notion of its homogeneity and renders it place and time specific.[11]

In its desire for privilege, the story of whiteness is as old as the story of mankind and begins with what Alexandre Kojève, following Hegel, called the first fight for recognition that produced a master and a slave, and without which there would be no man and no history. Kojève calls this history a "universal history," which he sees as a conceptual whole that conceals the existence of discrete histories formulated in response to specific desires.[12] This seeming wholeness of universal history encodes a split between a symbolic totality consigned to the abstract and actuality. Taken as a concept, whiteness resembles Kojève's "universal history" insofar as it can only operate in the realm of the conceptual and consists in a struggle for privilege and attendant recognition. This über whiteness, which is only accessible as a concept, calls into being disparate whitenesses, always internally differentiated, contingent, relational, and heterogeneous.

Any stratification of society relies on its subjects' recognizing their position within an established order. This act of subjective differentiation and reaffirmation is predetermined by social, political, cultural, and historical forces not only unique to but also dominant in a given place. These variations within whiteness, or "shades of whiteness," indicate the existence of a prescribed decorum that guarantees acceptance within its fold or spells banishment.[13] The Irish in nineteenth-century America did not earn the label of "degraded and savage people" as a punishment for their lack of visible whiteness—that was beyond doubt. Their only flaw was their Catholicism, which went against the values of American Protestantism and, thus, against a norm of recognized whiteness. Franklin recounts a similar case of metaphorical shellacking in his *Autobiography* that predates the "blackening" of the Irish by about a century. This time the objects of shellacking are the Quakers, who constituted the majority of the governing Assembly in Philadelphia, and whose religious convictions frequently placed them at odds with the governor. Following an altercation with the Assembly, Franklin reports, the governor was asked why he had not expelled the Quakers from the governing body. Franklin interposes, answering on the governor's behalf: "The governor, says I, has not yet blacked them enough." It was not for lack of trying. Indeed, Franklin observes that the governor "had labored hard to blacken the Assembly in all his messages but they wiped off his coloring as fast as he laid it on and placed it in return, thick upon his own face." And, for fear of being "negrified himself," the governor resigned from office. In the anecdote, Franklin justifies the blackening of the Quakers and the Irish on the grounds of religious difference. What these examples reaffirm is that whiteness transcends color and that being identified or identifiable as white, is not analogous to holding a claim to whiteness. When metaphorical shellacking can be conducted with impunity, the optics become null and void.[14]

The threat of metaphorical shellacking, of being off white, forms a fulcrum on which religion pivots, and Christianity is no exception. In the Western tradition, Christianity has furnished enduring ideals in the figures of Christ and the Virgin Mary who, Richard Dyer argues, embody whiteness proper. The epitome of white femininity is associated with such qualities as "passivity, expectancy, receptivity," "motherhood," "purity," "cleanliness," and "virginity." The masculine model follows the paradigm of Christ and possesses a duality of nature, where the spiritual and the human wrestle for primacy, which leads to the concept of suffering as emblematic of "spiritual and physical striving." Valerie Babb reworks this list by adding "sexual restraint" in men, mirrored by the asexuality and weakness of women—attributes that not only resonate with Christian ideals, but are also, in social and cultural terms, predominantly associated with the upper classes. It is not a coincidence that these are the very ideals that Scott, writing in nineteenth-century Scotland, in *Ivanhoe*, attributes to Anglo-Saxons, but a result of a long-cultivated perception.[15] In nostalgic echoes, they reverberate down through the pages of history back to courtly love and chivalry, implicitly suggesting that nobility, chastity, or restraint have little to do with mundane reality.[16]

Yoking whiteness, the upper classes, and privilege does not sit easily with religion that postulates the rights of the poor and the downtrodden. Yet, this discrepancy becomes indispensable when it comes to perpetuating and reconstructing whiteness, and is something that Christianity endorses through its insistence on a split between the mind and body—the latter perceived as inferior, a repository of sin or conducive to sin. The presence of Christ and the Virgin Mary is reificatory in that it offers a promise of a truth founded upon the assumption of inherent, irreducible, and transcendent values, the attainment of which culminates in whiteness proper.[17] Yet, the incorporeality of the figures of Christ and the Virgin Mary as paradigms of whiteness proper renders the gap between biblical antecedents and earthly aspirants unbridgeable, engendering difference in its wake. This scenario both spells the death of whiteness because it marks its unattainability and perpetuates its discourse, the striving for the attainment of the elusive ideal.[18]

Not only biblical antecedents are crucial to creating and maintaining a sense of continuity and whiteness. The South imported from Europe and adopted what Frederick Turner terms a parental model of kinship, which allocated ancestry pride of place. Heredity, history, breeding, blood, and the like became laden with meaning, frequently harking back to the old continent, and inextricable from the Southern lexicon of whiteness. It was not a question of privilege belonging by default to those with white skin; rather, it became the question of the foundation on which such privilege rested, of irreducible gradation underlying superficial homogeneity. The European ancestors to be proud of were those of the blue blood variety; their Southern progeny in the male line was the aristocratic planter. Amply endowed with such lofty qualities as culturation, civility, chivalrous to his equals but equally capable of benevolence and kindness to those deemed less worthy, he ruled supreme on his inherited acres. While the "unworthy" may be recipients of the aristocratic benevolence, they cannot, by virtue of being unequal, inspire chivalry. Inseparable and integral to the construct of the aristocratic planter is his female counterpart, the Southern belle.[19] Cast in the mold of a medieval lady, she acts as the receptacle of qualities that inspire chivalry, namely: chastity, piousness, purity, and asexuality. If, like Dyer, one adds suffering to the mixture, the Southern belle becomes a hybrid creation, a composite of the medieval lady presiding over a court of love, and the Virgin Mary. As reconstructions of such attributes, the benevolent planter and Southern belle transform into embodiments of whiteness, unique to the region. The idea of the Southern whiteness they epitomize owes as much to Christianity as it does to the veneration of heredity, both in a symbolic and material sense. These discrete characteristics of Southern whiteness embodied by such figures acquired a new significance during the post-Reconstruction era, when the abolition of slavery combined with harsh post-war realities effectively re-inscribed the relationship between land and its inhabitants as well as the region and the newly reunited country. And it was precisely the harshness of the newly altered political climate that proved conducive to the glorification of the past and reimagination of Southern whiteness, at the heart of which lay phantasmagoric historic continuity and mimetic reproduction.

FAVORABLE CLIMATES

Vital to preserving a sense of historic continuity is the hereditary possession of land. Allen Tate, David Landis Barnhill, and Patrick D. Murphy are among those who observe the symbiotic relationship between culture, history, and land, whereby each exerts influence on shaping perceptions of the other.[20] This idea of bipolarity, of irreconcilable difference engendered by the natural environment, found a fertile ground in nineteenth-century United States and led to the development of the concepts of the North and South as distinct places that influence the dispositions of their respective inhabitants. In 1851, Emerson declared that "the North and South are two nations. It is not slavery that separates them, but climate." Emerson was by no means the first to cast climate as a crucial factor in character formation. Aristotle declared that "the nations that live in cold regions and those of Europe are full of spirit, but somewhat lacking in skill and intellect." Vitruvius, the Roman writer and architect, was of the opinion that "the southern nations" possessed "minds made acute by heat;" while "northern peoples, infused with a heavy atmosphere and chilled by moisture because of the density of the air, have sluggish minds." Southerners shared the opinion of Aristotle and Vitruvius, that "civilization is an exotic in all cold latitudes. It belongs naturally to temperate climates."[21] To nineteenth-century Southerners, the self-proclaimed "descendants of the cavaliers of Charles II," in whose veins flowed "the genius of Chivalry and the spirit of fealty," such ancient convictions served to confirm their claim to cultural superiority and genteel heritage. That was certainly the belief of Thomas Nelson Page, who, in recounting the foundation of the colony, observed that among the first colonists were "four carpenters, twelve laborers, and fifty-four gentlemen." The tale paints a picture of a predominantly aristocratic society even in its nascent day. History paints a different picture—one of general misery, enforced migration, and social decay that have little to do with gentility. According to Page's history, however, thanks to the preponderance of the genteel over the base, the ethos of gentility "flourished for two hundred and fifty years," until the Civil War brought it to an end.[22] If gentility acquired a regionally racial dimension in the nineteenth century, it was partly the direct result of this bipolar outlook and not without a contradiction: the Southerners might have readily agreed with Aristotle and Vitruvius, but their chivalric models derived from their own northern European heritage, along with the broadly understood and adapted southern European tradition of chivalry itself.[23]

Unlike the Northern settlements, since the day of their founding, the Southern colonies "were rooted in the faith of England from which they came—political, religious, and civil." Having arrived armed "with the consent of the crown" and "the blessing of the Church," it was the duty of the newly fledged colonists to repay this favor with loyalty and monetary gain. The Northern colonists, on the other hand, were a bunch of "religious zealots and revolutionists," who sought "freedom to exercise their religious convictions" rather than "the enlargement of their fortunes," and whose removal to the New World was probably viewed as a blessing by the crown.[24] The Southern aristocratic myth, the myth of Southern whiteness, was an imported commodity that conquered the vagaries of the crossing with the first settlers and stemmed from a conviction of moral superiority partly grounded in an adaptation of English history and partly in an imagined ideal. Over time, it evolved through direct references to the natural environment seen as instrumental in the cultivation of aristocratic qualities. Here, the warm and temperate climate replaced the grand Puritan vision of the "citty upon a Hill," affording distinction from the North as a cold and hostile place.[25]

Page's voice is one of many singing the praises of Southern genteel civilization in the nineteenth century. The self-proclaimed Anglo-Normans, the descendants of English Cavaliers, were utterly devoid of "misanthropy, hypocrisy, diseased philanthropy, envy, hatred, fanaticism, and all the worst passions of the human heart," which constituted "the ruling characteristics of New England Yankees" who worshipped "no God but mammon." These grievous flaws were direct results of "the coldness of their climate and the sterility of their soil." Such an insalubrious climate also prevented the germination of gentility among women and men. Writing in 1860, J. T. Wiswall, an Alabamian writer and advocate of the Southern way of life, concluded that Northern women, unlike their Southern counterparts, were the embodiment of "nervousness, fanaticism, and superstition" as a direct result of "sedentary life through winters over hot stoves."[26] One scarcely dare imagine what irreparable damage such cold winters would have inflicted on Northern masculinity.

Out of the mutual campaign of slander, the South, as a region, created its own mythology and methodology of whiteness, which distinguished it from the national model or the "universal Yankee" model.[27] With Northern industry, frugality and pragmatism, the Southerners juxtaposed a feudal model of society in which lords ruled benignly and wisely and ladies radiated beauty, piety, chastity, and refinement in equal measure. The fact that the gentlemanly caste constituted a fraction of the population did not mitigate the universal appeal of Southern whiteness to the inhabitants of the region. Noble descent, supported by the possession of land, took pride of place in the Southern pantheon of whiteness. The nobility of birth as a prerequisite to Southern whiteness required spatial reification, a tangibility separating the worthy from the unworthy. The plantation house furnished the ideal set piece as both a monument to whiteness and testament to the higher values of its inhabitants. Like a feudal castle, it became both a focal point and symbol of the endurance of the civilization that erected it.

The end of the Civil War and the austerity of Reconstruction, with its influx of carpetbaggers, created a favorable climate in which narratives of Southern whiteness could be retold. It was not just a question of giving "whiteness color," as Grace Elizabeth Hale would have it; rather, it was the question of reinvention aimed at the legitimation and preservation of the genteel ethos. Retold from the perspective of post-Reconstruction, the story of Southern whiteness inevitably begins with the mythologized plantation and its antebellum splendor that graced the verdant fields of the Old South. The Old South then becomes a systematically mythologized receptacle of gentility and nobility of spirit inherited from the Cavalier settlers.[28] Thus conjured from a fantastic place and time, the Old South that emerges from the upheavals of Reconstruction is nothing more than a reconstruction of an already imagined region existing in a largely imagined past. But thanks to the artificiality of its construction, the Old South acquires a timelessness and placelessness that detach it from its geographical location and furnish it with a plasticity that is both conducive to reimagination and inaccessible like the biblical ideals. Planted in its fertile soil, Southern whiteness becomes as phantasmagoric as its place of origin. Any attempt to reproduce the wholeness of the antebellum ideal undertaken from the perspective of the post-war realities of the New South must, of necessity, transcend *a priori* difference enshrined in the unbridgeable gap between the imagined site of origin and reimagination. This differential condition of Southern whiteness—born out of the fusion of transcendence and interpretability of biblical values and genteel ethos—is evident in the works of Page, Glasgow, Chesnutt, and Dunbar-Nelson, for whose protagonists it remains elusive and unattainable.

REGIONALISM AND WHITENESS

By the end of the nineteenth century, the nationwide appetite for distinctiveness and all things Southern had grown. The South may have lost the war, but in the literary contest it could certainly hold its own. As Richard Gray notes, the re-united states wanted to hear the story of the South, although for different reasons: the vanquished Southerners could re-live the glories of the golden antebellum days, while the victorious Northerners could satisfy their curiosity and rest content in the belief that they set the South on the road to progress. Bill Hardwig notes the correlation between the rise in popularity of the travel narrative and regional writing, which he ascribes to the desire of Northern audiences to experience the region, even if vicariously.[29] More prosaically, however, for Southern writers, the road to success led through the North. Looking back over her literary career, Ellen Glasgow admitted that there was "more truth than wit in the gibe that every Southern novelist must first make his reputation in the North." This necessity, she complained, was responsible for many Southern novelists writing of "the South as if it were a fabulous country."[30] And, inadvertently, such an exercise led to the formulation of labels such as local-color fiction, meaning nothing more than hackneyed humorous sketches of dubious literary, if not entertainment, value and the more "refined" regionalism.

Yet, as Hardwig proves, such labored classifications collapse in the face of stringent analysis, and they certainly did not exist for contemporary writers and readers. For Page, Glasgow, Chesnutt, and Dunbar-Nelson, whose works engage with social, economic, and racial concerns, these issues would have been as much of regional as of national importance. The Old South and the plantation house may still be present, but this presence serves to foreground the plight of the region and its inhabitants, black and white alike. If anything, the works of these writers demonstrate that writing from or about a geographically determined place does not impair the realistic merits of such fictions. For Hamlin Garland, an advocate of local color, the literary and aesthetic merits of the genre lie in a writer's ability to reflect spontaneously "the life that goes on around him. It is natural and unrestrained." Far from being second-rate provincial writing, local color or regionalism is an organically de-centralized form by virtue of place, but not necessarily focus.[31]

Focus operates in two dimensions—the geographic and the temporal—and both are equally important to the Southern novelists of the post-Reconstruction period. Allen Tate observes of Southern regionalism that it is unlimited in time—"a literature conscious of the past in the present." This consciousness, although not indifferent to the broader issues that plagued the region in the aftermath of Reconstruction, such as impoverishment, industrialization, race, or reintegration into the national fabric, is responsible for a certain atavism of Southern literature that consists in looking to the past and its reimagination. The turmoil of Reconstruction and the post-Reconstruction years not only made such retrospection appealing, but also turned it into a celebration of the good old days. For Southerners only mildly interested in returning to the bosom of the nation, reimagining the past became a means of preserving regional distinctiveness, including the conceptualization of Southern whiteness.[32] The Old South and its genteel ethos feature prominently in Thomas Nelson Page's *Gordon Keith* and *Red Rock: A Chronicle of Reconstruction*, while both warn of the dangers of capitalism, whether in the guise of iniquitous Northern carpetbaggers or unscrupulous industrialists bent on squeezing every last cent from the land. Ellen Glasgow, although more circumspect in glorifying the golden antebellum days in *The Battle-Ground* or *The Voice of the People*, still found it difficult to relinquish the myth of gentility and see the common man triumph.

Just as the loss of the Civil War spurred the glorification and promotion of the myth of the Lost Cause, the bleakness of the post-Reconstruction years generated an appetite for the invention of Southern whiteness through the recreation of a viable past that would furnish an alternative to viewing the region through the prism of slavery. Such regeneration becomes important in the wake of social and political upheavals that threaten collective identity and consists in "invariance," in re-constructing aspects of social and cultural life as "unchanging."[33] In a region whose more affluent inhabitants prided themselves on their genteel pedigrees, an alternative narrative of whiteness was readily available to Southern writers. But to make it historically credible and legitimate, post-Reconstruction Southern writers like Page cast their nets wider, to encompass England and, by default, further into the past. It was more than literary caprice or poor historicity aimed at romanticizing the Southern genteel ethos; rather, it was a deliberate effort to forge a new tradition of Southern whiteness of which Southerners could be proud. Sir Walter Scott proved a versatile weapon in the arsenal of Southern writers, a fact much lamented by Mark Twain, who held him solely responsible for the Civil War. Baron Bradwardine of Scott's *Waverley; or 'Tis Sixty Years Since*, always "on hospitable thoughts intent" and overflowing with good-natured bonhomie, became the blueprint for many a Southern gentleman planter. In the hands of post-Reconstruction Southern writers, this natural conviviality and hospitality happily commingle with an aptitude for classical scholarship.[34]

The borrowings from Scott in the post-Reconstruction years were both overt and widespread. Page, Glasgow, and Chesnutt all use Scott, albeit for different purposes. Page writes in earnest to create a historically viable narrative of Southern whiteness through the re-establishment of continuity between the genteel ethos of the Old World and the South. Glasgow also uses Scott as a means of acknowledging the significance of this historic connection, but she recognizes the futility of reviving old gods well past their expiry date. In *The House behind the Cedars,* Chesnutt uses the trope of Scott and chivalry to acknowledge the centrality of this narrative to Southern conceptions of whiteness and debunk it as empty rhetoric bearing no correlation to the here and now.[35] The novel inveighs against the destructive influence of past traditions that hold the present in an iron grip.

Such explicit borrowings from Scott set postbellum Southern writers apart from their antebellum compatriots like William Gilmore Simms or John Pendleton Kennedy.[36] Although they share in the Southern genteel heritage, they write from different historical vantage points and thus to distinct agendas. Through a blend of humor and irony that mocks rather than celebrates, Kennedy exposes to ridicule what he sees as the ubiquitous foibles of the Southern genteel ethos. He is able to do so because he writes about the South as is, without an underlying agenda of historic embellishment or regional aggrandizement. By contrast, Page—and, to certain extent, Glasgow—faced with the unavoidable decline of the genteel class as a result of Reconstruction, engage in an act of regenerative historicity, essential to which is the establishment of continuity, however tenuous, between the old and the new.

The notion of continuity, whether as a form of resistance to change or an indictment of the rusted *status quo,* forms an inextricable part of the story of Southern whiteness that extends beyond mere nostalgic retrospection. The means of approach and methodology, however, depend on the vantage point of the writer. In the case of Page and Glasgow, both descendants of Virginian aristocracy, Southern whiteness is the product of a particular tradition and mythology, which finds expression in verisimilitude of description and characterization. Page frequently borrows Scott's method of introducing the region through an outsider's eyes. Glasgow, though no stranger to this approach, uses it only once in *The Deliverance: A Romance of the Virginia Tobacco Fields.* In his collection of stories, published as *In Ole Virginia,* Page pairs a newcomer to the region with a former slave who regales him with tales of the old time with ingenuous simplicity, although in his later novels he dispenses with the faithful dependent and contents himself with a stranger. The technique is more than a literary strategy and was just as successfully employed by Gerstein in *Hart of Dixie,* where a quirky Northerner takes her first tentative steps on Southern soil. Its merit lies in the freshness and seeming objectivity of perception that a stranger's perspective offers, which functions as a vehicle for converging the past and the present. It furnishes an organic means of comparison that is unobtrusive yet evocative of sympathy with the heroes' predicament, and by extension the region's.[37] Yet another, and this time implicit borrowing from Scott, are the seemingly ordinary and flawed heroes Page and Glasgow create, and through whom they offer a viable means of continuity in the unlikely union of endurance, history and fiction resulting in a historically conscious adaptability.[38]

Scott's formula proved as useful to debunking whiteness as it did to its construction. Chesnutt, the son of free persons of color, stood on the opposite end of the social spectrum, and his plight of being a black white made visible the absurdity of racial classifications. Although he inveighs against and mocks the ethos of Southern gentility and its pernicious rhetoric, he does so using the trusted methodology favored by Page. In *The Conjure Woman and Other Conjure Tales*, it is a former slave, Uncle Julius, who instructs the Northern newcomers and owners of the plantation in the ways of the South. In *The House behind the Cedars*, the reader catches his first glimpses of Patesville as reflected in an outsider's eyes. The same principle of organicity, of producing the effect of a seemingly natural and unbiased impression, operates here, and its aim is to undermine the ethos of Southern whiteness. Chesnutt's position is clear and calls for a politics of meritocracy based on individual achievement rather than outdated notions of hereditary privilege. Meritocracy over hereditary gentility is also the message Alice Dunbar-Nelson sends in her story "The Stones of the Village."[39] Dunbar-Nelson's mixed heritage meant occupying a marginal position in relation to the privileged elite. But her work stands out because it eschews the well-established techniques exploited by Page and Chesnutt. On the point of Southern whiteness, Dunbar-Nelson's position in "The Stones of the Village" resembles Chesnutt's approach in its emphasis on individual merit and social advancement. Yet, unlike Chesnutt, she exposes the internal conflict that is the price of social advancement, or aspirations to Southern whiteness, which leads to a crisis of individual identity unable and unwilling to extricate itself from the allure and stranglehold of the genteel legacy. This preoccupation with the Southern genteel legacy, with what it means to be white and off white, is the thread connecting these four writers who, despite sharing a regional affinity, write from diametrically opposed positions. The Southern whiteness they re-imagine is ambivalent and inaccessible, either by virtue of the impossibility of resurrecting the past or by the intrinsic imperfection of its antecedents.

Off Whiteness looks at this ambivalence of Southern whiteness from three distinct vantage points: place, ideality, and repeatability. Its thematic division into three parts allows for an examination of individual authors' conception of Southern whiteness shaped in response to historically and culturally constructed narratives. Part I, "Passing place—imagined or real," examines the role of place and the monumental space of the plantation house in the construction of Southern whiteness. Part II, "A touch of the tar brush, or the ambivalence of whiteness," focuses on the conflict that arises between an ideal and its reconstruction, and how it plays out in the embodiments of Southern whiteness, the gentleman planter and his sidekick, the Southern lady. Part III, "Monster mash—or a paler shade of white," interrogates the notion of continuity through repetition, which condemns the subjects of whiteness as sites of monstrous mutation.

PART ONE

PASSING PLACE — IMAGINED OR REAL

ONE

THROUGH A STRANGER'S EYES
Nature, Place, and Whiteness in Thomas Nelson Page

The end of the Civil War and the period of Reconstruction created a fertile climate for the germination of Southern whiteness. That germination, however, required mythologizing the Old South and reimagining key players in the performance of whiteness: the gentleman planter and the Southern belle. Eric Hobsbawm observes that traditions emerge at points of discontinuity and as a result of social or political trauma. Their primary aim is to preserve a sense of continuity, however tenuous, between what has been and is no more and the here and now. At the point of loss ushered in by the South's defeat, the gentleman planter and Southern belle became the hallmarks of the continuity of tradition and furnished ready material for its remolding, particularly as they were still living embodiments of the past and what many Southerners believed to be the South's own Augustan Age. Michel de Certeau observes that places acquire meaning through usages that they inspire and influence, effectively creating a place-inhabitant dialectic. And, although the South-whiteness dialectic is no exception, this reciprocity extends further, beyond mere habitation, to include the hereditary possession of land. After all, it was the concentration of vast landholding, the clement climate, and the fertile land that, together, facilitated the emergence of cotton and tobacco monocultures that dominated the region and promoted what came to be known as the Southern way of life.[1] At this point of convergence of nature and culture, the South acquired a distinct sense of place, which then contributed to the emergence of unique constructs, such as the aristocratic planter or the Southern belle. These epitomes of Southern whiteness became endemic to the region and, in Patrick D. Murphy's terms, "ennatured"—

defined by the hereditary possession of land and cultural practices associated with it. Speaking of adaptations and alterations to natural environment as a result of cultural practice, Murphy suggests that they are more likely to occur in conjunction with a migration of culture. The culture transplanted to the South, that eventually formed the upper echelons of society, was predominantly Anglo-Saxon, moderately Protestant, and with strong Royalist leanings.[2] The place of origins and antecedents, preferably those with a drop of blue blood, mattered, adding new significance to such notions as heredity, history, breeding, and blood, which hark back to the old continent and become a permanent fixture of the Southern lexicon of whiteness.

These four concepts accrued fresh meaning in the post-Reconstruction South. Post-war austerity ushered in a period of retrospection, which led to a re-evaluation of the relationship between the land and its inhabitants as well as the region and the country. Hand in hand with this newly emerged context was a reimagination of Southern whiteness, one that emphasized gentility of breeding, blood, and history. In short, it was a model of whiteness of which to be proud, and it conveniently de-emphasized the role of slavery in its creation, thereby furnishing a more palatable alternative. Its trajectory resembles Certeau's theory of the concept of the city, which attains idealized, timeless, and universal signification as a subject through a revival of tradition, and begins with the conception of the Old South. Imbued with a continuity of tradition and frequently imagined as a prelapsarian idyll, the Old South becomes both impersonal and universal—a perfect place in which the seeds of postbellum Southern whiteness can germinate.[3] Thomas Nelson Page eulogized the Old South, writing that it "combined elements of the three great civilizations, which since the dawn of history have enlightened the world. It partook of the philosophic tone of the Grecian, of the dominant spirit of the Roman, and of the guardfulness of individual rights of the Saxon civilization." He saw this cultural splendor as steeped in "a softness and beauty," and "the joint product of Chivalry and Christianity."[4] In this reimagined South, cobbled from a variety of traditions, antiquity sat comfortably alongside the Saxon civilization transplanted from England, while adherence to the codes of chivalry and Christianity ensured a lasting tranquility for the region. Such a felicitous convergence of traditions, augmented by the possession of land, led to the emergence of the myth of Southern whiteness and created the attendant fiction of its continuity and resilience. But this tenuous sense of continuity was only possible through retrospection, a constant looking back to the past and mining the fecund soil of the Old South to reconstruct Southern whiteness and inject it with timeless impersonality as the idealized place of its origin. Such reificatory reimagining reinforces the status of whiteness as a simulacrum, which thereby becomes inseparable from the site of its conception.

This sense of place emerges at the juncture of a geographical locale and atemporality of tradition, and is a standard feature of Page's reconstructions of Southern whiteness. Criticism of Page's works has not changed much since the publication of his first stories in the 1880s. Page's contemporaries saw in him a redeemer of the South, somebody to speak up for the region and tell the Southern version of its story. An article announcing Page's address to the Society of Virginia University Alumni, which appeared in the *Louisville Courier-Journal* in 1891, hailed him as a hero capable of responding to "the South's dire need"—and the need was setting the record straight and preventing "the World" from "misjudging her children." His "middling literary talent," as one critic writing for the *New York Times* put it some twenty years later, did not hinder Page from becoming "the recognized interpreter of the South—the old South—to the rest of the country." Modern-day critics tend to substitute "apologist" for "redeemer" and, although they do not go so far as to accuse him of "inveterate sentimentality," find fault with his tales of nostalgic reminiscence and deliberate mythologizing of the good old days.[5]

If Page had an agenda, it went beyond nostalgic reminiscence to include a historicity with the aim of fashioning an alternative and viable model of Southern whiteness; a model that predated the peculiar institution and was thus capable of existing independently of it. A glance at his own family tree would have furnished Page with enough material to fashion the figures of many a Southern gentleman and lady. He was born at Oakwood plantation, in Hanover County, Virginia, to John and Elizabeth (né Nelson) Page in 1853. Of aristocratic stock, his family occupied pride of place among Virginia's finest. A cousin of Page, Dr. Richard Channing Moore Page, traced the elaborate family genealogy and published some of his findings in the *Baltimore Sun*, in an article titled "Virginia Heraldry." According to his kinsman, Page was the grandson of John Page, the thirteenth governor of Virginia and, if that was not grand enough, on both his father's and mother's side he could also claim descent from General Thomas, the fourth governor of Virginia and one of the signatories of the Declaration of Independence.[6] But the idyllic life that such a pedigree guaranteed came to an abrupt end when Page was still a boy. If he knew privilege, he also became acquainted with hardship and poverty. The war was a turning point for Page because his family lost everything in the conflict. When still a boy, Dexter Marshall reports for the *Baltimore Sun*, Page "had to milk the cows and do other farm work." The misfortune did not end there; he also had to "walk five miles daily to school." The family's altered circumstances naturally had an impact on his later life, a problem he would return to in his later novels, notably *Red Rock: A Chronicle of Reconstruction*, *Gordon Keith*, and *John Marvel Assistant*. Although he attended Washington and Lee and later the University of Virginia Law School, his financial circumstances prevented him from completing his studies in either institutions. But, Page did not let the lack of formal qualifications stand in the way of opening a law practice in Richmond and going on to have a successful career in diplomatic service, a career of which his ancestors would have heartily approved.[7] The war may have deprived Page of his share in the family's wealth, but it left intact his reverence for Southern tradition and pride in genteel descent and ethics—all part of the posture of Southern whiteness.

Page's literary career began in 1884, with the publication of a short story titled "Marse Chan," later included in the collection *In Ole Virginia*, published in 1887. The chosen venue for his first literary airing was *Century Magazine* where, two years later, "Meh Lady," another of his stories appeared. The stories in the collection are unique not because of the juxtaposition of two unlikely characters, the faithful ex-slave and a Northerner, but because of the way Page uses black dialect to invoke and build the image of the Old South. The speech of the former family retainer lends veracity to his account which, considering the source, never fails to overcome the skepticism and prejudice of his Northern interlocutor. The hapless Northerner has no choice but to trust the narrator, not only because he is a flesh and blood remainder of the antebellum South, but because he is, despite his speech, astute and discerning, and had experienced Southern genteel ethos first hand.

The image of the Old South emerging from the stories remains somewhat blurred, an impression rather than a fully formed picture. Yet, despite this lack of crystallization (after all, it was Page's first foray into *belle lettres*), the impression is of gaiety and harmony—give or take the occasional neighborly feud. What takes form are distinct qualities of whiteness which, in "Marse Chan" and "Meh Lady," because the stories are told from a postbellum vantage point, acquire a timelessness. In "Marse Chan," as in his later novels, Page introduces the scene through the eyes of a newcomer, in a ploy designed to add a disinterested objectivity that a non-Southern perspective affords. Page uses a calculated naivete in the stranger's account of what he sees to comment on the otherness of the unfolding scene and transform the Old South into a site of familiarity. Through a dispassionate description of the scene around him, "now fast falling to decay," the visitor invokes the splendor of what must have been the Old South. It is but a fleeting glimpse, but it leads the observer to remark that "distance was nothing to this people; time was of no consequence to them." This innocuous remark establishes the Southern attachment to tradition and the abiding hold that the past has on the present. Soon, the stranger happens upon Sam, a former slave, and the story proper begins. Sam, with his quaint speech and exclamations of "Lawd, marster," is a relic of the past, not because he symbolizes the old order, but because he reveres Southern values and distinctiveness—or, as Hardwig terms it, "southern exceptionalism."[8] From Sam, the stranger learns of Marse Chan's chivalry, which manifested when he was still a boy, his inbred sense of honor, constancy, courage and, finally, heroism on the battlefield. Told by a former slave, or as he calls himself a "body-servant," and thus somebody who should resent rather than admire his "marster," these virtues and components of Southern whiteness acquire a veracity that is hard to refute.[9]

Similarly, in another story from the collection *In Ole Virginia*, "Unc' Edinburg's Drowndin," also narrated by an ex-slave, the stranger learns of Southern hospitality in no uncertain terms. The servant, dispatched to fetch the visitor from the station, upon glimpsing his modest luggage greets him with the unexpected "mistis say as how you might bring a trunk."[10] Nonplussed at this turn of conversation, the visitor excuses the lack with a "short visit" and is duly informed that "dee don' nobody nuver pay short visists dyah." In this story, Southern hospitality, an integral part of the genteel ethos, connects the present to the past and the Old South which remains in the background; the zeitgeist may have changed but the values endure. The tale that follows tells of another aspect of Southern whiteness—blood legacy—more explicitly than "Marse Chan." When Marse George falls in love with Miss Charlotte, who happens to be a step-sister of Mr. Darker, a telling name for somebody who turns out to be a first-rate scoundrel, his parents try to dissuade him from marrying the lady by pointing out the unsuitability of her relations. George refutes the charge by pointing out that Darker is "on'y de step-brurr of de young lady, an' ain' got a drap o' her blood in he veins." The point is hard to miss: blood will tell and, in Darker's case, the name symbolizes a deviation from the Southern standard of whiteness as a composite of genteel blood, honor, and integrity.

Blood and breeding also remain at the center of "Meh Lady." The story opens with a chance meeting between a former slave, Uncle Billy, and a stranger. It tells of fortitude and sacrifice in the face of the disaster that was the Civil War, loyalty to cause and principle, and honor, shared equally by men and women who are "jes' dat ambitious 'bout it."[11] Marse Phil perishes on the battlefield, while "mistis," his mother, and "meh lady," his sister, struggle through the years of the conflict, enduring poverty and indignity at the hands of the Northern invaders, the latter much harder to bear. Speaking of the family's resilience and fidelity to the Cause, Uncle Billy declares that "de thorybreds goes wid dee heads up till dee drap." In this most explicit reference to breeding in the collection, Page goes beyond drawing a mere comparison with horses. Breeding, he implies, is comprised of courage, endurance, honor in both men and women as well as female passivity and acceptance; in short, the many threads that converge in the composite of Southern whiteness. Page returns to the image of a horse as a metaphor for blood and breeding in one of his later stories, tellingly titled, "Bred in the Bone."[12] In "Meh Lady," however, Page treads cautiously, perhaps careful not to antagonize the Northern audiences, and has Uncle Billy verbalize what he sees as the quiddity of Southern whiteness. The caution pays off and, because of being voiced through the medium of Uncle Billy, the notion of breeding becomes all the more exalted.

The right breeding, by which Page understands Southern gentility, is indeed bred in the bone; it cannot be shaken off like an inconvenient habit. When Colonel Wilton arrives on the plantation with a Northern regiment, he acts honorably by preventing the looting of the place. And Page loses no time in explaining his actions: he is "the son of Colonel Churchill Wilton," who was "mistis's" husband's cousin. Although she acknowledges the chivalric gesture, the claim of kinship makes little impression on "mistis," who replies: "Churchill Wilton was a Virginian, do' he lived at de Norf."[13] In this instance, loyalty to the South takes precedence over familial ties; it is possible to be a Southern gentleman and live in the North, but it is impossible to remain one when fighting the South. Wilton learns that lesson the hard way when he proposes to "meh lady," who rejects him. It is not until after the war, and with the deathbed blessing of "mistis," that "meh lady" finally accepts him—by which time he is no longer "the half-Virginian" he was at their first meeting. Hardwig sees the union as indication of a reconciliation between the South and the North.[14] This particular reconciliation resembles a capitulation. After all, Wilton's acceptance is conditional, dependent on his embracing the Southern values he inherited from his father; it is the story of a prodigal son returning to the land of his forefathers.

"Meh Lady," and indeed all the stories in the collection, met with favorable reviews. "Marse Chan" and "Meh Lady" received particular praise for being "vivid," "tender," and "touching," and for giving "a wonderfully graphic picture of Southern life."[15] Another critic, writing for the *Atlanta Constitution*, admired Page's spontaneity and directness in the treatment of his subject, which he saw as "the flower and fruit of his genius." Yet, it is perhaps Samuel M. Smith, a reviewer for the *Raleigh Weekly State Chronicle*, who came nearest to Page's intention. He hailed the collection as a protest against what he called "this late gospel of the Almighty Dollar" and "a page of unwritten history." Strong words, to be sure, combining as they do an indictment of the present, with a thinly veiled allusion to Northern capitalism, and an endorsement of a historic truth of the past. The Southern gentleman, "careless, heedless, happy, brave, opportunistic, courteous [and] chivalrous," is the undisputed hero of this "unwritten history." In this "incarnate manly perfection," Smith gushed, Page unites these distinct components of Southern whiteness, tying them neatly with the Old South. Perhaps because of its hero's ability to unite all of these traits, "Marse Chan" collected the accolade for the best story—not only in the collection but among publications at large.[16] Its popularity stood the test of time. When the *Louisville Courier-Journal* reported in 1907 that "the famous Virginia novelist" was set on trying his hand at breeding mules and had acquired a pack of them, the newspaper speculated that the finest specimen would be called Marse Chan.[17]

"Marse Chan" and *In Ole Virginia* made Page's reputation both as a writer and a spokesman for the South. With celebrity came lecture tours and an opportunity to tell the story of the Southern genteel ethos, all the more tempting to the public because the raconteur was the member of that very class. By the time the fruit of his first foray into novel writing, *On Newfound River*, appeared in 1891, Page had firmly established his literary reputation. And the reviews were good. A critic for the *Dial*, although he saw the novel as an elaboration of Page's short stories in terms of plot and character, nonetheless called it "a charming story of Old Virginia." The *Catholic World* found in Page's stance "a certain cosmopolitanism" and "an absence of aggressive sectional assertion or equally aggressive sectional deprecation." Another reviewer praised the novel's accuracy in historical delineation of its characters, as "the typical ones common to the times and place." Some critics enthused about the novel's "air of reality" and "lifelike portrayal of a type of civilization which is now extinct, and which never will be duplicated." For others, the novel was proof of the existence of "good Southern fiction beyond the short story."[18]

Unlike modern critics of his works, Page's contemporaries did not dismiss the novel as an unrealistic attempt at mythogenesis, which suggests that the story of Southern whiteness this gentleman was telling, and which predated the peculiar institution, was both a viable and plausible alternative at the time. In *On Newfound River,* this alternative story crystallizes and gains substance. The short stories foreground the particular genteel qualities that form a composite of Southern whiteness such as honor, chivalry, loyalty and the right kind of breeding, but they communicate a vague sense of the region, as if looking through misted glass. In *On Newfound River,* Page intensifies the narrative and begins to hone in on the plantation house and the significance of hereditary land ownership as requisites of Southern whiteness.

The interdependence of Southern whiteness and place lies at the heart of this story set in antebellum Virginia that tells of the fortunes of the patrician Landons. Unlike in the short stories, Page does not introduce place through the eyes of a newcomer, opting instead for a blend of omniscient and retrospective narration that both conveys objectivity and establishes a detachment between the events narrated and the telling. In the intervening years, the narrator explains, enemy armies trampled and destroyed the settlement and "the civilization which existed there in the old days." The narrator tactfully omits the name of the war, an example of Page's lack of sectional hostility— observed by one of the critics; but the destruction of civilization to which he alludes leaves no room for doubt. The antebellum setting of the novel is not a mere indulgence in nostalgic reminiscence of the golden days, but a deliberate effort to draw an alternative sketch of Southern gentility through a shift in focus from slavery to heritage and land. Newfound is a place that both bore the brunt of and emerged altered from historic upheavals. Its very name suggests a proprietary attitude, a claim of ownership, and hybridity born out of its colonial past. The Landons were among the first settlers and have "ruled unquestioned in an untitled manorial system" ever since. In this pseudo-feudal class ecosystem, everybody knows his or her place in relation to the Landons, and it is always one of inferiority, that of "part friend, part retainer."[19] The universal prestige and respect the family enjoys stem not so much from their wealth, which they owe to the fertility of their lands, but from "the fact that they held their lands under the same grant which had been issued by Charles II to the first of the name who had crossed the seas."[20] The royal connection affords historic legitimacy to the Landons' claim to whiteness and anchors it firmly in this place, where it has become something of a tradition.

Page wastes no time establishing the family's genealogy and genteel status. The Landons have been in possession of the land for six generations, and the present custodian is the irascible, but still likeable, Major Landon. He resides at Landon Hall with his wife, Lucy, a former belle blessed with an inexhaustible store of patience and kindness, and Bruce, his heir apparent, who is the favorite of the Newfound community and whose stubbornness exceeds even that of his father. The major's felicity would be complete if it were not for an imprudent ancestor in the fourth generation who lost a parcel of the granted land to a neighbor in a game of cards. The land, although not valuable in material terms, is priceless in historic terms because it contains the dwelling the first Landon built—Landon Hill. Page, however, seems far from castigating the irresponsible ancestor's actions and, instead, hastens to dissociate him from the sin of gambling: he did not lose the house because he was an inveterate gambler, but because he was too polite to refuse the bet when his neighbor "had badgered him." The accommodating ancestor found himself in an impossible situation: to renege on the wager would mean the loss of honor, while honoring it would mean losing tangible evidence of the family's gentility. Either solution, however, diminishes his claim to whiteness. A duel and numerous offers to repurchase the property at inflated cost all fail, and two generations later—and despite the family's continued prosperity—the major still acutely feels the loss of "the old place," which was "Naboth's Vineyard" to him; the fact that his ancestor acted honorably brings him little comfort.[21]

The old place, ever visible from the windows of the new residence, is a stubborn reminder of a lost heritage. Henri Lefebvre, discussing the place/usage dialectic, concludes that to signify as a monumental space a place must combine three modes of usage: "the perceived, the conceived and the lived." The old house signifies as such monumental space because it enshrines these three modes of usage. Perceived and conceived as "the cradle of the race," it is also a tangible testament of the lived experience of the four generations of Landons. The possession of such monumental space, Lefebvre suggests, fixes in the collective mind the social image of its owner. Social image, even when inherited, determines and safeguards one's place in the collective mind. For the major, the loss of the old place equals the loss of the Landons' historic legitimacy—all the more galling because the "family prided itself on being an older branch than that which remained in England, and on having brought its landholding instincts across the water." More than a dent in social image, it is a rupture of family tradition, a grievous misfortune to the major, who prides himself on his descent and who understands the significance of hereditary possession of land to his social standing. It is, therefore, a reciprocal relationship between gentility and hereditary possession of land that defines the major's whiteness. He may benefit from the land in material terms, but he reveres it because of the historic legitimacy it redounds. And, it seems, this quality sets the major apart from the other inhabitants of Newfound.

Sam Mills, one of the locals, and "part-friend, part-retainer," observes that the major "thinks as much o' that lan' o' his as if it was a gold mine."[22] Mills is an exponent of a lower class who understands value in strictly monetary terms. It is therefore not only his speech that marks him as off white, but also the lack of comprehension of the significance of the hereditary possession of land to the legitimacy of the major's gentility.

Gentility and its attendant class difference manifest in the attitude toward and relationship to place and land. When the new owner of Landon Hill, Dr. Browne, arrives at Newfound with his granddaughter and two servants in tow, the major, as behooves a Southerner and a gentleman, pays him a visit. He finds Dr. Browne "not at home to visitors," a blatant violation of the sacred custom of Southern hospitality that provokes "the aversion of the major, and the suspicion of the rest of the community." Only Bruce remains on friendly terms with Dr. Browne's granddaughter, Margaret, who is his junior by several years. But the major swiftly puts a stop to the friendship, calling Dr. Browne and his family "low and worthless, and unfit associates for a gentleman." Bruce's protests to the contrary fall on deaf ears, and the major sends him away to school. The major bases his harsh judgment on Dr. Browne's lack of hospitality and, by extension, breeding. Yet, Bruce's encounters with Margaret reveal that, very young though she is, she already displays a respect for tradition and history. In a series of hints too obvious to miss, Page suggests that there may be more to Margaret and Dr. Browne than meets the eye. When Bruce first meets Margaret and introduces himself, Margaret exclaims, "Bruce, prince of Scotland." The family pets bear the grand names of King Alfred, Banquo, and George Washington, all of which point to a felicitous marriage of histories and traditions, not unlike the creed to which the Landons subscribe, making Landon Hill itself a symbol of the merging of two cultures and a fitting place of residence for Dr. Browne, despite his breach of Southern etiquette.[23] The doctor's charitable work and kindness in tending to the sick, upon which Mrs. Landon remarks, testify to a nobility of spirit and disinterestedness of purpose commensurate with gentlemanly behavior.

The major, however, remains unshaken in his classification of Dr. Browne and his granddaughter as "worthless," and it is with increasing alarm that he observes the growing attachment between Bruce, now a young man freshly returned from university, and Margaret. He determines to nip the romance in the bud by confronting Margaret and demanding she promise not to marry Bruce. When he comes within full view of Landon Hill, the major's anger rises again because "the house of his fathers" has been "allowed to grow up in a wilderness; worse than any poor white's place."[24] The outward shabbiness and neglect of the place reinforce the major's conviction of Dr. Browne's non-whiteness. No gentleman possessed of historic self-awareness and familial pride could countenance such disrepair.

The major is not immune to associations between place and social image, and the decrepitude of Landon Hill precipitates certain conclusions about the condition of its inhabitants—the worst assumption imaginable because the label of poor white invites connotations of not only thriftlessness but also moral degeneration.[25] This is why the major's first encounter with Margaret, whom he mistakes for a visitor, begins inauspiciously for both and resembles that between a master and a servant. He dispenses with any sense of chivalry and civility he may possess and addresses Margaret without dismounting from his horse, removing his hat, or looking at her. Upon hearing Margaret's "placid [and] melodious" voice in reply and finding her "a beauty and quite a lady" in deportment, if not in dress, he hastily checks his manners and feels "embarrassed by finding her so different from what he expected."[26] That Margaret, and not the major's behavior, is the source of his embarrassment reaffirms the inter-dependence between place and social impression and merely casts her as an exception to the rule.

Yet, the revelation does not divert him from the purpose of his visit, and he succeeds in securing Margaret's promise not to marry his son on the grounds that Bruce "is a gentleman." When Bruce discovers the reason for Margaret's refusal of his proposal, he confronts his father and demands he release her from the contract. The major does so while calling him "a shame and disgrace" to the name of Landon, and disinherits him. This is a test of Bruce's mettle in gentlemanly conduct because he must choose between his birthright and fidelity to Margaret. Because he chooses Margaret, he acts honorably and chivalrously. But Page cannot leave his hero penniless and without his hereditary acres, even at the risk of weakening the plot. Later that day, when Bruce is waiting for Margaret at their favorite spot, Pokeberry Green, his long-time sworn enemy, ambushes him and hits him on the head, and thus Margaret finds him, unconscious and bleeding. Pokeberry Green is a shady character who incites slaves to run away only to sell them again, and whose "strong accent and familiarity with the purlieus of a great city led to grave suspicion of his origin."[27] Page the gentleman writer is not as reluctant to promote regional assertion and deprecation as the critic in the *Catholic World* suggests. He may not name places, but the reference to accent and big city unmistakably points to one direction: the North.

Nearly slain by a Northerner, Bruce winds up in Dr. Browne's house, where his father finds him and for the first time confronts the doctor. In reply, the doctor cries that he has "no name" and is "no one," but Margaret's "name [and] blood" are equal to the major's because she is "Charles Landon's great-granddaughter."[28] This sentimental denouement reveals the doctor to be the major's long lost and presumed drowned brother, Bruce, who, following a quarrel with their father, renounced his name and assumed an alias. The doctor's admission to his family name marks his return to gentility, which is mirrored in the family's restoration to Landon Hill and the renovation of the old place. The restoration of Landon Hill marks the completeness of the Landons' whiteness, if one is willing to overlook the major's lapses in gentlemanly behavior. The marriage of Bruce and Margaret, though suspiciously incestuous by modern standards, both prefigures and safeguards the continuity of the family's gentility and, by extension, Southern tradition. Margaret, in particular, becomes a living icon of the endurance of the Landon blood because of her striking resemblance to her great grandmother, so much so that "she looked as if she had stepped out of the old picture over the piano at Landon Hall."[29] Page takes up the motif of woman as preserver of Southern whiteness and tradition in his later novel *Red Rock: A Chronicle of Reconstruction*, transforming it from passive to active involvement.

If the plot of *On Newfound River* sounds naïve and, perhaps, implausible in places, that is because it is, but it is also in keeping with its being "a charming story," as the *Dial* critic puts it. And, while Page's treatment of Southern whiteness in the novel is partial, as it is in *In Ole Virginia*, it places the plantation house and hereditary possession of land at the heart of the concept. If the Southern whiteness he delineates in *On Newfound River* is capable of attaining wholeness, it is only so because it hinges on the recovery of the old place and because Page consigns the narrative to the past. Only when Page attempts to unite all the distinct attributes of whiteness, such as blood and breeding, honor and chivalry, with the plantation house and hereditary possession of land to create the narrative of its permanence, as he does in *Gordon Keith*, do cracks appear in the image.

Gordon Keith, Page's third novel, appeared in 1903. Compared to the reviews *On Newfound River* garnered, reception of *Gordon Keith* was relatively lukewarm and praise scant. The reviewer at the *Minneapolis Journal* commended the novel for "its message" that "rings true and clear" and its "elevated" tone, but did not remain oblivious to "certain inconsistencies in the narrative" and its general naiveté.[30] For the critic at the *Dial*, *Gordon Keith* suffered from the lack of definite "historical background," but deserved the somewhat muted compliment of "reasonable coherency." Others were not so kind. Jeanette L. Gilder, writing for the *Chicago Daily Tribune,* called the novel "old fashioned," and slammed its length, saying "there is enough material in it for half a dozen ordinary stories." The reviewer for the *Louisville Courier-Journal* echoed Gilder and belabored Page's outmoded and expansive style: *Gordon Keith* contained "capital material," but the trouble was that there was enough of it "for a dozen stories." The most scathing review came from a critic writing for the *Washington Times,* for whom *Gordon Keith* "can hardly be properly called a novel," because "it is more like a biography of a fictitious character."[31]

While the last review is remarkable for its ignorance of literary terminology, after all *Gordon Keith* is a novel and a *bildungsroman,* the other reviewers hit the mark: it is overcrowded, fraught with digressions and, generally, immodestly prolix. It is either a sign of the zeitgeist and the changing sensibility associated with the dawn of literary modernism that the novel failed to impress, or simply proof that Page went a step too far in expanding his once successful formula. The ingredients are all there, but the dish is decidedly over-seasoned. *Gordon Keith* follows the changing fortunes of the eponymous Keith. Gordon, the scion of the Keith family, witnesses his family's fortune and plantation dwindle and perish in the aftermath of the Civil War, vows to recover his ancestral seat, patiently but tenaciously struggles to achieve his goal, and finally returns victorious to the South. Gordon's wanderings take him away from the South, to New York and Appalachia, before Page finally restores him to his rightful place. Early on in the novel, and similar to *On Newfound River,* Page establishes a connection between the Keiths' claim to whiteness, heritage, and place through the act of naming. This time, however, Page turns to Scotland for inspiration, and the connections are more explicit. Both Gordon and Keith are of Scottish origin and, as cognomen, imbue the Keiths' whiteness with a particular historicity and tradition, thus emphasizing its uniqueness.[32] Page stresses the exceptionalism of their Scottish heritage through yet another name—Elphinstone—the Keiths' ancestral plantation. The word "stone" carries connotations of permanence and immutability, and "Elphin" links this permanence to Scottish royalty, aristocracy, and folklore.[33] The significance of Elphinstone as a place name lies in its convenient convergence of mythical, folkloric, and royalist ties with Scotland. Page not only fetishizes the Southern genteel tradition, but also establishes its historic provenance, the greatness of which dissociates the Keiths' history from slavery.

Elphinstone both inscribes and externalizes the interconnectedness of Southern whiteness, history, and tradition, which Page accentuates by introducing the place through the eyes of a visitor, a technique that, despite its common association with regional fiction, owes its popularity to Sir Walter Scott. In *Waverley; or, 'Tis Sixty Years*, when Edward Waverley travels to pay a visit to Cosmo Comyne Bradwardine of Bradwardine in Scotland, he first passes through the hamlet of Tully-Veolan, suitably inferior to the grandeur of the mansion, toward which leads an avenue that is "straight, and of moderate height, running between a double row of very ancient horse-chestnuts, planted alternately with sycamores, which rose to such huge height, and flourished so luxuriantly, that their boughs completely over-arched the broad road beneath." From there, "half-hidden by the trees of the avenue, the high steep roofs and narrow gables of the mansion, with ascending lines cut into steps, and corners decorated with small turrets," are visible. To Waverley, "the solitude and repose of the whole scene seemed almost monastic." The effect is close to sublime and owes its potency to the freshness of outlook, unspoiled by previous encounters: Waverley is a stranger, beholding the scene before him for the first time. Considering the popularity of Scott in the nineteenth-century South, the adoption of this method by Page, and to a lesser extent Glasgow and Chesnutt, is not incidental. Page deliberately emulates Scott's technique of introducing a place through the eyes of a stranger to reinforce the connection with Scotland and enunciate the whiteness of his protagonists. Glasgow's and Chesnutt's use of this method, however, subverts the notion of place as a monument of gentility as, frequently, the inhabitants of those places who have little, or nothing, in common with hereditary gentility belie the grandeur that surrounds them.

Scott's Waverley, his ingenuous character notwithstanding, could not fail but be equally impressed with Elphinstone, if he were to travel in the region. When Elphinstone first comes into view, it looks as it might have to a "stranger passing through the country prior to the war."[34] This brief preamble endows the description with objectivity, while both distancing the past from the present and reinforcing the sense of continuity already enshrined in its name. What the stranger would have seen first were "long stretches of rolling fields well tilled," then "a grove on a high hill," on top of which perched the "mansion" in "proud seclusion amid its immemorial oaks and elms." At the foot of this natural and constructed splendor lay "a small hamlet."[35] This feudal setting establishes the plantation as a pinnacle of greatness. Surrounded by fertile and verdant fields, it materializes as an ennatured emblem of civilization. Its setting not only establishes it as a part of nature, but, indeed, as its most salient spot. The location, in an organic fashion, sets it apart from the suitably inferior and conveniently located hamlet, creating a natural gap between their respective inhabitants.

The idea of natural environment as a mirror of moral and physical greatness has a long tradition. According to the proto-fascist philosopher Julius Evola, ascending a mountain has been historically the privilege of gods and heroes and, in the case of the latter, involved the attainment of immortality; while Certeau observes that the vantage point altitude affords generates the illusion of knowledge.[36] It is not just the elevated setting that separates the owners of Elphinstone from the denizens of the hamlet below, but also a claim to divinity that stems from the conjunction of mountain and knowledge. The plantation house, situated on a hill, possesses a significance that, although deriving from its physical setting, transcends its ontological presence. More than Landon Hill in *On Newfound River,* Elphinstone is a representational space *par excellence,* symbolizing the gentility of its occupiers; its possession becomes the first component in the fiction of the Keiths' whiteness, both Gordon's and his father's. Within the walls of Elphinstone, as befitting the cradle of gentility and knowledge, the visitor would have met with gracious hospitality; he would have encountered "culture with philosophy and wealth with content," and been "charmed with the graciousness of his entertainment." Indeed, if the traveler happened to reside outside the South, he would have left the place "with a feeling of mystification."[37] Little wonder, perhaps, because Page packs the picture with layers of signification and, through the metonymy of plantation, introduces both the values of Southern whiteness, among which he casts hospitality, graciousness of manners, knowledge, philosophy and culture—in short, all attributes associated with gentility—and its commensurability with the region. Gordon's world was the plantation "rimmed" by the very "woods" that had belonged to "the Keiths' for generations," over which the spirits of his saintly mother and many illustrious ancestors who found glory on the battlefields of the Revolution and the Mexican War kept watch. Gordon's heritage predestines him for gentility. His father, the epitome of the aristocratic and benevolent planter, governed the plantation without needing to raise his "voice," because "his word had a convincing quality of a law of nature."[38] The Keiths' gentility, and thus their whiteness, is not merely a matter of social status, but also a natural phenomenon, endemic to the place.

Such endemicity is only possible, Lefebvre suggests, because place attains its status as a lived reality through historically validated activity and, in doing so, delimits that very activity. Gentility and its attendant attributes, such as hospitality, graciousness of manners, and knowledge, can only signify as unique components of whiteness in the South in general and, as far as the Keiths are concerned, at Elphinstone, in particular, to which the "history of two hundred years bound" them. In that time, they "had carved" Elphinstone "from the forest" and "held it against the Indian." The Keiths wrote themselves into the place and transformed it as much as it transformed them, so much so that their heritage, "all the sanctities of life—were bound up with it." It is therefore fitting that, for Gordon, as for Faulkner in *Requiem for a Nun,* "the past is never dead. It's not even past."[39] This distinct place-history dialectic shaped their gentility and ensured its continuity by providing a link between the present and the past. Yet, in the aftermath of the Civil War, when pecuniary circumstances force General Keith to sell the plantation to Mr. Wickersham—a capitalist from the North—the link between the past and the present breaks, and with it the general's claim to whiteness. Although he remains on the plantation, he becomes, in Gordon's words, "nothing but an overseer." His presence on the plantation becomes transgressive, caught in the no-man's land between his former status as a gentleman planter and the much reduced position of a subordinate and Wickerhsam's employee. Werner Sollors defines such crossing of boundaries, whether enforced or voluntary, as passing—the condition of being what one is not.[40] Since the general's historically constructed function—that of the aristocratic planter residing at Elphinstone—determines his whiteness, with Elphinstone's passing from their hands, all the other hereditarily cultivated attributes associated with it, such as hospitality, graciousness of manners and knowledge, can only facilitate the Keiths' passing for gentlemen.

Yet, despite the Keiths' displacement from their ancestral seat, Page continues to use Elphinstone as a medium to evoke the individual attributes of their gentility. He does so through comparisons with others that allow him to incorporate a thinly veiled critique of the Northern parvenu nobility. When Wickersham entertains at Elphinstone, it is the Keiths' old servant Richard, who, when asked by the host his opinion of "our guests," the gentlemen present, replies: "Nor, suh; dee ain't gent'mens; dee's scalawags! . . . I been livin' heah 'bout sixty years, I reckon, an' I never seen nobody like dem eat at de table an' sleep in de beds in dis house befo."[41] Like the faithful retainers of *In Ole Virginia,* Richard is a former slave, and one of only two black characters in the novel. Yet, Page never alludes to his skin color, which allows him to divorce the Keiths' whiteness from the binarity of blackness manifested in hue; the simple reverence of a faithful servant for his one-time masters reifies their gentility. Richard's praise of the Keiths is doubly significant because it reaffirms that being called a gentleman is the highest commendation in the South. It reifies the aristocratic status of the Keiths by invoking the idea of the benevolent planter of the Old South. Despite the narrator's circumspection of expression, the scene turns into one of ingratiating usurpation, in which Wickersham mimics the ways of the general by using the plural possessive "our," a mode of expression reserved for royalty. This unfavorable comparison leaves little doubt as to whom Richard considers off white.

Throughout the novel, Page draws on the idea of being off white to resurrect Gordon's or his father's status as gentlemen. When Gordon displays a propensity for scholarly education, and his father cannot afford to send him to college, an "old cattle-dealer," Squire Rawson, unexpectedly comes to the rescue. Although the squire's "edication didn't cost twenty-five dollars," he is astute enough to "admit blood counts for somethin'," and he is "half minded to adventure some" on Gordon's. The Keith blood and the family's once-superior standing in the community are the only securities the squire needs to loosen his purse strings. It is the behavior of a Southern gentleman, although the squire's vernacular speech undermines his status as such. Discussing dialect writing in the nineteenth century, Gavin Jones observes that it served to enunciate the difference between the social standing of the characters and narrator. The squire's speech reifies Gordon's claim to whiteness in a similar way to the black narrators of *In Ole Virginia*. The fact that the squire does not "care anything about security or interest" or "want any bond" suggests another quality of whiteness that he believes the Keiths possess: that of honor.[42] Page mines every situation to its full potential to extol regional virtues. This display of disinterested generosity, coming from an exponent of a lower social stratum, evokes the notion of Southern generosity, with which all inhabitants of the region are blessed, and which places them in direct opposition to the Northern "scalawags."

Following a period of sedulous study and graduation from college, Gordon takes up a position as a teacher in Ridge College; here, again, environment provides a natural contrast between Gordon's gentility and the lack thereof in others. A part of Gordon's aristocratic legacy that places him on par with Evola's gods and heroes is his acute awareness of the beauty of nature. Mountains are a particular source of inspiration to him and, upon climbing one, he reflects on the past and the future. He wonders if "the Alps could be higher or more beautiful. A line he had been explaining the day before to his scholars recurred to him: 'Beyond those mountains lies Italy.'"[43] The act of climbing the mountain becomes a gnostic, consciousness-raising experience. His awareness of the mountainous grandeur forces him to acknowledge the loss of his home—the kernel of his gentility and heritage. The allusion to the Alps and Italy links Gordon, and the civilization he represents, to antiquity—the cradle of Western civilization—and, incidentally, to Romantic visionaries like Shelley and Byron. Through the allusion to the Alps Page transforms Gordon into a living symbol of the continuity of both traditions, the classical and the Southern. But, despite Page's efforts to join the two in a symbolic marriage, Gordon is no longer the heir to Elphinstone, and his gentility can only be incomplete.[44]

The only thread that ties Gordon to Elphinstone is the memory of the plantation. Although this link is strong enough for the latter to become a haunting presence, inseparable from Gordon's consciousness, its role in the projection of Gordon's whiteness is deconstructive rather than regenerative. The memory of Elphinstone both validates Gordon's tenuous claim to gentility and negates it by virtue of being a recollection of what is lost. The memory returns with a particular force whenever Gordon finds himself surrounded by the natural grandeur of the mountains. Depending on his vantage point, the mountains both symbolize his family's fall from grace and offer a healing vision of a way forward. It strikes Gordon that "others had crossed the mountains to find the Italy of their ambition." The force of this sudden revelation propels Gordon to stand upright, with "his face lifted to the sky, his nerves tense, his pulses beating and his breath coming quickly." At this cathartic moment, with his gaze lifted heavenward, Gordon partakes of a divine revelation, like that of the ancient heroes who ascended the mountain, and one that is possible because of his heritage. He vows that he will "conquer and achieve honors and fame, and win back his old home, and build up again his fortune, and do honor to his name." Honor, name, fame, and fortune are ideals worthy of a hero; and, that he mentions the recovery of his home among his future exploits implies they can be lived out in one place—a sentiment voiced by one of the protagonists, Miss Brooke, who grimly concludes that "one week in New York" will ruin "any gentleman of good manners."[45] Page's treatment of regional difference may be tactful, but it still hits the target by inviting unfavorable comparison: New York as a symbol of the North and its relentless capitalism and the cult of the self-made man is anathema to the Southern genteel ethos that glorifies nobility of birth, honor, chivalry, knowledge, and the past.[46] These values of Southern whiteness, Page implies, can only thrive in certain places, and New York is not one of them.

Yet, it would also appear they are not as widespread in the South as Page would wish. To Gordon, the mountains symbolize inspiration and ambition, and he defines both in relation to Elphinstone; but they exert no such influence on his pupils. The line from Emily Dickinson's poem that Gordon recollects reading to his students, "Beyond the Alps lies Italy," sent his lips aquiver "with feeling," whereas his young listeners meet it with "listless eyes and dull faces."[47] Partaking of a less lofty heritage, his scholars are incapable of comprehending either the significance of the line or the splendor of the mountains in the shadow of which they dwell. Because they represent an off-white end of the spectrum of whiteness, they cannot aspire to the genteel sensibility that constitutes Gordon's refinement. Yet, it is precisely their close proximity to nature, the source of raw experience without any connotative properties, that defines their status as off white.

Unlike Gordon's upbringing on the plantation, the Dennison boys, who are among Gordon's listless scholars, live in a "'cove'" surrounded by mountains. Their mother, Mrs. Dennison, is "a small, angular woman with sharp eyes, a thin nose, and thin lips, very stiff and suspicious," someone who would not have been averse to setting the family's "dog" on Gordon when he visits.[48] A far cry from the idealized Southern belle, such a mother can only produce "listless" offspring who, living at the foot of the mountain, possess neither the means nor the inclination to aspire to greatness as Gordon does. For Page, blood indeed tells, and the gulf separating the sensibilities of these inhabitants of the South, including Mrs. Dennison's decidedly un-Southern lack of hospitality, is seemingly unbridgeable. In this unfavorable comparison, Page introduces class difference by stereotyping Mrs. Dennison and uses the opportunity to showcase Gordon's gentility by juxtaposing it with her silent hostility and lack of manners. Even the kind Squire Rawson, Gordon's benefactor and staunch supporter throughout his career, despite accumulating considerable fortune following, in his words, "years of hard work on the mountain-side, sweatin' o' days, and layin' out in the cold at nights, lookin' up at the stars and wonderin' how I was to git along—studyin' of folks jest as I studied cattle," falls victim to Page's class discrimination. Unlike Gordon's, his relationship with the land is not that of an aesthete capable of understanding its symbolic significance—a fact that Page again emphasizes through the squire's vernacular speech—but that of a simple farmer. He is the salt of the earth to Gordon's cream; Gordon is simply a paler shade of white. The squire is a man of simple sensibility, for whom "land's land," and its significance is primarily utilitarian.[49] The squire's pecuniary circumstances may place him above Gordon, who works as a teacher, but his lack of aristocratic heritage invalidates his claim to gentility, at least in the region.

Gordon's love of the region and attachment to Elphinstone are peculiarly Southern traits which, like the South itself, become as fully transparent as the grandeur of the plantation house when observed by a non-Southerner. The stranger is Alice Yorke, a visitor to the region from New York, who becomes the recipient of Gordon's love and adulation. Alice is not entirely immune to the beauty of the place, but seems incapable of forming a spiritual bond with it. She finds the idea that "any one [sic] could have so much feeling for a plantation" incomprehensible. Alice's Northern sensibility occludes her understanding of the bond between Gordon and Elphinstone—the ties that transcend mere ownership of land to encompass tradition and heritage. Alice's regional affinity prevents her from understanding both this bond and Gordon, whom she finds wanting "in that quality of sound judgment which she recognized in some of her other [Northern] admirers." Gordon's shortcoming is his lack of business acumen, which Alice ascribes to his culture: Gordon "was too romantic."[50] Once again, through regional stereotyping, Page places Southern chivalrous gentility and romanticism at loggerheads with Northern industry and pragmatism.

Page disassociates Southern whiteness from dollar-worship early in the novel, when Gordon's father informs him that "there are some things that gentlemen never discuss at table. Money is one of them." This simple scholium from father to son confirms the existence of an unwritten code of practice obtaining among gentlemen that consigns money to the realm of the unmentionable. The gentlemanly disdain for matters pecuniary and the accumulation of capital are of particular importance to Page, who returns to them further in the narrative. Using General Keith, the living exponent of antebellum gentility, as his mouthpiece, Page concludes that riches *qua* riches are "one of the most despicable and debasing of all the aims that men can have." But Gordon's brush with Northern pragmatism in the person of Alice Yorke redefines riches, so that "wealth appeared to him just then a very desirable acquisition."[51] Depending on viewpoint, to mark the expansion or contraction of Gordon's ideals, Page writes a dramatic episode into the narrative when Gordon finds Alice lying unconscious on a peak. She has fallen from her horse, and Gordon, in a tide of chivalric spirit, carries her down the mountain. The act itself appears proleptic as it foreshadows Gordon's subsequent quest for wealth and his altered sensibility occasioned by the encounter with a lady from the North. The descent from the mountain symbolizes the change in Gordon's sensibility, rendering his heroism anti-heroic, as it prefigures his partial abandonment of his hereditary ideals.

Gordon's quest for wealth, begun with his descent down the mountain, takes him away from the region—to Appalachia and New York, where he finally accomplishes his goal of becoming rich. He recovers Elphinstone, but continues to reside in the city that made him prosperous, until he realizes that "he was sailing under false colors."[52] The accumulated wealth cannot elevate him to the metaphorical peaks where he once sought his ideals, because it is acquired and, as such, not reconcilable with his heritage. In his pursuit of wealth, "he had almost lost sight of the life that lay outside of the dust and din of that arena," and forgot "that life held other rewards than riches." Gordon's apathy is not merely the result of an insalubrious city life devoted to making money that he led in New York, but of spiritual starvation. He knows that the only remedy is to return to "the calm and tranquil region" where his father walks with calmness and serene thoughts elevated "high above all commercial matters," in communion with "statesmen, philosophers, and poets," steeped in "universal gentleness and kindness," while the spirit of his mother breathes "the purity of heaven" over the scene in benediction.[53] Page turns Elphinstone into the perfect metonymy so that, in Gordon's imagination, it signifies more than a brick-and-mortar edifice. It encompasses gentility, learning, heritage, gentleness, selflessness, all of which apotheosize Southern whiteness and ground it in the region. Only in Elphinstone, surrounded by history and the ghosts of his past can Gordon recover his gentility, and thus his whiteness.

Unlike in *On Newfound River,* where serendipity intervenes on Bruce's behalf and restores him to Landon Hill through marriage, what complicates Gordon's vision are the terms of his return: he does not inherit the plantation but purchases it with the capital he has accumulated over the years—an act that indelibly distinguishes his gentility from that of his father. This break in the historic chain of inheritance means that he can never return to the innocence that his wistful imagination has conjured up. Page, perhaps unconsciously, signals the impossibility of such a return to a state of purity, uncontaminated by capital, through another allusion to the environment. On his return to the region, Gordon sees the moon "slowly sinking toward the western mountaintops"; however, he remains a passive observer.[54] The scene is reminiscent of "*ragnarokkr,* the destined twilight of the divine." This act of passive observation marks the end of Gordon's quest—one that began with his descent down the mountain—and foreshadows the incompleteness of his now-acquired gentility. This scene holds nothing of the hustle and bustle of renewal present in the closing pages of *On Newfound River.* The "twilight of the divine" signifies the permanence of the lost whiteness and changes the function of Elphinstone from a space of lived experience to a mausoleum of a lost ideal. Yet, despite the impossibility of Gordon's mythical return to the whiteness of the past, Elphinstone, as the monument of Old South, remains the site of origin and an emblem of the endurance of Southern genteel values. Certeau observes of proper names that their power lies in their connotative properties which sustain believability.[55] As a proper name,

Elphinstone creates the meanings of whiteness to which Gordon subscribes and that encapsulate gentility and heritage as well as tradition and knowledge. In propagating this particular fiction, Elphinstone's power is twofold: it evokes the permanence and continuity of such a fiction thus binding both to the locale; however, by furnishing this fiction with believability, it places it within the realm of the abstract and ensures its status as a fiction. Because facts are subject to verifiable, empirical knowledge, and fictions only need to be believable, Gordon's fiction of whiteness requires him to return to Elphinstone, where the ghosts of his ancestors still reside.

TWO

ELLEN GLASGOW AND THE PLIGHT OF RETROSPECTION

The times may have changed, but the plantation house, that relic of a bygone era and emblem of Southern whiteness, remained a permanent fixture of the Southern landscape and worldview. The loss of the Cause ushered in the birth of another cause whose aim was the preservation of the genteel ethos of the antebellum days. This zeal to preserve, regenerate and, in many cases, re-invent the Southern way of life became the chief objective of the post-Reconstruction Southern writers for whom, unlike their predecessors, the Lost Cause of the War was simply a *fait accompli*. Page responded to this call with alacrity, painting the picture of an idyll not only despoiled by the armies of the North but also destroyed by the unconscionable politics of Reconstruction. Yet, despite the ruin, Gordon Keith's chivalrous spirit lingers amid the embers and, while Elphinstone stands, the return to a semblance of gentility, albeit with coffers filled in the North, is still a possibility. What anchors Keith's claim to whiteness and facilitates the continuity of its fiction is the monumental space of the plantation house as the place of a lived historical experience. It is an inspiring and benevolent presence that motivates Keith to remain true to his heritage. For the protagonists of Ellen Glasgow's *Deliverance: A Romance of the Virginia Tobacco Fields*, however, it is both a burden and a constant reproach that keeps them rooted to the spot; it evokes the ghosts of the past and invites questioning of the legitimacy of the genteel heritage it represents. Although its presence looms just as large as that of Elphinstone in *Gordon Keith,* the Blake Hall in *The Deliverance* disrupts the fiction of whiteness based on hereditarily predetermined claims. Glasgow's South is a region blighted by such outdated notions, which arrest its development by constantly harking back to what once was. To emphasize the anachronism of such sentiments, Page's benevolent planter and his accomplice, the Southern belle, are all but absent from Glasgow's narrative, supplanted by an array of characters who find themselves out of place, literally and metaphorically.

The novel, published in 1904, is the second in a series on the social history of Virginia and begins immediately after the end of Reconstruction, spanning the years from 1878 to 1890. In *The Deliverance*, and in the series, Glasgow, by her own candid admission, set out to "treat the static customs of the country" and "portray the different social orders," which she saw as endemic to the place. She called the series "a history of manners" that examined those "aspects of Southern life" with which she was "acquainted." As it happened, those aspects included Virginia and its inhabitants of the genteel extraction. Glasgow was born in Richmond, Virginia, and, with the exception of a few years passed in New York and Europe, spent her life there. She wrote all her books, except one, in Richmond. On her mother's side, she could trace her lineage back to the early Tidewater plantation days and boasted a Colonel Randolph among her progenitors. Her ancestors on her father's side subscribed to the Calvinist creed and had come from Scotland, via Ulster, to stand "among the stalwart pioneers in the upper valley of the James River."[1] Although by the time she was born, the years of the war and Reconstruction Acts "had swept away" the family's possessions and they "had little left," there was still enough to employ Mammy Lizzie, of whom she was exceedingly fond. Despite the conflict, or maybe because of it, the Southern sensibility had not changed much, and Glasgow grew up "in the yet lingering fragrance of the Old South," and in her "blood" coursed the "remote inheritances of the past three hundred years in Virginia." Yet, despite her love of "the imperishable charm" of the Old South, Glasgow acknowledged its constraining allure and, in her own words, "revolted from its stranglehold on the intellect."[2] To break this stranglehold, Glasgow wrote, the South needed "blood and irony"—blood because it "was satisfied to exist on borrowed ideas" and irony because it is "the safest antidote to sentimental decay." Both also go against the grain of "the superficial picturesqueness of 'local color'"—a label that Glasgow passionately resented.[3]

Although critics have attempted to affix a literary label to Glasgow, they spared her regional typecasting. Frederick McDowell and R. H. W. Dillard observe that Glasgow, like many of her contemporaries, subscribed to a diluted version of social determinism with Darwinian inflections. Whether Glasgow would have endorsed such evaluation is rather doubtful. A self-confessed rebel, she resented any kind of literary or cultural regimentation, although she did admit to being affected by Darwin's *The Origin of Species*. Against realism as conceived by W. D. Howells and concerned with depicting "nothing more and nothing less than truthful treatment of material," she held its superficiality and inability to penetrate into individual experience. She despised Southern evasive realism of the Page school for its "solitary purpose" of defending "the lost" combined with a triteness of insight. The task of the true realist, she wrote, was to "illuminate experience, not merely transcribe it."[4] And, for Glasgow, that human experience was to be found in the changing scenery of the South, where the old order of *noblesse oblige* refused to give up its ghost and still reverberated in the hallowed but now simply hollow walls of the plantation house. In *The Deliverance*, as in *The Battle-Ground* or *The Voice of the People*, the notion of Southern whiteness or gentility, becomes entangled with the hereditary possession of land and its hallmark, the plantation house. In this place, where the possession of land is thus qualified, the disinherited aristocrat and the *nouveau riche* face a similar predicament; they are both off white.

The Deliverance poses a challenge to the corrosive influence of the Old South mythology, particularly in the characters of Mrs. Blake and her daughter Cynthia, both of whom literally live on "borrowed ideas." Unlike Page's tale, however, Glasgow resists "the elegiac impulse" and hers is, in Richard Gray's apposite paraphrase of John Donne, "a Valediction to the Old South, forbidding mourning." The story unfolds in postbellum Virginia, where first the vagaries of war and then Reconstruction have irrevocably altered the fortunes of the once-patrician Blake family. So far, the story resembles Page's formula. In this place, the notion of whiteness is intricately woven into the fabric of everyday life and resonates as loudly as if the war had never been. Mrs. Blake sagaciously advises her son to "remember to be a gentleman," and he will "find that that embraces all morality and a good deal of religion." What matters most when choosing a spouse is "family connection" and then "personal attractiveness." Wealth "counts for very little beside good birth." Wafting strongly of anachronism, the sentiments that Mrs. Blake voices encapsulate the quiddity of Southern whiteness: suitable heritage, breeding, and morality, all of which boast divine sanction. Sarah Gardner suggests that Mrs. Blake symbolizes the post-war South that is unable to face the economic and social challenges posed by post–Civil War realities. Yet, blind and paralyzed, she also stands as the emblem of the endurance of the antebellum genteel mythology, clinging with passionate fidelity to "the ceremonial forms of tradition." Pitiful and misguided as she may appear, one thing is certain:

in this place, where such anachronistic legacy obtains, she is not groping alone. For Mrs. Blake and the inhabitants of this corner of Virginia, the old ideas are far from dead, let alone buried.[5]

The rules of "good breeding" and their attendant hereditary possession of land dictate the classification of society and that, accordingly, "good people," the "lineal descendants of English yeomen" dwell alongside "good families" of the planter aristocracy. "De tribble wid dis yer worl'," as Uncle Isam, one of the Blakes' former slaves remarks, is that "w'en hit changes yo' fortune hit don' look ter changin' yo' skin es well." The simplicity of these words is only skin-deep and conceals an ambiguity that renders them equally applicable to Uncle Isam's and the Blakes' situations. The change of skin acts as a metaphor for displacement and, in the Blakes' case, dispossession. Despite their impoverished status, they are unable and, in the case of Cynthia, unwilling to shed the skin once habitually worn. What decides their categorization are the past and local lore, woven out of reminiscence from which escape is futile. To their neighbors, they are still a "good family," although Christopher Blake has tilled the strip of land remaining in the family's possession for fifteen years, since he was ten. But he is still Mr. Christopher to his once less fortunate neighbors like the storekeeper, Tom Spade, or Marse Christopher to the former slaves. The title itself, as Aunt Sadie, the former overseer's sister now residing at Blake Hall reminisces, is a hereditary privilege accorded to Christopher in memory of his father, also Christopher, for whom she "used to open the gate" when she was a child. And, indeed, as far as gentlemen go, she "don't recon thar was a freer or a finer between here and London." Aunt Sadie is not alone. The other inhabitants of this place subscribe to the principles of Southern whiteness "where ancestry, gentility, and the backward view counted most."[6]

Christopher's status rests upon the past that sustains it through living memory. From the very beginning, however, Glasgow emphasizes the precariousness of such positioning. *The Deliverance* is Glasgow's only novel in which she opts for an "indirect approach" and introduces the hero through "a stranger's eyes."[7] The stranger in question is Mr. Carraway, a lawyer, summoned by his client, Mr. Fletcher, to Blake Hall on a matter of business. The visit affords Carraway the pleasure of observing the surrounding countryside and the benefit of Sol Peterkin's commentary. Peterkin, a local tobacco farmer, with a "wiry, sun burned neck," from whose mouth "a thin stream of tobacco juice" trickled, fits the stereotypical description of a "redneck." The narrator's account of Peterkin sets the tone for the ensuing narrative and indicates its distance from the refinements of the mythical South. It is from Peterkin that Carraway learns that "tobaccy's king down here, an' no mistake," and that the Blakes' fortune depended on its cultivation. With pride and fondness, Peterkin reminisces about the grandeur of the family's estate: "you might stand at the big gate an' look in any direction you pleased till yo' eyes bulged fit to bu'st, but you couldn't look past the Blake land for all yo' tryin." Indeed, the fields they are passing were once "set out in Blake tobaccy time an' agin." Peterkin's narrative enunciates the interdependence between the conception of whiteness and place. Speaking of the construction of subjectivity, Neil Evernden observes that it is context and place dependent.[8] What defines and revitalizes the story of the Blakes is the possession of this vast plantation and the cultivation of tobacco. That Peterkin consigns his narrative to the past foreshadows the Blakes' fall.

Deprived of his inheritance by the cunning of his father's former overseer, Fletcher, Christopher Blake labors in the fields with other common laborers. To Carraway, however, he appears a hybrid, "molded physically perhaps in a finer shape than they," but also "the product of the soil on which he stood." Inadvertently, Carraway contrasts his newly acquired knowledge of Christopher's heritage with the actual, attempting to discover traces of his family's gentility beneath the laborer's exterior. Peterkin's assessment is free of such intellectual gyrations and, despite his diminished status, Christopher is simply "a Blake, skin an' bone, anyhow, an' you ain't goin' to git this here county to go agin him."[9] The respect accorded Christopher is largely, but not solely, based on his family's former standing in the community; it is also grounded in blood. Indeed, blood, Peterkin wisely remarks, "will tell, even at the dregs." Blood symbolizes the superiority of Christopher's lineage which his appearance externalizes. His resemblance to his father is uncanny, if not entirely flattering. Christopher, Peterkin observes, is "the very spit of his pa, that's so', and 'he's got the old gentleman's dry throat along with it." In a world irrevocably altered, where "de overseer is in de gret house, and gent'man's in de blacksmiff shop," Peterkin's narrative provides a continuity between the past and the present, and Christopher is the embodiment of this connection. In Peterkin's estimation, Christopher's lineage places him above the other denizens of the region; whereas to Carraway, whose assessment does not partake of the same historicity as Peterkin's, Christopher is only "an illiterate day-laborer," albeit of a finer stature.[10]

Frederick McDowell observes that the South's defeat left intact the Southerners' instinctive respect for class distinction.[11] Glasgow was not alone in her inability to shake off the "stranglehold" of the old South. It is Peterkin's inbred respect for Christopher that effects his claim to gentility—

and, consequently, whiteness. Told and retold by Peterkin, the fiction of Christopher's whiteness becomes endemic to the place; its discourse enters into a mutually reciprocal relationship with the place. Its construction depends on the place, while its fiction adds to the uniqueness of the place. In telling the story, Peterkin actively produces the fiction of Christopher's whiteness, the fiction that Carraway's comment simultaneously undermines. But the uncharitable remark upon Christopher's reduced circumstances does not alter Carraway's conception of gentility. In a conversation with Fletcher, Carraway voices the connection between property, heritage, continuity, and place, observing that: "The property idea is very strong in these rural counties. . . . They feel that every year adds a value to the hereditary possession of land, and that when an estate has borne a single name for a century there has been a veritable impress placed upon it."[12] Effectively, like Page, Glasgow uses Carraway to express an indispensable component of Southern whiteness, namely the hereditary possession of land. Since the Blakes had occupied Blake Hall for two hundred years, the relatively short period of Fletcher's tenancy cannot erase the impression left by its previous occupants, the impression that has passed into local lore.

Once Carraway becomes acquainted with the local history, he cannot remain unaffected by it. He imagines, perhaps a little fancifully, that the forced departure of the rightful owners stripped the place of a "peculiar spirit" that "makes every old house the guardian of an inner life—the keeper of a family's ghost." Blake Hall, or "the Hall," as it is known during Fletcher's occupancy, forms an inextricable part of the Blakes' fiction of whiteness that the family's changed circumstances cannot alter. Yet, the presence of the Hall is deeply ambivalent and both facilitates and undermines the fiction of whiteness not only of the degraded Blakes but also of the upwardly mobile Fletchers. Murphy sees place as a formative element of self-awareness because of the historical and environmental values enshrined in it. An active participation in a place exceeds mere passive observation to include reformulation of old histories associated with it.[13] It demands an active engagement with one's heritage and history as constituents of self-awareness, while self-awareness becomes a historical construct. As long as the Hall endures, the outcome of the stories of the Blakes' and the Fletchers' whiteness, actively told and retold by the region's inhabitants, is already predetermined; a modified version of Darwinism gone sour or the crux of Southern philosophy, where memory and tradition replace survival of the fittest.

Fletcher's adaptability is no match for the endurance of memory and tradition that the place represents. The "Blake portraits" may have vacated the premises with the previous owners, but they left behind "dust-marked squares" and "lines that the successive scrubbings of fifteen years had not utterly effaced." These empty, discolored spaces irrevocably tie the story of the Blakes' whiteness to the Hall and mark the tangible failure of Fletcher's efforts to untell it. Fletcher's uncouthness and lack of noble lineage, which Carraway observes, achieve the opposite effect and serve only to accentuate the gentility of the previous occupants of the house. When, at supper, Fletcher's grandson observes that Mrs. Blake has spring chicken every night, Fletcher's contempt for such blatant lack of economy spills over. The Blakes are "fools" to dine on spring chicken "when they could get forty cents apiece for 'em in the open market." Fletcher's mercantilism, in which avarice meets budding capitalism, is a far cry from Mrs. Blake's privileging of breeding over monetary gain. Not that Mrs. Blake's dictum would sway Fletcher. His ambitions of social rising are for his grandchildren, William and Maria, for whose education Fletcher spares no expense. Maria's refinements are so genteel that, as Carraway observes, "she's like a dressed-up doll-baby" who looks as if "all the natural thing has been squeezed out of her, and she's stuffed with sawdust." In the harshness of Carraway's assessment, Glasgow asks whether an individual is capable of rising above his inherited class predispositions, which, in this place, amounts to becoming a lady—the feminine acme of whiteness.

Compared with her grandfather's former occupation as an overseer on the Blakes' plantation, her father's lowly station as a blacksmith and alcoholism, and her mother's illiteracy, Maria has indeed come a long way. According to Valentin Vološinov, self-awareness is born out of socialization and is the product of an endless positioning of oneself against social norms, evaluations, and affinities, so much so that self-consciousness becomes inseparable from class consciousness.[14] Such positioning, while influencing conformity and mimicry, invariably fosters difference, and this difference itself stems from social, political, cultural, and historical discourses that are not only unique to a given place, but also linked to environmental factors. In the South—and in contrast to the North—the agriculturally based orientation and consequent stratification of society was a direct corollary of a conjunction of socio-historical heritage with natural environment, which resulted in the emergence of a particular genteel ethos whose beginnings reached back in time to England and the settlement of the colony of Virginia. This is precisely why, to Carraway, armed with the foreknowledge of her ancestry, Maria's refinements are unnatural, jarring with the place that had sheltered her betters.

As accomplished as Maria may appear, Fletcher, nonetheless, pins his hopes of the family's social rising on William. Having summoned Carraway to discuss his will, Fletcher intends to bequeath everything to his only grandson, William, who will one day "make his mark among the gentility;" while his granddaughter, Maria, will "receive a share of the money," which will "make her child-bearing easier" and, as far as Fletcher is concerned, "that's the only thing a woman's fit for." He would "as soon keep a cow that wouldn't calve" than "a childless woman." Fletcher's lack of chivalry and undisguised disdain for women emphasize his plebeian status, which even his possession of Blake Hall cannot expunge. Though he resides in the region, as an exponent of the lower class, Fletcher does not worship at the altar of femininity. He sees a woman's purpose as purely utilitarian, a sentiment that "Carraway as a man of 'old-fashioned ideal' finds deeply offensive." Glasgow juxtaposes Fletcher and Carraway to destabilize the notion of the South as a homogenous region and offset Carraway's gentility. And the attitude to women is not the only thing that separates them. Fletcher's attitude to that time-and tradition-honored ambition of scholarly prowess—to which every landed gentleman should aspire—is equally utilitarian. Greek and Latin are "a good thing to stop a mouth with," and his own lack of knowledge has cost him many a bargain. Indeed, in Fletcher's experience a "line of poetry spurted on a sudden in one of them dead-and-gone languages" brings a negotiation to a desired end much more speedily than "taking the Lord's name in vain."[15] The logic may be flawed, and certainly is far removed from genteel ideals, but it is Fletcher's sole reason for putting William "on 'em from the start," because it "dose him well with something his neighbors haven't learnt." This may be an instance of a vicarious one-upmanship, yet Carraway considers Fletcher's renouncement of personal ambition to be his only redeeming feature, which invests his "racial" scheme to socially advance his grandchildren "with a kind of grandeur." In this place, former overseers do not qualify as "good families" or "good people," and the occupation is as much a class as it is a racial denominator. This brief exchange, while emphasizing Fletcher's lack of genteel breeding, effects Carraway's claim to gentility by highlighting his subscription to the "old-fashioned ideal." The very setting of the exchange, Blake Hall—"a manifestation in brick and mortar of the hereditary greatness of the Blakes"—makes it doubly offensive. Set against the backdrop of this hereditary grandeur, adorned with "the clean white Doric columns" harking back to antiquity, Fletcher's lack of gentlemanly manners alienates him from the place, while evoking the ghosts of the Blakes' past.[16]

Maria Fletcher, who inherits the residence after her brother has reverted to the shiftlessness of his father and returns it to its rightful owners, acutely feels her inadequacy to occupy the plantation house. Having been educated to become a lady, Maria observes of returning to Blake Hall: "When I come back here I seem to lose all that I have learned, and to grow vulgar, like Jinnie Spade, at the store." Blake Hall seems to unmake Maria's tenuous claim to gentility, which her education and grandfather's wealth have furnished. What causes such a transformation is an awareness of transgression—a pretending to be what one is not that is emblematic of passing.[17] When confronted with the heritage of the Blakes that the Hall represents, Maria realizes that, despite her acquired gentility, in this particular place, she only passes for a lady. To Maria, Blake Hall's "very age is a reproach to us, for it shows off our newness—our lack of any past that we may call our own."[18] Though formulated in a more sophisticated manner, Maria's sentiment echoes that of Peterkin in that they both see notions of the past and heredity as crucial to one's status. Maria's statement seems the more poignant as it emphasizes her precarious status in passing as a lady by rendering acute her awareness of her lack of an acceptable past—her lack of a genteel legacy.

Blake Hall, an emblem of the conjunction of localization and history, becomes a key factor in the formation of Maria's self-awareness. Both within its walls and in the region, where the individual and collective social and historical consciousness do not admit of change, Maria's ambiguous status as passing for a lady has long been sealed. Before her marriage to Wyndham, her trousseau sends shock waves through the community. Gathered in Tom Spade's shop, the locals who have it on good authority that Maria's "very stockings have got lace let in 'em" cannot contain their disdain for such extravagance. Sol Peterkin's judgment is as swift as it is contemptuous: "them lace let in stockin's ain't" to his "mind."[19] If the offensive garments were to belong to Mrs. Blake or one of her daughters, the neighborhood would be spared the sanctimonious outrage. The real cause of dismay is not the stockings, but an instinctive irreverence for the Fletchers, stemming from localized historical knowledge. The idea of the former overseer's granddaughter owning silk stockings is simply irreconcilable, even in her current circumstances; it is a case of misplacement on both counts. The world may have changed Maria's fortune but "hit don' look ter changin" her "skin es well," and she cannot outgrow an instinctive reverence for the Blakes. Even before she falls in love with Christopher, she bows to the gentleman lying dormant beneath the exterior of a field laborer when she exclaims: "you would make three of me—body, brain and soul." What motivates her decision to return the property to Christopher is the need to mend past wrongs and restore the rightful order. In an impassioned appeal to Christopher to accept the gift, she calls herself "a dependent—a charity ward who has lived for years upon" his "money," and whose "education," "culture," and "refinements" rightfully belong to Christopher's family. In this natural reversal to type, putting her in a socially and historically allotted place, which she communicates to Carraway, Maria forces him "to modify his conservative theories as to the necessity of blue blood to nourish high ideals."[20] Yet, despite the selflessness of her deed, Maria's acknowledgement of being out of place and Carraway's questioning of old truths highlight the nature of her whiteness as a fiction based on wealth and education—devoid of the indispensable endorsement of acceptable heritage. The altruism of Maria's actions may bring her closer to the venerated sanctity of the female ideal. Yet, here, where the past shapes the present, she can never be a lady.

Christopher's claim to whiteness, by contrast, rests on heredity and historicity. Reduced to near penury, Christopher, together with his frail mother whose Southern belle fame still reverberates in a nostalgic echo across the region, dwells in the former overseer's cottage. Cramped into the hovel with its "soiled whitewashed walls" adorned with "a noble gathering of Blake portraits in massive old gilt frames" are Christopher's two sisters, Cynthia and Lila, a cousin of Mrs. Blake and Civil War veteran, Uncle Tucker, and several of their former slaves. Painting, Chad T. May notes, captures the past but divides it from the present.[21] But, paintings do more than separate the past from the present; they are both windows to the past that stubbornly insist on the connection between the past and the present and points of comparison offering a possibility of reconciliation, however futile. The intersection of the historical and the personal encoded in the portraits revitalizes the metaphor of blood as heritage and safeguards the memory of the Blakes' gentility. From this memory, which returns like a revenant, there is no escape, as Christopher finds out. When the disinherited William Fletcher kills his grandfather in a violent confrontation, he runs to Christopher for help, and the portraits bear mute yet expressive witness to their exchange. Feeling culpable for William's degradation because he designed and fostered the breach between the grandson and his grandsire as part of his revenge on the Fletchers, Christopher takes the blame upon himself and is imprisoned. The decision to do so is cathartic and comes as his eyes fall upon the portrait of his grandfather Bolivar Blake. At this critical moment, Christopher remembers his grandfather's "dying phrase:" "I may sit with the saints, but I shall stand among the gentlemen."[22] In admitting to aiding and abetting a murderer, Christopher regains his familial sense of honor and fortitude.

Honor and fortitude rank high on Mrs. Blake's list of gentlemanly prerequisites, and in this respect, she is as much a relic of the past as the portraits adorning the walls. Mrs. Blake has been living in darkness—literally and metaphorically—for the past twenty years. The stroke she suffered before Fletcher took over Blake Hall left her blind and paralyzed. In this state she continues, unaware of the family's altered circumstances; for Mrs. Blake dwells in a world in which "the Confederacy had never fallen," where "the three hundred slaves" are constantly present in her visions "tilling her familiar fields." When Carraway, at Fletcher's behest, pays a business visit to Christopher bearing an offer to purchase his land, the deference with which he treats Mrs. Blake owes everything to the past. As the two become acquainted, Carraway recalls an incident from his childhood when he was "taken out upon the street corner merely to see" Mrs. Blake pass him on the way to a ball.[23] Mrs. Blake delights in the recollection but, more importantly, Carraway's memory confirms that she is in the presence of one of her kind, so much so that she offers him hospitality and invites him to spend the night beneath their roof, which once "has had a privilege of sheltering General Washington."[24] That Washington's visit adds a historic gravitas to Blake Hall is certain, but evoking the association in the shabby surroundings of the overseer's cottage throws into relief the extent to which Mrs. Blake is passing for a lady and the family's sham attempt at maintaining a facade of gentility.

Mrs. Blake's dislocation from the here and now elucidates the family's poverty. Glasgow builds the effect of hopeless decay gradually, through Mrs. Blake's relentless conjuring of the past and its customs, which cannot but reflect negatively on the present. And so Christopher, she admonishes her son, should betake himself to the library to discuss matters of business "over a bottle of burgundy," as was his "grandfather's custom" before him.[25] In Mrs. Blake's condition, Glasgow literalizes the principles of Southern whiteness whose *modus operandi* is the replication of tradition, however debilitating it may be in the present. Ironically, this instruction in gentlemanly conduct yet again undermines the facade of gentility that her family has painstakingly maintained. This scholium on the importance of upholding tradition effectively forces Christopher to pass for a gentleman, since he feels obliged to postpone his discussion with Carraway until they can retreat to the library. What seals the failure of the endeavor is the lack of a library in their cottage, and, with it, Christopher's passing is foiled.

Gentility and tradition constantly occupy Mrs. Blake's thoughts, and she never misses an opportunity to impart wisdom to her offspring. Only a gentleman, she informs Christopher, "who has taken the enemy's guns single-handed, or figured prominently in a society scandal, is comfortably settled in his position."[26] Christopher, however, is "an ordinary gentleman" and, since they "are not likely to have another war," he "really ought to marry." But, marriage is a delicate business and, when Lila proclaims she cares not for blood, Mrs. Blake cannot hide her dismay: "Not care about blood, indeed! What are we coming to, I wonder." Mrs. Blake's horizon, just like that of her plebeian neighbors, is circumscribed by notions shaped by historic precedent. And, thanks to the efforts of her family, who have woven "the intricate tissue of lies" around her, Mrs. Blake can pass for an aristocratic matron—the epitome of Christian charity who graciously gives audiences to her inferior neighbors such as Jim Weatherby. Before Jim can present himself before her illustrious personage, Mrs. Blake instructs Cynthia "to make him wipe his feet." Only when reassured of the cleanliness of her visitor does Mrs. Blake nostalgically remark: "I remember his father always was [clean]—unusually so for a common laborer."[27] In a paradoxical twist, belied by her surroundings, such remarks both emphasize Mrs. Blake's displacement and provide a means to effect her own whiteness and superiority. This blunt enquiry leaves implicit the notion of Mrs. Blake's own cleanliness, which constitutes a *fait accompli*. To paraphrase Dyer, the cleanliness of a former belle is the norm, but the cleanliness of a common laborer is an exception. If cleanliness belongs among the attributes of whiteness, then Mrs. Blake certainly aspires to it, at least in her own estimation. Interestingly, Mrs. Blake's remark about Jim's father's cleanliness sets the Weatherbys apart from other laborers and reaffirms the existence of off-white hues, inadvertently validating their tenuous claim to whiteness. Later, Jim's marriage to Mrs. Blake's daughter Lila legitimizes this claim.

Lila and Jim's courtship and marriage meet with a strong opposition from Cynthia, the eldest of the Blake siblings, who guards genteel values with the might of the mythical Cerberus. Just like her mother's, Cynthia's main objection is the product of socio-historical legacy that places blood heritage above personal merit, and whose resonance is all the louder because of the close spatial proximity of the two families and their shared memory. Cynthia meets Lila's declaration of her wish to marry Jim with an outraged exclamation of "who was his Grandfather?" When Uncle Tucker intervenes and points out the folly of sacrificing oneself for "a relic," Cynthia accuses him of having no "consideration for the family name," which is all they have left. The nuptials mark, at least in Cynthia's estimation, the ultimate degradation of the family and, after the happy event, she concludes that the Blakes have fallen "to the level of the Weatherbys and—the Fletchers."[28]

Cynthia's worries, however, prove to be unfounded. In this place, where the past haunts the present, the Blakes cannot eschew passing for gentility. By virtue of birth and *noblesse oblige,* Christopher risks his life to help a former slave, Uncle Isam, who sends for him because his family has been dying of smallpox. The call of the former, though now severed obligation, overrides all other concerns, and Christopher strips off his overalls to don the shoes of a benevolent planter. To the farmers present when Uncle Isam's message arrives, Christopher's action is reckless and quixotic. Cynthia, however, understands the motivation behind Christopher's decision and simply concludes that "there was nothing else" for him to do. On the one hand, the fiction of the Blakes' whiteness is propagated by their formerly poor, but now financially equal, neighbors for whom the very connection with the Blakes stands for an elevation in status. Mindful of Lila's heritage, the Weatherbys treat her as the belle that she never was, so much so that Sarah, Jim's mother, "would ruther work her fingers to the bone than have that gal take a single dish cloth in her hand."[29] On the other hand, the family writes their own fiction of whiteness, equally populated by the ghosts of their past. Cynthia spends her nights plotting "all sorts of pleasant lies" that she can relate to her mother, "about the house and the garden, and the way the war ended, and the Presidents of the Confederacy" whose names "she made up." Since the Blakes' whiteness is bound up with the Old South, it is imperative that the place be reinvented in order for Cynthia's narrative to be believable. In re-inscribing their whiteness, Cynthia re-inscribes the history of the region. Cynthia's reconstruction of their whiteness, grounded in a resurrected and rewritten story of the Confederacy, inadvertently confirms the signification of the construct as a simulacrum.[30] Not only did a precedent for it never exist, but its story was conjured alongside the reinvented history of the region, which exacerbates its imaginary character. Christopher may be "a Blake by force of blood and circumstance," but in his altered circumstances such notions reify the status of his gentility as a thing of the past.

To their neighbors, the Blakes' whiteness stems from their genteel heritage, but Christopher perceives the untenability of such fiction. The close proximity of Blake Hall is a constant reminder of who he might have been and how low he has fallen. He has long buried his childhood ambition of being "a gentlemanly scholar of the old order," sitting in the library, reading Horace and eventually completing his father's translation of Homer's *Iliad.* Lofty ambitions, indeed, that hint of continuity of tradition and place Christopher in direct opposition to the mercantile baseness of Fletcher's motive for scholarly advancement. The clash of sensibilities that Christopher and Fletcher represent is symbolic of the collision between the Old South mythology and the emerging new order. When Maria offers to restore Blake Hall to Christopher, he bluntly answers her that "it is too late," and she "can't put a field-hand in a fine house and make him a gentleman."[31] Christopher's retort at once evokes Maria's own sense of being out of place in Blake Hall and problematizes it by highlighting the futility of claims to whiteness based on lineage and heritage alone. Without his ancestral home and the adjunct acres, hereditary whiteness becomes an empty signifier. Having tasted "the abject bitterness and despair of those years" when he "tried to sink to the level of the brutes—tried to forget that [he] was any better than the oxen he drove," Christopher places himself beyond the pale of whiteness.[32]

Unlike Page's Gordon Keith, Christopher sees the futility of a rebirth through a return to the past, vehemently declaring: "No, there's no pulling me up again; such things aren't lived over, and I'm done for good." In Christopher's case, Glasgow offers a twist on social Darwinism, in which the lived experience and his enforced metamorphosis into a field laborer override the call of historic and familial legacy. He will never be able to rise above his station in life and, in his self-professed powerlessness, Glasgow withdraws the possibility of a reconciliation between the old and new orders. When the truth about Fletcher's murder finally comes to light and Christopher, exonerated, returns to his family, it is not the sight of Blake Hall that he finds revitalizing and inspiring, but the sight of tobacco fields. His transformation is complete. A similar social determinism guides Maria's actions. Whenever in Christopher's presence, Maria feels "the appeal of the rustic tradition, the rustic temperament; of all the multiplied inheritances of the centuries, which her education had not utterly extinguished."[33] What Christopher resents but accepts, Maria finds appealing because of her lowly descent—which no amount of education can elevate. Just as Maria's lowly legacy invalidates the accomplishments that her grandfather's wealth helped to acquire, Christopher's status as a field laborer belies his hereditary claim to whiteness. Implicit in his status is a different relationship to the land. In other words, the land provided and the land hath taken away.[34] Christopher's words both bring into sharp relief the disparate totalities of whiteness—hereditary possession of land and lineage—and reify the existence of a class among whom he counts himself but whose claims to whiteness are denied. His forefathers may have supervised the cultivation of tobacco, but Christopher's participation is literal and occurs at the elemental level: when the hands touch the soil. Such engagement leaves an indelible mark.[35] "The smell and the stain" of tobacco are so "well soaked in" that, Christopher bitterly wonders, whether "all the water in the river of Jordan could wash away the blood of the tobacco worm."[36] Glasgow thus transmutes the blood of the tobacco into the stain of the original sin, which even the waters of Jordan cannot cleanse, and this is what will always preclude his rebirth into whiteness. Even if he is restored to Blake Hall, for Christopher it can only be a passing place, just as it has been for Maria.

The Deliverance met with an enthusiastic reception from the critics. Even before its publication, an advertisement in the *New York Post* hailed it as "the first important book of 1904," but given that the advertisement appeared on January 4, 1904, the praise may have been a little premature. William Morton Payne, writing for the *Dial,* praised Glasgow for the characterization of Christopher and Maria, who reflected "all the subtle psychological processes of the years."[37] Another critic, in a piece titled "A New Field in Southern Fiction," claimed that "so sincere and unprejudiced representation of Southern life" had never before flowed from under the pen of "an author in that region." His praise extended to Glasgow herself, whom he commended for tackling "the psychic conditions" of the plot and character development that "the average southern novelist ignores."[38] Fattened on the fare of Southern romances, the critics must have found *The Deliverance* a breath of fresh air. But these psychic conditions that Glasgow so masterly captures stem equally from her refusal to view the South through roseate glasses and a unique interdependence of conceptions of gentility and place as formed through individual and collective socio-historical experience. In Glasgow's South, the answer to the question of whether blood will tell has already been predetermined by the cult of genteel tradition, which renders the dispossessed aristocrat and the parvenu off white.

THREE

THE INEVITABILITY OF PASSING IN CHARLES WADDELL CHESNUTT AND ALICE DUNBAR-NELSON

Narratives of Southern whiteness and passing converge in Glasgow's *The Deliverance* and Page's *Gordon Keith*. Although glorification of the values of the Old South inadvertently plays up the difference between the *hic et nunc* and the past, Page remains oblivious to this convergence. Glasgow, whether more perceptive or, perhaps, less interested in writing a paean, hones in on the duality of the plantation house, which creates and unmakes Southern whiteness. In *The Deliverance* and *Gordon Keith*, Southern whiteness as passing becomes a reality, but it is a new reality contingent upon the vicissitudes of Reconstruction and, in Page's case, stubbornly resisted. For their fellow Southerner and contemporary Charles Waddell Chesnutt, this confluence of Southern whiteness and passing is an inevitable reality born out of the rigidity of the paradigm that polices admission and safeguards the ineptitude of those already admitted. It is an institution rotten to the core.

Chesnutt experienced first-hand this rigidity when he found himself excluded from the purlieus of Southern whiteness by virtue of his heritage—a heritage that placed him on the wrong side of the color line. White but black by dint of possessing even so much as a trace of black blood, Chesnutt embodied the paradox of the one drop rule that rendered external appearance subordinate to connotative predetermination. In an entry in his journal made in 1875, the young Chesnutt recalls an incident when an "old fellow" points to him and says to his companion "'look here Tom, here's a black fellow as white as you air.'"[1] The words imply a reality that extends beyond the obvious and the visible, and points to a historically and socially predetermined positioning, diametrically opposed to that of Page and Glasgow.

Chesnutt's pedigree did not boast a single aristocrat, self-proclaimed or otherwise, although it included a well-to-do farmer, Waddell Cade, who over time increased his landholding in the vicinity of Fayetteville, North Carolina, and from whom Chesnutt inherited his middle name. His surname was the legacy of his grandmother, first a mistress of and then a housekeeper to grandfather Cade. Chesnutt, a free man of color on both his father's and his mother's side, was born in Cleveland, Ohio, where his father, Andrew Jackson Chesnutt relocated in the 1850s in search of opportunity. After the Civil War, Andrew Jackson Chesnutt and his family, including Charles, returned to Fayetteville, where he set up a grocery store. The move, although not especially lucrative in business terms, proved a golden opportunity for Charles because he could benefit from instruction at the prestigious Howard School, a joint effort of the Freedman's Bureau, Northern philanthropy, and black Southern community, which included Chesnutt's father. Juggling learning with the more prosaic chores at the shop could not have been easy, yet he managed it. His diligence and hard work paid off and, in 1874, he obtained a teaching certificate from the State Colored Normal School in Charlotte, North Carolina. The certificate came with a pay check of forty dollars and an opportunity to teach in country schools in the vicinity of Charlotte, on which he reflected in his journal and which reinforced in him the conviction of his difference and led him to formulate his own definition of Southern whiteness. The charms of the country did not detain this ambitious man long, and he returned to the State Colored Normal School. In one of his journal entries in the summer of 1879, he elevated himself to the title of "Professor of Reading, Writing, Spelling &c in the State Colored Normal School of N C." Shortly after this closet elevation, he assumed the headship of the school.[2]

For many of his contemporaries, securing such a position would have been the pinnacle of professional ambition. But not for Chesnutt, who later, like his father before him, moved his family to Cleveland, Ohio, learned stenography and set up a successful business there. For this self-taught man, constantly on the lookout for improvement and advancement, this was all a prelude to the career he dreamed of carving out for himself—that of a writer. The noble objective of his writing, which he confided to his diary on May 29, 1880, "would not be so much the elevation of the colored people as the elevation of the whites." As befitting an educator, it was to be instruction combined with amusement to combat not just regional but national prejudice by undermining the idea of white moral and cultural perfection; a crusade that is still ongoing and as much in need of combatting now as it was then. Chesnutt's liminal position of being, in his own words, "neither fish, flesh, nor fowl," not only propelled his constant need to prove himself—to rise above what was expected of him—but also taught him that there was more to whiteness than being white.[3]

Tackling this complexity of whiteness demanded an examination of its composite parts in an effort to demonstrate—or, indeed, educate, his predominantly white readers, that as often as not it transcended the color line. It became a recurrent motif in his works, beginning in the mid-1880s, with the publication of short stories in *Cleveland News and Herald* and *Atlantic*.[4] Despite some difficulty that the black dialect presented to an unaccustomed eye, the stories were commended for "being well studied" and hailed as "acquisitions" to American "folklore."[5] Chesnutt's first essay into novel writing was *Mandy Oxendine*, completed toward the end of 1896, or early in 1897.[6] The novel did not see the light of day until 1997, when Charles Hackenberry's edition appeared. This was not for the lack of trying. The hopeful author sent the manuscript to Walter Haines Page at Houghton Mifflin. The reply was a blow: the novel possessed "elements of truthfulness, and some novelty of situation," but the powers that be could not persuade themselves that they "should find publication a safe venture." As unequivocal as it is oblique, the editors' verdict has led to speculations. William L. Andrews sees the novel's resistance to common conceptions of femininity and its reluctance to accommodate itself to the protocols of "'tragic mulatta fiction,'" unlike *The House behind the Cedars*, as the likely obstacle to commercial success. Matthew Wilson suggests that the novel's representations of a Southern gentleman as a lecherous villain and his lower class counterpart as a sex-obsessed halfwit would have been equally unpalatable to white audiences.[7] White libidos remain firmly in check in Chesnutt's second novel and leave the heroine's virtue intact, but the scathing attack on the institution of Southern gentility could not have been easily digestible to white readers. Yet, the novel was published, despite the resemblance of its plot to *Mandy Oxendine*. Nor was Chesnutt the first writer to cast a white Southerner of the planter class as a villain: Glasgow's Christopher Blake blurs the fine line between hero and villain, as does Jonathan Gay in *The Miller of Old Church*. For Hackenberry, the answer lies in the structural weakness of the novel, characterization that is wanting in depth and overemphasis on plot combined with a rigidity of narrative voice.[8] Sloppiness of execution and structural naivety of the *deus ex machina* ending speak of an author who has not cut his teeth yet and who, as a result, does not qualify as a safe investment.

Despite its flaws, *Mandy Oxendine* is not just a story of crossing the color line; it is an indictment of the ethos of Southern whiteness enshrined in the notion of hereditary gentility. The novel is set in Rosinville, North Carolina, after Reconstruction. Its chief protagonists are the eponymous Mandy and Tom Lowrey, once-upon-a-time sweethearts now separated not only by the desire for social betterment, but also by the choices they make in its pursuit. Both Mandy and Tom are white in appearance and black by custom. Whereas Tom, like Chesnutt, chooses to pursue opportunity through improvement and study, Mandy takes a shortcut, relocates to Rosinville where nobody knows her, passes for white, and hopes to improve her standing through marriage. The path to advancement Mandy decides to follow is, as Hackenberry observes, one of the three available to people of mixed ancestry. The other two are advancement through education, which Tom pursues, and relocation to the North.[9] Although Chesnutt refrains from overt criticism of Mandy's choice and actions, he makes it clear that his sympathies lie with Tom.

The narrative begins when "a tall young man, somewhat fair of complexion, with grey eyes and light slightly curly hair" dressed in "a loosely-fitting grey suit that had seen some wear" and carrying an "apparently heavy valise" alights from the train at Rosinville station. The man in question is Tom Lowrey, a newly qualified teacher appointed to run the Sandy Run Colored School. His motive for relocation to Rosinville is twofold: the necessity to earn "his own living" and to find Mandy. Two things become immediately apparent from the narrator's description of Tom: he may be a stranger to Rosinville, but he is no stranger to the state or, more broadly, the region. Neither the "long rows of yellow rosin-barrels, encrusted with amber exudations" nor the sign reading "this Waiting-room for White People Only" is a surprise, although the latter angers him.[10] Seemingly at a loss at finding nobody to meet him, Tom approaches "an elderly negro" who has been scanning the train carriages. Introductions are made and the elderly man, now revealed as Deacon Pate, exclaims: "I never would a dremp' you wuz de teacher. I wuz lookin' fer a dark man, er a yaller man f'um de secon'-class kyar. I wuz'n' lookin' fer no white gen'leman f'um de fus'—class kyar." This encounter is vital because it introduces a difference, which Chesnutt methodically reinforces through the remainder of the narrative, between Tom and the other inhabitants of Rosinville. Despite the somewhat shabby attire, Tom's deportment, no doubt the result of his education, marks him out as a gentleman. His refusal to pass, when he informs Deacon Pate that although he is "not very highly colored," he is "sufficiently so," only intensifies this impression. It bespeaks honor and integrity only a true gentleman possesses. But, most importantly, Chesnutt uses the meeting to suggest that gentleman is a loaded term and detaches it from the edifice of the plantation house.[11]

The plantation house occupies a marginal position in the opening pages of the novel, foreshadowing the corruption of the institution of Southern whiteness it symbolizes. On the way to Deacon Pate's house, where he is to lodge, Tom passes two plantation houses that stand in close proximity but differ in appearance. The first, "a stately mansion, in the colonial style, with broad two-storied piazzas" is surrounded by "wide stretches of cotton and corn," and boasts "an extensive vineyard" as well as "numerous outhouses."[12] The only praise the narrator has for the other is that its "fields were planted" and the house large. The general air of disrepair and "neglect" that "pervaded the premises," the narrator notes, speak volumes of its present custodian and owner, "Mistah Bob Utley." Utley, Deacon Pate explains, is soon to be married to Florence Brewington, "Kunnel Brewin'ton's only daughter" and heiress to the impressive plantation where she resides with her aunt, Mrs. Ochiltree. Florence is Utley's cousin, his betrothed and co-owner of the dilapidated estate where Utley lives, and which "ole Miss McIntyre" left "ter her niece and neffy."[13] While these revelations seem to leave little impression on Tom, the picture Deacon Pate paints is of cultivated separation with a hint of incest. Absent is the natural elevation of Page's hilly setting and, with it, the idea of the family's superiority. Although Deacon Pate spares Tom no details in relating the Brewingtons' and Utleys' familial connection, he has nothing to say on the subject of the families' ancestry and history or, indeed, lands granted by royal charters. What emerges is a counter-narrative to Page's panegyrics to Southern gentility, in which Chesnutt subtracts the distinct requisites of Southern whiteness to lay the foundation for an alternative paradigm.

Chesnutt places Tom at the center of his narrative of whiteness but, in a move as subtle as it is subversive, he chooses Deacon Pate to outline its principles. In a conversation on the eve of Tom's arrival, the deacon, fortified by a hearty meal of chicken, gives his opinion on education. He has nothing against "book-larnin,'" he declares, but "larnin', aftuh all, is jes sump'n ter git sump'n e'se wid—a kin' of hook ter go fishin' wid." And, since "it'll he'p you to read de' Bible and to understan' religion" and "he'p you 'arn money fer ter buy chickens wid," the deacon gives it his vote.[14] Deacon Pate's simple philosophy goes to the heart of Chesnutt's model of Southern whiteness, which casts education and achievement, not hereditary gentility, as the hallmarks of moral worth and the means of social and professional advancement; not exclusive, but inclusive. Using Deacon Pate as his mouthpiece and lacing his speech with dialect allow Chesnutt to verbalize his counter-model of Southern whiteness, which, to his white readers, would have appeared revolutionary; while making it possible to dismiss the speech as the ramblings of an uneducated black yokel. Chesnutt's reticence to adopt a more forceful position is understandable: educating white people of culturally and racially jaundiced outlook takes time and effort, and a budding novelist of precarious standing must tread cautiously to ensure he gets into print.

This caution extends to Chesnutt's characterization of Tom Lowrey, who is to serve as a paradigm of the reformulated Southern whiteness. Carrying the torch of knowledge to the backwoods of North Carolina, where he hopes to be reunited with his former sweetheart, Tom cuts a hybrid figure, part Prometheus part knight errant, but not a parvenu bent on filling his pockets. Tom's guiding principle, initially, is the "love of learning" that a Northern teacher "had implanted" in him. The seed, thus planted, grew, "fed by such books as he could find," eventually transforming itself "into a burning desire for a better education, a broader culture, and a higher life," sentiments not unlike those of Page's Keith or Glasgow's Blake. As Tom leaves to pursue his studies, he learns to cultivate a reverence for history, tradition and antiquity. A pride in personal achievement combined with humility replaces the outdated notion of hereditary privilege. Tom's is a progressive variety of Southern whiteness where gentility of character, not of birth, matters. But, Tom is also pragmatic enough to know, as he tells Mandy before he departs, "that with learning he could gain wealth and position for her."[15] In making Mandy the sole reason for Tom's ambition of financial gain, Chesnutt distances him from wealth *qua* wealth and draws him in the likeness of the Southern gentleman of the old school, not unlike Page's General Keith. Tom, however, is also a new kind of Southern gentleman, one who embodies the loftier ideals of Southern whiteness, such as cultural refinement and learning, and demonstrates that these attributes can be progressive and not regressive. In this exercise of literary eugenics, Chesnutt creates a new species: a self-made man who privileges the intellectual over the material.

Yet, Tom's emancipation and progressiveness fail to impress Mandy. Chesnutt paints Mandy as a victim of in-betweenness who yearns for a stable identity and who has not yet realized that gentility may transcend the color line. She is the antithesis of Tom, whose regressiveness is the reason for his progressiveness. When Tom tracks her down in Rosinville, where she has moved with her mother and is now passing for white, Mandy reproaches him for abandoning her. Tom remonstrates with her, painting a picture of their future together, in which they will "go away," he will "work and study," and "having a white man's chance," he will make her "a white lady." Mandy rejects the offer and informs him that she is going to marry someone who "is a gentleman; he is white, he is rich, he rides on horseback, he lives in a big house." The man is no other than Bob Utley and little does Mandy know that these are but superficial qualities. Even when Tom points out to her the improbability of any gentleman marrying "a sand-hill mulatto" or "a sand-hill poor white girl," Mandy remains unconvinced. Although Chesnutt mitigates Mandy's stance, observing that she understood "the essential element of difference in the status of the two races" and "felt that it was not learning or wealth, or even aspiration—but opportunity," the defense seems half-hearted.[16] Mandy deals in binaries, which makes her situation all the more ironic; a sand-hill poor white and a sand-hill mulatto both stand beyond the pale of whiteness. With such an outlook, Chesnutt suggests, Mandy lacks the intellectual mettle to rise above her station in life; marriage with Tom will not be enough to remove the chip from her shoulder.

Because of her naiveté, Mandy becomes Chesnutt's vehicle for a critique of Southern whiteness, with its emphasis on particular surface-deep traditions. The narrator describes Mandy as possessing "the statuesque lines of a noble figure" with "a luxuriant head of nut brown hair, with varying tints of golden gleams," which she gathers "into a Greek knot," either by "intuition or inspiration."[17] On another occasion, Mandy appears "singing an old song" that was once sung by "gallant cavaliers" and "loyal ladies" of the Stuart days, and that crossed the ocean with Flora McDonald and "Scotch exiles."[18] A Cleopatra with Scottish ancestry may sound like an unlikely combination, but it spells out Mandy's affiliation with the two cultures glorified in the region. This is Chesnutt's first attempt in the novel at unmasking the speciousness of gentility formulated on a flimsy connection to the Old World, a theme that he subjects to closer scrutiny in *The House behind the Cedars*. If Mandy's pedigree appears implausible, it is no more so than the Utleys' or the Brewingtons'.

Although Chesnutt shows no inclination to entangle himself in the gnarled branches of the Utleys' and the Brewingtons' genealogies, the fact they still own—or partly own, as in Utley's case—a plantation predetermines their descent from the self-proclaimed Southern aristocracy. On seeing Utley riding from the direction of the "Lumberton plankroad," Brer Revels, one of the farmers in the local colored community, informs Tom that he must be "up ter some debilment." So low is Brer Revels's opinion of Utley that he refuses to sell him his mare because he would "lack to see de money fer 'er, an' Mistah Utley's mighty po' pay."[19] The implication is clear: Utley is not so much unable to pay as he is unwilling. Honor, Chesnutt suggests, is a virtue that Utley does not possess. His gentility, just like Mandy's idea of it, is cosmetic and, as the novel unfolds, so does Utley's mendacity and villainy. He promises marriage to Mandy, hoping it will smooth the way to seduction and, when it fails, he attempts to rape her. Fortunately, another admirer of Mandy, the fanatical preacher Gadson, intervenes and kills him. While Utley is the sexual predator in a gentleman's trappings, Lowrey is the gentleman in a school teacher's garb. He takes upon himself the role of Mandy's protector and, while he watches over her meetings with Utley, his "love of fair play as well as a sense of self-respect kept him from listening to what they said."[20] The image of Lowrey the gentleman and Utley the scoundrel solidifies with every turn of the page.

Utley as a character is as flawed as the rhetoric of Southern whiteness that fostered him. And, he is not the only character whose moral fiber has been worn to shreds. His Aunt Ochiltree, who is also Florence Brewington's aunt and guardian, despite knowing Utley's faults, still presses for the match. She urges Utley to pay court to Florence because his "credit" and "good name are dependent upon this marriage." This outright mockery of the Southern code of chivalry turns Utley into a cad, his aunt into nothing more than a procuress, and Florence into hapless prey. Florence, despite her "stately" beauty, "refinement," and "style," is no different from Mandy in that she "wished no better fate than to become" Utley's wife. Like Mandy, she falls victim to Utley's facade of gentility, believing in the power of her influence over him now that "he had fallen under her compelling charm." That she can be so easily deceived makes her situation more pitiable because, her education notwithstanding, it reveals her to be as regressive as Mandy, believing in the clichéd notion that Utley's "essentially noble heart," and by extension the heart of every Southern gentleman, overrides "mercenary consideration."[21] It does not. Despite its emphasis on chivalry, nobility, and honor, "monetary consideration" is not antithetical to the Southern conception of hereditary gentility.

Hereditary gentility is a myth, and one that is built on shaky foundations. A gentleman, Chesnutt acknowledges, may be a term infused with historical and cultural significances, but in Rosinville, it is a signifier without a signified. Utley, a gentleman in name if not in deed and the most eligible bachelor, is also a thwarted rapist. The lynch mob that gathers to hang Tom after he admits to killing Utley in order to save Mandy, upon whom suspicion has fallen, are just rabble that follows "the onwritten law of the Southe'n States," yet they call themselves "gentlemen." The only person who makes no claim to the appellation is also the most deserving one. Tom's rejection of the title in principle if not in action signals Chesnutt's re-appropriation of the term and the tenets of Southern whiteness as a discourse of meritocracy. To drive the point home, Chesnutt casts the South as the passing place for the likes of the Utleys, the Ochiltrees, and the lynchers, who not only exist on borrowed ideals, but are also their living caricatures. The only person who does not pass is Tom and that is because he surpasses others "in intellect, in culture," and "in energy," and is capable of looking forward.[22]

A forward outlook akin to Tom Lowrey's is something that the protagonists of Chesnutt's second, but first published, novel also lack. *The House behind the Cedars* appeared in 1900, and in this study Chesnutt continues to undermine the validity of claims to whiteness based on heritage and possession of land alone. Despite its similarities to *Mandy Oxendine* in plot and setting, the novel garnered positive reviews. In a section titled "The Year's Most Notable Book," a critic for the *Pittsburgh Post* opined that the novel had "genuine interest and literary skill." Its author received praise for "a clear style and a keen sense of dramatic effect." It seems that Chesnutt succeeded in the objective of educating white readers and, the critic suspected, the novel had "done a great deal toward opening the eyes of those" who would "be willingly ignorant."[23] The *New York Times* commended Chesnutt for being one of the first authors to write "sympathetically and comprehensively from both view points [sic]" on the question of racial prejudice. The novel, the same critic enthused, was "a brilliant performance—clear, to the point, keen in interests, penetrating in its presentation of character." More astutely, however, the critic noted Chesnutt's treatment of the present as "ever present realities which [had] grown out of the past." This "novel of purpose" and "more than ordinary merit," through its author's "strong, delicate, [and] artistic" treatment of a difficult topic, earned "a unique place in American literature." The reviewer for the *Richmond Times*, however, tempered his praise with the prediction that the novel would flop in the South, where the readers were not likely to find the subject palatable.[24] The fare that the Southern readers would find hard to digest was not the iniquity of race relations in the region, a *status quo* in which they participated more or less willingly, but the critique of notions of blood and heredity as inimical realities of the present shaped by the past.

This is the reality, where the past holds sway over the present, which Chesnutt paints in the pastoral setting of Patesville, North Carolina. In introducing Patesville, Chesnutt utilizes the familiar technique of viewing it through a stranger's eyes. The stranger is John Warwick, whose attire, comprising "a suit of linen duck," "a panama straw hat, and patent leather shoes" combined with his tall stature and "straight, black, lustrous hair and very clean-cut, high-bred features," convinces the hotel clerk of his status as a gentleman. Judging Warwick's apparel, the clerk, familiar with all things local in matters of business, draws the only possible conclusion—that this must be "one of the South Ca'lina big bugs," whose fortune derives from "cotton, or turpentine."[25] Chesnutt uses the clerk as a mouthpiece to establish the source of John's gentility, and his claim to whiteness, through an association with the region and its resources, cultivated or natural. Although the stock image of the plantation house is absent from Patesville, it is still a place where certain hierarchies obtain, according to which its patrician citizens reside on the elevated peak of the "Hill"—"the aristocratic portion of the town." Like Page, Chesnutt employs natural terrain to signify a preordained boundary separating aristocracy from plebeians. It is also a place where certain customs are cultivated, which, as John reminisces, "once made, like our sins, they grip us in bands of steel; we become the creatures of our creations."[26] John's words both indicate the existence of a code according to which Patesville's inhabitants construct gentility and its antithesis, and emphasize the artificiality of such creations.

John learns the guiding principle of this code, which operates on the basis of exclusion and is place-specific, when still a boy. The instructor is Judge Straight, who informs John in a moment of almost unguarded liberalism—almost being the operative word—that he "need not be black, away from Patesville." That Judge Straight, one of the most illustrious denizens of the town whose name and office indicate moral rectitude and infallibility, gives John a lesson in the relativity of his blackness points to the speciousness of the laws he upholds. The irony is unmistakable, and Chesnutt exploits the duplicity of the situation to its full potential. When the judge, acting either on a philanthropic impulse or genuine concern, indulges John's wish to become a lawyer and offers him the position of an office boy, he stipulates: "To the rest of the town you will be my servant, and still a negro." What mitigates the judge's beneficence is his adherence to "certain customs" that demand that John, to borrow from W. E. B. du Bois, be kept in his place.[27] Although the judge voices no objection to John's reading his books when "no one is about" and being "white" in his "own private opinion," this covenant is to be kept secret: "But mum's the word." The judge's words clearly separate whiteness from white as skin color, but his actions establish conformity to Patesville customs as a means of maintaining his genteel status. In order to perform the role of a benefactor, which in this instance replaces that of the benevolent planter, and to retain his privileged position as a gentleman, his relationship with John can only be that of master and servant; while John's servile status becomes a matter not of hue but of blood and heritage. The judge's benevolence rests on his re-enactment of the role of the beneficent master, which he can only perform in the presence of an inferior servant. In this reinterpretation of the Hegelian master/slave dialectic, the oppressor becomes the oppressed and is, literally and metaphorically, immobilized in his own social role as the result of his own actions. In other words, John's inferiority and aspiration to become a lawyer precipitates the judge's benevolence while making impossible his escape from the bondage of his social role.[28] Nor can he escape the duplicity of his actions; hence, the need for secrecy, because John's aspirations depend on the judge's averting his gaze. The fact that the charade is to be maintained before "the rest of the town" reaffirms the existence of rigid customs that, paradoxically, by the very virtue of policing the boundaries of gentility transform it into passing.

Unbeknownst to the judge, his questionable beneficence sets John on the path to gentility, culminating in the metamorphosis of John Walden into John Warwick. John—now a respectable lawyer and owner of his own plantation—returns to Patesville to assist in the transformation of his sister, Rowena, into a lady. A year later, Rowena Warwick—ironically named after the archetype of Southern whiteness, the noble heroine of Scott's *Ivanhoe* and epitome of Saxon beauty and virtue—makes her debut in the Clarence society at a jousting tournament. Unlike Page's veiled allusions to Scott, Chesnutt's narrator observes acerbically that both the idea of tournaments and "Scott's novels of chivalry appealed forcefully to the feudal heart." This spectacle of medieval chivalry perpetuates the myth of the nobility of the Southern civilization, the myth that is simultaneously belied by the presence of "the poorer white and colored folks [who] found seats outside, upon what would now be known as the 'bleachers.'" The "bleachers" sublate the validity of the myth of a homogenous Southern nobility, while suggesting that watching the spectacle will provide the means of ennoblement for the less worthy and reification of status for the "best people," entitled to take their place in "the grand stand." Needless to say, both John and Rowena find themselves among those seated in the grandstand, where John, in response to a remark from one of the ladies, pronounces the spectacle "the renaissance of chivalry," which, however, "must adapt itself to new times and circumstances." John's words imply that the unfolding events are already a simulacrum, an idealized copy, as are the values that the spectacle promulgates. In the here and now, when the "knights are not weighted down with heavy armor," when "a wooden substitute" replaces "an iron-headed lance," such re-enactments yield palimpsests passing for "Southern knights."[29] Clarence, just like the less poetically and nostalgically named Patesville, materializes as a passing place, a fact emphasized by John and Rowena's passing for white. If, according to

Peter Schmidt, Scott is an essential author for understanding narratives dealing with the reclamation of nationhood, then John and Rowena's presence at the tournament acquires new meaning, since in their veins flows united the blood of two discrete "races."[30] They are the symbols of the convergence of both blood and culture. Their presence at the tournament marks an attempt to reclaim their heritage, their claim to Southern whiteness, which, according to English law, constitutes their undisputed patrimony. It is the reinvented law of the colony that turns their gentility into a fraud.[31]

At the tournament, in a clichéd turn of events, Rowena meets her "knight in shining armor" in the person of George Tryon. His "inherited two estates," "lots of land, and plenty of money," combined with his faultless manners, make Tryon an undisputed gentleman. The sound of his inherited property strikes a false note with his name, which implies both aspiration and usurpation, and casts a shadow over his pedigree. M. Giulia Fabi observes that the names of Chesnutt's male protagonists connect them with such historical personages as "Warwick the Kingmaker and George Duke of Clarence."[32] Yet, Chesnutt's choice of names resonates more deeply than a surface replication, adding another dimension to John Warwick and George Tryon. Both the Kingmaker and Clarence, his son-in-law, were guilty of treason against Edward IV. While the Kingmaker died an honorable death on the battlefield, Clarence was tried and executed. What Chesnutt conceals under the veil of allusion is that betrayal constitutes the historical legacy of both John Warwick and George Tryon, and underpins their conduct: Warwick betrays his heritage by electing to pass for white, and Tryon betrays Rowena.[33]

Chesnutt uses Rowena the ingénue to amplify the trope and drama of betrayal, and inject pathos into the narrative. Following a brief courtship, Tryon proposes to Rowena and is accepted. Honest, innocent, and aware of her heritage, Rowena is soon beset by pangs of conscience and feels obliged to confess her secret to Tryon, yet fears his reaction. Upon her request, John sounds Tryon on his views on heritage and confesses to him their lack of aristocratic background. Not only do they "have no connections of which you could boast and no relatives to whom [they] would be glad to introduce" Tryon, but they "are new people." Tryon meets John's circumspect honesty with an impassioned denunciation of there being any "advantage in belonging to an old" family. Despite Rowena's lack of heritage, Tryon is ready to embrace her, particularly since, to him, she "carries the stamp of her descent upon her face and in her heart." To demonstrate his apparent disregard for heritage, Tryon confesses a secret of his own: "My maternal great-great-grandfather, a hundred and fifty years ago, was hanged, drawn, and quartered for stealing cattle across the Scottish border. How is that for a pedigree? Behold in me the lineal descendant of a felon!" Whereas in Scotland, as Colin Dayan observes, crimes of treason or felony meant the "forfeiture of property to the king" that invalidated laws of descent and carried the stigma of corrupted blood, in the South, the Scottish heritage, reinvented, secures Tryon's respectability and with it, his gentility.[34]

Tryon's confession, however, undermines his own claim to whiteness and reinforces the region's status as a passing place. If a "week in New York" can divest a gentleman of his manners, so three generations of residence in the South can turn a felon into a gentleman. While both transmutations ground the ideal of a gentleman in the South, the latter threatens the possibility of the stability and purity of such an ideal. Indeed, Tryon's "corrupted blood" is soon put to the test. Before the nuptials take place, Rowena and Tryon, unbeknownst to each other, travel to Patesville: Tryon on business and Rowena to nurse her sick mother. Their respective visits there literally turn Patesville into a passing place where, as the *New York Times* reviewer observes, "the personages are always stumbling over one another."[35]

Chesnutt uses this stumbling to undermine any notion of truth in the ideal of Southern whiteness by revealing it as inherently unstable and untenable. Patesville is a bastion of the customs of Southern whiteness, where its tenets never slacken their hold: here, by his own admission, Tryon—"the lineal descendant of a felon" is hailed by Judge Straight as a representative "of the old blood"—a statement that inadvertently highlights the shaky ground upon which Tryon's gentility rests. The judge's effusiveness is quite understandable considering that Patesville is a place where "the ties of blood" are "cherished as items of value, and never forgotten," and where a gentleman must be "treated with genuine Southern hospitality." In Patesville, the uniquely Southern commodities of blood and heritage are traded cautiously and with utmost frugality: blood establishes, however tenuously, one's status as a gentleman and validates one's claim to the right kind of heritage. Both become accessories in what Dayan terms legal "rituals of banishment," which serve to marginalize those branded unworthy. That both are accorded to Tryon serves to reify the dubiousness of not only his claim to gentility but also the rhetoric and ethos that sustain it. When Tryon finally learns the truth of Rowena's descent, he sends a letter to her brother, breaking off the engagement. Rather tellingly for somebody of "corrupted blood" and a name that implies opportunism and lack of steadfastness of purpose, Tryon confesses in the epistle that he "would have doubtless been happier" if he "had gone through life without finding" Rowena's secret out.[36] Possessing the knowledge, however, he must break off the engagement, as it might jeopardize his gentility by tainting the already "corrupted" purity of his ancestral whiteness. Faced with this mock-Faustian pact, Tryon proves himself a true beneficiary of his heritage. Chesnutt uses Tryon's faux gentility to emphasize that whiteness and being white are not synonymous. Although Tryon cannot think of John "as other than a white man," he "cannot marry" his sister. Indeed, his "repugnance," he admits, is "not to the woman," but "merely to the thought of her as a wife."[37] What makes his marriage to Rowena impossible is her heritage because of which he cannot accept her as his equal; and, considering his own lineage, his conduct appears doubly ironic.

Yet, despite his conduct, Tryon is not the ultimate villain; it is the ethos of Southern whiteness that claims both Tryon and Rowena as its victims. Tryon's rejection of Rowena leads to her "civil death," a phrase that Dayan uses to describe a legally imposed condition on those who are legally disenfranchised, in that she is barred from living the life she has chosen for herself, soon to be followed by her actual death. It is the place, Patesville and, by extension, the South, that imposes and supports its own "rhetoric of banishment;" and though Tryon recognizes this rhetoric as a blend of "reason, common-sense, the instinctive ready-made judgments of his training and environment," he is powerless to liberate himself from its spell. When he eventually defies custom and tradition, and decides to marry Rowena, filled with love fueled by a newly found conviction that "custom was tyranny," he arrives too late: Rowena is dead.[38] Through Rowena's death, Chesnutt reveals the proliferation of the metaphor of passing. While alive, she passed for the ideal, in passing she becomes the ideal, divested of flesh and blood, perpetually virginal and asexual, a status that Mandy Oxendine never achieves. Rowena's death literalizes the metaphor of whiteness as death—whiteness as passing *ad infinitum*. What is more, her unattainability as the ideal will ensure the continuity of Tryon's passing for a gentleman.

In an ironic twist of plot, on his way to Patesville, Tryon meets a woman whose claim to whiteness, according to the Southern custom, would be greater than Rowena's. He observes that "she was white enough, with the sallowness of the sandhill poor white," and in her hand she held "a bottle, the contents of which had never paid any revenue tax." Through recourse to stereotype, Chesnutt has Tryon acknowledge and voice the paradox on which Southern whiteness rests: the woman was "white enough," but "she was not fair, and she was not Rena." The comparison does not erase the ambiguity of the construct. On the contrary, Chesnutt compounds it by using the term "fair," which carries connotations of beauty and gentleness as well as lightness of complexion. While the woman does not possess any of these attributes, she certainly espouses the notion of Southern hospitality as she "tenders" Tryon "the bottle with tipsy cordiality."[39] It avails her naught because the stringent customs obtaining in the region place both beyond the reach of whiteness: the sandhiller woman because of the shiftlessness that her appearance bespeaks, which testifies to her lowly descent, and for which even her attempt at hospitality cannot atone; and Rowena because of her descent, regardless of her fairness and gentility. Rowena's gentility, like that of Tom Lowrey, owes nothing to her descent; it is a product of learning and cultivation and, as such, does not require the monumental space of plantation to sustain it. Chesnutt reserves the plantation house for the likes of Tryon, and its shadowy rather than monumental presence symbolizes his equally shadowy past. Tryon needs all the props to pull off his gentility and, in the end, finds himself lacking. In drafting the characters of Tryon and Rowena, Chesnutt aims at more than just a representation of race relations. He penetrates the core of the rhetoric of Southern whiteness to reveal its inherent instability and ambiguity based on the perpetuation of a flawed and impossible ideal.

A similar ambiguity characterizes the stories of Alice Dunbar-Nelson. Younger than Chesnutt, Dunbar-Nelson was born in New Orleans in 1875. Like Chesnutt, despite humble origins that included a father who was in the merchant navy and a mother who was a seamstress, Dunbar-Nelson received a thorough education. She attended public school, graduated from Straight University in 1892, and embarked upon a teaching career in her hometown. Not content with resting on her laurels, she moved to the North four years later, studied at Cornell, Columbia, and later the University of Pennsylvania. A number of teaching appointments followed, among which was one at Howard High School, the school that Chesnutt had attended some years before. An activist, writer, newspaper editor and aspiring screenwriter, Dunbar-Nelson, as Gloria T. Hull describes her, had "the breeding, education, culture, looks, and manners of the 'higher classes,'" but not the financial wherewithal that accompanies them. Her diary entries reveal that the numerous lecture appointments Dunbar-Nelson kept did not offer much in terms of remuneration and, sometimes, left her out of pocket. She began her literary career with the publication of a collection of poems in *Violets and Other Tales* in 1895. Three years later, she tried her hand at prose, publishing a collection of short stories titled *The Goodness of St Rocque*.[40]

If fame was what she was after, then she had to share it with her late husband, poet and writer Paul Laurence Dunbar. The lingering connection with her first husband could not have been entirely distasteful to her because, as Hull notes, she never dropped his name.[41] The reviewers certainly continued to yoke her to Paul Laurence Dunbar. Writing in 1899, a critic for the *New York Times* had little to say about the stories other than "her tales deal with Creole life and character, and the scenes are for the most part laid in the vicinity of New Orleans." He did not omit to say, however, that the stories would appeal to readers who had "shown an interest in the poems, short stories, and single novels of Paul Laurence Dunbar." The *Washington Times* reviewer played a similar tune, saying that "the fact that the author is the wife of Paul Laurence Dunbar" added a "particular interest to the collection." Whatever praise he managed to squeeze in grudgingly in the review for Dunbar-Nelson for "individuality and charm" of the collection, he quickly tempered by adding that it shared those qualities with "the work of her husband." At least the review that appeared in the *Oakland Tribune* gave Dunbar-Nelson the credit she deserved, praising her for "delightful humor" and a "style" that is "simple, direct, and convincing." The stories, the critic wrote, contained "delicate touches of true pathos" that attested to the "author's keen insight and broad sympathies."[42]

New Orleans, with its unique history and attendant social climate, including culturally and racially ambiguous designations like Creole, Quadroon, and Octoroon, was a place that inspired broad sympathies. Given Dunbar-Nelson's social positioning as a woman of color who, like Chesnutt, visibly lacked color, hers was a similar predicament. The ambiguity of her interstitial position made her doubly sensitive to the instability of such labels as whiteness and blackness, and their separateness from reality. Recalling in her diary the meeting with President Harding, during which she and a number of black delegates presented him with a petition for clemency for black soldiers who had been unfairly incarcerated following the Houston riots of August 1917 and the president's biased and insipid response, Dunbar-Nelson calls him "the nigger in the White House," which, she adds, is "his general cognomen."[43] What earns Harding the title is his mendacity and moral cowardice, which prevent him from directly confronting the unfair incarceration of the black soldiers. Some eighty years later, surrounded by the unsavory aroma of sexual scandal, Bill Clinton earns the moniker of "our first black president." Toni Morrison, the black author and activist, bestows the title, but this time its undertones are far from derogatory. Morrison finds analogy between the treatment Clinton receives, which rests on perceptions of him as standing outside the establishment, including the blackening of his character and violation of privacy, treatment that has historically been meted out to the black population.⁴⁴ But, it is the ease with which the label sticks that matters because it shows the malleability and ambiguity of the term that rest on connotation rather than visibility of difference.

Although Dunbar-Nelson remains aware of the pernicious power of connotation and the untenability of claims to whiteness resting on appearance alone, she is not blind to the existence of a paradigm policing its boundaries. In "In Our Neighborhood," Dunbar-Nelson, like Chesnutt, purposefully blurs the distinctions between black and white, and casts aspiration and place as yardsticks against which whiteness is measured.⁴⁵ In the story, it is not a plantation house but the "Avenue" that serves as a site of aspiration. The actual setting is a nondescript square whose inhabitants are separated by more than distance from the "Avenue." Dunbar-Nelson's capitalization of the name highlights its influence on those dwelling in its vicinity. The "Avenue," just like the "Hill" in *The House behind the Cedars*, functions as, in Pierre Macherey's terms, a "half-presence" that enacts the "true absence" of the genteel values encoded in its name in the neighborhood.⁴⁶ The Harts, whose name reflects the ambiguity of the symbolism of the mythical hart connoting innocence, purity, and elusiveness, are a family with aspirations. With a distinct air of disapproval, the neighborhood watches as they prepare for a party. The Hart children run "to and fro, soliciting the loan of a few chairs, 'some nice dishes,' and such like things, indispensable to every decent, self-respecting party." The lack of such essentials in the Hart household transforms their efforts into a collective enterprise, suggesting that they still have a long way to go to attain the kind of respectability that the "Avenue" exemplifies. Mrs. Tuckley, a passive observer of the hustle and bustle of the preparations both identifies and undermines the individual steps of the Harts' attempt at social ascent. First comes her neighborly wonder at "how them Harts do keep up," questioning their financial resources. The comment follows immediately after Dunbar-Nelson describes the frantic borrowing of dishes, and she uses it to create a situational irony in which actions belie intentions. The second step Mrs. Tuckley identifies is pretension, which manifests in "them girls" dressing "just as fine as any lady on the Avenue." The third step, and possibly the most poignant one, that Mrs. Tuckley notes, and which "'pears mighty, mighty funny" to her, is "the airs they do put on!" Without overemphasis but through a deft application of vernacular speech and constriction of spatial setting, Dunbar-Nelson succeeds in subverting the Harts' attempt at effecting difference between themselves and their neighbors. Although ultimately futile, the effort foregrounds the endurance of the paradigm enshrined in the "Avenue."⁴⁷

The "Avenue" may constitute a site of inspiration and incite aspiration, but in this particular neighborhood such aspirations are, by virtue of the location, downgraded to second rate palimpsests and decidedly off white. Whereas in "In Our Neighborhood," the "Avenue" provides a site that both inspires and foils its denizens' aspirations to gentility, in "Tony's Wife," Dunbar-Nelson limns a neighborhood that acts, literally, as a passing place. The title functions as a metaphor for passing. Dunbar-Nelson uses its innocuousness and deceptive simplicity to foreground the prevalence of pretense as a necessary way of being. The effect is all the more powerful because the revelation comes at the very end of the story, when it turns out the marriage is a sham. Tony, a brute of Italian extraction, runs a shop with a self-effacing German woman. Although his accent may have lost its original inflection, his manners and status mark him as less white than his customers. Their neighbors are "fine enough" to "look down" on those in trade, Dunbar-Nelson notes, hinting at a difference within as well as without. This locality, she writes, is "the sort of neighborhood where millionaires live before their fortunes are made and fashionable, high-priced private schools flourish, where the small cottages are occupied by aspiring schoolteachers and choir singers."[48] It is a passing place in a dual sense: it is simultaneously a purgatory, through which those with aspirations pass and, possibly, emerge improved enough to attain a semblance of whiteness, at least in their own estimation; and a carrot on a stick. The institutions, while titillating with the possibility of attaining whiteness through a blend of education and morality, do not boast aristocratic heritage as a curricular item. Without this constituent part of whiteness proper, all efforts at improvement inadvertently yield pseudo-gentility. Here, as in "In Our Neighborhood," another place, "the old-time French quarter," acts as a "half-presence," a source of aspirations to whiteness and, as such, its meaning, as that of the "Avenue" or the "Hill" or Page's and Glasgow's plantations, goes beyond the literal, soaring to the lofty heights of genteel notions and aristocratic legacy.[49] In this locality, whiteness begins and ends with a dream of aspiration sustained by the spectral presence of an imagined site of genteel ethos.

For Dunbar-Nelson, as for Chesnutt, Page, and Glasgow, the idea of place as a site of whiteness appears indispensable, if ever-fraught, to writing its fiction. To these authors, whiteness is not only a fiction, but also one with synecdochal properties. Glasgow once remarked of writing at the turn-of-the-century that "an extravagant amount of energy had to be wasted merely in proving that things were not what they seemed, and that they were, in fact, seldom known by their right names," and this sentiment seems particularly pertinent to the fiction of whiteness.⁵⁰ In the South, it becomes synonymous with hereditary gentility, with its own fictions of blood and tradition, that find their visual representation in the monumental space of the plantation house and have grown in significance commensurate with the cultivation of cotton or tobacco that sustains them. Each tale of whiteness is contingent upon the staples of the plantation house, heritage and blood; and, in the absence of one of these components, Southern gentility falls short of the ideal. None of Page's, Glasgow's, or Chesnutt's protagonists can boast of possessing a plantation, aristocratic descent, and purity of blood concurrently, perhaps with the exception of the senile Mrs. Blake. For them, the South in general, and the distinct localities in particular, become passing places where the disparate fictions of whiteness can never be united in a totality. In Dunbar-Nelson's stories, the absence of the plantation house is palpable, for it emphasizes the lack of claims to whiteness of her protagonists, which she establishes through references to other places where genteel values obtain. In doing this, Dunbar-Nelson renders her protagonists as hopelessly passing—a status exacerbated by the futility of their desire for redemptive whiteness. Whiteness places the desiring subject at a disadvantage because it consists in positioning oneself in relation to the ideal, whether in spatial, historical, or social terms, of gauging one's distance from the standard that inadvertently culminates in an admission of lack.

PART TWO

A TOUCH OF THE TAR BRUSH, OR THE AMBIVALENCE OF WHITENESS

FOUR

LIVING WITH SPECTERS
IN THOMAS NELSON PAGE

In the particular places evoked in Page's, Glasgow's, and Chesnutt's fiction, or their spectral traces in Dunbar-Nelson's, Southern whiteness becomes synonymous with hereditary gentility. The Southern gentleman planter and lady, ensconced on inherited land, with appropriately aristocratic blood coursing in their veins, signify as the living embodiments of the enduring aristocratic tradition, a tradition that depends upon convoking and ontologizing the genteel ideals of the Old South. Jacques Derrida sees the politics of inheritance as intrinsically antagonistic because it is impossible without reconciling oneself with "some spectre."[1] Derrida's specter is *a priori* difference, inescapable from the discourse of inheritance that marks the inheritor as different from the ideal, not least because of a temporal divide. A striving toward maintaining a sense of continuity between the site of origin and reconstruction is already haunted by this *a priori* difference, which is constant and cannot be overcome. This dynamic of inheritance places the Southern gentleman and lady on the wrong foot. The whiteness they reproduce—overshadowed by the ghost of the ideal—becomes a locus of approximations. As repositories of antebellum gentility, they perpetuate alterity that is predicated upon the impossibility of uniting the three factors indispensable to gentility: hereditary land ownership, blood, and tradition; and predetermined by the discontinuity from the site of origin: the Old South.

In *The High Place: A Comedy of Disenchantment*, James Branch Cabell sees this hysteric striving as a tragi-comedy of a particularly Southern kind, and its "first act is the imagining of the place where contentment exists and may be come to."² This is the "high place" of the novel's title. The words, spoken by the fiend Horvendile employed by the devil Janicot who assists Florian in his quest for the sword Flamberge, sound the note of warning and futility. The "high place" is an imagined place of perfection, the Old South in all but name, and its power is deconstructive rather than constructive because it encodes the irreconcilability of the past and the present.

The Old South was never old until it entered the post-Reconstruction era, when it gradually aged into legend. This place, which, according to James Branch Cabell's memorable words, "had died proudly at Appomattox without ever having been smirched by the wear and tear of existence," gained new status and currency as a pristine site of origin and became crucial to the reconstruction of Southern whiteness.³ Page was no stranger to its significance in the preservation of the genteel ethos, infusing misty recollections into his short stories, *Gordon Keith*, and even *On Newfound River*, in which he marks the contrast between the Old South and the desolation of the post-war South. Blurred in transparency but heavy in substance, the image of the Old South that Page creates, though open to interpretation, admits only one kind of reading: as the cradle of Southern gentility.

Page's second novel, *Red Rock: A Chronicle of Reconstruction*, treads the familiar path of a lost arcadia and gentility in distress. When it appeared in 1898, the critics, already familiar with Page's work, were generally kind. *Red Rock* had "much of the same note which made 'Marse Chan' famous," wrote one reviewer, and was "a romantic love-story."⁴ Others were more astute. The critic reviewing the novel for the *Scranton Republican* hailed it as "dramatized history" that dealt tactfully with "a time of the greatest sectional bitterness and misunderstanding" and deserved the label of "American in the best and highest sense." Another reviewer called it simply "a good story, historical, [and] valuable" that afforded unprecedented "insight into the dark scheming, the base intrigues, the scum rising to the agitated surface of social and political life."⁵ On this broad—although, according to another critic—"flatter canvas than the genre pictures of 'Marse Chan' and 'Meh Lady,'" Page offers a tantalizing glimpse into the reconstruction of the Southern ideal of whiteness built on the unstable foundations of an imagined place and past.

In *Red Rock*, as in *Gordon Keith* and *On Newfound River,* Page begins by exploiting the relationship between the reconstruction of Southern whiteness and the notion of place as a site of origin. And he does not stray far from the familiar trope of an aristocratic family fallen on hard times. This time, however, the novel traces the tempestuous fortunes of two patrician families: the Grays and the Carys. The narrative begins on the cusp of secession, follows the heroes on to the battlefields of the Civil War, and continues into Reconstruction—"the era [that] represented the worst abuses heaped upon a righteous civilization." In the "Preface," Page establishes a connection between place and myth. The Red Rock plantation lies *in the South, somewhere in that vague region partly in one of the old Southern States and partly in the yet vaguer land of Memory*."[6] Such a precarious setting, suspended between the *hic et nunc* and memory, serves a constructive purpose because it inscribes Red Rock with timelessness. Yet again, Page conjures a proper name that accentuates the relationship between gentility and place. Just like Elphinstone, Red Rock carries connotations of permanence and indelibility. The plantation, owned by the Grays, takes its name "from the great red stain, as big as a blanket, which appeared on the huge bowlder [sic] in the grove, beside family grave-yard." The blood on the stone belonged to "the Indian chief who had slain the wife of the first Jacquelin Gray who came to this part of the world: the Jacquelin who had built the first house at Red Rock, around the fireplace of which the present mansion was erected, and whose portrait, with its piercing eyes and fierce look, hung in a black frame over the mantel, and used to come down as a warning when any peril impeded above the house." The provenance of the family speaks of hardship, conquest, and loyalty. The roots the first Jacquelin planted in this place reach across the Atlantic to England, where "he was a scholar and had been a soldier under Cromwell and lost all his property." The same Jacquelin later "fell in love with a lady whose father was on the King's side, and married her" before packing his bags and setting sail for the South.[7]

The rock from which the plantation derives its name drips with an historically inflected significance that links the Grays to both the Stuart England and Scotland and, as the hint of the loss of property implies, its more affluent class. In the descendants of Jacquelin, the puritan sympathies coexist happily with royalist ones to create a unique brand of aristocratic gentility. The conquest and death of the Indian chief cements the legitimacy of this gentility and, rather tellingly, seals it in blood. The blood stain, still visible upon the stone, literalizes the metaphor of blood as heritage. Even the deeds to the house are stamped red by the feet of Jacquelin's descendant, Rupert Gray, who "while playing in the hall," dabbed them in red paint thus marking the floor and the papers that the wind happened to scatter on it. Rupert's mother, Mrs. Gray, in a gesture reminiscent of Mary Queen of Scots, "would never allow the prints to be scoured out, and so they have remained."[8] In this allusion to Mary Queen of Scots, Page offers his version of historic regeneration as a viable means of continuity in the unlikely union of endurance, history, and fiction by borrowing from the master inventor of Scottish tradition, Sir Walter Scott.

In the "Introduction" to *The Fair Maid of Perth or St. Valentine's Day,* Scott includes an account of the murder of David Rizzio—Queen Mary's favorite. Discussing the authenticity of the blood stains, which are still visible on the floor in Queen Mary's apartments in Holyrood Palace, and which are reputed to be Rizzio's, Chrystal Croftangry offers the following explanation to his cousin, Mrs. Baliol: "The constant tradition of the Palace, says, that Mary discharged any measures to be taken to remove the marks of slaughter, which she had resolved should remain as a memorial to quicken and confirm her purposed vengeance." In one fell swoop, Page has Mrs. Gray imitate the behavior of Mary Queen of Scots and perpetuate the continuity between the Grays, Scotland, and royalty. Scott, who saw the potential of the trope of blood to arouse historic consciousness, includes a similar legend of blood stains that enhances the teller's claim to nobility in *Waverley,* where Mrs. Rachael Waverley regales her nephew, Edward Waverley, with a tale of his ancestor's heroic deeds. Following the battle of Worcester, Lady Alice, endangering her life, "offers a day's refuge" to the future King Charles II. When Cromwell's soldiers approach "to search the mansion," she orders her son to gather the servants and "to make good with their lives an hour's diversion, that the king might have that space to escape." During the diversion, the son receives a mortal wound and, according to Mrs. Racheal, one "may trace the drops of his blood from the great hall-door, along the little gallery, and up to the saloon, where they laid him down to die at his mother's feet."[9] Blood thus spilled in noble cause yokes heroism to aristocracy. It both symbolizes the continuity of tradition and furnishes it with a historicity and materiality of a tangible proof. Although Page's allusion to Mary Queen of Scots is rather subtle, the conjunction of Red Rock, tradition, and blood serves to enunciate the aristocratic heritage of the Grays and reinforce the ties with Scottish nobility. In refusing to have the prints removed, Mrs. Gray displays a historically conscious adaptability, actively perpetuates the Gray tradition and reinforces the family's hereditary hold on the place wherein lies their claim to gentility.

Blood as heritage, immortalized in stone, forms an inextricable component of the Grays' gentility, while its visible marks invoke its continuity. What is interesting is that Page, like Scott, assigns equal share in the perpetuation of the Grays' fiction of whiteness to women and black servants, the disenfranchised by law. First, it was Mammy Celia who instilled in Jacquelin Gray, a descendant of the first Jacquelin and heir to Red Rock, a reverence for his formidable ancestor by telling him that if he misbehaved "the 'Indian Killer' would see him and come after him."[10] Mammy Celia was also Jacquelin's instructor in gentlemanly decorum and inspired in him a respect for the past. When the plantation is unjustly repossessed by Hiram Still, a former overseer, it is one of the Grays' former slaves, Doan, who, as the only witness to Rupert's exploits, is able to verify the authenticity of the bond and becomes instrumental in effecting the Grays' claim to Red Rock and, consequently, to the whiteness that the place represents.

Told and retold, the Grays' whiteness becomes endemic to the place, part of the local folklore, perpetuated in the stories "believed by the old negroes (and perhaps, by some of the whites, too, a little)." Thanks to such stories, Red Rock, in the eyes of the locals as well as the Grays, becomes synonymous with hereditary gentility, courage, justice, and benevolence—the seat of the Southern "truth" of whiteness. The perpetuation of a myth, Lefebvre observes, depends on the "symbolic space"—"practice" dyad.[11] Grounded in Red Rock, such stories acquire a mythical dimension in practice that is the act of telling and, through evocations of the Grays' ancestry and courage, they construct the Grays' whiteness, rooting it firmly in place. The allusion to the Indian blood neatly endows it with a continuity that predates the colony's establishment.

Page's effusiveness in painting the pastoral borders on hyperbole. This cradle of gentility, he writes, is "a little world in itself—a sort of feudal domain: the great house on its lofty hill, surrounded by gardens; the broad fields stretching away in every direction, with waving grain or green pastures dotted with sheep and cattle, and all shut in and bounded by the distant woods." Like the Keiths' Elphinstone, the elevated setting of the place is a natural reflection of the status of the owners of Red Rock, separating them from the other inhabitants of "*the Red Rock section*." Mr. Welch, an entrepreneur from the North and a visitor to the South, sees the natural splendor of the place as "evidences that the Garden of Eden was situated not far from that spot, and certainly within the limits of the State." As in *Gordon Keith*, Page builds a holistic image of gentility through evocations of the natural environment. Having a Northerner sing praises of the family and region adds a touch of objectivity to the picture. There may also be another motive: by extending the pastoral of the place to the whole region, Mr. Welch voices the difference between the idyllic South and North; while the allusion to Eden firmly mythologizes Red Rock and grounds it in Christian tradition. Unlike the path to Cabell's "high place," the path to this place leads "by the highway of Sincerity and Truth."[12] Quixotic as the remark appears, it nonetheless reifies the notion that truth can only be found and cultivated in one place: Red Rock. It endows Red Rock with the conceptual qualities to build an image of Southern whiteness that combines the tangible and the abstract. Sincerity and truth compound this image because both imply a purity of purpose and knowledge, notions that the elevated location emphasizes.

The notion of honor is such a quality that constitutes one component of this truth and features highly on Dr. Cary's list of gentlemanly values. In his impassioned speech against secession, Dr. Cary, the owner of Birdwood who is related to the Grays by blood since his sister married Mr. Gray, proclaims that "war is the most terrible of all disasters, except Dishonor." Yet, despite his anti-war sentiment, when the conflict erupts, the doctor joins the Confederate Army because his honor demands it. This heightened sense of honor extinguishes commonsensical pragmatism and, in Red Rock, becomes an element of Southern whiteness. Honor also demands that one be kind to one's servants. On the eve of his departure for war, General Gray leaves Hiram Still in charge of the plantation "as long as he treated the negroes well." As befitting a conscripted benevolent planter, the general's sense of honor encodes a moral obligation toward those in his care so that the tradition of planter benevolence can be carried on *in absentia*. Because running the plantation involves dealing with financial matters, the general leaves it in the hands of the overseer, whom he believes to be "the best business man." His orders to his son, Jacquelin—a gentleman in the making and heir apparent to the plantation—are to care for his mother and younger brother, Rupert. Above all, however, Jacquelin must "keep the old place. Make any sacrifice to do that. Landholding is one of the safeguards of the gentry."[13] A safeguard it may be, but it encodes an unwritten distinction between a nominal ownership and practical involvement. Consequently, Jacquelin, in whose name Page evokes the perpetuation of tradition, is not privy to the financial circumstances of the family, which will have disastrous consequences. Instead, he receives an invaluable lesson that his gentility is inextricably bound up with possession of land, both as heritage and its quotidian manifestation . There is one more paternal command: as his brother's guardian, Jacquelin must "see that he gets an education. It is the one patrimony that no accident—not even war—can take away."[14] This proviso allows for the preservation of a semblance of whiteness, but it cannot outweigh the importance of the hereditary possession of land imbued with historic legitimacy.

His father's dictum remains etched deeply in Jacquelin's memory, and later, when the plantation eventually passes to Still, it reveals, perhaps unintentionally, the complexity of Southern whiteness based on the notion of historic inheritance. Jacquelin's inheritance is haunted because it relies on the ghost of what once was and is no longer. Haunting is the primary *modus operandi* of inheritance and works on both a metaphorical and literal level. When Jacquelin returns to the region after an absence of several years, he is still "Marse Jack" to Waverly, an old servant. So striking is the resemblance that Waverly mistakes him for the "ole marster—er de Injun-Killer."[15] Page, it seems, never tires of allusions to Scott, and Waverly supplies another direct link with Scotland. As somebody whose name internalizes the continuity of tradition, Waverley is a fitting mouthpiece for Jacquelin's hereditary claim to gentility, which his uncanny similarity to his ancestor externalizes. A double haunting occurs as the past is literally revitalized in external appearance and metaphorically through the historic and hereditary connotations that Jacquelin's name evokes. This is the only place where Jacquelin can signify as "Marse Jack," and where his name encodes the convergence of past and present. Because Jacquelin is no longer a plantation owner and master of slaves, the title becomes an empty signifier. Ironically, it is Waverley, a former slave, who evokes Jacquelin's whiteness and voices its incompleteness.

The loss of Red Rock, his "high place," sets Jacquelin on course to the re-enactment of the next two acts in Cabell's tragi-comedy of Southern whiteness, the second of which "reveals the striving toward, and the third act the falling short of, that shining goal,"[16] With the militant blood of his ancestors running in his veins, Jacquelin vows to recover Red Rock. Assuming the authority of his ancestors, he confronts Still and announces to him: "you will not be in this place always. We are coming back here, the living and the dead."[17] Page casts the recovery of Red Rock, Jacquelin's ancestral home and the place where the ghosts of his forefathers serve as constant reminders of his heritage, as crucial to the reconstruction of his gentility. Because Jacquelin's whiteness is as much the discourse of the living as it is of the dead, the trajectory of its reconstruction must begin with recovery of the tangible emblem of the ideal and idealized genteel past that it represents.

Such reconstruction, however, is only possible in response to historic antecedents and will, of necessity, convey their absence, marking them as other than the present, other than Jacquelin. Jacquelin begins from the position of displacement because the act of recovery, as Derrida observes, "recalls the repetition of the same, of the same thing as a ghost."[18] Undertaken from the vantage point of the present, such recovery is doubly problematic because it implies both a re-discovery of this historic other, elevating and confirming its status as an ideal or a truth, and marks its disjunction from the here and now. Implicit in Jacquelin's reanimation of Southern whiteness are, therefore, death and rebirth. As such, its nature is atavistic since it consists in looking back to the past for reification, a reification whose significance increases exponentially with the change occasioned by the end of Civil War. In Red Rock, as in Elphinstone, Page implies, the past can never be past because it is a site of inspiration and historic legitimacy that will always forbid its being laid to rest. This sensibility is not unique to Jacquelin. Dr. Cary shares Jacquelin's reverence for place and land as receptacles of genteel tradition. In the wake of adversity and devastation in the aftermath of the war, he reminds his wife and daughter: "we have—the land. It is as much as our forefathers began with."[19] This land, framed by "the far-off mountains [that] rose blue and tender," is more than a site of inspiration; it is a constant, visible, and ennatured link to the past. The possession of land enables Dr. Cary to transform himself from benevolent planter into benevolent employer and retain an element of his former gentility. The transition, however, tarnishes his genteel benevolence and strips it of the presupposed innocence enshrined in hereditary wealth because it depends on borrowed money, and no gentleman should concern himself with pecuniary matters. The possession of land becomes deconstructive as it reveals Dr. Cary's gentility to be an attenuated replica of his forefathers' legacy.

This genteel legacy encompasses a respect for land that Jacquelin and Dr. Cary share, and that Page uses to establish a difference between them and those representing a darker shade of whiteness or, indeed, nonwhiteness. Still, the former overseer, who unlawfully takes over the Red Rock plantation, vehemently declares: "I know good land, and when you've got land you've got it, and everybody knows you've got it."[20] Although Still acknowledges that the possession of land signifies as "more"—it denotes prestige in this place—he does not recognize that it is the hereditary possession of land on which such prestige, and thus gentility, rest. Unlike Still, Dr. Cary is fully aware of this symbolic value of land; however, even such awareness cannot withstand the dire necessity of taxation that forces him to sell part of his property to pay off his debts. To accomplish this, he travels, accompanied by General Legaie, to the city to meet Mr. Ledger, a banker from the North. Mr. Ledger, true to his name, has eyes for profit only and remains unmoved by the doctor's laudatory evaluation of his land from which "not an acre has ever been sold from the original grant," a fact that in the doctor's estimation "manifestly added to the value of the terms offered." As in *On Newfound River*, Page uses the royal connection to showcase the difference between the Southern and Northern sensibilities, inviting a comparison in which the North, represented by Mr. Ledger, is the unnamed villain. The doctor does not doubt that the connection to the royal grant aggrandizes the place. That it fails to impress Mr. Ledger suggests that he possesses no reverence for heredity so esteemed by gentlemen. Incomparably rich in sentiment, Dr. Cary and General Legaie lack Mr. Ledger's Northern business acumen, so much so that, according to Mr. Ledger, "they are about as able to cope with the present as two babies." Lucinda MacKethan observes of Dr. Cary and General Legaie that, as symbols of loss, they foreground the difference between the Old and New South.[21] Arguably, this is not their only purpose. Mr. Ledger fails to discern the motivation behind the doctor and General Legaie's resistance to the demands of the zeitgeist—namely the loyalty to tradition that characterizes their whiteness and sets them apart from Mr. Ledger. The parallel with babies, unwittingly expressed by Mr. Ledger, goes beyond mere emphasis of the innocence of the two gentlemen and the values they espouse; it adroitly transforms criticism into praise and tacitly inveighs against a context that sees such values as outdated. Page uses the encounter between Dr. Cary and Mr. Ledger to offer an image of Southern whiteness that comes into focus at an intersection between gentility, benevolence, disdain for matters pecuniary, and a crucial lack of these attributes in usually, but not exclusively, Northern others.

Page returns to the ploy of negative comparison elsewhere in the novel. When Mr. Welch, accompanied by his daughter, Ruth, returns to the region with a view to settling there, they are accidently—or serendipitously—directed to Dr. Cary's. The latter has by now lost his plantation and resides in a little cottage; however, even amid such impoverished surroundings, the doctor's nobility of breeding shines brightly. He enthralls Ruth by the bow he makes to her "with an old-fashioned graciousness" that "sets her to blushing." The exchange unmistakably marks the Northerner, Ruth, as the gauche ingenue, not the provincial and impecunious doctor. Her admiration of the doctor's nose, which is "finer even than" her father's is a tacit acknowledgement of his patrician heritage, while the direct comparison with her father, a Northerner, juxtaposes the two regions. The conclusion inevitably invites itself: such gentlemanly manners are endemic to the South, but alien to the North. Ruth's admiration extends to the doctor's daughter, Blair, whose "figure was so slim" and her "face so refined" that they compensated amply for the plainness of her dress adorned only with "a brass button." What astonishes Ruth even more are Blair's "manners," which she finds "as composed and gracious as if she had been a lady and in society for years," which is precisely what Blair has been raised to be.[22] Ruth's genuine admiration for Dr. Cary, and Blair's performance of Southern gentility, evokes the ghosts of gentlemen and ladies past, and reveals their "striving toward" and "falling short" of those ideals.

The scene descends into a spectacle of difference as praise. Ruth is the Northern other, Page implies, because she lacks a sense of historic consciousness. Although she observes the brass button adorning Blair's dress, she remains immune to its symbolic significance: it is a Confederate uniform button and, as such, imbued with a dual significance. On the one hand, it is a symbol of the Lost Cause acting as a link to the mythical South as the source of the gentility that Ruth so admires; while, on the other, the button highlights the doctor and Blair's imitation of gentility in the present, branding it as a lost cause. To a Northerner like Ruth, however, such intricacies of history and tradition are beyond comprehension, as are they to her mother, Mrs. Welch. As befitting one hailing from the North, Mrs. Welch is an industrious woman who has "no time to spend in the sort of hospitality practiced by her neighbors," whereby "the idea of going over to a neighbor's to 'spend the day,'" or "of having them come and 'spend the day' with her as they did with others, was intolerable."[23] Mrs. Welch's outward condemnation of Southern hospitality transforms it into a virtue and a lesson in the unabating difference in regional sensibilities. The same Southern hospitality and genteel manners prevent Dr. Cary from asking Mr. Welch whether he is a carpetbagger, a term he finds offensive, combining as it does opportunistic materialism with Northern occupation. Page offers a stereotypical rendering of the carpetbagger in the character of Jonadab Leech, who "arrived one afternoon with only a carpet-bag." Leech, who combines Northern avarice with duplicity, has relocated to the South to "bleed" the country dry. And he proves true to his name. Steve Allen—Jacquelin's cousin—compares him to a vampire "sucking the life-blood of the people." Page does not hide his contempt for Leech the carpetbagger and what he represents. He is the only character in the novel who "turns nigger," a phrase that constitutes an indictment of the highest order. When, following the arrest of the local gentlemen, Steve Allen kidnaps Leech and holds him in a secret location in order to exchange him for the prisoners, Leech, fearing being handed over to the Klan, climbs up the chimney. When Steve Allen pulls him down, Leech has literally and metaphorically, through his lack of courage, "turned nigger." Seeing him, Steve Allen observes: "You wouldn't know yourself from a nigger." Being a "nigger," Frantz Fanon writes, indicates a combination of obsequiousness and fear that anticipates punishment even in the absence of a threat.[24] The term then transcends race and, in Leech's case, serves to dissociate him from the values of Southern whiteness. No wonder, therefore, that the doctor "would not insult" Mr. Welch under his roof by evoking the appellation that he finds offensive because it is synonymous with theft and exploitation and, therefore, sin—metaphorical blackness.[25] Carpetbaggery is an unforgivable offence, yet one must be presumed innocent until proven otherwise. Despite his suspicion of Mr. Welch's purpose, Dr. Cary's conduct toward him cannot be faulted: it is that of a gentleman.

Both Blair and Dr. Cary's conduct toward the strangers harks back to the ideal of Southern gentility characterized by the display of hearty hospitality that they replicate in the real. The problem with such replications, Derrida suggests, lies in the slipperiness and spectrality of an ideal that can never materialize as a whole and tangible presence. In evoking the ideal, the very thing that cannot manifest itself, both Blair and Dr. Cary effectively open the gap between the promise of the ideal and the reconstruction they represent, and become inadequate replicas of that very promise.[26] What they embody are permutations of the truth, or the ideal of gentility, that come into being at the moment of re-enactment, which itself marks the fissure between the site of origin and the copy. Such a process of replication simultaneously evokes a preconceived truth and renders each act of mimetic reproduction incomplete and lacking. Like his protagonists, Page appears stuck in the second act of "striving toward" reproducing the imagined ideal of antebellum whiteness, which makes him studiously oblivious to Blair's and Dr. Cary's shortcomings: a lack of the prerequisites of land and plantation.

Lack of the material attributes of whiteness is not the only factor distancing the protagonists of *Red Rock* from the ideal. Dyer sees Christ and the Virgin Mary as essential antecedents of whiteness, and its male and female incarnations. Christ embodies asceticism and self-denial which lead to suffering as the ultimate expression of striving, both spiritual and physical; while the Virgin Mary acts as a paradigm of feminine virtues of docility, passivity, and purity, features that found their way from the sacred to the secular world of courtly love and chivalry. Although colonial Maryland seems far removed from the refinements of the mythical courts of love, the notion of female purity acquired a particular significance there and led to the establishment of "civil distinctions" based on the threat of "'loathsome copulations.'" The white female became the embodiment of this threat of sin, a distinction she owed to her status on arrival. Those women who arrived in Maryland, as elsewhere in the South, did so with one goal in mind: to offer their reproductive capacity in return for marriage and, if luck was on their side, the possibility of upward mobility that came with a wealthy husband. An indentured servant and resident of Maryland in the 1660s, George Alsop, wrote of such unions as "copulative marriages." In this fair without vanity, the lower-class woman gained a reputation for unbridled fecundity that would prove difficult to shake off, and later became the characteristic of the lowest of the low—the white trash. As class divisions crystallized, "copulative marriages" evolved into the threat of "loathsome copulations," which, as Felipe Smith proves, was less successful in securing eternal damnation than in neatly classifying white femininity because only white women who were indentured servants were deemed capable of engaging in such acts. Thus constructed class consciousness limited the danger, and potential spread, of contaminated femininity to the lower stratum of society.[27] This palliative measure effectively contained the threat of pollution and made purity and sexual innocence the purview of the genteel woman, who could then act as an ideal in need of protection.

Purity, the *sine qua non* of female gentility, became indispensable to projections of male whiteness, which could then develop along axes of asceticism and self-denial. It is, therefore, metaphorical blackness, the possibility of fallibility and imperfection that underlies the construction of both male and female ideals of gentility. This need to preserve the ideal of female purity creates a paradox: for the ideal to remain immaculate, it must be divorced from its corporeal presence and function. Klaus Theweleit, discussing depictions of women in fascist literature, concludes that the world the fascist man inhabits is a world to which the presence of women is essential but only when accompanied by female biddability.[28] It is a world of semi-exclusion of women, one that qualifies their presence in order to carve out a space for masculinity. The principle operates in reverse in the South. The Southern gentleman replaces such pseudo-repudiation by valorizing and elevating the purity of the genteel lady. The fiction of the Southern gentleman depends on safeguarding the ideal of the genteel lady in the quotidian—on the negotiation of the dissonance between the ideal and corporeal reanimation. This interdependence of the two constructs points to an ambivalence of whiteness predetermined by the unattainability of its ideals through the perpetuation of which it comes into being.

Yet, this ambivalence is indispensable to the construction of Southern male whiteness as it inaugurates the struggle inherent in the protection of the female ideal from the specter of pollution. Even when docile and meek, the presence of the Southern lady constantly evokes the "absent presence" of the ideal to which it alludes. This "absent presence" of the ideal, however, spurs the elevation of the Southern lady to the status of the ideal since only then can Southern male whiteness come into signification. The ambivalence of this interdependence between the Southern gentleman and lady for signification is evident early on in the novel, in the roles Mammy Celia and Mrs. Gray play in instilling and preserving Jacquelin's gentility. And it continues throughout the narrative, where it soon becomes apparent that, in Red Rock, behind every gentleman stands a Southern lady. As befits a gentleman in the making and heir to the Red Rock plantation, Jacquelin has always harbored a respect for women. Since childhood, Blair Cary, his blue-blooded cousin and heiress to the neighboring Birdwood plantation, has shaped his behavior.[29]

Born to the felicity of the antebellum South, suitably edulcorated by their aristocratic heritage, Jacquelin and Blair grow up carefree. But, even the innocence of their childhood games betrays a division of roles with Jacquelin—Blair's senior by a handful of years—assuming the position of a judicious mentor. When Jacquelin jumps from the roof of a barn and Blair, unheeding of his command not to jump, follows suit, the incident marks a turning point in their relationship. Jacquelin vows to "guard her," and this vow has "sweetened to him the bitterness of having to confess to his father." And so, despite being "mightily afraid," he behaves "like a man," recounts "the whole story alone without the least reference to Blair's part in it, taking the entire blame on himself."[30] Blair's misdemeanor kindles Jacquelin's chivalric spirit, which results in his vow to protect her and safeguard her honor as a budding lady for whom jumping off barn roofs exceeds the acceptable decorum. In one fell swoop, Page transforms Jacquelin into Blair's protector and defender of the ideal of femininity she represents. What remains, however, is the irreducible ambivalence of his position in that a lie undermines the honorability of his deed, and marks his departure from the gentlemanly ideal to which his status preconditions him. Blair's apparent unbiddability frustrates Jacquelin's genteel aspirations because it reveals the irreconcilability between loyalty to his father and chivalry; yet another Eve that leads Adam astray. As embodiments of the ideal of Southern whiteness, both are flawed: Blair because of her disobedience and Jacquelin because of the falsehood he tells. In this discourse of reciprocity, imperfection fosters imperfection, and Jacquelin's gentility is as flawed as the ideal that inspired it.

The fissure between the ideal of Southern femininity and Blair's action propels Jacquelin's initiation into the role of gentleman. On his return from the war, Jacquelin finds Blair changed. She has "sprung up to a slender young lady of 'quite seventeen,' whose demureness and newborn dignity were the more bewitching, because they were belied by her laughing glances." To an impartial observer, Blair's modesty and flirtatiousness may appear irreconcilable, but to Jacquelin "she was no longer mortal: he had robed her in radiance and lifted her among the stars." The elevation of Blair among the celestial bodies marks a continued effort of pedestalization on Jacquelin's part, the effect of which Blair's description as a carefree teenager somewhat belies. Yet, such desexualization serves a purpose. In his discussion of the unity of a fascist soldier, Theweleit evokes the concept of the "white wife" who brings order to the home, presides over matters domestic, and guards against sexual contamination. Such devivification, Theweleit continues, both renders the "white wife" subordinate to the soldier and central to the projection of the wholeness of his body-ego.[31] In Jacquelin's imagination, Blair becomes a "white wife" in all but name. Only the desexualized and devivified Blair may move closer to the purity of the ideal, enabling Jacquelin to assume the role of a protector so essential to the conception of himself as a Southern gentleman. This complex reciprocity both foregrounds the interdependence between the projection of male and female incarnations of whiteness and renders them lacking. Speaking of the conception of the wholeness of the male body, Theweleit notes that it requires other "external totalities" against which it may define itself.[32] The mechanism also works for the projection of whiteness. Jacquelin's devivification of Blair invokes the ghost of the ideal, the woman beyond blemish, because in doing so he can merge the corporeal with the perfect image into a totality. This convergence is essential to Jacquelin's delineation of his own perception of whiteness as a distinct totality. The process, however, reveals Blair to be nothing more than a synecdoche because her physical presence inexorably points to the specter of the ideal that she represents in the real. Because the two are essentially irreconcilable, Jacquelin substitutes the defense of the ideal for the protection of its embodiment.

That the scenario strongly suggests a medieval courtly romance where the cult of femininity and heroic knights ruled supreme is not surprising given Page's agenda to create the cult of Southern whiteness. Jacquelin is merely a single manifestation of what Page casts as a ubiquitous trait among Southern gentlemen, to whom "the honor of the female sex" ranks higher "than money or life." When Jonadab Leech, a former carpetbagger now elevated to the rank of provost, initiates a search of Confederate homes to confiscate arms, his conduct merits universal condemnation because it is deemed offensive to ladies. As a result of Leech's transgression, Steve Allen— Jacquelin's older cousin who also grew up on the plantation—leads a deputation to Captain Middleton, who commands the Northern regiment stationed there. During the interview, Steve asseverates: "before we will allow our women to be insulted, we will kill every man of you."[33] What may seem an overreaction on Steve's part is yet another example of Page's ability to avoid direct confrontation on the matter of regional difference. But it is present in Steve's impassioned declaration, in which he professes his loyalty to the passivity enshrined in the ideal of the Southern lady. Like Jacquelin, he needs to protect this ideal because failure to do so would undermine his projection of whiteness. Page uses this overarching quest for the protection of Southern women to homogenize the male incarnation of gentility. After all, Steve leads a delegation of like-minded men who, united in the defense of the ideal, epitomize culture and education. The signification of male whiteness that this defense inaugurates, as will become evident in Ellen Glasgow's *Battle-Ground*, applies only to a "woman of culture" who "satisfactorily fulfills her functions of representation."[34] In other words, it can only be inspired by a genteel lady who approximates the ideal of female whiteness. The promise of attaining the wholeness of the ideal that the lady embodies exceeds her physical presence, transforming her into a metonymy and pointing to the abstract concepts of purity, chastity, docility and male gentility.

Yet, this excess of meaning also points to a lack in the ambivalent space where meaning transcends the sign or the imitator. To reconstruct his whiteness, the Southern gentleman must reimagine female gentility in the ordinary to fit the mold of the ideal, which involves negotiating the space between the two totalities: the ideal and its actual embodiment. Ironically, it is a woman who first voices the ambivalence of the Southern male whiteness conceived in response to perceptions of Southern femininity. The lady is Jacquelin's spinster aunt, Thomasia, a relic of the Old South. When Blair complains to her about Steve's blaming "all his shortcomings" on "the example set him by a woman," Aunt Thomasia stoically replies: "They all do it, my dear, from Adam down." Elsewhere, Aunt Thomasia makes an equally astute assertion: "Men like to fancy themselves broader and more judicial than women."[35] Aunt Thomasia goes to the heart of the matter: the female ideal is a male invention, an invention intricately woven into the tapestry of Christian tradition. Unlike the men who continue to subscribe to this fiction, Aunt Thomasia is aware of its irreconcilability with the real. Her words reaffirm the haunting influence of the female ideal on the constructions of male whiteness, particularly the comparative forms of the adjectives "broad" and "judicial," incidentally in the case of the latter formed through the quantifier "more." The inclusion of women among the "broad" and "judicial" seals their status as "cultured women" and, consequently, a fitting site for cultivating Southern male gentility. Aunt Thomasia, however, labors under no illusion and notes the disparity that obtains between the Southern female ideal and its embodiment. Her remark confirms their status as distinct and irreconcilable totalities.

For a person who is aware of the irreconcilability of the ideal and the reconstruction, Aunt Thomasia's life stands as testament to the alluring power of Southern whiteness and the inescapabability from such awareness. Her choice to remain a spinster and her resistance to General Legaie's interminable addresses stem from her loyalty—the trait characteristic of male whiteness—and feminine docility. Having given her heart to a gentleman "who had loved her," but who "had not been strong enough to resist, even for her sake, the temptation of two besetting sins—drink and gambling," Aunt Thomasia "had obeyed her father and given him up."[36] The gentleman's vices symbolize metaphorical blackness and undermine his gentility. Besmirched by sin, he lacks yet another quality associated with whiteness—that of the sacrifice of self-denial. His susceptibility to temptation marks a lack of reverence for the ideal that Aunt Thomasia represents and invalidates his status as a "cultured man." His failure to convert from the path of iniquity flies in the face of virtue as a hereditary trait characteristic of gentility. But Aunt Thomasia does not escape unscathed. In obeying her father, she fulfills her filial duty and acts according to the standard of ideal femininity—that of a woman doing others' bidding. Such unconditional obedience secures her claim to whiteness and concurrently problematizes it by preventing Aunt Thomasia from fulfilling one of the duties that Dyer links to the concept of ideal female whiteness, namely motherhood. The purity of her intentions notwithstanding, Aunt Thomasia's whiteness remains incomplete: the distinct qualities she possesses may constitute discrete signifiers of whiteness, but they never converge as a totality. Instead, her incarnation of a genteel lady remains synecdochal which, while pointing to the ideal, betrays a lack. Aunt Thomasia intends her disclosure to Steve Allen—coincidentally her ill-fated suitor's son—to prevent him from following in his father's footsteps. But, its success is only partial: "I will not say I will never drink again; but I will promise you not to gamble again, and I will not drink to excess any more."[37] Steve may not be immune to the appeal of a genteel lady; however, he consciously retains his father's legacy of metaphorical blackness. Although Aunt Thomasia's tale initiates Steve's struggle for whiteness, his failure is a *fait accompli,* predetermined by his reluctant promise that spells his "falling short" of the "shining goal" before the quest even begins. Steve's whiteness transcends the color line and can only signify as black whiteness.

The ambivalence of Steve's whiteness is twofold because it is predicated upon the incompleteness of the ideal that inspires it and is undermined by his conciliatory promise. Unlike Aunt Thomasia, Steve is unaware of the dissonance between the ideal and reproduction. In a conversation with Aunt Thomasia, Steve declares that "there aren't any of 'em [ladies] like you nowadays. The mould's broken." Steve reiterates the familiar story of gentility destroyed by war, without pausing to consider its essence. He venerates the ideal that Aunt Thomasia represents but, by consigning it to the past, inadvertently evokes its death and pronounces it beyond the reach of other aspiring ladies, such as Blair. Blair shares his opinion. Of visits to Aunt Thomasia, she declares, each "was like reading one of Scott's novels; that she got back to a land of chivalry."[38] Blair endows Aunt Thomasia's gentility with a mythical status that, while it may inspire emulation, cannot be reconciled with the present.

Aunt Thomasia may seem out of place because her saintliness and antebellum ways hark back to a bygone ideal, but Blair is equally misplaced because she departs from it. To help her father meet tax payments on Birdwood, Blair betrays a truly enterprising spirit and sets about making and selling preserves. Andy Stamper, whose parents Aunt Thomasia describes as "one of our poor neighbors," and his wife lend a helping hand. Their cooperation, to the displeasure of Mammy Krenda, marks Blair's departure from the Southern belle ideal. Although the selflessness of her intentions bespeaks her whiteness as encoded in the impossible ideal of the Virgin Mary, it simultaneously taints it by performing manual labor, which is incommensurate with the construct of the Southern belle. And it is Mammy Krenda, like Jacquelin's Mammy Celia, who is her sternest critic and insists on Blair's maintaining a facade of gentility. When Captain Middleton finds Blair cooking, Mammy Krenda ingenuously exclaims: "I don' know what she air doin' in heah." Her efforts are wasted when Blair admits to Middleton: "I do nearly all the cooking since our cook went off, but she thinks it's beneath my dignity to be caught at it."[39] If, as Fanon writes, black symbolizes "evil" and "sin," Mammy Krenda's lie, although essentially springing from good intentions, is a "natural" corollary of her skin color, whereas Blair's truthfulness reaffirms the purity encoded in whiteness. What undermines such a supposition, however, is Blair's well-intentioned, but nonetheless duplicitous conduct toward her father from whom she conceals her preserve-making enterprise. Blair's candid admission both renders superfluous the indispensability of blackness as a manifestation of skin color to constructions of whiteness and reifies the undecidability of the Southern belle as the incarnation of the ideal of Southern whiteness.[40] Blair embodies the conflict between the ideal and its actual representation, between what she ought to be and what she has become by choice: a working woman. But the instability inherent in Blair's positioning allows her father to maintain a facade of gentility, effectively transforming her into an "enabler" of the ideal of the Southern gentleman.[41]

It is, similarly, the enterprise of Blair's mother and aunt Thomasia that, though marking their departure from the ideal, maintains the facade of gentility of Dr. Cary and General Legaie. These gentlemen's shirts are "made from an under-garment of one of the ladies," and this very fact seems to endow them with transformative powers. The general declares that "he had felt on putting it [the shirt] on that morning, as a knight of old might have felt when he donned his armor prepared by virgin hands." Literally, the ladies' labors enable the general's gentility by negotiating the fissure between the past and the present. In this supplementary role, they vacillate between transgressing and respecting the ideal of whiteness.[42] The gentility they resurrect is a product of this vacillation between the transgression of, and respect for, the antebellum ideal and, as such, encodes difference predicated upon the impossibility of the resurrection of antebellum whiteness. The best they can hope for is a collage of pieces, but never a whole. The shirts' genesis reveals the untenability of the passivity enshrined in the ideal of the Southern lady, consigned to occupy a purely representational space. In the ordinary, the representational space transmutes into a constitutive space, and the genteel lady, comfortably or not, straddles both. But, it is precisely because of the fissure between the ideal and its actual representation that, in Steve Allen's words, one can "don his gray jacket [and] play gentleman once more."[43] Steve's playing gentleman "once more" implies a haunted performance that points to an *a priori* condition: a revenant that, while promising continuity, marks such re-playing as different and finite. Despite Page's effort to create a viable and sustainable paradigm of gentility, capable of bridging the gap between the past and the present that offers a hope of continuity, the picture and the characters unravel into abortive fictions of verisimilitude who invariably betray the touch of the tar brush.

FIVE

ELLEN GLASGOW AND THE AMBIVALENCE OF IDEALS

The touch of the tar brush may seem like a questionable term to apply to a discussion of Southern whiteness, yet it captures perfectly the plight in which Page's protagonists find themselves—that of being defined by the past and found wanting. Although the phrase lends itself all too easily to suggestions of a visible imperfection such as, for example, a drop of "negro blood" made manifest in the color of skin, Fanon equates the symbolism of darkness with "evil, sin, wretchedness," and "death."[1] What the touch of the tar brush foregrounds is an innate imperfection—a metaphorical blackness—that is the inescapable reality of reproduction precisely because of its distance from the ideal. Page is aware of this ambivalence of darkness; after all, he has Jonadab Leech "turn nigger" because he is ultimately lacking in courage and honor (and he is a carpetbagger to boot). The ambivalence of the whiteness of the gentlemen and ladies populating the pages of *Red Rock* is of a different kind: it is an innate imperfection that stems from their inability to replicate the perfection of the antebellum ideal. Intent on preserving the myth of Southern whiteness, Page remains if not oblivious then grudgingly reluctant to recognize the ambivalence of the constructs he creates as its paradigms, and whatever shortcomings they may be guilty of are justified by the vicissitudes of Reconstruction. Not so Ellen Glasgow, whose *The Battle-Ground* offers no such justification and, instead, holds up the very notion of the ideal to close scrutiny.

This "wonderfully rich and charming" novel was published in 1902 and is the first in the series of the Commonwealth. The narrative begins in "Virginia—the school for gentlemen," before the outbreak of the Civil War, follows the fortunes of its protagonists through the conflict, and ends on the cusp of Reconstruction.[2] Although the narrative ends before the reforms of Reconstruction begin, its relevance to the reimagination of the postbellum Southern gentility is twofold. Showing how outmoded notions of breeding, musty chivalry, and transgression persistently shadow the development of the key players in the novel allows Glasgow to question the presupposed ubiquity of antebellum gentility. At the close of the story, rather than propose a model of spurious continuity of the imagined whiteness, she salvages the individual traits of what she sees as the Southern character, such as nobility of spirit, loyalty, endurance, to hint at a future of productive adaptability. This is not so much a reconstruction as a healing deconstruction.

The narrative journey is long, spanning fifteen years, from 1850 to 1865. Critics like McDowell see this as a narrative ploy that helps Glasgow to foreground the contrast between the idyll of the antebellum South and its resistance through the years of the conflict and beyond. This extended narrative is not unique to *The Battle-Ground* or unusual for Glasgow, whose *The Voice of the People* covers the distance of twenty eight years. In *The Romance of a Plain Man*, she goes even further, stretching the narrative over the period of thirty five years.[3] As a narrative method, it works, not only because her characterization is effective and vivid but also because it lacks Page's pathos. The extended narrative allows Glasgow to foreground the minutiae that shape individual experience. As a literary technique, it remains indebted to Sir Walter Scott's reconceptualization of the historical novel. What the genre lacked before Scott, Georg Lukács writes in his seminal study *The Historical Novel*, was the creation of character as part of the lived historical experience. Unlike his predecessors, Scott made history accessible by recreating the ethos of the past and he did so through the device of average and ordinary heroes who cannot remain unaffected by the historical events they witness.[4] The result was a fictionalization of history, in which the mundane and the trivial met historical fact and presented it as lived experience instead of dry statistics; a conjunction that earned Scott unprecedented popularity and rubbed off on Glasgow.

Glasgow's exposure to *belle lettres*, and more prosaically, orthography, began with Scott's *Old Mortality* and *The Waverley Novels* retold by "dear old Aunt Rebecca." And his influence persists in the way she approaches her subject matter. Her intention in writing *The Battle-Ground*, "was to write, not literally a novel of war, but a chronicle of two neighboring families." The Civil War, the game-changer in the history of the South, takes a back stage, despite a section of the novel covering Dan Montjoy's military exploits. This lack of direct involvement with the war was a deliberate choice that, on occasion, put her at odds with her fellow Richmonders. In 1913, shortly after the publication of *Virginia*, Glasgow recalls a visit from "one of the perpetual widows of the South" who magnanimously agreed that there was "truth" in her book but thought it "a mistake for Southern writers to stop writing about the War." Having pronounced her judgment, she expressed the hope that either Glasgow "or Annie Cabell's son [James Branch Cabell] would write another *Surrey of Eagle's Nest*."[5] Her hope remained unrealized.

It is doubtful that the widow would have approved of Glasgow's protagonists of *The Battle-Ground*, which, notwithstanding its title, talks of a battle less militant. The narrative centers on two aristocratic families, the Lightfoots residing at Chericoke and the Amblers inhabiting the neighboring Uplands. The surnames which, as Richard Gray observes, convey good breeding by inviting comparison to horses, signal the nature of the battle Glasgow pitches: it is a metaphorical battle that questions the validity of the Southern ideal of gentility and its female and male incarnations, at the heart of which stands breeding. Unlike the rigid uniformity of Page's Grays and Carys, who are the chips of the old block of Old World finest, Glasgow's Lightfoots and Amblers are a mixed breed with skeletons in their closets. Here, as in *Red Rock,* place names possess connotative power, which speaks of the quality of those dwelling within their walls. The name of the Amblers' estate, Uplands, evokes ideas of noble spirit and gentility. Unlike Uplands, the Lightfoots' residence, Chericoke, betrays little of the character of its inhabitants; instead, the narrator draws attention to its fame, which derives from the portrait of "great-great-aunt Emmeline," who "was the beauty and belle of two continents," and who still is "the abiding presence of the place."[6] This deliberate omission enunciates a difference between the pedigree of the two families and destabilizes the idea of a homogenous Southern aristocracy. Even among the self-proclaimed Southern finest, whiteness comes in many hues, as the Lightfoots' grandson, Dan Montjoy discovers. The thought of this illustrious ancestor immortalized in the portrait hanging in the parlor sustains him during his two-hundred mile walk to Chericoke following the death of his mother and the Lightfoots' estranged daughter. The legend of Aunt Emmeline, told and retold by his mother, becomes synonymous with Dan's patrician heritage, and women are the medium through which it is perpetuated. Glasgow uses the portrait to frame the narrative of *The Battle-Ground*; it welcomes the young Dan Mountjoy to the home of his ancestors and, after the plantation has been burnt down by Union soldiers, "the radiant image" survives to welcome Dan again—this time as a war veteran. R. H. W. Dillard pronounces women "veritable icons of the Old Order," and the portrait, set amid humble surroundings, represents a silent but salient reminder of their antebellum gentility; it is the revenant *par excellence* because it figures a dead woman who is also emblematic of the spirit of whiteness, the reincarnation of which it prefigures.[7] The portrait encodes a compulsion to continuity that acquires a mythical dimension, not unlike predestination: there is no escape from the past but none is sought and the burden willingly embraced.

The portrait is a tangible remainder of the past that further congeals the metaphor of blood as heritage. It is not just a window to the past that stubbornly insists on the connection between the past and the present, but also a point of comparison offering a possibility of reconciliation, however futile. The portrait possesses a dual signification that derives from the intersection of the historical and the personal. For Dan, it constitutes a physical representation of his antecedent and, in doing so, provides a haunting but tangible link to a historic past and legitimation. The link, however, is tenuous because, by virtue of being a copy, Aunt Emmeline's portrait brings into sharp relief the unbridgeable gap between the ideal and its reconstruction. It foregrounds the "absent presence" of the ideal, both literally—since Aunt Emmeline has long departed from the place; and metaphorically—since her departure marks the unattainability of the ideal.

The still perfection of this ideal sets off the imperfections of the genteel ladies who dwell in its shadow. Aunt Lydia, the Amblers' relation living with them at Uplands, feels acutely the need to maintain the veneer of a genteel lady. Aunt Lydia, who "had read Scott, and enshrined in her pious heart the bold Rob Roy," like Page's Aunt Thomasia, establishes a link to the past that reaches beyond the Old South to the Scotland of heroic exploits. Aunt Lydia's fondness for Scott betrays an unhealthy preoccupation with tradition and a devotion to upholding its rigidity. According to her creed, "the proper place for a spinster is her father's house," a dictum she is wont to deliver with "her conventional primness, and send, despite herself a mild imagination in pursuit of the follies from which she so earnestly prayed to be delivered." The mixture of awe and fascination in which she holds Mrs. Ambler's grandmother, who was "the most finished dancer of her day," dilutes the image of a spinsterly variety of whiteness that she projects through her outward primness. Despite deeming dancing "the devil's own device," her "timid pride" in recollecting this bold but sinful personage betrays Aunt Lydia's desire for metaphorical blackness—for that which is forbidden by the dictates of spinsterly gentility. Since desire alienates the desiring subject from itself by evoking the chasm between the desired and the actual, Aunt Lydia's immodest yearnings reify the instability of the ideal that she projects and point to the futility of her aspirations to whiteness; as long as "the blood of the most finished dancer circulated beneath the old lady's gown and religious life," Aunt Lydia's incarnation of the genteel lady will remain touched with the tar brush.[8]

Futile it may be; however, Aunt Lydia's adherence to the ideal of spinsterly whiteness becomes a site of constant struggle in which desire is mediated by the necessity to maintain the preordained decorum. Although Julia Ambler has ordered a new bonnet for her, in matters of attire, according to Aunt Lydia, "a plain black poke" only befits her status as a spinster.[9] To reconcile the temptation the bonnet represents, Aunt Lydia seeks guidance in the Scriptures, in "Saint Paul on Woman." Having consulted the biblical authority, "when she came down a few hours later, her face wore an angelic meekness. "I have been thinking of that poor Mrs. Brown who was here last week," she said softly, "and I remember her telling me that she had no bonnet to wear to church. What a loss it must be for her not to attend divine service." Hearing Aunt Lydia's remark, Mrs. Ambler replies: "Why, Aunt Lydia, it would be really a charity to give her your old one!" Her conscience thus assuaged, Aunt Lydia consents that indeed "it would be a charity."[10] Aunt Lydia may seek the conformation of the ideal of female whiteness in the Bible, but she actively re-interprets it, which allows her to transform an otherwise unseemly vanity into Christian charity. Such a re-interpretation of the ideal exacerbates Aunt Lydia's ambivalent position as an inchoate imitation and casts Mrs. Brown, who represents a darker hue of whiteness, as an unwitting enabler of Aunt Lydia's dubious claim to Christian charity. Because Mrs. Ambler solicitously encourages her to keep the bonnet, she becomes equally implicated in the charade that is the maintaining of Aunt Lydia's facade of gentility.

The preservation of this facade does not come without sacrifice. When offered apple toddy at Christmas, Aunt Lydia declines: "she was fond of apple toddy, but she regarded the taste as an indelicate one, and would as soon have admitted, before gentlemen, a liking for cabbage."[11] Through Aunt Lydia's expert performance of a genteel lady, Glasgow reveals the factors influencing the behavior: an aesthetic concern indicating etiquette a lady should observe in the presence of gentlemen. Something as earthly as apple toddy may degrade the ideal of female whiteness in the eyes of the gentlemen, so, as a preventative measure, Aunt Lydia devivifies herself to protect the sanctity of the ideal. What belies the sincerity of her refusal of the offending potation is a tacit admission to a fondness for it which, inadvertently, reveals a crack in the facade of the genteel lady she so painstakingly maintains.

The example of gentility that Aunt Lydia sets is metonymic in that it is partial, haunted by the perfection of the ideal but irreducible to it; it exceeds her incarnation of gentility and renders it lacking. Such lapses notwithstanding, Aunt Lydia extends her unceasing preoccupation with the protection of the ideal of female whiteness to her niece, Betty, whom she implores not to sample the toddy because "it will give" her "a vulgar color." Flushed cheeks, it appears, are unacceptable in a genteel lady. Through the denial of her desire for apple toddy that results in a quasi asceticism, Aunt Lydia escapes the treacherous flush of the cheek and preserves her virtue. In the characterization of Aunt Lydia, Glasgow inveighs against the very notion of conformity to imagined ideals, which leads to the caricature of the subject. She compounds this critique in her later novel, *The Sheltered Life* (1932), where she has a young doctor, John Welch, voice the constraining effect of living by a standard. "People who have tradition," he muses, "are oppressed by tradition, and people who are without it are oppressed by the lack of it—or by whatever else they have put in its place." It is a no-win situation and his is a first-hand experience of watching the decline of his cousin Eva Birdsong. Eva, who brought him up and who has been avowed by one and all in Queenborough to be the earthly incarnation of the ideal of Southern belle, succumbs to depression following an illness. The illness invites retrospection and forces an unwelcome admission. She is "worn out," she admits, "with being somebody else—with being somebody's ideal."[12] Eva shoots her husband, the person whose idealization of her turned her into a perpetual prisoner to tradition. In *The Sheltered Life*, Glasgow abandons caricature in favor of overdramatization of Eva's story to showcase the deconstructive power of ideals.

Eva's "sheltered life" has been a "battle-ground" to conform to the inherited expectations that are the legacy of Queenborough. The endurance of the paradigm of Southern genteel femininity she represents depends upon cultivating a particular view of history and historic continuity, a view that is uniformly shared by the fellow denizens of Queenborough. Michel Foucault sees history and historic continuity as intrinsically antagonistic, for they foster discontinuity in the place of uninterruptedness which they imply. Historic continuity in Foucault's formulation is a fiction and an insidious one because it leads to a double estrangement of the subject: from the self and from the paradigm it reproduces by virtue of temporal separation between the past and the present. Betty Ambler, whom Glasgow considers one of "the best liked" of her "heroines," personifies, at least initially, the struggle to preserve appearances.[13] In Glasgow's hands, Betty becomes the medium for exposing the fatuity of living up to preconceived standards.

Betty's has been a life of non-conformity interspersed by a desperate desire to conform, which has only enunciated her difference. Even Betty's looks conspire against her embodying the ideal of Southern female gentility. Betty's red hair both marks her divergence from the ideal of Southern femininity and hints at her centrality to the narrative. Twain mercilessly mocks the ideal of Southern femininity by naming one of his heroines Rowena, after Scott, and by describing her as "nineteen, romantic, amiable, and very pretty, but otherwise of no consequence." Betty is neither of these, and her lack of conformity is a constant concern to her Aunt Lydia and her sister Virginia. In an attempt to bring Betty closer to the Southern ideal of female whiteness, at least in the looks department, Virginia brings her a pitcher of buttermilk and consolingly remarks that it "isn't usual for a young lady to have freckles." To remedy this particular shortcoming, Betty "must rub this on and not wash it off till morning" and then "get down on" her "knees" to "ask God to mend" her "temper";[14] a hopeless endeavor, it seems, and crowned with the dubious success of pointing out yet another flaw—Betty's temper. Although she obediently "laved her face in buttermilk," Betty obstinately refuses to pray, reasoning: "I don't reckon there's any use about the other," and "I believe the Lord's jest leavin' me in sin as a warnin' to you and Petunia." As disarming as Betty's honesty is, her vernacular speech further belies her meager effort at improvement and, because it evokes the kind of vulgarity of manners associated with the lower classes, marks her as a shade darker than Virginia. Glasgow uses Betty's remarks to destabilize the notion of truth inherent in hereditarily predetermined ideals. Betty sees herself as an embodiment of sin—metaphorical blackness—and thus a warning to Virginia and her Negro slave, whom she considers more virtuous and, like Virginia, possessing a stronger claim to whiteness. Unlike Virginia, "a pretty, prim little girl" who "carried her prayer book in her hands when she drove to church," Betty acts as an antithesis to the ideal of perfection that her sister embodies. As a proper name, Virginia connotes not only chastity and purity, but also gentility through its evocation of the state hailed as its cradle.[15] Virginia's meek conformity devivifies her, and her path to sanctity culminates in her death in childbirth when she attains the ultimate devivification, and takes her place alongside Aunt Emmeline.

Virginia's death is symbolic in that it stands for the demise of a paradigm incompatible with the ordinary. Glasgow allows Betty to live and prosper to demonstrate the ambivalence of ideals and the fluidity of attributes associated with them, which, as often as not, cross the rigid boundaries delimiting the male and female incarnations of gentility. Betty's conviction of her imperfection amplifies the ambiguity of her positioning because it inaugurates her quest for betterment and endows her with the characteristic associated with the male ideal of whiteness—namely struggle. Because desperate struggle calls for desperate measures, Betty resolves to dye her hair. It is not a question of vanity but, it seems, of propriety. The act, as Betty explains to her mother, may not be "ladylike" but "red hair isn't ladylike either."[16] Being the lady that she is, her mother objects, and Betty abandons the scheme, but her resolution reveals that Betty's being is haunted by her conception of the ideal that casts her as inferior.

What makes Betty's predicament doubly poignant is her recognition of it: "She had been really a double self from her babyhood up." Betty recognizes the paradox inherent in the concept of female whiteness which, while consisting in replicating the ideal, can only result in a split-self—a corollary of the irreconcilability of the ideal and the quotidian; whether crowned with success or marred by failure, Betty's struggle toward the attainment can only be a struggle for approximation. Despite "the kindness brimming over from her eyes" and having inherited "her father's head and her mother's heart," Betty is a hybrid, possessing a heady mixture of male and female attributes of whiteness. In a place where "women do not need as much sense as men," Betty's father's intellectual legacy exacerbates the chasm separating her from the ideal of the genteel lady.[17]

Unlike Betty, her mother, who "was rare and elegant like a piece of fine point lace," whose "hands had never known no harder work than the delicate hemstitching" and "mind had never wandered over the nearer hills," embodies the ideal in the ordinary. To her husband's remark that she "might have been President, had [she] been a man," Mrs. Ambler replies that she is "quite content with the mission" of women and certain she would "much rather make shirt fronts" for her husband than wear them herself. In this display of wifely docility devoid of aspiration, Mrs. Ambler is the perfect example of what Smith terms the spiritual quintessence of the white family.[18] As a site of inspiration, she attains the passivity of the ideal, while actively perpetuating the construct of "a bland and generous gentleman" that is Mr. Ambler. Content to dwell in the shadow of her husband, Mrs. Ambler's humility and modesty secure her claim to female whiteness and enhance her husband's gentility. This exemplary union, caught up in emulating a code of behavior, reaffirms a truth that deems such emulations genteel. Both Mrs. Ambler and Virginia, McDowell observes, possess the "sanctified qualities" of "moral passivity," "emotional reticence," and a docile willingness to subordinate themselves to "masculine superiority," all of which Betty lacks, despite Aunt

Lydia's ministrations. Mrs. Ambler's projection of the ideal requires a fetish, an object for which she can sacrifice herself, and which in turn justifies her being as the incarnation of an idealized femininity. Initially, her husband fills this space but, after his death in combat, she finds another object, for which to sacrifice herself—the Cause. As dutifully as she once sewed his shirts, she now floats around the house, "grave and pallid as a ghost," eating "nothing that, by any chance, could be made to reach the army." Her ghostly pallor marks the process of devivification on which she embarks and foreshadows her death because only then will she be able to take her place among the likes of Aunt Emmeline and Virginia. But before she attains the sainthood, Glasgow seems unable to resist the impulse to take her down a peg to show again that, despite appearances, even Mrs. Ambler's saintliness is not without blemish. She may float around the house with "the unearthly light upon her face," but she adamantly refuses to sacrifice the family jewels to the Cause, an act that mitigates the selflessness of her conduct and casts her as an intrinsically imperfect imitation.[19]

Mrs. Ambler's neighbor and the wife of the irascible Major Lightfoot and Dan's grandmother similarly engenders the irreconcilability of the ideal and the actual, though her incarnation lacks the meekness and passivity of Mrs. Ambler. Capable of "weeping over 'Thaddeus of Warsaw,'" Mrs. Lightfoot displays an unmitigated disdain for an "untitled hero" and literature about "Sukey Sues, with pug noses, who eloped with their Bill Bates, from the nearest butcher shop." Indeed, upon reading one of Dickens's novels "about a chimney sweep—a common chimney sweep from a workhouse," the lady felt as if she "had been keeping low society." Mrs. Lightfoot's sentimentality may be questionable, but her sympathies undisputedly lie with the upper classes. When she learns that Rainy Day Jones, one of their less refined neighbors, whose name indicates ungentlemanly parsimony, sent his son to the university her grandson attends, Mrs. Lightfoot vehemently declares: "I don't care to have my grandson upon terms of equality with any of that rascal Jones's blood. Why, the man whips his servants." In order to prevent her grandson's contamination, she would rather send him to Oxford, as "it matters very little where he is so long as he is a gentleman."[20] Mrs. Lightfoot's sacrifice is predicated upon the desire to protect her grandson's gentility from lower-class contamination. In her tirade against Jones, she names one of the traits that characterizes the Southern gentleman—and the Lightfoots—and separates them from the likes of Rainy Day Jones. It is the benevolence enshrined in a paternal attitude toward their subordinates as opposed to profit-driven exploitation; the same attitude that Page's planters possess in spades.

Unlike Page, however, Glasgow uses Mrs. Lightfoot's class-conscious selectiveness to reveal the inbred bias of her opinions and undermine her and her husband's gentility. When her husband gambles and loses her carriage and horses, she accepts the news with surprising equanimity. The only reprimand she offers to the errant spouse, as their faithful servant—Big Abel—recollects, is: "Well, Marse Lightfoot, I'm glad you kep' Abel—en we'll use de ole coach agin."[21] Mrs. Lightfoot's restraint from criticism serves a purpose in that it protects the ideal of the Southern gentleman of which her husband falls abominably short. The awareness of her husband's transgression and its simultaneous disavowal effectively transform Mrs. Lightfoot into an "enabler" of her husband's quasi-gentility. Her conduct may stem from wifely duty to honor her husband (and confirm her status as a cultured woman), but it also evokes the "absent presence" of the ideal of a gentleman capable of resistance to temptation.

So closely intertwined are the two constructs that Major Lightfoot's misdemeanor tarnishes Mrs. Lightfoot's projection of the standard of Southern femininity. In 1860, writing for *DeBow's Review,* Mr. A. Clarkson expresses in no uncertain terms that the task of the Southern woman was "to guide us [Southern men], and lead us to heaven." The Southern woman, he eulogizes, was "the great moral angel" who could elevate men "above the brute creation"—eloquently expressed sentiments that grant an ennobling gloss to the second fiddle any Southern wife would have been forced to play. As "the great moral agent" of Clarkson's imaginings, Mrs. Lightfoot fails, for she proves singularly incapable of elevating her spouse "above the brute creation." Having escaped lightly, Big Abel recalls, the unrepentant Mr. Lightfoot declares her "en angel."[22] But, since Major Lightfoot bestows this divinity upon his wife following the concealment of his transgression, it is, like his gentility, tainted by metaphorical blackness.

Mrs. Lightfoot's tolerance, however, does not extend to Dan who, following a duel, has been expelled from university. That he fought the duel to defend female honor fails to mollify her anger. On this occasion, Mrs. Lightfoot assumes the authority of "the great moral agent," and sententiously declares that "the honor of a barkeeper's daughter" is not "the concern of any gentleman."[23] What she effectively does is question the gentility of her grandson who, it seems, has so far forgotten himself as to confuse virtue with a lower-class woman. Harsh as it may appear, Mrs. Lightfoot's judgment is only possible because of a long-established tradition, according to which the promiscuity of a lower-class woman is a done deal. Placing herself as the polar opposite of such pre-conceived immorality, Mrs. Lightfoot reaffirms her own claim to whiteness, if not to Christian compassion, as a lady beyond the suspicion of sin.

Glasgow's portrayal of Mrs. Lightfoot sets the politics of cultural and social affinities at the center of the conception of whiteness. It is a matter of continuous policing and interpreting of historically preordained boundaries that delimits the behavioral standards of the Southern gentleman and lady. As often as not, Dan does not get it right. His supposedly misguided chivalry reveals the inherent instability of his position, caught between the conception of what he should be and what he is. His attempt to follow a gentlemanly code of behavior jeopardizes his Lightfoot inheritance, the dictates of which demanded, according to the major, that they "fought like men and made love like gentlemen." Loving like a gentleman implies attachment to a lady of equal social standing, and dueling for such a worthy keeper of a gentleman's affections is, indeed, an honorable matter. Only then can a gentleman preserve his sense of honor and his claim to whiteness. What makes Dan's transgression doubly grievous is its implicit undermining of the notion of a Virginia gentleman because, after all, what precipitated the duel was the dubious conduct of another gentleman, who "insulted the girl" in Dan's "presence." The major, however, is quick to draw his own conclusions; his grandson's transgression is the result of the Montjoys' "dirty blood," which renders it impossible "that Jack Montjoy's son could be a gentleman."[24] Dan's fallibility to err is his legacy, a legacy that bars his ascent to the Lightfoot standard of whiteness. But what kind of standard is it?, Glasgow seems to ask. If Dan's father's blood is responsible for his imperfection, what about his mother's blood? The major himself provides the answer, albeit unwittingly, implicating his daughter who displayed "a dangerous taste," "the taste for trash," in Dan's disgrace. Implicit in the major's assertion are Dan's father's trashiness and his daughter's attraction to, despite her aristocratic descent, metaphorical blackness. Dan's legacy is, it appears, doubly tarnished, for he internalizes what Derrida calls the "preoriginary and properly spectral anteriority" of two others—his father's trashiness and his mother's predilection for it.[25] Blood tells, but what it tells, Glasgow suggests, negates the possibility of hereditary gentility.

Although Dan's gentility is haunted by the specter of his father's polluted blood, it is the transgression he commits in trying to emulate the gentlemanly code of behavior that leads him to re-evaluate the trappings of gentility and sets him on the path toward enlightenment and betterment. Following the confrontation with his grandfather, Dan leaves Chericoke and finds lodgings in an inn run by the Hickses—the local representatives of white trash.

Initially, he finds Mrs. Hicks's presence deeply offensive. Looking "at her faded wrapper and twisted curl papers, he flinched and turned away as if her ugliness afflicted his eyes." Mrs. Hicks, as a living antithesis of the genteel lady, repulses Dan, to whom her bedraggled appearance is proof positive of moral turpitude. Dan's instinctive revulsion anticipates the reaction of Mrs. Turpin, the heroine of Flannery O'Connor's short story "Revelation." A chance encounter with a woman of Mrs. Hicks's caliber in a doctor's waiting-room reveals an hysteric fear of disreputability associated with the lower class. It prompts Mrs. Turpin to admit that she would rather be "a neat clean respectable Negro woman, herself but black" than white and trashy. The similarity between Mrs. Turpin's and Dan's recoil from the perceived trashiness is striking in that it foregrounds the dissonance between white and whiteness; the conundrum that being white may disqualify one from whiteness. Dan eventually revises his opinion of Mrs. Hicks, but only after he is subjected, albeit unwillingly, to her life story. A part of this story relates to his mother's elopement with Jack Montjoy. The act of telling becomes a cathartic experience that enables Dan to write Mrs. Hicks into his own history. The knowledge effects a transformation of Mrs. Hicks, whose face, Dan notes, acquires "a new meaning," possessed of a quality "that made her look like Betty and his mother—that made all good women who had loved him look alike." This revelation allows him to overcome his initial revulsion and observe "only the dignity with which suffering had endowed this plain and simple woman."[26] Mrs. Hicks's suffering and passive acceptance of it hark back to the suffering of the Virgin Mary, enable her to transcend class boundaries, and take her place among genteel ladies. But, Mrs. Hicks's elevation, albeit temporary, inadvertently touches the other two women with the tar brush, for it implies a connection between the ideal and the antithesis, which reifies the ambivalence of Southern female whiteness as a prerogative of the upper class.

Dan's realization of the ambivalence of preordained ideals has a trajectory that takes him full circle, from the poverty of his childhood when he was fed stories of the Lightfoots' superiority, through the years of sampling the benefits of a privileged upbringing at Chericoke, to the final fall from grace and return to the inferiority of his early years. If he is slow to learn, it is because converts make the best zealots. When the awareness comes, it hits him with the force of a revelation. Only when he matures, does he become worthy of Betty's idea of the ideal man. Betty, because of her own peripheral positioning in relation to the ideal of Southern female gentility, has always been aware of the impossibility of the reconciliation of the ideal with the ordinary. Her ideal is "a man with a faith to fight for—to live for—to make him noble. He may be a beggar by the roadside, but he will be a beggar with dreams." Betty dispenses with the conventional criterion of Southern whiteness encoded in hereditary gentility, instead valorizing striving as the only path leading to the nobility of spirit and whiteness proper. Because striving is inseparable from imperfection, Betty inadvertently places the ideal beyond attainment and, in doing so, exorcises its ghost. In investing striving with ideality and futurity, Betty severs the link with antebellum antecedents and renders the replication of these ideals superfluous. When Dan returns from the war, an invalid, to find Chericoke reduced to ashes and its grandeur a distant memory, it is Betty who inspires his truly heroic declaration: "There's some fight left in me—I am not utterly beaten so long as I have you on my side."[27] Only when he is stripped of the trappings of gentility is Dan's nobility of spirit manifest. Though he now approximates Betty's ideal of male whiteness, he is irrevocably separated from the concept of Southern whiteness as enshrined in the construct of the gentleman planter to which he once aspired. In *The Battle-Ground,* Glasgow suggests, the only escape from the touch of the tar brush that guarantees the attainment of ideal whiteness, the kind of whiteness the portrait of Aunt Emmeline symbolizes, is through death, which divorces the ideal from its corporeal reanimation.

At least one critic recognized the antagonism between the ideal and its reanimation as the force driving the narrative of *The Battle-Ground,* although not the complexity behind it. The elements of the story, he wrote with an astuteness betraying naivete, "are not at all unusual: the factors are much the same as one finds in other tales of the period." The "originality" of the novel, he added, lay in the way "the material" had been "bandied." And Glasgow "bandied" it in a way that allowed her to imply the imponderable: that Southern gentility is not only an antiquated paradigm, but one divorced from the ordinary. Others praised her ability and flare for description and the feeling with which she rendered the predicament of her class. M. D. McLean, a reviewer for the *Boston Post,* expressed a view quite similar to that of the "perpetual widow" from Richmond, complaining that Glasgow did not have "very much to say, all things considered, of the actual fighting." Such literal mindedness in a critic is lamentable but, if Glasgow took such reviews to heart, this was the one charge she did not have to worry about when *The Miller of Old Church* was published in 1911. The critics were ecstatic. The reviewer for the *San Francisco Call* all but places her on a plinth, claiming that she "has reached a place now in American literature which is almost unassailable and she occupies it alone."[28]

Unlike in *The Battle-Ground,* in *The Miller of Old Church* the sound of the guns had long since died away. Nobody has much to say about the conflict, but the preoccupation with the ideal of gentility has not diminished. The book was hailed as "the strongest and truest of all the half dozen or more" that Glasgow had written. It was "close, deft, and even in its construction." Glasgow received praise for style, for "a quite striking facility for making neat, terse turns of phrase." Her place as a literary historian of the South was secured, wrote one critic for the *Brooklyn Daily Eagle*, and "the history of the reconstruction period will never be well written without large drafts from her novels for the spirit and atmosphere of this time." If the novel had a weakness, it lay "in the disproportionate amount of sex pursuit." However, it is far from the wanton promiscuity the reviewer seems to suggest. Rather than "disproportionate," the "sex pursuit" is vital and, in a novel where the ideal and mésalliance walk in tandem, inevitable. This tapestry of "romance and realism," as Glasgow called the story, is set in the Southside province of Virginia from 1898 to 1902.[29] Just as in *The Battle-Ground*, in *The Miller of Old Church* the touch of the tar brush is not a corollary of the Reconstruction exigencies, but rather an inevitability that stems from the constructed nature of the ideal of Southern gentility. In *The Miller of Old Church*, more emphatically so than in *The Battle-Ground*, Glasgow casts women as active agents in the propagation and destabilization of the female ideal of whiteness and, consequently, its male counterpart.

Peopled with quaint characters, a fact duly noted by one critic who called them "a wonderful group of rustics," and replete with bucolic wisdom, the novel tells the tale of a struggle for and against conformity, where the notion of being touched with the tar brush is as inevitable as it is divorced from skin color.[30] Both Old Church and the neighboring plantation, Jordan's Journey, are places where ideals of female and male whiteness are esteemed and cultivated, irrespective of class. One of the protagonists, the eponymous miller—Abel Revercomb—observes the struggle inherent in the pursuit of ideals: "The world he moved in was peopled by a race of beings that acted under ideal laws and measured up to an impossible standard." Such an invocation of a preconceived truth, according to Foucault, stems from the reverence for bygone continuities, and turns each attempt at mimetic reproduction into a disconnection. What makes Abel's remark so poignant is not only his awareness of the existence of a truth, but also his conviction of its unattainability, which, inevitably, marks all reproductions as haunted approximations.

Notwithstanding the acuteness of his observation, Abel's life has been that of struggle, which, were it not for his humble origin, would furnish a claim to whiteness. While "Abel's ancestors had got out of the habit of trying" to measure up to the "impossible standard," so much so that his father died "in the odour of shiftlessness," Abel overcomes his legacy and prospers. The sole reason for Abel's striving to overcome his white trash legacy is Molly Merryweather, the granddaughter of the overseer at Jordan's Journey and illegitimate offspring of its late owner, Jonathan Gay. Molly's illegitimacy constitutes a *bar sinister* invalidating her claim to whiteness as hereditary gentility; however, the stigma of illegitimate birth does not prevent Abel from setting her up as an ideal and dreaming of "a happiness that was suited to the ideal figure rather than to the living woman." In Abel's case, such pedestalization goes hand in hand with aspiration. Little wonder, then, that he idolizes Molly despite his conviction of the impossibility of ideals since, as Mrs. Bottom—the proprietress of Bottom's Ordinary—astutely observes: "when it's b'iled down to the p'int, it ain't her, but his own wishes he's chasin'."[31] The pedestalized Molly becomes a receptacle of Abel's ambition of social elevation. So important is the preservation of the ideal to Abel that while Molly expresses her doubt of ever being "little or innocent," Abel obstinately assures her: "I don't believe you know yourself as you are, Molly." Abel's privileging of the imagined ideal of Molly over its actual representation is essential to his budding aspiration to whiteness. Ironically, it is Molly who deconstructs the image he constructs. Noting his hebdomadal finery, complete with a "starched collar" and complemented by "hair" which "was brushed flat on his head," she observes that "he had never looked worse, nor had he ever felt quite so confident of the correctness of his appearance."[32] Molly's uncharitable remark evokes the ghost of the ideal of male whiteness, which renders Abel's reconstruction a poor imitation by showing his dissociation from the very paradigm he strives to emulate.

Glasgow emphasizes the futility of Abel's aspirations to limn boundaries that cannot be crossed. Molly is the perfect messenger because of her illegitimacy and avowed non-conformity, a potent convergence of circumstances both beyond and in her control that dictate her position in Old Church. Molly's rebellion against the *status quo* only accentuates the ideals to which she is expected to subscribe: "The rector thinks that I'll marry him and turn pious and take to Dorcas societies, and Jim Halloween thinks I'll marry him and grow thrifty and take to turkey raising—and you [Abel] believe in the bottom of your heart that in the end I'll fall into your arms and find happiness with your mother. But you're all wrong—all—all—and I shan't do any of the things you expect of me."[33] Not particularly tempting options, they form ideals of femininity commensurate with the stations of the suitors. Although they have nothing in common with the über whiteness of gentility, they share a common trait—conformity—offering Molly an opportunity to become "the spiritual essence of the house." Molly refuses to trade independence for the conformity that attends these meager offerings of respectability, and that would ensure whiteness of a darker tone.

The phrase "darker tone" characterizes Molly's legacy. In a deliberate move to accentuate the impossibility of freeing oneself from the all-pervading influence of the ideal of Southern femininity, Glasgow orchestrates a dramatic change in Molly's circumstances. On her twenty-first birthday, Molly finds out that her father, the late Jonathan Gay, has bequeathed her a considerable legacy. There is a caveat, however: that she come and live at Jordan's Journey with his sister-in-law—Miss Angela, her sister—Miss Kesiah, and his recently arrived nephew and namesake—Jonathan Gay. Molly is transformed overnight into an almost genteel lady with the material wherewithal to support it. In accepting her father's legacy, Glasgow implies, Molly embraces another form of conformity—the ideal of the genteel lady. But this particular ideal will remain unattainable to Molly by virtue of, as Miss Angela puts it, "the strain of Merryweather blood, of the fact of her being born in such unfortunate circumstances," which manifests "itself in a kind of social defiance that would always keep her from being just—oh, well, you know—."[34] The unspoken speaks volumes about the ambivalence of Molly's heritage, which concurrently facilitates and negates her claim to the ideal of female whiteness. The rise in Molly's circumstances only reaffirms the undecidability of the ideal of female whiteness by cementing her incarnation of the Southern lady as a synecdoche that always points to a negative excess—illegitimacy and diluted aristocratic blood.

Molly's precarious positioning allows her to unmask the impossibility of the female ideal of whiteness and the futility and duplicity of the male ideal grounded in the projections of perfect femininity. When the Reverend Orlando Mullen, one of Molly's unfortunate suitors, delivers a fiery sermon on the virtues of the ideal woman, "Molly's lips trembled into a smile," and considering the self-aggrandizing pompousness of his homily, her merriment is justified. According to the reverend, "what the womanly woman desired was to remain an Incentive, an Ideal, an Inspiration," sacrificing herself for the advancement of her husband and sons. Indeed, "self-sacrifice was the breath of the nostrils of the womanly woman," and it was for this "that men loved her and made an Ideal of her." Only by emulating the self-sacrificial example of the Virgin Mary can the "womanly woman" aspire to whiteness. The only respite from the rigors of idealhood is to be found in "ministering to the sick and the afflicted." In this saintly life of duty, the "womanly woman" should not concern herself with whether she is "ugly or beautiful," but instead should find comfort in the fact that "no God-fearing man would rank loveliness of face or form above the capacity for self-sacrifice and the unfailing attendance upon the sick and the afflicted."[35] It is a double bind, in which self-sacrifice and compassion characterize the "womanly woman" and secure her claim to whiteness; but the recognition of these qualities delineates an ideal man. Curiously, it is the reverend's disparagement of beauty that betrays his duplicity and casts him as a caricature of an ideal man, of which Molly wryly observes: "It was all very well for the rector to say that beauty was of less importance than visiting the sick, but the fact remained that Judy Hatch visited the sick more zealously than she—and yet he was very far, indeed, from falling in love with Judy Hatch! The contradiction between the man and his ideal of himself was embodied before her under a clerical waistcoat."[36] His zealous delineation of the female ideal smacks of epicurean pleasure and Jeffersonian eugenics, revealing a fissure between the standard and praxis. "The circumstance of superior beauty," wrote the Virginian Thomas Jefferson in 1787, "is thought worthy attention in the propagation of our horses, dogs, and other domestic animals; why not in that of man?"[37] Judy Hatch's piousness and self-sacrifice go unnoticed because she is not comely. The reverend's actions undermine the veracity of his sermon, while emphasizing, unwittingly, the ambivalence of the female ideal of whiteness. The disparity between the reverend's idea of himself and the reality transforms this saintly man into a "no-God-fearing man," revealing him to be the antithesis of his sermon. Contrary to his teaching, the female embodiment of the ideal must first and foremost be pleasing to the eye.

The reverend is not the only one with a firmly fixed idea of the female ideal. Jonathan Gay imagines the "ideal woman" to be "submissive and clinging." Indeed, he has always considered meekness "the becoming mental and facial expression for the sex." Jonathan's conception is guided by an ulterior motive; since meekness connotes defenselessness, it is capable of inspiring chivalry and contributes to Jonathan's projection of gentility. Contrary to his imaginings, it is not Blossom's meekness that moves him when he meets her, but her beauty, or more precisely, her embodiment of a particular type of female beauty: "She was of an almost pure Saxon type—tall, broad-shouldered, deep-bosomed, with a skin the color of new milk, and soft ashen hair." Yet, being the miller's niece, Blossom is more than a shade darker than Jonathan, a fact emphasized by her speech, which, Jonathan observes, is "simple" and "direct." But, Jonathan—a veritable votary of beauty—is more than willing to overlook this flaw because the very perception of this Saxon ideal evokes a sense of hereditary pride characterized by the reverence for beauty that is "in the bone and ... is obliged to come out in the blood;" as his predecessors did before him, Jonathan will cultivate this dubious inheritance and "go on ogling the sex."[38] This susceptibility to female beauty forms a constitutive part of his genteel heritage which, along with the inherited acres and plantation, endows it with continuity.

But Jonathan's ready response to this legacy also brands him as different from the site of origin because, driven by his passion and having reassured himself that she looks "every inch a lady," Jonathan marries Blossom. Unfortunately, there is a difference between looking and being, as Jonathan discovers, and when Blossom becomes clinging, his ardor is tempered by "a serious annoyance." This change of heart is not simply a matter of inconstancy; rather, Glasgow suggests, it stems from the need to constantly reimagine the female ideal that always sets it at variance with the actual and leads Jonathan to replace the once-vaunted meekness and clinging with "a perpetual virgin in perpetual flight."[39] Jonathan's reformulation betrays an indebtedness to the ghost of courtly love, which dictates that the female ideal "be like a mother: remote, superior," and "unattainable."[40] Enmeshed in the net of Western logic, the sentiment acquires a universality that transcends the borders of Old Church. While the knights of old may have mellowed into vapid aristocrats, the strength of the logic has not waned. Placing the female ideal beyond attainment fuels male striving and self-denial and, consequently, becomes indispensable to male aspirations to whiteness. For Jonathan, the only way to revive this struggle is to render perfection imperfect; to perform a ghostly transference that renders the sensuous non-sensuous.[41] Only by divorcing it from the actual can he protect the notion of the female ideal and preserve his claim to whiteness. Imperfection, then, becomes the *modus operandi* of whiteness, as it both perpetuates its ideal and exacerbates its ambivalence; while the essence of the ideal consists in its unattainability, which, while fueling desire, negates the possibility of its fulfillment. Irrespective of Blossom's approximation of the ideal and a claim to gentility that their union guarantees her, she can no longer aspire to the ideal purity enshrined in the figure of the Virgin Mary. Glasgow sees the pursuit of the ideal of whiteness as a relentless process of substitutions inextricable from the desire for imagined perfection. The interdependence of the two paradigms breeds defective subjects. The imperfection of Jonathan's conduct mirrors the imperfection that inspired it, only accentuating the ambivalence of whiteness as an ideal that cannot be replicated.

Nowhere does Glasgow make the ambivalence of the ideal of female whiteness more pronounced than in the characters of Miss Angela and Miss

Kesiah, whose patrician descent seemingly seals their claims to whiteness. In the treatment accorded to both ladies, Glasgow mocks the very notion of hereditary whiteness. Miss Angela, a former belle and "a still pretty woman of fifty years," presents a worthy contender to replicate the ideal of female whiteness in the quotidian. The reverend believes it impossible "for any woman to approach more closely the perfect example of her sex." As for the existence of Miss Kesiah, Mr. Chamberlayne, a lawyer and family friend, asserts that it is "an outrage on the part of Providence that a woman should have been created quite so ugly." Miss Kesiah's patrician heritage avails her naught because it is not augmented by the quality that all God-fearing men should spurn: physical beauty. Her plainness fails to inspire and affronts "openly a man's ideal of what the sex should be."[42] Miss Kesiah externalizes the ambivalence between the notion of the female ideal of gentility and its representation; irrespective of her rank, she stands as close to the antithesis as the trashy Mrs. Hicks in *The Battle-Ground*. Even the life of self-sacrifice that she leads at the side of her sister is a travesty. It may be the mark of a womanly woman but, instead of filling the gap separating her from the ideal, it only exacerbates it. For saintliness does not count unless it is selfless, and hers derives not "from inclination, but from the force of necessity against which rebellion has been in vain."[43]

The vividness of the image of Miss Kessiah as an ultimate victim of conceptual femininity rests on comparisons with her sister, Miss Angela, which Glasgow exploits expertly. Miss Kesiah's "false front only extinguished sentiment" and failed to inspire chivalry, while her sister collects all the accolades due the "womanly woman." Described as "clinging and small and delicate," Miss Angela embodies the holy trinity of reverend Mullen's sermon: incentive, ideal, and inspiration. More deadly than this combination, Glasgow suggests, is Miss Angela's awareness of being vaunted as the ideal of female gentility, which, combined with her superficial docility, enables her to dominate "not by force, but by sentiment," to surrender "all rights in order to grasp more effectively at all privileges," so that she rules with a "remorseless tyranny of weakness."[44] This external projection of the passivity of the ideal enables Miss Angela to exert her influence over others.[45] Miss Angela internalizes the ambivalence of the ideal of female whiteness: her submissiveness and docility carry no traces of self-sacrifice, and her purity is an assiduously cultivated fiction. To Jonathan's enquiry about Molly's status and financial security, Miss Angela replies: "I am a woman and should know nothing of such matters." Through her feigned innocence, she purports the purity of the genteel lady by dissociating herself from any knowledge of Molly's illegitimacy. The fact that she knew about the late Jonathan's love for Molly's mother but "thought he had forgotten it" and remained true to his "spirit worship" for her reveals Miss Angela's innocence as a lie.[46] Her lack of humility bespeaks a conviction of herself as the embodiment of the ideal and reveals indifference bordering on callousness. What distresses her is not Jonathan's indiscretion, which precipitated his death, but the fact that he strayed in his devotion to her by "thinking of that woman [Molly's mother]" when he lay dying. Jonathan's death atones for this lapse in judgment and, in Miss Angela's eyes, removes the possibility of contamination and restores him to the status of a gentleman who worships at her feet. This is why, Miss Kesiah observes, Jonathan "means much more to her dead than he did living."[47] The irony is unmistakable because, in his attempt not to distress Miss Angela, Jonathan forsakes Molly's mother, which marks his conduct as ungentlemanly. Since the same concern for Miss Angela's health prevents her son from revealing his union with Blossom, she is also responsible for his ungentlemanly conduct. In her zeal to guard the ideal of Southern whiteness, she becomes the unmaker of gentlemen.

A critic writing for the *Brooklyn Daily Eagle* pronounced Miss Angela "the triumph of the book." It is through the portrayal of Miss Angela that Glasgow caricatures most eloquently the ideal of Southern gentility and invokes its inherent instability and contradiction. Miss Angela praises her son Jonathan for being "free from those dreadful weaknesses of other men," meaning imprudent liaisons, after he has already succumbed to Blossom's charms and married her. Outwardly, Miss Angela condemns such worshipping as weakness; inwardly, she considers it essential to the perpetuation of the ideal of the genteel lady. This is why, she tacitly admits, "she herself preferred adorers to lovers."[48] Since adoration implies a lack of corporeality, it invests its object with a divinity that places it beyond the specter of pollution. If promiscuity is a marker of lower-class femininity, then Miss Angela's preference of adoration over love reifies her status as a genteel lady. Inherent in the notion of adoration is repression, which can only exist where there is desire.[49] Miss Angela understands fully that the preservation of the female ideal of whiteness requires that she fuel desire, but defer its fulfillment at the bodily level. Once the ideal acquires corporeality, it ceases to be an ideal. Miss Angela's preference of adoration over love betrays her awareness of the impossibility of the reconciliation of the ideal with its quotidian representation.

When it comes to the necessity of maintaining the unattainability of the ideal as the only means to ensure its propagation, Miss Angela and her son display a like-mindedness. Adoration, just like "the perpetual virgin in perpetual flight," while evading consummation leads to a devivification and separation from bodily functions, thus implying purity. Ironically, in performing the split of the ideal from the body, Miss Angela, unwittingly, condemns her incarnation of female whiteness as deficient. So deadly is the power of the adored ideal that Miss Angela "has drained her sister" so that "there isn't an ounce of red blood left in her veins."[50] Miss Angela is a parasite that metaphorically sucks the living force out of others, which, literally, makes her responsible for three deaths: her brother-in-law, Jonathan, Molly's mother, and her son Jonathan, all fall victim to Miss Angela's projection of the ideal of whiteness. In her doggedness to protect the purity of her family's gentility from lower-class contamination, Miss Angela prevents the marriage between the elder Jonathan Gay and Molly's mother, Janet. Forsaken by her lover, Janet succumbs to madness and dies. It is not long after Janet's death that her former suitor is found shot, his unexplained fate supplying an inexhaustible grist for the mill of local speculation. Finally, motivated by his concern for Miss Angela's health, Jonathan resolves to keep his marriage to Blossom a secret, and persuades his wife to do likewise. The secrecy surrounding their union rouses the suspicions of Blossom's father, Abner Revercomb. Convinced of what he imagines to be Blossom's disgrace, Abner decides to avenge his daughter's honor and shoots Jonathan. As he lies dying, Jonathan refuses to disclose the name of his assassin, for he sees his death as a punishment for his misconduct toward Blossom. In claiming that it was "an accident," Jonathan finally acts honorably and selflessly, partially redeeming his whiteness with a lie.[51]

Despite the saintliness encoded in her name, Miss Angela apotheosizes metaphorical blackness—what Fanon associates with evil, sin, and death. Without Miss Angela's "soft yet indomitable influence," Molly observes, Jonathan, like his uncle before him, "would never have lied in the beginning, would never have covered his faithlessness with the hypocrisy of duty."[52] It is the need to protect the ideal engendered in its irresistible power that underlies their dishonorable conduct. Veneration of the female ideal of whiteness, Glasgow says, literally destroys the men lured by its culturally and socially shaped appeal. Her critique of Southern whiteness foregrounds its ambivalence because she bases it on the irreconcilability between the ideal as an abstract concept and its physical reproduction. There is no sugar coating the pill and shifting blame; its pernicious effect maims the subject, for it marks him as lacking. The indictment, powerful though it is, never questions the validity of the paradigm, betraying perhaps a degree of class bias.

SIX

DEBUNKING THE IDEAL
IN CHARLES WADDELL CHESNUTT

Glasgow, by her own admission, chose to write of people, places, and the lingering flavor of the Southern way of life with which she was familiar. In any writing, a tincture of bias is as unavoidable as it is dependent on the social and cultural positioning of the author. Objectivity works much better in principle than it does in practice. When Glasgow's "near and distant relatives," as she recalls, had finally resigned themselves to her chosen calling, they did not fail to sound a note of caution, telling her that if she "must write," she should "write of Southern ladies and gentlemen."[1] If their idea of what writing of Southern ladies and gentlemen should be about resembled the view of "the perpetual widow" of Richmond, it is doubtful they would have wholeheartedly approved of Glasgow's heroines and heroes. Nor would the United Daughters of Confederacy, an organization devoted to the arduous task of edifying the Old South and waxing lyrical on its fallen heroes.[2] Noble as the enterprise may appear, Glasgow could not bring herself to endorse such outright adulation because she was aware of the antagonism that underpins the proposition. Although she admitted to loving the "imperishable charm" of the Old South, she was pragmatic enough to realize that any attempt at emulating the past or animating the legend became "the eternal warfare of the dream with reality."[3] The protagonists of *The Battle-Ground* or *The Miller of Old Church*, genteel or plebeian, are all subject to this conflict, which cultivates stagnation, frustrates social advancement, and fosters pretense as a form of defense against downward mobility. Glasgow saw the elevation of historic continuity to an overarching and guiding principle in the preservation of Southern gentility as the region's cultural heritage as a crippling and regressive influence that, inevitably, ended in proving just the opposite; that the ideal was far removed from actuality.[4]

Glasgow's view of Southern whiteness runs counter to the narratives preferred and endorsed by the United Daughters of Confederacy, which tend to shift the blame for the decline of the South onto the rapacious North. The fault, she suggests, lies much closer to home, in the inherent instability of the notion of an ideal that always manages to wiggle out of its historically, socially, and culturally preordained boundaries. The United Daughters of Confederacy would have fought tooth and nail to deny the possibility of such transgressive indeterminacy. Charles Waddell Chesnutt wielded his pen to prove the opposite. Like Glasgow, Chesnutt's *The Marrow of Tradition* destabilizes the notion of whiteness as an attainable totality. Glasgow's exploration of whiteness leads her to examine discrete totalities—asexuality, chastity, self-sacrifice, and beauty—that characterize the female ideal; and chivalry, honor, and self-discipline that mark its male incarnation. She succeeds in demonstrating that these qualities never unite in the construct of the Southern lady and gentleman and, as often as not, transcend class boundaries. The pursuit of the holy, or unholy, grail of perfection inevitably brings them back to the starting point, which is the concept of the ideal. It is a doomed quest, as James Branch Cabell's Jurgen and Florian discover, who having tasted by means fair or foul of the ideal readily return to the dreariness and mediocrity of the everyday, healthily purged of illusion.[5] Although Glasgow limits her interrogation to representatives of the white caste, she still manages to undermine the correlation between whiteness and skin color as her protagonists, despite their lack of visible tint, are always touched with the tar brush.

Chesnutt takes the notion of transcendence a step further in *The Marrow of Tradition*, across the color line. The novel, published in 1901, presents a fictionalized account of the race riot that broke out in Wilmington, North Carolina, in 1898. Wilmington boasted a vibrant black population, professionally active and economically and socially on the rise. The seeds of the riot had been sewn a few years earlier, in 1896, when the black Republicans of North Carolina joined forces with the white Populist Party. As a result of the coalition, the prominent offices in the county passed from the hands of Democrats with supremacist leanings who found the new *status quo* decidedly unsavory. The supremacists' victory in the 1898 elections to the city council was not enough to erase the bitter taste of their previous defeat, and they orchestrated the riot to unseat the remaining Republican office holders.⁶ Chesnutt substituted Wilmington for Wellington, but preserved its location in North Carolina. The substitution did not fool anybody. One reviewer questioned Chesnutt's judgment in publishing the novel so soon after the event, fearing it could arouse "bitter resentments in politics and personal relations." "It may be questioned," he continued, "whether it is wise to force public sentiment in this direction by presenting the involved question in the form of a novel in which the writer's feelings are neither obliterated nor skillfully concealed."⁷ As if there were a better time or medium to address the issue. Even more scathing was the attack by a critic writing for the *Richmond Dispatch* who called the novel "infamously libelous to the last degree." He belabored Chesnutt for his "misrepresentations of the whites," which included representatives "of all professions and vocations" in a thinly veiled attempt "to establish white degeneracy" and, the worst horror of all, "southern women" who were "made to figure in dishonorable plots."⁸ This harangue displays the kind of naïve and racial bias Chesnutt inveighs against in his work and that presupposes an inherent nobility of whites.

Other reviewers saw merit in Chesnutt's argument and were less eager to accuse him of prejudice or excuse whites of all culpability. One critic observed that although it was "natural that Mr. Chesnutt's novel should be a brief for the defendant," his arguments were "predicated in a spirit of fairness and justice." Another asserted that Chesnutt had "far outstripped his earlier successes." He was not the only one to compare the novel favorably with Harriet Beecher Stowe's *Uncle Tom's Cabin* and praise its author for a "strong and accurate character delineation."⁹ A critic reviewing the novel for the *Davenport Daily Republican* hailed it as "Mr. Chesnutt's masterpiece" that was "beautifully written, powerful and interesting story." Only one reviewer, whether spurred by honesty or insightfulness, offered less than platitude or condolence on the plight of black upward mobility, and he did so by presenting the South as a heterogenous region with rigidly policed class hierarchy. "The poor whites of the South," he wrote, "were despised by the slave and the slave-holder alike" because they had "no tradition of gentility, no wholesome pride of family to maintain." And he was not afraid of pointing fingers, either. It was they, "the descendants of this class," who were "burning and shooting the colored people."¹⁰ Fast forward to 2016 and the general election in the United States, and it was Mexicans in particular, and Muslims in general, who were guilty of impeding the upward mobility of those on the lower rungs of the social ladder—or so Donald Trump would have us believe. The story has not changed much, and what drives it is the idea of whiteness, of betterment, privilege, upward mobility, of whom to include and whom to exclude.

The critic was not wide of the mark, either, when he said it was "the economic subject" that "first provoked Mr. Chesnutt's attention." Having grown up in the South, Chesnutt would have been all too familiar with the value placed on gentility, parentage, and heredity. He was also all too aware that for those unfortunate enough who could not claim the right kind of descent, upward mobility was the only path to earning respectability. Education, respectability, and economic success—in this order—were key to social and cultural elevation and whiteness. In a diary entry made in June 1875, Chesnutt reports a conversation he had with a black farmer with whom he was boarding at the time. The man was bemoaning his lot and complaining about being unable to make ends meet. Chesnutt's reply was as unsympathetic as it was unequivocal: "'Now, I'll tell you. You say you are all renters, and get cheated out of your labor, why dont [sic] you send your children to school, and qualify them to look out for themselves, to own property, to figure and think about what they are doing, so that they may do better than you?'"[11] If the elevation of black people, or any marginalized groups for that matter, was possible through education leading to moral and financial gains; it was equally possible that the process could work in reverse and the degeneracy of those deemed superior by virtue of birth was not unthinkable.

Chesnutt places this possibility at the heart of *The Marrow of Tradition*. The choice of words is a masterful stroke that satirizes and surprises, far subtler in its undertone than Page's "Bred in the Bone." Marrow conjures up images of essence, quiddity and quintessence, while tradition amplifies the effect, evoking stability, history and continuity. The title stands at variance with the content and, as the story unfolds, the marrow liquifies into slime and tradition turns into a signifier short of signifieds. Little wonder, the novel chilled some critics to the marrow. Matthew Wilson observes that Chesnutt presents his white readers with "a counterhistory," a counter narrative that defies and rewrites the dominant view of history from a place-specific standpoint.[12] Chesnutt starts from the particular lived experience and works outward to undermine the image of a historic totality. A counter history, as its name suggests, places itself in opposition to a dominant proposition or propositions, to reveal cracks and inconsistencies, finally presenting an alternative possibility of interpretation. The cracks and inconsistencies that Chesnutt uncovers in *The Marrow of Tradition* concern the treatment of black and white people alike. Yet, it is not just a rant against injustice or privilege, but a measured challenge of long-held and cherished customs that make up the Southern tradition. Chesnutt's novel is not a single counter history, but counter histories that include the destabilization of the concept of hereditary gentility, the negation of the notion of inherent black ineptitude and the formulation of an alternative paradigm of a color-transcending whiteness free from the fetters of heredity.

The story delineates the events precipitating the riot, beginning with the formation of a secret coalition among the city's male elite and its efforts to "blacken" its prosperous black citizens. It culminates whilst the riot is still raging around its now either dead, or horrified, perpetrators. Critics variously read Chesnutt's reason for revealing the moral degradation of the white citizens of Wellington as an attempt to deprive white readers of "the privilege of whiteness" and denaturalize it.[13] Deprive and denaturalize are in and of themselves essentialist terms that do not admit of a different possibility of interpretation. If anything, Chesnutt's own pedigree makes him an unlikely candidate for harboring and peddling essentialist standpoints. Although he divorces the image of whiteness from the upper class, he does so to subvert the Western conception of blackness which, according to Fanon, rests on the principle that casts sin as negro and virtue as white.[14] In allowing whiteness to transcend the color line, Chesnutt liberates it from the strictures of its ontic manifestation—the binarity of black and white. In *The Marrow of Tradition*, Stephen P. Knadler notes, Chesnutt emphasizes that whiteness is "inflected in terms of gentlemanliness."[15] But what Chesnutt challenges is precisely the conception of "gentlemanliness" understood as hereditary whiteness. Chesnutt's scrutiny of the paradigms of whiteness—the Southern gentleman and lady whose gentility rests on the pillars of honor, chivalry and aristocratic heritage—reveals the hollowness of these constructs. The novel's protagonists—Major Carteret, Olivia Carteret, Clara Pemberton, Polly Ochiltree and Tom Delamere—despite boasting a hereditary claim to whiteness fall abominably short of the ideal; whereas others like Lee Ellis, Dr. Miller and Janet Miller possess honor, moral restraint and the ability for self-sacrifice in abundance, yet their heritage precludes them from ascent to whiteness.

Chesnutt begins the story in the conventional way, pioneered by Page and his ilk, to give a flavor of gentility in distress. Major Carteret, one of the male protagonists, hails from "one of the oldest and proudest" families "in the state," but the war has left him "hopelessly impoverished" and "swallowed" his "ancestral home." This reversal in the family fortunes leaves this lord apparent without a manor. Carteret owes the subsequent improvement of his circumstances to his marriage to Olivia Merkell, with whose "money he had founded the Morning Chronicle" that became "the most influential paper in the State."[16] His tenuous claim to whiteness, Chesnutt implies, augmented by "the fine old house in which they lived," is restored through marriage, and not inherited as tradition dictates.[17] A narrow-minded bigot, Carteret is possessed of a remarkably flexible conscience which, if required, he can trick "into acquiescence." The existence of "that docile organ" predestines him for sin, for it implies moral lassitude contradictory to the gentlemanly code of behavior. Thanks to the biddability of his conscience, Carteret's convictions appear rather contradictory. He may believe "in the divine right of white men and gentlemen;" however, his response to Dr. Burns belies the truthfulness of his conviction. When Dr. Burns, a specialist from the North, asserts: "I am a gentleman, sir, before I am a white man," Carteret avers that "the terms should be synonymous."[18] Betraying a certain naivety with regards to the treatment accorded to the blacks in the North, Chesnutt has the Northerner, Dr. Burns, separate gentility from the white hue. But the real purpose of the exchange is to divorce white from whiteness. Because Carteret conflates the terms white and gentleman, he turns white into the prerogative of a gentleman. Compared with Dr. Burns's liberality of outlook, Carter's rejoinder marks unfavorably his regional difference and narrow, class-circumscribed horizons. The "divine right," historically the preserve of kings, is far from being the privilege of white men in general, if white and gentleman are synonymous. What Carteret believes in are the divinely sanctioned gradations of whiteness, a taxonomy that leaves out all those without genteel heritage.

Carteret's dealings with General Belmont and Captain McBane emphasize his conviction of gentlemanly superiority and the narrowness of the category. Together, the men form a triumvirate, the aim of which is to restore the antebellum order.[19] When Captain McBane and General Belmont present themselves in his office, Carteret greets the Captain "with an unconscious but quite perceptible diminution of the warmth with which he had welcomed the other." In drawing the scene, Chesnutt demonstrates the dynamics of class distinction based on inherited notions of descent. The coolness of manner with which he greets McBane is a direct response to his tainted heritage. As "the descendant of the indentured bondservant and the socially unfit," McBane is a social upstart whom, regardless of the fortune he has amassed from "a contract with the State for convict labor," Carteret deems unworthy of the cordiality he accords to Belmont who is "aristocratic by birth and instinct."[20] Carteret's reserve betrays class aversion that is unapologetically Jeffersonian. Jefferson considered overseers "the lowest feculum of beings" and "the most abject, degraded and unprincipled race," certainly no better than indentured servants most of whom arrived in America to avoid incarceration for debt.[21] McBane is the descendant of this undignified breed and no fit acquaintance for a gentleman. His wealth, though it marks one of the criteria of gentility, carries the unsavory stench of new money. It is certainly not enough to buy him membership in the gentlemen's Clarendon Club, for he lacks the other essential attributes that guarantee admission to the institution—"birth" and "breeding."[22] McBane's predicament marks the first instance in the novel when Chesnutt highlights the disconnect between white and whiteness, of always being out of step with the ideal.

McBane's acquired gentility offends Carteret's genteel sensibilities. Yet, needs must and, although he finds it distasteful "to rub shoulders with an illiterate and vulgar man of no ancestry," his flexible conscience goes into overdrive and he concedes that McBane's "wealth and energy" make him useful to their cause.[23] Carteret's admission proves that Chesnutt, like Glasgow, is fully aware that ideal whiteness is a composite of distinct totalities, totalities that antagonize themselves. McBane's dubiously acquired fortune both furnishes and invalidates his claim to whiteness; it transforms him into a member of the upper class and, simultaneously, emphasizes his lack of education and suitable ancestry—the two attributes that should go hand in hand with hereditary gentility. Wealth alone, Chesnutt implies, cannot guarantee ascent to whiteness proper, if it is not haunted by aristocratic ancestry. In a place where gentility is venerated, it acts as an excess that exacerbates the lack of attributes associated with it.

Chesnutt is aware that this negative excess requires a field of comparison to function as excess. Carteret's alliance with McBane is that of expedience which, incidentally, augments his own claim to gentility. McBane's dubious legacy of overseers and indentured servants betrays an "inbred" tendency to metaphorical blackness which Theweleit associates with "the masses," "floods" and "filth." As an exponent of this human detritus, McBane becomes the perfect site of unfavorable comparison. Chesnutt uses the interaction between the two to demonstrate that whiteness operates through a complex network of division and reciprocity. Carteret may rub shoulders with McBane because his uncouthness validates Carteret's gentility and allows him to dissociate himself from McBane's offensive plebeianism. In Carteret, Chesnutt presents the politics of gradation that underpin Southern whiteness at work, and lock the subject in an endless cycle of comparison. In comparison with McBane, Carteret cuts a gentlemanly figure well enough; but, what belies Carteret's gentility is his awareness of the disparity between his incarnation of the ideal and old Mr. Delamere's whom he considers the "ideal gentleman of the ideal past."[24] Chesnutt's whiteness, formulated as a composite of traits, as an active process of positioning and re-positioning in response to another shows that when compared with McBane, Carteret is a gentleman, whilst a comparison with Mr. Delamere reveals him to be an inadequate exponent of that elite. Carteret's and McBane's unstable positioning is just a prelude to the debunking of the very ideal of Southern whiteness. The conjunction of "the ideal gentleman" with "the ideal past" is as telling as it is subversive, for it transforms Carteret and his contemporaries' gentility into imperfect imitations.

The trouble with ideals, whether be it of gentleman or past, is that they seldom materialize in the ordinary and, if they do, they do not necessarily keep to preconceived boundaries. Transgression, Chesnutt suggests, is part of the concept of ideal as it is of those who aspire to embody it, successfully or not. To unmask Carteret's phony gentility Chesnutt uses no other than the upstart McBane, the man whom Carteret finds detestable on a good day and contemptible most of the time. McBane becomes Chesnutt's unlikely mouthpiece who verbalizes and exposes Carterett's duplicity. During a discussion upon who from among the black citizens is to be expelled from the city, Carteret declares his wish "to be strictly impartial in this matter, and to take no step which cannot be entirely justified by the wise regard for public welfare." McBane finds this lofty speech hard to swallow and asks: "What's the use of this hypocrisy, gentlemen?" The rhetorical question requires no answer and so McBane continues, but in more explicit terms: "Every last one of us has an axe to grind! The Major may as well put an edge on his." Ironically, Carteret's reaction to the speech furnishes the answer to McBane's question and confirms that virtue is anything but white. Inwardly, Carteret is dismayed to hear McBane speak so of their undertaking because it robs "the enterprise of all its poetry and put[s] a solemn act of revolution upon the plane of a mere vulgar theft of power."[25] McBane's blunt remark debunks Carteret's gentility by pointing out the hypocrisy of his purpose, but it is Carteret's own comment that removes the cloak of honor from the otherwise ignoble enterprise. When the gloss dulls, Southern whiteness is nothing more than keeping up appearances to minimize the impact of what becomes, at least to Chesnutt, a questionable ideal. Theweleit observes that the dissociation from the vulgarity of the mob equals an escape from an innate darkness or, indeed, sin that has been historically deemed the prerogative of the Negro.[26] In this endeavor, Carteret fails irrecoverably and his failure enunciates the ambivalence of the ideal of whiteness. Effectively, McBane—the antithesis of the ideal of gentility—foils instead of shoring up Carteret's position in the supposedly morally superior elite.

This exchange is just the beginning of Carteret's inevitable fall from whiteness which, rather tellingly, coincides with the riot that he has helped to mastermind to protect the ideal of gentility. In a somewhat melodramatic turn, Carteret's only son contracts the croup during the riot. As a consequence of the fighting, there are no white doctors available to treat him and Carteret is forced to seek the help of a colored doctor—Dr. Miller. He hopes that Miller, as "a man of some education" and "fine feeling,—for a negro," will not refuse a "professional call," despite being once refused admittance to Carteret's house. This is the kind of dubious honor that no colored doctor should resist and refuse. As it happens, Miller refuses because his own son has been killed in the riot, for which he holds Carteret responsible. As Carteret leaves, he is filled with an "involuntary admiration" for Miller and concedes that "in Dr. Miller's place he would have done the same thing."[27] The recognition of Miller's refinement and honorableness, albeit belated, confers upon him a claim to whiteness otherwise denied him by virtue of his descent. In the encounter, Chesnutt has Carteret and Miller trade places. The meeting reveals to Carteret the futility of his pursuit of the ideal of whiteness by displacing it onto Miller—its socially and culturally constructed antithesis. Ultimately, the exchange leaves Carteret decidedly off white and Miller whitened.

Carteret's only redeeming quality that betrays a smattering of gentlemanly honor is his belated realization that white does not equal a gentleman any more than black equals a sinner. Despite what the *Richmond Dispatch* critic wrote about the novel's "misrepresentations of the whites," Chesnutt does not treat Carteret as a degenerate beyond improvement. Quite the contrary, he is a character for whom, perhaps, there is still hope should he decide to climb down from the self-constructed plinth of entitlement built on shaky foundations. Just how unstable these grounds are Chesnutt demonstrates through another character, Tom Delamere. More so than Carteret, Tom Delamere, the grandson of the old Mr. Delamere, did not inherit honorableness along with "birth" and "breeding." In his case, the innate darkness spills outwards. Tom's gentility, Chesnutt suggests, is hereditarily preordained as befits the last scion of the patrician Delameres, yet his countenance "negativated [*sic*] the idea of manliness." By manliness Chesnutt does not mean physical brawn, but integrity of purpose, honor, and ability to resist temptation; in short, the attributes associated with the male ideal of whiteness with Christ as its paradigm that dissociate it from the stigma of sin. Tom's unmanliness bespeaks metaphorical blackness which, as the novel unfolds, Chesnutt makes manifest through his conduct to emphasize the untenability of the concept of hereditary gentility. A drinker, gambler and eventually murderer, Tom, more than any other character in the novel is aware of the power of keeping up appearances on which his gentility precariously balances: "He had reached that degree of moral deterioration where, while principles were of little moment, the externals of social intercourse possessed an exaggerated importance."[28] The more Tom's awareness of the travesty that is his gentility grows, the more conscious he becomes of the power of projection.

What constitutes Tom's heritage is a penchant for projection, a trait that Chesnutt exploits to its fullest potential. Tom is already a "nigger" on the inside, a person marked by moral turpitude, cowardice and meanest servility, like Jonadab Leech, Page's carpetbagger in *Red Rock*. Like Leech, although not accidently, he can also literally "turn nigger" and imitate Sandy, his grandfather's servant, to such perfection that he wins the cakewalk "much to the surprise of his sable companions, who were about equally swayed by admiration and jealousy." [29] Tom is an expert at "turning nigger" and when he resorts to this stratagem again, it is to implicate Sandy in the murder of his aunt Polly Ochiltree, which he commits himself. Chesnutt uses Tom's ability to pass freely across the color line as a reflection of his innate blackness. There is a difference, he implies, between Carteret's and Tom's conduct. Carteret passes for a gentleman because of the unattainability of the ideal; Tom's passing is necessary to project the ideal of gentility since his social position demands it. Passing for and projection are not worlds apart and both constitute indictments of an ideal that is only capable of producing faux gentility, the kind that even offends the sensibility of an ex-slave, Sandy.

There is a distinct whiff of stereotype in Chesnutt's portrayal of Sandy as an ex-slave possessed of undying devotion to the Delameres. Yet, Chesnutt uses Sandy's loyalty as a perfect foil to Tom's lack of moral fiber. As a former slave, Sandy has grown up on the stories of the family's honor and greatness, and knows when he sees an impostor. When Tom turns to him to borrow money to settle the most pressing debts, Sandy reluctantly agrees "fer de sake er de fam'ly honuh." But, when Tom, in a surge of feigned gratitude, calls him "a good darky," Sandy is appalled at his lack of genteel manners: "in all de yeahs I has wo'ked fer yo' gran'daddy, he has never called me, a 'darky' ter my face, suh. Co'se I knows dere's w'ite folks an' black folks,—but dere's manners, dere's manners, an' gent'men oughter be de ones ter use 'em.'"[30] Each instance of passing produces slippage, a detail that betrays the passer as an imitation. In Tom's case, it is his attitude toward Sandy that is devoid of the paternalism commonly associated with the gentleman planter. Sandy corrects Tom's slippage and, in doing so, accentuates the difference between Tom's grandfather and Tom. Their kinship notwithstanding, the message is clear: Tom is no gentleman. Instead, the hereditary gentility, like Tom, skipped the color line and passed to Sandy, endowing him with a sense of ancestral honor and pride. Sandy unmakes what remains of Tom's already grievously undermined gentility.

In case Sandy should prove an unreliable attestor to Tom's degradation, Chesnutt whips up another witness, Lee Ellis. Chesnutt molds Ellis as an inversion of Tom: where Tom's claim to whiteness is belied by his ungentlemanly conduct, Ellis's conduct is beyond reproach, but his Quaker heritage blights his attainment of whiteness proper. Another no-win predicament, it seems, that prevents social advancement of the deserving and fosters stagnation in the name of the trumped up ideal. Despite not hailing from "their caste," Ellis is received "cordially" by the "'best people'" of Wellington, including the Carterets. Interestingly, Chesnutt's use of inverted commas belies the epithet and bespeaks a darkness beneath the finest paragons of Wellington's gentility. Even his membership at the exclusive Clarendon Club cannot eradicate the fact that he is Carteret's employee and a Quaker, whose "father never owned any slaves."[31] This inexcusable ancestral lack of foresight reaches from the past into the present to mark Ellis as unworthy of the appellation of a gentleman. If Ellis, a man of high moral integrity and honesty whose family never tainted themselves with the despicable institution of slavery, is unworthy of being called a gentleman, then who is? The answer is unequivocal and damning: in Wellington, nobody. In Wellington, and by extension the South, whiteness is like the proverbial smoke and mirrors. Pretenders and permutations obfuscate the paradigm that Chesnutt considers inherently flawed because it privileges antiquated notions of entitlement based on breeding.

The emphasis placed on breeding is the undoing of the self-styled Wellington finest, including the ladies, a fact belabored by the *Richmond Dispatch* reviewer. Carteret's half-sister, Clara Pemberton's claim to gentility is partial because her mother "married Daniel Pemberton, who was not of so good a family" as the Carterets. Clara may possess a "fair countenance" that bespeaks "a pure heart and a high spirit," but this cannot change the fact that her incarnation of the ideal is intrinsically tainted by association with the lower classes.[32] Inappropriate parentage blights Clara's claim to whiteness, as it does Ellis's. Chesnutt reserves a degree of sympathy for these characters whose station in society is predetermined by factors outside their control. They are trapped in a process of rigorous policing that places them on the margins and from which there is no escape. Chesnutt's scorn finds its full outlet in the characterization of Miss Polly Ochiltree, a person whose very actions cast her outside the pale of gentility. And this time, parentage is not at fault, either.

Miss Polly, as her surname suggests, comes from sturdy Scottish stock whose ancestors are bound to have braved the pitfalls of colonial life and prospered, though Chesnutt remains silent on the matter.[33] Ochiltree seems to be Chesnutt's preferred name for a villain. In his first novel, *Mandy Oxendine*, Miss Ochiltree is an equally unsympathetic character; she is appointed a guardian to her niece, whom she pushes into a marriage with a philanderer and gambler despite being fully aware of the prospective groom's vices. When Chesnutt finally strips the facade of the genteel lady that Miss Polly—Olivia Carteret's aunt—maintains, it is to reveal a thief. When Olivia's father lies on his death-bed, Miss Polly overhears his conversation with Julia—Olivia's half-sister, Janet Miller's mother—whom he informs of the whereabouts of his will, in which he has left her a considerable bequest. Hidden in the same spot is also their marriage certificate confirming Janet Miller's legitimacy. Miss Polly intercepts the documents and, when she finds Julia searching for them, brands her a thief and, showing "no mercy," banishes her from the house.[34] A far cry from the Marian ideal of compassion, Miss Polly herself negates her own claim to whiteness, ironically, doing so to protect and project the image of the ideal in the ordinary. In branding Julia a thief, Miss Polly externalizes the darkness within herself. The deed is particularly repugnant because, as a Southern lady, Miss Polly should be the embodiment of angelic kindness, passivity, and compassion. Chesnutt withholds judgment and lets actions speak for themselves, but he ensures that Miss Polly does not escape punishment. This thief masquerading as a lady meets her death at the hands of another thief, her nephew who, in turn, comes to steal from her. If Miss Polly's death is symbolic, it is so because it discredits the very notion of Southern whiteness as moral superiority bred into successive generations of the Delaweres, the Ochiltrees, the Carterets, and their ilk.

The only inheritance these families share, Chesnutt implies, is the obsessive policing of access to the privileged class. Like her aunt Polly, Olivia, a proud woman, fiercely guards her claim to whiteness by refusing to acknowledge her half-sister, Janet Miller, who is her mirror image. When, after her aunt's death, she discovers the papers confirming her father's marriage and bequest left to Janet Miller's mother, Olivia chooses to throw "the offending document into the fire." Acknowledging Janet as her half-sister would mean a scandal, something that Olivia "could not have endured."[35] Her primary concern is protecting the ideal of gentility that she projects. But, in destroying the documents, she consciously, like her aunt before her, elects to depart from the dictates of the genteel ethos that valorizes honor and truth. Dishonor, on the other hand, breeds dishonor. In a domino-like effect, Olivia's dishonorable deed removes the stain of inter-racial mésalliance from her father's gentility and, simultaneously, negates this very gentility by concealing his honorable conduct toward Janet's mother. Olivia's actions confirm her lack of purity and selflessness, both of which form fundamental pillars of female gentility. When her child lies dying, despite her husband's explanation of Dr. Miller's honorable right to refuse the call, Olivia rushes to the Millers' house. There, she confronts her half-sister and finally acknowledges the bond between them. Olivia resolves to "shrink at no sacrifice" to save her son, and the sacrifice in question involves offering Janet a claim to her father's name "and to half his estate," and thus a right to hereditary whiteness. Although the scene wafts strongly of melodrama, it serves an important purpose. Janet consents to her husband's treating the child, but she rejects "this tardy recognition" because "it is tainted with fraud and crime and blood."[36] Janet's utter condemnation of Olivia's offering is Chesnutt's most direct indictment and redefinition of the notion of Southern whiteness. The much-vaunted heredity is nothing more than a fraudulent sense of entitlement, enforced through the servitude of others and sealed in blood—literally and metaphorically.

Blood possesses dual meaning in the novel: it refers to the blood spilled in the riot because of trumped up and ultimately spurious notion of superior breeding. It is Janet who emerges from the encounter with her honor intact because she spurns the tainted whiteness Olivia offers and proves herself capable of compassion to those who have wronged her. She comes closest to the Marian ideal of selfless sacrifice and suffering. Olivia's sacrifice consists in acknowledging the kinship with Janet, while Janet's sacrifice lies in her forgiveness and repudiation of the whiteness she had desired. What necessitates Olivia's sacrifice is saving her son and, because of that, it can never be selfless. It lacks the purity of Janet's motivation, which stems from the rejection of the privilege her connection with Olivia would bring. Janet's sacrifice reinforces her claim to the ideal of female whiteness and inveighs against the construction of gentility as a conjunction of "birth" and "breeding." Through the confrontation, Chesnutt effects the transference of a claim to whiteness from Olivia to Janet, and negates the notion that whiteness is skin-deep. Knadler sees Janet as the savior of white society, but her ultimate repudiation of the kinship with Olivia condemns rather than redeems that very society.[37] For Janet, as for Chesnutt, whiteness constructed on the false premises of birth and blood can only be black. Its ambivalence lies in the struggle to guard the impossible ideal pitted against the inherent imperfection of its alleged embodiments. Olivia and Miss Polly Ochiltree exemplify this rupture between the ideal and its reconstruction. Janet does not hesitate to reject Olivia's offer because she knows that, in accepting it, she would be swapping her conviction of moral superiority for a pseudo gentility. With the exception of Janet Miller and her husband, pseudo gentility is the most that Wellington's elite can boast. Chesnutt keeps his Southern ladies, the promoters of gentility in Page's and Glasgow's novels, busy not with needlework but with actively unmaking gentility through their efforts to protect it. Through the construction of his characters, Chesnutt debunks the notion of hereditary whiteness as a conjunction of nobility of descent and spirit.

Alice Dunbar-Nelson follows the trail blazed by Chesnutt insofar as she demonstrates that the attributes of whiteness defy class categorization and are capable of transcending the color line. "The Stones of the Village" follows Victor Grabért's rise from obscurity to prominence. From his childhood spent in a neighborhood beyond the pale of whiteness, Victor emerges with the stigma of a "white nigger," with which he is unanimously branded by "white and black and yellow" boys.[38] Inherent in the appellation is the seemingly irreconcilable dichotomy of black and white; a combination of virtue and sin. Dunbar-Nelson leaves no doubt that Victor's appearance aids his ascendancy and helps him to pass the color line. Yet, his passing acquires a duality. On one level, it begins with crossing the proverbial color line, attending white college, marrying into an aristocratic family, and becoming a judge; on another level, it is inaugurated by his realization that "he hated the traditions his wife represented." What precipitates his hate is the realization that, in following the dream of gentility, he has "turned nigger," for his actions have always been motivated not by "his convictions," but as a result of "prudence and fear and cowardice." He pays dearly for the dream of gentility that relies on material gain and pretension to a heritage that is not his to have. The discovery that cowardice and lack of honor—and not his origin—undermine his claim to whiteness ensures that the dream will never be fully realized. The lesson Grabért learns is that he is ultimately responsible for compromising the moral integrity that Dunbar-Nelson, like Chesnutt, situates at the heart of whiteness. Only when he acknowledges his own failure and admits that his conduct "blackens" him does he realize that whiteness can transcend color. This revelation tarnishes his triumph in court over a black lawyer and fills him with self-loathing; for, in Pavageau, he recognizes "the abler man."[39] Pavageau is "the abler man" because he internalizes the courage and honor that Victor has left behind in his pursuit of the genteel ideal.

In Dunbar-Nelson's hands, Grabért becomes an object of pity, and his social elevation a marker of his failure rather than success. What he lost in the process of gentrification gives the measure of the man he could have been. He is a fool who succumbed to the romanticized ideal and only succeeded in proving its unattainability and untenability. Miss Sophie in Dunbar-Nelson's "Little Miss Sophie," also acts imprudently, but her folly displays a remarkable sense of *noblesse oblige*. In the story, honor and courage feature highly on the list of genteel attributes and are, indeed, a matter of heredity, though not necessarily synonymous with gentility. Here, Dunbar-Nelson evokes an object, a Roman ring, which is a tangible emblem of the continuity of that particular tradition praised in the South, the possession of which symbolizes attaining ideal whiteness. The ring was once given to Miss Sophie by Louis Neale, who has since found a different object of adoration and married. Sophie, who "had not always been poor," now lives in abject poverty, eking out a meager existence as a seamstress, and the ring has been pawned. When Sophie learns that Neale stands to lose his inheritance and face ruin unless he produces the ring, she vows to redeem it. Although this means tripling her workload, "telling" Neale that "he might redeem it was an impossibility," and would have meant "that good, straight-backed, stiff-necked Creole blood" rising and choking her.[40] Blood enters the scene again, only to muddy further the waters of whiteness and color classification, raising questions about Miss Sophie's heritage.

In the nineteenth century, "Creole" as a classificatory term underwent re-appropriations and semantic redefinition, the trajectory of which took it from denoting pure Latin descent to mixed-blood. Dunbar-Nelson lets the ambiguity hang to emphasize her point that blood legacy as a driving force behind the construction of gentility does not and should not matter. Regardless of what blood courses in her veins, Latin Creole or Creole diluted, Miss Sophie possesses a nobility of spirit surpassing that of others who occupy higher rungs on the social ladder. Since the ring was bestowed upon her "as a present," honor demands that "as a present should it be returned."[41] For Sophie, contrary to Neale, honor and self-sacrifice are inseparable, and this conjunction decides her claim to whiteness. Through her sacrifice, Sophie redeems the ring and dies clasping it in her hand. Despite her relatively lowly station, she, not Neale, is the worthy keeper of the ring. Her death, which is foreshadowed by comparisons with the Virgin Mary, marks her attainment of the biblical ideal of whiteness and severs it from the ordinary.

Dunbar-Nelson, like Chesnutt, sees the concept of ideal whiteness as underpinned by a conviction of truth which, ineluctably, cannot be reconciled with its embodiments. Enshrined in this concept of über whiteness is a coalescence of whiteness denoting spiritual nobility and hereditary whiteness encompassing blood, tradition, and the possession of land. A remarkably tall order and, for Theweleit, who sees the concept of a whole as a force obscuring constituent parts, impossible. If the ultimate whiteness operates on a pretense to such truth, the operation requires the concealment of that which is deemed flawed, inappropriate, and unworthy. Any struggle to protect the wholeness of ideal whiteness, as Chesnutt's and Dunbar-Nelson's protagonists prove, reveals the split nature of the ideal that is beyond reconcilability. This wholeness of the ideal whiteness is not the truth but an illusion, always already mediated by its disparate attributes, the existence of which both fosters and foils its attainment. When Daniel Hudley, a nineteenth-century lawyer from Alabama, wrote that "the genuine Southern gentlemen, like all real gentlemen, are not quite so plentiful as blackberries in summertime, or New-England robins in spring," he may have been closer to the truth than he had imagined or intended in his class taxonomy of the South.[42]

PART THREE

MONSTER MASH,
OR A PALER SHADE OF WHITE

SEVEN

THOMAS NELSON PAGE AND THE BURDEN OF HERITAGE

Writing in nineteenth-century Alabama and keen not to strip the South of its pretense to aristocracy while providing a viable account of class hierarchy, Daniel Hundley kept the comparison tame. Saying that genuine gentility is not "so plentiful as blackberries in summertime, or New-England robins in spring" has a much more positive ring than as rare as unicorns.[1] Perhaps unicorns would have been a better analogy. After all, they have the advantage of myth that comes from the conjunction of folklore and mysticism, providing a thrill that stems from constantly deferred pleasure, the possibility of seeing one against all odds and logic. They are, incidentally, white and inaccessible. And they do not exist. Indeed, these words could describe Southern whiteness—inaccessible and non-existent. Certainly, this is the image of Southern whiteness that emerges with some force from the pages of Chesnutt's novels and Dunbar-Nelson's stories. Glasgow's is a less damning account, but even she cannot stop herself from critiquing the pernicious nature of ideals. Page's work, so far, has been the most optimistic and the most contestable narrative because of his determined myopia. In *John Marvel Assistant,* Page comes closest to abandoning the romanticized vision of the attainability of Southern gentility by drawing a more realistic picture of American society, one more attuned to class difference and less inclined to class flattery. What he does not abandon, however, and what he shares with the other writers, is a vision of Southern whiteness based on the notion of true, or ideal whiteness, which they equate with hereditary gentility. From their postbellum standpoint, its essence consists in replicating the perfection and wholeness of the antebellum ideal that flourished in the imagined Old South.

This wholeness is merely an illusion that conceals the fragmented nature of Southern whiteness and renders its embodiments—the gentleman planter and lady—perpetually lacking.

When subjected to closer scrutiny, whiteness and wholeness emerge as mutually exclusive terms. Part of the problem stems from the rhetoric of Christianity, which, as Dyer observes, while germane to conceptions of whiteness, promulgates a split between the spiritual and the corporeal, casting the latter as inferior. This split condemns earthly embodiments of whiteness as monstrous mutations, for it prefigures rebellion against the loftier ideals of whiteness such as Marian passivity, purity, and expectancy, the kind of waiting and acceptance adorned with a beatific smile; and Christ-like striving and the denial of self-gratification.[2] Translated into Southern parlance, this split is further problematized because these antecedents of whiteness are endowed with worldly goods that do not sit comfortably alongside notions of asceticism: specifically, hereditary possession of land that is inextricably bound up with its concomitant adjuncts—tradition and blood. This heady mix of distinctive attributes, both divine and genteel, ensures that Southern whiteness becomes doubly split and intrinsically heterogenous. The Southern gentleman and lady become loci of conflict through whom the unattainability of the ideal manifests in the actual, rendering their reconstructions of Southern whiteness more or less successful—but never complete—approximations of the ideal. Chesnutt and Dunbar-Nelson use this incompleteness to propose an all-inclusive paradigm of whiteness based on meritocracy and individual achievement. Neither Page nor Glasgow conceals it, though for the former it is not for lack of trying. The protagonists of Page's *Gordon Keith* or Glasgow's *The Deliverance* all fail to combine genteel lineage with possession of land; or material wealth with aristocratic pedigree; or augment genteel breeding with angelic goodness.

Henry Glave, the hero of Page's *John Marvel Assistant* fares no better when it comes to unifying the genteel and divine attributes of Southern whiteness. The novel, published in 1910, met with muted praise. In a review entitled "Socialism or What? Mr. Page's New Novel," the critic softened the blow by expressing his conviction that "Mr. Page could not write anything unreadable, so this novel entertains and interests." The novel, he conceded, had "elements that make popularity," but "a little more planning, more care in developing, more definiteness of aim would have improved it a hundred percent." The reviewer for the *Houston Post* sounded a similar note, calling it "an interesting and straightforward story" that, nonetheless, was "somewhat unconvincing," with "a tinge of conventional melodrama."[3] Nor did the "touches of melodrama" escape the attention of another critic, who noted "some irrelevant happenings which after all are found to fit into their places like bits of mosaic." Page's style also came under scrutiny and was found lacking. This novel, "full of action, even of melodrama," failed to generate "excitement" because Page's "style" was "as placid and leisurely as a May morning, and so charming that even the descriptions of some of the horrors of slum life scarcely ruffle the reader." There were some kinder voices, too, one of which admired Page's craftsmanship in the drafting of the opening chapters, which possessed "some of the delicate appreciation of local color" he demonstrates in *Red Rock*. He even went so far as to call it "perhaps the best of Mr. Page's charming stories."[4]

In his praise he displayed a substantial lack of judgment. A novel that deals with "various phases of corruption—political, economic, and social" hardly fits the bill of a charming story.[5] In *John Marvel Assistant,* Page steps outside of his usual customary setting of the Southern plantation, and sets most of the scenes in one of the burgeoning cities of the middle West. But, although he changes the scene, he does not adjust the voice and manner, which leads to the dissonance between style and subject matter that some critics observed. The result is a curious blend of nostalgia, hopelessness, squalor, and poverty, all rendered in dusky pastel tones characteristic of a writer who is, indeed, reluctant to ruffle any feathers. The novel bears a resemblance to *Gordon Keith* insofar as it is a *bildungsroman*. Absent from the narrative, however, is the prudish morality that permeates *Gordon Keith*. Instead, Page serves the tale of a reformed prodigal, Henry Glave, whose reward is a happy ending if not the attainment of whiteness proper. The retrospective narrative compounds the effect of Henry's imperfection or, indeed, otherness, for it benefits from hindsight wisdom that betrays his awareness of not only the ideal of gentility, but also his departure from it.

Henry's otherness is a matter of his social and cultural legacy. His gentility is a burden rather than a blessing in that it stunts, at least initially, his moral development, alienating him from himself and his antecedents whose example he should follow. Jacques Lacan observes that otherness is inseparable from the discourse of inheritance in which the subject forms one of its links. Lacan exemplifies this point with the discourse of the father, which the subject must reproduce, for there is no escape from the chain of inheritance.[6] In this scenario, the subject is powerless and has no agency of his own. The best he can hope for is an aberrant reproduction that places him at odds with the discourse he reproduces. The implication is clear: heredity cannot exist without aberration, which marks the successor as inherently other than the predecessor. In *Gordon Keith*, Gordon's capitalist ambition taints his espousal of his father's genteel legacy; while in *The Deliverance*, Glasgow juxtaposes Christopher's striking resemblance to his father with his severely diminished circumstances, which exacerbates the loss of his genteel legacy.

Like Gordon Keith or Christopher Blake, Henry cannot escape the circuit of inheritance and lineal mutation. Mutation implies distortion, lack and dilution—in short, monstrosity. The term monster has always carried inflections of visual imperfection thanks to its Latin root "monstrare," meaning to show, demonstrate, or manifest.[7] Historically, the ugliness of the monster bespoke vice, iniquity, and general wickedness which spilled over to claim the subject as their own. The vices that deserved particular condemnation, however, left their mark on the soul and not necessarily on the body. They were the flaws of moral and spiritual weakness and wickedness such as, Chris Baldick suggests, "ingratitude," "rebellion," and "disobedience" to the authority of progenitors and blood kith and kin. This emphasis on moral iniquity becomes particularly pertinent to reconstructions of Southern whiteness, which rely on the premise of continuity. To be a monster is to transgress those boundaries of filial obedience to ancestral worship. If there is a vice of which Southern whiteness is guilty, albeit inadvertently, it is filial rebellion. Rebellion signals difference and brings the cycle back to Lacan's inescapable repetition of the discourse of the father, which creates abortive subjects. The essence of monstrosity lies in the discursive impossibility of the repetition of sameness which, paradoxically, fuels fantasies like that of Southern whiteness, which rest on securing continuity.[8] Page's, Glasgow's, Chesnutt's, and Dunbar-Nelson's protagonists, perhaps with the exception of Miss Sophie in "Little Miss Sophie," are all guilty of the vice of filial rebellion. What determines their monstrosity is the failure to conflate the antebellum and biblical ideals and to reproduce them in a non-aberrant form.

Page's Henry Glave fits the aberrant mold. His tale reveals that the gentility he replicates is flawed on two counts: his failure to reproduce like for like, and the imperfection of the construction when he actually does preserve the likeness to the model. In Henry's case, the circuit of inheritance extends to encompass not only the father, but also the rhetoric of gentility that the father symbolizes, and the interpretability of which leads to distortion. Page does not disclose the actual setting of the novel, but Henry's brief family history leaves no doubt as to the region from which his ancestors hail. The path looks and sounds familiar. Henry's "family was an old and distinguished one," and its genealogy "could be traced back about two hundred years." Several of his "ancestors had accomplished enough to be known in the history of the State," and his father "fought through the war, rising to be a major and surrendering at Appomattox." While the family "had formerly been well off," and "prior to the Revolutionary War owned large estates," that time of greatness is now only in the realm of fond reminiscence. Despite Henry's father's "slender patrimony" being "swept away by the war," "by much stinting" he manages to send him to college. The impoverished circumstances of his family, however, do not dent Henry's pride in his descent, leaving him "quite satisfied at college to rest" on his ancestors' "achievements" and feeling "no need to add to its distinction by any labors" of his own.[9] Armed with hubris, Henry basks in the knowledge that his gentility is secured by virtue of his descent from such illustrious personages. His heredity guarantees his claim to whiteness and, in his estimation, exempts him from striving. Heredity gives, and heredity takes away, for it facilitates a departure from the model practiced by his ancestors and the spiritual ideal of male whiteness. In other words, it erases the possibility of like proceeding from like, casting mutation as the only constant and irreducible force.

Henry's belief in the hereditary virtues of gentility contradicts his father's conviction that "a king can make a nobleman," but "it takes Jehovah to make a gentleman." The maxim is fit for a king and, it seems, Page again indulges in historic intertextuality and borrows it from one. Henry VIII, following a nobleman's complaint of rough treatment received at the hands of his court painter Hans Holbein, is reported to have replied: "I can make of seven peasants just as many lords, but of seven lords I cannot make *one* Holbein." Henry VIII speaks of talent and his divine right to make or unmake nobility. Henry's father also speaks of gentility as a divinely ordained state that no earthly being can strip. The difference lies in the conception of nobility as a quality that is part of spirit and therefore unquantifiable, rather than a quantifiable acquisition that may be measured in honors or material wealth. Henry may admire such principles but disapproves of them. They mark his father's "inadequacy to the new state of things" and lead Henry to consider himself his sire's superior "in all practical affairs."[10] This tacit conviction of superiority marks Henry's filial disobedience to the model of gentility espoused by his father and makes him guilty of the sin of ingratitude toward those of his own blood. Effectively, Page, uncharacteristically so, finds flaws in both Henry's and his father's incarnations of whiteness: the father's because it disposes with the hereditary aspect of gentility, and Henry's because it relies solely on heredity, disregarding its spiritual facet.

Henry's college years deepen the gulf separating him from the whiteness of his ancestors. Whereas the father harbors "a high idea of classical learning," the son prides himself on being "a good poker-player."[11] By his own admission, Henry "loved pleasure too much" to work diligently, and "was too self-indulgent to deny" himself "anything." Gone are the ideals of striving and self-discipline of which Jehovah might approve; what remains in their place is a hubristic conceit. Solely by virtue of being a gentleman, Henry firmly believes, he will "bear off the more shining honors of the orator and society-medalist." In the end, Henry's hopes are dashed and, although he finally receives his lawyer's diploma after "many tribulations," he loses "all the prestige and pleasure of receiving it along with" his "class." Henry's semi-success forces him to acknowledge his arrogance and admit that he did not succeed precisely because he "was so certain of winning." Before Henry formulates this conviction, a combination of conceited pride and self-assurance leads him to despise "the plodding ways of cold-blooded creatures like Peck even more" than "the dullness of John Marvel," leaving him blind to the attributes of whiteness that others possess—including the eponymous John Marvel. What is more, Henry's admission reveals the permeability of boundaries separating Southern whiteness from monstrosity. His departure from the model of gentility espoused by his forefathers and father transforms him into what Judith Halberstam, speaking of the constructedness of monstrosity, terms a distorted product of social conventions.[12] But, it is also through the perpetuation of such "social conventions" that Henry can maintain a facade of gentility, for they are socially and legally permissible. More than any other of Page's heroes, Henry embodies not just the dissociation—but also the contradiction—between theory and practice. This is Page looking at gentility without rose-tinted spectacles. He dwells on Henry's weaknesses to show him, to borrow from Mary Shelley, as a "hideous progeny," a monstrous distortion of the ideal of Southern whiteness. But this distortion is only possible, he suggests, because certain vices are permissible, tolerated, and gentrified. Henry never stoops to tumbling wenches in the hay, but this is the first, deliberate hint from Page that gentility is not all white and innocent.

Page allows Henry to find redemption, but never lets him reach or live the ultimate dream of Southern whiteness—of being the morally superior, landed descendant of a long line of blue-blooded aristocrats. This is the one fantasy that Page, a staunch supporter of the Southern genteel myth, finally admits can only be half-lived. Speaking of fantasy, Slavoj Žižek concludes that it is a primal lie, a smoke-screen concealing its own negation; for fantasy to exist, it cannot be attainable. Unattainable but sustainable, fantasy operates through essentially conflicting "unwritten rules," rules that are simultaneously "*transgressive*" and "*coercive*"; transgressive because in order to be effective they require that the subject always be positioned at a disadvantage from the fantasy, and coercive because they ultimately restrict or deny the fulfillment of the fantasy. Robert Penn Warren's *All the King's Men* shows the *modus operandi* of fantasy in vivid paradox.[13] Despite his phenomenal rise to power and fortune, Willie Stark, the son of a poor Southern farmer, seeks constant revalidation of his status as a governor through the erection of imposing edifices. The intention is to translate into visible permanence what he lacks in pedigree, to put himself on par with the aristocratic Stantons, one of whom was the state governor before him. This, of course, he cannot do, so he projects forward, hoping to found a dynasty. In any established order of social stratification, a Willie Stark starts from the transgressive position of an upstart who, lured by the prospect of upward mobility, seemingly defies the stasis that characterizes class categorization, but never completely succeeds.

Transgression presupposes and sustains fantasy, and Southern whiteness is no exception. It forms part of a distinct ideology that was shipped across the water with the first indentured servants, while those who financed the enterprise stayed at home and rubbed hands with glee in anticipation of financial rewards. Even before they set foot in the New World, the new arrivals, mostly criminals guilty of more or less grievous misdemeanors, would have grown up in the shadow of gentility and on the wrong side of the law, the standards of which condemned them as monstrous. Those fortunate enough to afford a passage came in search of betterment through upward mobility. For most, there was not much that separated them from the effluvium of indentured servitude, but a great deal that stood between them and gentility. For the landless and the poor, the fantasy of upward mobility was the only viable alternative that kept them safely in their place and ensured they would never achieve it. For the lucky few, extensive land grants furnished the material wherewithal to lay a claim to a semblance of gentility.[14] The hereditary possession of land may have been the marker of gentility in the country of origin, but theirs was a new gentility, an offshoot of the old tree but without roots of its own.

This newness added new significance to concepts of tradition, birth, and blood. There is hardly a Southern nineteenth-century novel that does not feature a major, a colonel, a general, or a judge of long and admirable lineage.[15] Self-made men are scarce and generally do not prosper. But even the generals of unprecedented and incomparable valor do not live up to the standard of Southern whiteness because the convergence of the genteel and biblical ideals presupposes the impossibility of its attainment and transforms it into a rhetoric spawning monstrous subjects. What underpins the politics of the fantasy of Southern whiteness are tacit rules that police its boundaries and facilitate a re-construction of gentility in relation to an other who stands farther down the pecking order. It is precisely such commonly accepted commandments that enable Henry to reconstruct his flawed gentility by placing others beyond the boundaries of what is deemed respectable or acceptable. Henry eventually realizes that the perfection of gentility consisting in an amalgamation of the divine and genteel models is merely a fantasy, but initially he asserts his whiteness by turning others into monsters.

Henry's first recollection of John Marvel is far from charitable and not devoid of class stereotyping. Marvel, whom Henry describes as "round-faced, round-bodied, bow-legged" and a "moon-faced, slow-witted Saxon," arrives at the institution to study "for the ministry." Although Page, always the gentleman, refrains from using the adjective "shiftless" in describing Marvel, the readiness with which he has students accept "a rusty man with a frowzy beard, and a lank, stooping woman" to be his parents suggests that a "slow-witted Saxon" is Henry's euphemism for plebeian. Social norms dictate that Marvel, as an exponent of the lower classes, should remain dim-witted and slow. Soon, however, Marvel, whom Henry tutored in Latin, "had come to understand the language better than" he. Unpleasant as the admission is, at this point Henry does not realize that what he took for Marvel's "plodding" is a symptom of the strength of his character and striving—qualities that Henry lacks. In this reversal of roles, where complacency and striving transcend their socially preordained boundaries, revealing in the process the permeability of whiteness and monstrosity, the student literally masters the master. Through the Henry-Marvel dyad, Page divorces the concept of monstrosity from visual imperfection. Beneath Marvel's "awkward exterior" lies "a mine of true gold," whereas Henry's blemish-free physiognomy conceals an inner imperfection that turns him into "an idle dog."[16]

In dispensing with the ugliness as a mark of spiritual imperfection, Page subjects one of his own class to harsh critique. This is not, however, the only example of Page's seemingly revised outlook on whiteness. Enter Leo Wolffert, a student with whom Henry is assigned to share quarters upon his arrival in college. If Henry's acquaintance with Wolffert reveals anything, it is an in-bred sense of superiority based on hereditary entitlement and religious bias. Henry's first impression of Wolffert, unlike that of Marvel, is favorable. Wolffert appears to him "an affable, gentlemanly fellow, and very nice looking," with a "broad brow," "curling brown hair," "dark eyes," and "a nose the least bit too large and inclining to be aquiline." The impression is as ephemeral as Henry's conviction of his own grandeur and both evaporate as soon as he learns that Wolffert is Jewish. This knowledge alone is enough to alter Henry's perception and turn "the ridge" of Wolffert's "well-carved nose" into a monstrous flaw. In Henry's estimation, Wolffert's descent erases his claim to gentility, which, combined with his father's rise "from poverty to the position of chief merchant and capitalist" as well as "elected mayor," makes him an unsuitable roommate for a gentleman of deep convictions of the virtue of heredity.[17] This encounter with Wolffert is the exact reverse of Henry's first meeting with Marvel. In Marvel, he expected to find a dullard and was disappointed; Wolffert's appearance and demeanor convinced him he was meeting a gentleman.

Appearances mislead, Page seems to suggest, and one would do well to avoid hasty judgments. There is not much Henry does well, but he can certainly judge a book by its cover and arrive at a firm conviction. Following Wolffert's disclosure, Henry promptly vacates the lodging in his absence, justifying his action with a lie that he had met "an old friend who was very desirous" of sharing his quarters with Henry.[18] The lack of courage that Henry's action betrays places him in direct opposition to his forefathers and father's standard of gentility against which he unwittingly rebels. The harder he tries to preserve his gentility, the further he departs from the ancestral archetype. Page emphasizes Henry's predicament through juxtapositions of his idleness with Wolffert's "acquirements and ability," which have no equals. Unlike Henry, Wolffert is capable of striving and self-denial. Wolffert's father, hoping that his son would desist from his chosen path and become a capitalist, "cut him down to the lowest figure on which he could live."[19] Here, Page presents another instance of filial disobedience to a father, but Wolffert's rebellion earns him a claim to the kind of whiteness that Henry's father extols. In a liberal move, uncharacteristic of his view of gentility already witnessed in *Gordon Keith* or *Red Rock*, Page allows Wolffert and Marvel to break out of the stereotypes of their inheritance. He leaves Henry to blunder in the haze of outdated assumptions of genteel righteousness.

The bildungsroman as a genre, arguably, requires a degree of blundering which is necessary to showcase a character's growth and development. But in dwelling on Henry's errant ways, Page indicates an altered perception of Southern whiteness not unlike the view Henry's father espouses. It is a view Henry learns, albeit slowly, to value. Part of this learning process is the acknowledgement of virtue in others to whom societal and cultural norms deny it. Once Henry realizes that Wolffert is a man of a disinterested purity of purpose, who sees "beneath the stony surface of the commonplace the ideals and principles that were to reconstruct and resurrect the world," he feels "ashamed" of his "poltroonery in leaving him." Henry's admission of shame at his conduct marks a dawning awareness of his own imperfection. If, as Page writes, "courage" and "fidelity" as well as "honesty, and truth" distinguish the Southern gentleman, then Henry falls abominably short of this paradigm. Avital Ronell observes of monstrosity that it works as a dialogic relationship between the monster and its opposite. In recognizing and positioning this other as its antithesis, the monster's conception of itself as a monster awakens.[20] It is thus that Henry's acquaintance with the two men offers him a glimpse of his own inadequacy and the untenability of claims to whiteness based on heredity. The realization irrevocably dawns that Marvel and Wolffert internalize the qualities that Henry lacks and become symbolic of the spiritual model of whiteness. Compared with them, Henry is not only a paler shade of white, but also monstrous within.

Although the paths of the three men will cross again, following their graduation they separate, and soon correspondence ceases. Full of grandiose schemes, Henry sets up as a lawyer in a neighboring city. Before he leaves home, his father advises him to "be careful with other people's money and keep out of debt." Betraying monstrous ingratitude, Henry wastes this valuable piece of paternal wisdom. After a promising beginning, arrogance and misplaced pride lead him to decline cases that he considers "too small to satisfy him" or "below" his "abilities." It is not long before he is "welcomed in the poker-game of 'the best fellows' in town" and has little time to do anything else "than enjoy" his "social success." Page has Henry repeatedly revert to type only to accentuate that it is not the type of gentility his father represents. Just as he did during his college days, Henry opts for idleness instead of self-discipline and, in due course, begins "to speculate—just a little at first; but more largely after awhile [sic]." This is the kind of conduct of which neither Page's nor Henry's father would approve. Even in his choice of profession, Henry stands in breach of the Southern genteel tradition. The acceptable and honorable profession for "every young Southerner of good social connection who was too poor to live without work, or too ambitious to be contended with his plantation," Page observes, was the law.[21] A limited choice and one that does not admit the possibility of speculating as a respectable means of earning a living for a self-respecting Southerner. Yet, again Henry transgresses the Southern standard of whiteness and, though his newly earned wealth enables him to keep "a pair of horses" and engage in "other gay pleasures" the town has to offer, this display of wealth transforms his gentility into a gaudy display far removed from the symmetrical lines of a plantation house harking back to classical Roman architecture.[22] These are the things that last and stand testament to tradition, while Henry's dubiously acquired wealth bespeaks an ostentation with which an arriviste may wear his gold

Henry's lucky streak does not last long; nor is it meant to, because it contravenes all that Southern gentility stands for. His ambition "to go to Congress" and his wealth come to an abrupt end when, through an unfortunate accident, a scheme in which he has invested all collapses, leaving him bankrupt. Penniless, Henry relocates to another city to start afresh. Upon arrival, he puts up at a respectable boarding house, Mrs. Kale's, and dutifully returns to a respectable occupation, setting up to practice as a lawyer. Yet, even here certain "unwritten rules" of gentility prevent him from developing the selflessness enshrined in the paradigm of Christ, which manifests in an instinctive revulsion toward anything that does not appear genteel. Henry's neighbors are two elderly ladies whom he spots one day carrying parcels. He offers to relieve them of the burden, but "at heart" feels "rather ashamed to be lugging two large bundles for two shabby-looking old women."[23] The chivalric deed becomes a monstrous masquerade that reveals Henry's untenable position as gentleman *manqué*. It opens a gap between his behavior and his conception of gentility. Both menial labor and accompanying ladies less than finely attired are damaging to one's gentility: the former because it is incommensurate with it, and the latter because it carries the threat of lower-class contamination. His feelings of shame betray his awareness of the ontological instability of his position and highlight the acuteness of his need to preserve a semblance of whiteness.

A semblance of whiteness becomes the operative phrase and the best Henry can hope for. Page exploits Henry's circumstances to highlight the ontological instability of his position, which manifests in his constant need to reassert his gentility. Henry admits he had "no association in the town except the poor" and "had come to know some of them well," but immediately qualifies the admission by adding "as well as a man in a good coat can know men in a workman's blouse." Considering his pecuniary circumstances, Henry's insistence on class distinction is both misplaced and emphasizes the chasm separating him from the standard of the Southern gentleman. The law may be a suitable profession for a gentleman only insofar as it acts as "the surest stepping-stone to political preferment." Henry's foremost ambition, however, is not a glittering political career but the rather more prosaic and utilitarian aim of earning a living. This very necessity of having to earn his own keep marks Henry's departure from the model of hereditary gentility and foils his attempts at reasserting superiority. His projection of whiteness betrays a "lack" and "excess," both of which characterize the monster: it exceeds the actual while pointing to a monstrous lack of the divine and earthly prerequisites of whiteness. The critic reviewing the novel for the *Detroit Free Press* called it a "medium" through which Page presents "his ideas on various subjects of present-hour interest, especially Christianity and socialism."[24] And he was correct, particularly in relation to Marvel the selfless minister and Wolffert the revolutionary fighting for social justice. But looking at the two ideologies, both of which rely heavily on the fantasies of ultimate reward after death and equality in life, allows Page a good vantage point from which to review, if not revise, the concept of Southern whiteness, which owes a debt to both Christianity and socialism; the former supplies paradigms for emulation, the latter for disavowal and dissociation. Page has Henry constantly struggle to distance himself from those whom he believes to be below him by virtue of inferior birth if not financial position. He is a man desperately trying not to relinquish that phony notion of inherited gentility. Only when he had "pawned everything pawnable" he possessed to augment his scant earnings, does Henry perceive the paradox inherent in gentility. Reduced to near penury, he contemplates reverting to his old habit of gambling because "gambling was gentlemanly—at least, gentlemen gambled." He resists the temptation, but the resistance does not stem from a nobility of spirit that his father admires, but rather from the conviction that "as soon as a man played for his living, he crossed the line and ceased to be a gentleman."[25] Henry's words reveal his dawning awareness that Southern whiteness is a self-negating fantasy. Though incongruent with the self-denial of the Christ model or the honesty of Page's paradigm of the Southern gentleman, gambling is ranked among gentlemanly pursuits. The gentlemanly code of practice therefore precludes the attainment of gentility, rendering its practitioners monstrous.

In an almost epiphanic moment, this paradox inherent in gentility reveals itself to Henry when he is in the gambling house. Upon overhearing a conversation between a young man and his companions at a card table, Henry learns that the gentleman is "one of the real upper class," and his "soul revolted at the thought of this man standing as the type of our upper class." The gentleman in question is John Carter, the son of a wealthy entrepreneur and "the *bon parti*, the coveted of aspiring mothers." What arouses Henry's indignation is less Carter's gambling, which after all is gentlemanly until it becomes a source of income, than his face "with marks of dissipation," in which he sees a reflection of his former self.[26] The clarity of this vision carries with it a realization of how far he had strayed from the whiteness espoused by his father. For the first time, Henry becomes fully conscious of his monstrosity, particularly as he entered the establishment with the intention to gamble. Following this failed attempt to bolster his finances, Henry is forced to abandon his lodging at Mrs. Kale's and moves "to the poorest part of the city." Although he admits that, while living at Mrs. Kale's, he "had been playing the gentleman," words that echo those of Steve Allen in *Red Rock*, he conceals the true reason for his removal from her for fear of coming "down in her esteem." A much attenuated, if not distorted, form of *noblesse oblige* that conceals a lie. According to Derrida, an example is "first of all for others" and always "beyond the self" and, whoever sets the example is never "equal" to it;[27] in this instance, Page deconstructs. Henry's unwillingness to abandon the pretense of gentility bespeaks dishonesty, which, although stemming from the need to protect the image of a gentleman, renders him unequal to the task of representing the standard that exceeds the actual embodiment, reaching beyond to the presupposed wholeness of the ideal.

Henry's pretension to whiteness is all the more monstrous because it springs from the awareness of his imperfection, the result of which is his "slipping down, down" and finding himself "near the bottom." The turning point comes when he finally accepts the blame for finding himself in such a predicament, which leads him to re-evaluate the standard of whiteness. Wandering the streets of the city, he observes that the vulgarity of displaying material wealth is a testament to the owners of such edifices who possess "no traditions and no ideals." There is nothing the facades advertise—no historic inheritance and no affinity to life beyond the material. This garish display and gaudy spectacle of wealth are monstrous distortions of gentility. The excessive grandeur of the display appears to Henry both transgressive and "only a counterfeit, a poor imitation of what" the bourgeoisie "imagine to be the manners of the upper class abroad whose indifferent manners they ape."[28] This observation enables him to redefine his whiteness as a matter of refinement grounded in tradition, which is, however, lacking the pecuniary resources that would furnish a gentlemanly lifestyle. Though Henry's reformulation of gentility begins to resemble that of his father, it also reveals the latter's model to be divergent from the archetype of Southern whiteness.

Whiteness and transgression become inseparable in the novel. Transgression presupposes and sustains every fantasy. Henry's mutated gentility is essential to supporting the ideal of Southern whiteness in its pure form. What Page avoids in his other novels, he finally utters in this one: Southern whiteness carries its own antagonism, which means that its reproductions must be partial and imperfect in order to sustain the idea of perfection. What springs to mind is the Lacanian concept of *objet petit a*, which is always found outside the feeling and perceiving subject. Because it points to a more than the subject, *objet petit a* renders him inadequate, always on the point of acceptance but never arriving.[29] It is a case of incompleteness promoting awareness; Henry only appreciates the loftier ideals of whiteness once he has departed from them. Only from the position of a monstrous mutation is Henry able to perceive "the spark of sentiment" that manifests itself in "a bit of a plant in a little pot" that symbolizes "struggling and striving," which is precisely why, once he stops "playing the gentleman" and moves to the poorest quarter of the city, he finds charming "a little house" with "a rose-bush carefully trained over the door."[30] The symbolism of the plant marks Page's reluctance to give up altogether on the institution of hereditary gentility. The rose bush supplies a link to land, the *raison d'être* of hereditary gentility, and stands for the finer sentiment of tradition to which Henry, despite his blunders, is instinctively drawn.

It is in this part of the city where his path crosses with Marvel and Wolffert, both of whom have renounced worldly glory and devoted their lives to the service of the poor: Marvel preaching and helping by any means possible, and Wolffert championing for the recognition of their rights. Marvel is the "simple follower of Christ" who is "threadbare like" the poor whom he serves, but it is Wolffert the Jew who dies "a Christian death," trampled by a striking mob, "in the act of supplicating for those who slew him." Although both Marvel and Wolffert embody the Christ-like nobility of spirit, Wolffert even making the ultimate sacrifice, both stand beyond the pale of whiteness proper by virtue of descent. They provide perfect foils for Henry insofar as they demonstrate the complexity of the paradigm of whiteness. Both are the yardsticks against which he measures his flaws, conceding "how much nobler both had always been."[31] This recognition of Marvel's and Wolffert's nobility is both redeeming and cathartic, for it points a way to improvement by emphasizing Henry's monstrous shortcomings: Marvel and Wolffert are marvels because, in meeting the Christian standard of whiteness, they surpass Henry's incarnation, which, ironically, turns Henry into a marvel because he departs from the model despite his hereditarily predetermined claim. With this admission, Henry seals his status as a monstrous aberration and accepts the unattainability of whiteness as an organic whole.

Page's construction of the three characters, though characterized by a naturalistic tendency to stereotype, inadvertently reveals the rigidity of whiteness and the malleability of the monstrous. Unlike in *Gordon Keith* and *Red Rock*, in *John Marvel Assistant,* Page engages with the complexity of the fantasy of whiteness. Henry, Marvel, and Wolffert embody distinct attributes of whiteness such as birth, candor, self-denial, and striving, which may add up to a totality of whiteness, but, collectively, symbolize the impossibility of such a merger, the impossibility of living the fantasy. Only partial incarnations are possible because of this inherently fragmentary nature of Southern whiteness, which, as a totality of disparate elements, can only function at the level of the conceptual. While each element reinforces the idea of a unified totality, it is never reducible to it.[32] If anything, Page demonstrates that the fantasy of Southern whiteness oppresses and terrorizes itself with the promise of a transcendence enshrined in the convergence of the unattainable Christian and impossible antebellum ideals that signify as inaccessible reality. Henry's hereditary gentility is nothing more than a burden of self-indulgent inertia that turns him into a monstrous mutation and relies on spawning monsters. Compared with *Gordon Keith* and *Red Rock,* the novel itself is a marvel, or indeed a monster, in its candid admission that, irrespective of the post-Reconstruction contingencies, only partial reconstructions and approximations are both possible and indispensable to perpetuating the ideal.

EIGHT

ELLEN GLASGOW'S FICTIONS OF VERISIMILITUDE

Thomas Nelson Page's distinctly gentlemanly and decorous approach to genteel flaws would have earned him praise from fellow Virginian and man of letters John Esten Cooke, who would have found *John Marvel Assistant*, and all his other novels, a fine example of literature. Cooke had no trouble with defining literature, although his definition seems remarkably puritanical by modern standards, and of a didactic bent not unlike that of Samuel Richardson, Cooke's senior by about a century and a half. Literature, wrote Cooke in *Virginia: A History of the People*, should be instructive in purpose and "notable for its respect for good morals and manners." It should never be "offensive to delicacy or piety" or, indeed, attempt "to instill a belief in what ought not to be believed."[1] Page excelled in this kind of literature of politeness, tirelessly papering over the cracks in Southern whiteness, pointing his finger at the evils of Reconstruction and post-Reconstruction years, but never attempting to question the ideal of gentility *qua* ideal. In this, he inadvertently added to the long tradition of disseminating what "ought not to be believed," though it is doubtful that Cooke, a staunch admirer of the myth of Southern genteel origins, would have chastised him for it.

Whether he would have extended equal tolerance to Glasgow, who dares to question and undermine the tenability of Southern whiteness, is uncertain. Not that her novels are disrespectful to "good morals and manners," but they certainly offend the "delicacy and piety" of those possessed of an unshakable belief in the veracity of the ideal of gentility. Glasgow differs from Page in that she refuses to disseminate an unblemished vision of gentility. Because of her sensitivity to the role of historic, cultural and religious re-appropriation and reconstruction in the process of ideal-making, Glasgow is able to *de*-idealize Southern whiteness. Never a *fait accompli*, but an ultimately futile struggle to remain true to the ideal of gentility underlies the plots and subplots of *The Battle-Ground*, *The Deliverance*, or *The Miller of Old Church*. She treads a similar path in *The Voice of the People*, a path that leads her to scrutinize the enduring appeal of the ideal of Southern whiteness while revealing the shambolic attempts of its embodiments to conform. Casting Nicholas Burr as the unlikely hero with a decidedly trashy background, Glasgow is able to demonstrate the hypocrisy and insularity that govern claims to gentility.

The story spans eighteen years—from 1870 to 1898. It begins in the fictional city of Kingsborough in Virginia, for which Glasgow used Williamsburg as her model, and later relocates to Richmond. She peoples the city with anachronistic characters who exemplify the hierarchical structure of the Kingsborough social milieu. McDowell opines that *The Voice of the People* portrays "a society in transition." But a more accurate description for Glasgow's Kingsborough would be a city that will resist transition at any cost, and Nicholas Burr's violent death at the hands of a lynch mob at the close of the novel stands as a symbol of this resistance, which is just as common among the affluent as it is among those deemed off white. Through the upheavals of the Civil War and Reconstruction, the narrator informs the reader, Kingsborough "clung to her amiable habits" —a euphemism for anachronism, perhaps.[2] Glasgow's acute sense of irony comes across forcefully in her description of Kingsborough, which sets it at variance with the genteel pretense of its elite. In Glasgow's Kingsborough, everything seems shabby, second rate, and down at heel. Once "a chartered city," Kingsborough now boasts "only a charter." Despite the denizens' valiant efforts to preserve the former grandeur essential to the continuity of the historic tradition out of which it had sprung, Kingsborough itself is emblematic of filial rebellion that, not once but twice, disturbed the wholeness of the body politic: first through participation "in the cause of American independence" and then through secession from the Union. A similar divergence characterizes the inhabitants of Kingsborough. They may present, like all Virginians, "a countenance that was unerringly Anglo-Saxon," but it is also a countenance that has been "modified by the conditions of centuries of changes."[3] Glasgow evokes the immortal, though by now a little worn, Anglo-Saxon ideal to suggest that whatever the residents of Kingsborough write is their own fiction of verisimilitude. Given the altered nature of the place and its residents, it is a fiction rich in sentiment but poor in fact.

This kind of sentiment, born out of nostalgia for the past, forms part of the collective consciousness of Kingsborough—and no one is immune or indifferent to its influence. Glasgow sees it as a force that simultaneously propels its inhabitants to replicate the ways of their antecedents and demonstrates the monstrous incompleteness of their reconstructions. When it comes to the monster mash of Kingsborough denizens, Glasgow literally inscribes the inherent incompleteness of their whiteness onto their bodies. Although the blemishes that Glasgow's protagonists sport hardly merit the appellation monstrous *per se*, they act as constant reminders of the tenuousness of their projections of gentility, which threaten to unravel at any moment. One of the more blue-blooded inhabitants of Kingsborough is Judge Bassett, through whose name Glasgow invokes the breed of a dog, the Bassett Hound, to convey the idea of breeding, a device she would return to in *The Battle-Ground* two years later, swapping dogs for horses.[4] The implication leaves an impression that Judge Bassett is the pure-bred exponent of the uppermost echelon of Kingsborough society. But the picture Glasgow paints is of shades and contrasts that foreground the notion of gentility only to undermine it.

Hinting at a continuity of superior breeding, Glasgow describes the judge as "a boldly limned composite likeness of his race." Yet, the judge's immediate surroundings, "the white paint" that was "fast peeling away" from the shutters of his study, testify to his altered circumstances and contrast unfavorably with the "rows of bygone Bassetts" who "looked down on their departed possessions—stately and severe in the artificial severity of periwigs and starched ruffles." The judge may be "a Bassett of Virginia," but what remains of the composite legacy of his antecedents has dwindled to a name and a former slave, now servant, Caesar. The bewigged Bassetts are the other in the dyad of the judge's gentility. Glasgow uses their still presence as a medium, which allows her to emphasize the atotality and spectrality of the judge's whiteness. The judge is a man out of step with time and, whether he likes it or not, his antecedents. "His classic head" jars with his "ill-fitting boots," which, combined with "an absent-minded, habitual friendliness" and "rich, beneficent smile" that he is wont to bestow on his inferiors transforms him into a parody of a feudal lord.[5] This is a spectacle of grotesquery that mocks the idea of an inherited privilege. Glasgow turns the mismatched compositeness of the judge's appearance into a visible proof of his departure from the gentility represented by his ancestors and a mark of futile resistance to transition.

The ill-fitting clothes and the giving of airs, Glasgow suggests, characterize a man whose position has become ambivalent, and whose actions compound the effect of this ambivalence. The judge's acceptance of Nicholas Burr, a boy whose family is commonly regarded as white trash, into the school he runs for the progeny of local gentry may be read both as an instance of benevolent kindness and a disregard for class-consciousness. He regrets the impulsive offer, albeit briefly, which suffices, however, to suggest that he feels guilty of a breach of genteel decorum. Although he stands firm and resists the insistence and scheming of Mrs. Dudley Webb—a former belle whom circumstances transformed into a sour lady—to have Nicholas removed from the school, the victory he gains "would have felt pleasanter had it been defeat. It was as if he had taken some secret advantage of a woman—of a widow." This glimmer of progressiveness places the judge in direct opposition to Mrs. Webb, who evokes the power of aristocratic tradition that makes "those who go counter to her wishes feel they have violated the loyalties which ought to command their deepest reverence."6 In opposing Mrs. Dudley Webb—a more somber and inflexible reincarnation of Blair Cary of Page's *Red Rock*—the judge inadvertently rebels against the model of Southern gentility and the dictates of chivalry upon which it is founded. The monstrous vice of filial rebellion rears its ugly head, irrevocably tainting the judge's gentility.

Such rebellion is possible because of the physiologic nature of the ideal of Southern whiteness. Ernst Kantorowicz traces the concept of the physiologic principle to the doctrine of the "*duplex corpus Christi*" or "the 'Lord's Two Bodies,'" in which Christ's natural body and his mystic body merge. The same physiologic law governs the idea of kingship, the conflation of a king's natural and mortal body with the enduring and "immortal body politic"; when one ends, the other continues, uninterrupted and sempiternal, in the body of the successor.7 A similar physiologic principle operates in the bodies of the Southern gentleman and lady whose whiteness is contingent upon unifying the perfection of the antebellum and biblical ideals of gentility and temporariness of their physical bodies. But, in a context drastically changed, as is the postbellum Kingsborough, such physiologic law undermines the very fiction of continuity it fosters, for the bodies carry indelible traces of alteration. The changes are all the more transparent because of the doomed struggle to ensure that the ideal continues.

The judge's is not the only body that caries visible signs of change, and the comparison to the periwigged ancestors underscores the point in that they belie rather than augment his status. Mrs. Webb—formerly Miss Dudley—married a Northerner who "was a jovial young buck, who lived in his cards and cups and loathed a quarrel as he loved a fight."8 With the outbreak of the war and "caring little for either cause," Julius Webb fought for Virginia and died in her service. The gentleman's frivolity and flexibility of conscience are hardly compatible with striving and denial of self-gratification, but his death in combat for the cause he never embraced expunges such flaws and elevates him to martyrdom, at least in his wife's eyes. On her husband's death, Mrs. Dudley Webb donned her weeds and has worn them proudly ever since. The only adornment of this somber attire is "a button that had been cut from a gray coat," which she pins "at her throat." In the Webbs' marriage of regional opposites, Glasgow pits Webb's Northern ability to adapt to circumstances with the Southern inflexibility of his wife's principles; and the loser is the South. The perpetual mourning in which she immures herself and the single relic of the past accrue to monumentalize lack: they point to a site of origin and emphasize her departure from it. Gone is the plantation that once furnished the life of leisure. Forced to support herself by renting "her spare rooms to student borders," Mrs. Webb's gentility is as patched up as the sleeves of "her black gown," which "she sat up far into the night to darn."⁹ According to Friedrich Nietzsche, "all great things," before they acquire eternal greatness beyond reproach, "must first wander the earth as monstrous and fear-inducing caricatures." It is a sobering reflection on the constructedness of ideality, itself a process of damage limitation, a continuous removal of warts, until a desired idea of perfection emerges. The irony is that Mrs. Webb's sutured whiteness is the crowning glory of this sanctifying process and is thus revered precisely because it is imperfect. Like a black guardian of remembrance and conscience, she is a "fear-inducing" caricature of her former self, the Southern lady. Her struggle to maintain a semblance of gentility makes General Battle "feel positively unworthy to sit in her presence," for her manner evokes his "past indiscretions," and there are some ancestral embarrassments locked in his closet.¹⁰

Mrs. Webb with her projected saintliness is the forerunner to Miss Angela in *The Miller of Old Church*, who reduces others' gentility to second-rate imitation. Sally Bassett, Judge Bassett's daughter-in-law, observes of her husband that he, "like all men, believed Mrs. Webb to be a martyr until I convinced him that she martyred others." Both are like parasites that feed off of others to sustain their projections of gentility; but Miss Angela is the more insidious because she exudes the air of kindness, gentleness, and pliability—all ruses that Mrs. Dudley Webb has yet to learn to perform , and for which she lacks a natural proclivity. Even at the sight of Nicholas Burr running to school without a coat in winter, her compassion remains unstirred and her "placid eyes would not darken."¹¹ Such indifference to the plight of her social inferiors may be imputed to the harshness of her reduced circumstances, the awareness of which makes the need to dissociate herself and her son from the stigma of poverty all the more acute. But even this mitigating factor cannot counter the impression that Mrs. Webb's embodiment of the biblical ideal is far from flawless. When it comes to defending her son's gentility and tradition, however, she demonstrates a determined single-mindedness truly incompatible with the passivity of the female ideal. Her son, Dudley, she declares, "is a gentleman, and will not submit to association with his inferiors. His grandfather would not have done so before him."[12] That her son's gentility is nominal only and based on the charity of her more affluent acquaintances transforms it into a signifier with merely one signified—blood legacy—and reveals its monstrous incompleteness. And, in evoking the comparison with the grandfather, Glasgow suggests, kinship alone is insufficient. She includes Dudley in the circuit of inheritance only to show the unsustainability of his claim, which has outlived its expiry date.

If Dudley Webb's claim to whiteness has expired, General Battle's smacks of a suspicious newness. He is one of Dudley Webb's benefactors and, along with the judge, a hefty pillar of Kingsborough gentility, "hefty" being the operative word. Contrary to his name, the only battles the general fights these days are with his former slaves—now servants—and obesity. A widower, the general is "a stout gentleman with a red face" whose "expansive shirt front" sports a "collar" that "had wilted away." The general's equipage fares no better. It comprises a vehicle "of an old-fashioned make, bare of varnish, with rickety, mud-splashed wheels and rusty springs," which mirrors the shabby splendor of the general's apparel. He could almost pass for the judge's cousin, whose equally distressed appearance bears traces of bygone finery, if it were not for his stoutness, which bespeaks a more sinister flaw in his projection of gentility. The bombshell drops from the horse's mouth when the general admits that his "great-grandfather Battle raised himself."[13] This is Glasgow's most direct indictment yet of the notion of hereditary gentility, not just in terms of usurpation and flying under false colors, but also in that it questions the contexts that validate and endorse such claims. The general's "jovial-faced" and "wide-girthed" gentility become physical symbols of his inflated claim to hereditary whiteness.[14]

Nor is his sister free from the malady. Miss Chris, predictably a belle in her youth, "as she passed middle age the family failing seized upon her, and she grew huge and unwieldy, the disproportion of her enormous figure to her small feet giving her an awkward, waddling walk." Resembling a stereotypical mammy rather than a lady, Miss Chris's stoutness, like her brother's, reveals her plebeian origin and transforms her gentility into a monstrous usurpation: a case of verisimilitude gone bad. Even her devotion to the service of her brother and his family, though truly Marian in its self-effacement, is prone to excess. When, alarmed by the mysterious disappearance of chickens, Miss Chris intervenes in the kitchen, Aunt Verbeny unceremoniously rebukes her and declares that "hit don't becomst de quality ter fluster demse'ves over de gwines on uv er low-lifted fowl."[15] Glasgow turns Miss Chris's zeal to protect the livelihood of her brother into an outward transgression of the boundaries of gentility that exposes her parvenu roots. The excessiveness of her and her brother's bodies reflects the untenability of their claim to whiteness and transforms them, literally and metaphorically, into monstrous travesties.

The indelible stain of the parvenu shows no signs of waning and only strengthens its hold on the family. The judge's son, Bernard, is "a bright-faced, snub-nosed boy" whose "girlish mouth" bespeaks a lack of honor and cowardice. Unsurprisingly, he grows up to be the seducer of a local grocer's daughter, who, in trying to preserve "the whiteness of his own skin," spreads a rumor laying the blame at Nicholas Burr's door.[16] The seduction is merely a prelude to his later misconduct, which culminates in charges of felony and self-imposed exile from the state to avoid prosecution. If anything, Glasgow's treatment of Bernard—and, later, Eugenia and Nicholas Burr—problematizes her own stance on whiteness. She sees the dangers of a blind attachment to tradition that advocates obedience to outdated ideals, obedience that only broadens the chasm separating her protagonists from their antecedents. The one constant is blood, although this alone is insufficient. The Battles' gentility is new, a product of upward mobility. Bernard is born into a gentlemanly life of leisure, but he turns into a villain, as if his natural proclivities propelled him to crime. The difference lies in the means of departure from the ideal of whiteness, whether precipitated by the impossibility of replicating its wholeness in the ordinary or a deliberate rejection of its precepts. Glasgow dramatizes the question by having Bernard take the latter course. If Bernard turns into a villain, is it because his predecessors were literally villains, tilling the land? If so, his misdeeds are an amplification of hereditary flaws, tarnishing by association his progenitors whose only crime was deception.

Glasgow's treatment of the Battles and their gentility weighs the merits of blood legacy against social advancement to probe whether the two are inseparable and interrelated. Does the wrong kind of blood, the blood that is common, preclude social mobility? The Battles' gentility, she suggests, in a monster-like fashion, undergoes mutation in each generation, so much so that Eugenia, the general's daughter, fears "getting fat" like her "forefathers." Glasgow's choice of the name for her heroine is telling: it alludes to eugenics and notions of a pure species, and denotes noble descent. In Eugenia's case, it is a misnomer because she literally embodies a divergence from the model of Southern femininity. "A plain, dark, little girl, with an unearthly pallor of complexion," she hardly presents a specimen of vaunted Anglo-Saxon beauty.[17] Her manners also lack polish. Uncle Ish, a family servant, disapproves of Eugenia's class liberality that "'ud mek Ole Miss tu'n in her grave to hear tell 'bout her gwines on. De quality en de po' folks is all de same ter her." Just like her aunt, Miss Chris, Eugenia does not know her place. Eugenia's other "gwines on," to which her mother might take exception, include "talking like a darkey," a failed attempt to wear breeches, which she was "made to get out of" by Miss Chris, and an aversion to hemming "cup-towels."[18] Such open dislike of feminine pursuits is a confirmation of what Eugenia's unnaturally white skin betrays: that she is off white. Eugenia's complexion heralds her non-conformity and foretells the unattainability of the ideal of which even Mrs. Webb with her heightened class-consciousness falls short. When Eugenia reaches womanhood, no transformation from an ugly duckling into a swan happens. The skin remains too pale, the forehead grows "too high" and the chin "too long." The nose that "isn't all that a nose should be" complements the assemblage. This irregularity of features borders on the excessive, becoming symbolic of Eugenia's legacy of usurped gentility, a legacy that never coalesces into a harmonious whole. Eugenia embodies a contradiction, a conflict of impulses that combines "a rooted aversion to duty" with selfless charity and would, in her father's words, "damn herself to do a kindness."[19] Such manifest non-conformity, not only of appearance but also sensibility, stems from the acquired status of her gentility, which negates the possibility of repeating the imagined perfection that inspired Grandfather Battle to raise himself, and that Linda Brigham says cannot be learned.[20] Like her father and aunt's gentility, her incarnation of whiteness is a distortion made visible through the imperfection of her countenance.

And it is Eugenia's awareness of her own unconventionality that draws her to Nicholas Burr. Echoing Betty in *The Battle-Ground*, Eugenia recasts the masculine ideal and professes that she would "rather a man would be clever than handsome." Unlike beauty, intellect is something with which nature has endowed Nicholas generously. In the Bassetts' and the Webbs' incarnation of whiteness, supported by the belief of "fellow citizens" in the unshakable value of "hereditary virtues," apathy and complacency, which do not even spare General Battle and his son, have replaced striving and denial of self-gratification. In Nicholas, however, Glasgow constructs an inverted image of the dissipated pseudo-aristocracy of Kingsborough. Nicholas Burr, as his surname suggests, sticks out, spoils the smoothness of the surface; he is there to rock the boat. Nicholas possesses such qualities of whiteness as striving, self-denial, and an unwavering sense of honor, despite his lack of genteel lineage. The son of Amos Burr, "a disorderly and procrastinating" peanut farmer, Nicholas hails from humble stock.[21] His physiognomy carries indelible traces of his father's legacy, which creates visible discord with the noble traits of his character. Beneath Nicholas's "red head," "freckles," and "ugly little face" lies ambition, which, in response to the judge's assumption that he will become "a farmer like his father before him," prompts him to declare boldly that "there ain't nothin' in peanut-raisin'," and that he would "ruther be a judge." This filial rebellion of sorts marks Nicholas's first step on the path to whiteness, and with it comes an awareness of the inadequacy of his aspiration. It is not until Nicholas joins the judge's school, however, that he feels "ashamed of his ugliness, of his coarse clothes, of his briar-scratched legs, of his freckles, and of the unalterable color of his hair." For the first time, Nicholas becomes conscious of the irreconcilability of his heritage and aspiration that renders him "common," in Dudley Webb's words, and "uncommon" in the judge's estimation.[22] Glasgow has Nicholas, literally, embody class difference that, while emphasizing his singularity, marks him as a doubly monstrous mutation, displacing him and threatening the preordained wholeness of the genteel ideal. The whiteness of the Bassetts and the Webbs may be flawed insofar as they depart from the ideal of gentility, but it is supported by virtue of descent; the legacy of peanut farming condemns Nicholas's aspiration to gentility as a monstrous excess. This is precisely why the general, even once Nicholas has become a successful lawyer, insists on discussing nothing but crops with him: "the boy's not a lawyer—only gentlemen belong to the bar, but there's nobody too high or too low to be a farmer."[23] Coming from a man whose great grandfather chose to elevate himself, it is a curious defense of the *status quo* which shows the hysteric need to guard the boundaries of gentility against intruders.

Boundaries, cultural and social, matter and decide one's place in the pecking order. Nicholas learns this early from his stepmother, Marthy Burr, who sententiously declares of handsome men: "they're pretty enough to look at when you're feelin' first-rate, but when you git the neuralgy they sort of turns yo' stomach."[24] Marthy suffers from chronic neuralgia, which Glasgow, still bent on testing the limitations of eugenics, casts as symptomatic of the flaw of her class. So constricted is Marthy's view that she has come to consider anything unafflicted in body or spirit a distortion. She would not look out of place in Erskine Caldwell's dystopian or realistic, depending on the standpoint, *Tobacco Road* where distortion is the norm. Glasgow's is by far the mellower view of distortion in terms of its manifestation, although it is as inflexible in the conviction of its ubiquity. Distortion is unavoidable as long as the physiologic principle supports ideality, but an awareness of distortion comes only when a subject reorients himself in new circumstances.

Glasgow casts Nicholas as the perfect example of such cultural reorientation that produces a shift in perception. The more time he spends in the judge's school, the more jaundiced his view of his family becomes: his stepmother seems "dried and brown like a hickory nut," looking at his half-sister, Sairy Jane, leaves him wondering "why she didn't have any eyelashes," and his younger brother, Jubal, "was all gums." Nicholas's alienation from his family grows commensurately with his ambition of betterment, as does his feeling of misplacement. When Eugenia and he are courting, Nicholas confides in her, not without a tinge of bitterness, that to the Battles he is "good enough in the fields, at the plough, or in the barnyard," but not as a prospective son-in-law. The educated Nicholas is conscious of his transgression, of the composite nature of his hereditarily blighted subjectivity that is indelibly etched in his "square-jawed, large-featured face," the "uncompromising ugliness" that is "the ugliness of individuality." He belongs nowhere. His "brains and education" support his claim to whiteness and, in Tom Bassett's words, set him apart from "those blasted people of his."[25] In this nod to Chesnutt's alternative view of whiteness, obtained through education and personal achievement, Glasgow concedes that elevation is possible. Yet, in Kingsborough, where conformity to the old gods is essential, the coarse assemblage that is Nicholas's face will always be a marker of not just his individuality but also non-conformity. Once he breaks out of his social sphere, the visibility of his appearance intensifies until it becomes a stigma of monstrous transgression, an externalization of the specter of the white trash monster who, though tamed, is ever ready to emerge.

Glasgow sketches the ambivalence of Nicholas's position with the intuitive knowledge of somebody who still harbors sentiment for the old ideal of gentility, but has no patience with the narrowness and untenability of its vision. She chooses Eugenia, whose grip on gentility is tenuous at best, as her medium to criticize the in-betweenness in which subjects aspiring to whiteness remain suspended. The undecidability of Nicholas's position manifests to Eugenia with staggering clarity when she meets Nicholas's father. Burr senior attempts to engage her on a matter of business and, "for the first time," she realizes "the full horror of the fact" that this "hairy, ominous," and "uncouth" man "was father to the man she loved." What precipitates the realization is a shift of context. Nicholas's association with the judge has shaped her conception of him, which allowed her to think of "his poverty and his people only in the heroic measures that related to his emancipation from them." This belated discovery of the vulgar in Nicholas's legacy demonstrates what Nietzsche calls the "will to truth-reversal, to untruth at any price," and which is a skill that the protagonists of Glasgow's *Virginia* hone to perfection.[26] In order to dissociate herself from the taint of Nicholas's family, Eugenia must recast Nicholas in unheroic terms that require that she concentrate on the surface, in which she sees reflected the inferiority of Nicholas's heritage. She can no longer look beneath the facade of ugliness because that would reveal Nicholas's nobility of spirit which, in turn, would violate the preordained integrity of hereditary gentility to which she aspires. In this ironic act of doubling, the distorted surface of Nicholas's face mirrors Eugenia's maimed claim to gentility. Her determination to preserve untruth leads Eugenia to acknowledge that Nicholas's ambition and striving will never emancipate him from the shadow of Amos Burr and are insufficient to support his claim to gentility, whether it be endorsed by the judge or not.

Context makes and unmakes the fiction of Southern whiteness, and Glasgow has Eugenia confirm it. Still shaken by the vision of Amos Burr, Eugenia admits that "had she, in the beginning, seen him side by side with his father, she could not have loved him."[27] Context is not a modern-day invention, as some critics would have it. Writing in 1643, Sir Thomas Browne pronounced the mob "the multitude, the numerous piece of monstrosity, which taken asunder seeme men, and the reasonable creatures of God; but confused together, make but one great beast, & a monstrosity more prodigious than Hydra." A change of context alters Eugenia's conception of Nicholas and allows Glasgow to reveal this plasticity of the monstrous; "taken asunder" from his father, Nicholas is a respectable man, but combined with his father he forms an inextricable part of the hideous multitude. Eugenia's rewrite of Nicholas's story traverses swiftly the distance between the nobility of spirit to the embodiment of an innate monstrosity. The process that began with the encounter with Amos Burr culminates in her ready acceptance of her brother's slander about Nicholas's dalliance with Bessie Pollard, for which Nicholas cannot forgive her, and they part ways. Recollecting his "convulsed features, the furrow" that, in a Frankensteinian fashion, "cleft the forehead like a seam," Eugenia glimpses in Nicholas "the man in whom, for its brief instant, evil was triumphant"—the evil of lower-class aspiration.[28] The implication is clear: Nicholas's ugliness, if confined to his social sphere, would be neither evil nor monstrous; however, because of the undecidability of his position, Eugenia, in a twist reminiscent of Jekyll and Hyde, imagines she can glimpse the hideousness of his plebeianism in his features.

This revelation leads to a Dorian Gray kind of reflection on the complexity of Nicholas's subjectivity and heritage that bear within themselves "strange legacies of thought and passion," tainting the flesh "with the monstrous maladies of the dead," and the still living. The epiphany, however, proves a double-edged sword, for it leads to the realization of the permeability of heritage and initiates a scrutiny of her own family. Looking at her relations, Eugenia suspects that beneath Miss Chris's candid "countenance," Bernard's "overwrought youthfulness," and "the apoplectic credulity of the general's" lay "latent possibilities—obscure tendencies, which were revealed to her now with microscopic exaggeration."[29] They may not appear as anomalous as Nicholas, but the very existence of such hidden capabilities renders them incomplete, hinting at something sinister lurking beneath. The fact that these "obscure tendencies" do not mark them as evil reaffirms the presence of a value system, according to which monstrosity and whiteness are graded. This is why, Nicholas reflects, Eugenia "would not have turned from the brother of her blood had he been damned in Holy Writ," as she did from him. This is a tempered version of social determinism, in which Glasgow presents individual struggles against the two indomitable forces she sees as shaping subjectivity in the South: heredity and environment. Both are responsible for Eugenia's betrayal and Nicholas's growing ambition, prompting him "to throw himself and his future into the service of his State" and culminating in his elevation to the governor of Virginia.[30] Unlike Eugenia, who surrenders to the dictates of heredity and marries within her social sphere, Nicholas throws off the shackles of social determinism, securing his transgressive distinctiveness. Success is possible, Glasgow concedes, but never a complete victory.

Nicholas's ambition and pursuit of gentility become obsessions that transform him into a lone messiah-like figure and prevent the formation of lasting bonds. He deems marriage "nonsense" for which he has "no time," and only belatedly realizes that "he wanted to be loved, if by a dog." As a self-made man who rose above the peanut-growing legacy of his forefathers, Nicholas has always been, and will remain, "an alien among his kind."[31] His is the fiction of partial success and ultimate failure. Having worked tirelessly to elevate himself, Nicholas dies from a shot fired by an exponent of the monstrous mass when trying to prevent a lynching in Kingsborough. Glasgow creates this melodramatic denouement to symbolize Nicholas's return to his former kind and define the nature of his failure: he fails because there is no room in Kingsborough for progressive thought among the plebeians or the elites. Sally Bassett, Tom Bassett's wife and Nicholas's fellow pupil in the judge's school, accepts his death all too readily and concludes that "it is perhaps better that he died just now. He would have tried to lift us too high, and we should have fallen back."[32] Sally's stoic and unsentimental response to Nicholas's death translates into Glasgow's rejection of the notion of hereditary gentility of the likes of the Bassetts, the Webbs, and the Battles, pitting the superior morality of the son of a peanut farmer against the inherited wisdom of treating this very superiority as a genteel privilege. Glasgow's rejection is all the more powerful because it is understated and leaves unspoken the name of the actual culprit. The suggestion is there, for those prepared to read between the lines; it is the stifling tradition of Southern whiteness that creates a hypocritical narrative that breeds mediocrity and deformity because they happen to be accompanied by a host of more or less blue-blooded antecedents. In this narrative, there is simply no room for Nicholas, and his death, however unexpected, produces an anti-climax that is in keeping with the wider fable of impossible gentility; it leads nowhere.

This lack of direction did not register on the critical radar. Critics compared *The Voice of the People* with Page's *Red Rock* and Mary Johnston's *To Have and To Hold*, both of which continued to extoll the virtues of genteel pedigree. Nicholas's plight of the "poor white" man's fight against the establishment did not go unnoticed insofar as its exploitative potential went, particularly for "a writer possessed of the philosophical bent that is an especial characteristic of Miss Glasgow."[33] Glasgow garnered praise for "humor and pathos," sketching "vivid vignettes of Southern character" and "excellent portrayal of social and political life in the South since the War." Certain flaws were noted, such as the novel's "lack of unity and dramatic sequence." But such voices were rare and drowned in the general acclaim of the novel as Glasgow's "masterpiece" that is "bound to live." In *The Voice of the People*, enthused a critic writing for the *San Francisco Call*, Glasgow "has given us a good, wholesome novel with a healthy, normal, moral tone, and yet fully as interesting as it is meritorious."[34] It is doubtful that Glasgow would have endorsed such unequivocal praise of her novel as moral, healthy, and normal, which is not to say that she would have rather had her work pronounced as immoral, toxic, or abnormal. What she shows in *The Voice of the People*, in the characterization of Nicholas Burr, Eugenia, and the wider Kingsborough elite, is that essentialist labels never reflect the complexity of the *status quo* and judgments are not only a matter of positionality but also of cultural and social conditioning, more commonly known as tradition and values. And these, as often as not, may run counter to the commonly accepted denominators of morality, creating a dissonance between what is and how it is perceived.

Glasgow further probes this dissonance between ideality and actuality in her fifth novel of the Commonwealth series, *Virginia*, selecting as her study subject the particularly Southern unhealthy attachment to tradition. Thirteen years intervened between the publication of *The Voice of the People* and *Virginia* and yet the inherent paradox of ideal worship, which maims the aspiring subject, showed no signs of waning. Published in 1913, *Virginia* occupies a category of its own, on a borderline between a paean and an indictment.[35] Glasgow's chief preoccupation is the scrutiny of the female ideal of Southern whiteness that consists in the emulation of the Marian paradigm. The result is an introspective narrative of the failure of Virginia, the titular heroine, not because she fails to live up to the ideal but because the perfection she embodies alienates her from those around her, in particular her husband, Oliver Treadwell, and later her two daughters.

In writing *Virginia*, Glasgow's aim was to "tell the life story of a woman in the transitional period," a woman who becomes a living proof of the relatively short shelf life of the supposedly timeless ideals. Critics responded favorably to the novel, and the plight of Virginia. Glasgow was praised for making "a most important addition to the growing list of literature, establishing the position of women in modern life." The resonance of the story, the critic raved, partook of a universality that crossed regional and state borders. If by universality he meant the burden the genteel tradition lays on women as its propagators, he would have encountered opposition from Glasgow. Although she conceded that "the gentlewoman" was a relatively ubiquitous creature, existing "more or less precariously, in all parts of the world," the Southern gentlewoman was a breed apart. Into her composition went "the native climate and soil of the South" with "its particular institutions to furnish for her species an appropriate background of fauna and flora." Given the composite nature of the ideal of the Southern lady, the habitat was ever prone to shrinking and, in the Dinwiddie of *Virginia*, it all but ceased to exist.

Because of Glasgow's readiness to admit the shrinkage, to paint a sordid picture of lives fed on and lived in the conception of ideality, the novel was hailed as her "best literary effort" and "an exquisitely told tale." The reviewer writing for the *Indianapolis News* concluded that the story was "dramatic because it was true to life" and full to the brim with "unerring faithfulness." If the novel had a weakness, he reluctantly conceded, it lay in "the superfluity of character description," which contributed to the overall impression of anti-climax.[36] The critic reviewing the novel for the *San Francisco Call* struck a similar chord. "Opinions may vary regarding the artistic quality" of *Virginia*, he wrote, but "there can be only one opinion regarding its breadth, its sincerity and its interest." He thought "the concrete example of a woman's sacrifice" unconvincing but necessary to the presentation of "certain abstract problems of womanhood in a manner that commands respectful attention." The flaws were so minor that they did not prevent him from including *Virginia* "among the more significant novels of the day." His criticism is not without merit, and what he finds unconvincing is precisely Virginia's saintliness that consists in self-effacement in the service of others. Yet, such exaggeration of Virginia's virtues is necessary to showcase the futility of living up to ideals of perfection. The tragedy of Virginia, as one critic observed, was the narrowness of her vision and stubborn, bordering on fanatical, insistence on following the path the genteel tradition had set for her. Virginia's "mistaken effacement," he concluded, caused her husband's "moral fiber" to break. Inadvertently, in elevating herself, she *de*-idealizes her husband and thus becomes superfluous to the construction she herself has created. As an ideal of female whiteness, Virginia occupies an unstable and untenable position, both a victim and a culprit. It was in the mold of a victim, however, that one critic cast her, suggesting that the novel should be titled "Oliver, the Brute."[37]

But should it really? Oliver, although he eventually leaves Virginia for an actress, hardly deserves the appellation. He respects Virginia and remains devoted to her but, as Glasgow puts it, becomes "a trifle weary of the dream-images" he has constructed.[38] The image that he has constructed possesses all the angelic goodness of the Marian ideal unfailing in devotion, but it also never fails in its duty to be an ornament, pleasing to the eye and firmly fixed on the pedestal of genteel femininity that tradition has fashioned out of inflexible prescriptions. It is a difference between projecting and being and, in Virginia, Glasgow creates the perfect foil to Miss Angela in *The Miller of Old Church*. Oliver's tragedy lies in his inability to accept Virginia, warts and all, which transforms his initial exasperation into pity and eventually resentment. From the vaunted embodiment of perfection, she becomes the woman scorned and, even then, incapable of fury. In Virginia's case, perfection is a double-edged sword; it is that which is sought but never realized because, at the moment of attainment, it turns on the seeker, revealing him as monstrous and lacking.[39]

For Glasgow, the perfection of gentility is never a *fait accompli*, but a continuous process, forever deferring fulfilment, leaving her protagonists on the cusp of being perfect but never perfect. Virginia's failure is the inability to live up to expectations; Oliver's is to have expectations. But neither of them, Glasgow suggests, is entirely to blame. "Every person in Dinwiddie," she says, "was linked in some obscure fashion" to Virginia's "tragedy, and with the larger tyranny of tradition." It is the kind of tyranny of unspoken rules and codes of behavior that, dictated by one's origin, determine his place in the milieu of Dinwiddie. Of Dinwiddie, Glasgow observes, that it is a place, like the South, suspicious of alteration and reluctant to change; a place where "the memorial wreaths on the battlefields" vie for supremacy with "the prophetic smoke of factories." It is a place of narrowed horizons that do not admit of anything beyond "an heroic attitude or a concrete image." The concerns of Diniwiddians are equally constrictive and follow the simple, if not infallible, doctrine that what lies beyond the borders of Virginia is "either Yankee or foreign, and therefore to be pitied or condemned according to the Evangelical or Calvinistic convictions of the observer."[40] And so, Dinwiddie and its inhabitants cling to what they know, if no longer have.

There are no plantations in sight, yet the echoes of the old days have not entirely died down. To highlight the pitiable fidelity of the Diniwiddians to an imagined past and contrast it to the present, Glasgow drops passing hints as to the pedigree of individual characters. The family of Virginia's father, the rector Gabriel Pendleton, once epitomized Southern whiteness, belonging to the cherished planter class. When the rector visits Aunt Mehitable at her summons, the narrator comments that his voice carried "the subtle recognition of all that she had meant to his family in the past, of all that his family had meant to her." There is a note of resignation and surrender in the rector's thoughts that transforms him into a living vestige of Southern whiteness, at least its material incarnation, which Aunt Mehitable symbolizes. A similar aura of resignation surrounds his wife, Mrs. Lucy Pendleton, who "was born a great lady" and "remained one when the props and the background of a great lady had crumpled around her." Any attempts at elevation belong to the past and are greedily treasured. Mrs. Treadwell, the bedraggled wife of Cyrus Treadwell, the richest industrialist in town, clings with desperation to the "secret consciousness that she was better born" than her husband.[41] It is the one consolation she may afford without selling the family silver that proves the old ideal of the superiority of genteel birth is still alive and kicking.

If Dinwiddie is out of step with progress, Glasgow implies, its inhabitants are equally out of step with actuality. Ideals, born out of historic consciousness, still reign supreme in Dinwiddie. The only use of time Dinwiddie makes, Oliver observes, is "to kill it." And there is certainly no room in this cultivated passivity for change or acceleration. The "middle-aged ladies" whom Virginia and her mother pass on the way to the market, "wearing crape veils and holding small black silk bags" are in perpetual mourning for the Lost Cause.[42] Some years later, Virginia will also embark on a train bound for New York carrying her own black silk bag, victim to the same veneration of tradition. These ladies clad in black, these living relics of the past, are also harbingers of a doomed present and a future that cannot live up to that very past, and those who dwell in it are reduced to shadows of a better time. Armed with an unshakable belief in the righteousness of their convictions, they haunt the streets of Dinwiddie as if in defiance of its smoking chimneys. Once genteel by birth, now only by reminiscence, they are cultivators of the art of misconception, of reimagining the world to fit a mold of a prescriptive and proscriptive worldview.

Glasgow sees this narrow and stagnant worldview as responsible for the fiction of verisimilitude that the townspeople spin for themselves. Just as in Kingsborough, its influence is destructive and succeeds only insofar as it produces difference. Derrida calls *différance* a movement that may be both active and passive and whose essence consists in the deferral of meaning, "delegation," and temporary suspense. Where there is signification, there is also *différance;* and the dictum applies to the construction of subjectivity and objectivity alike, both of which belong to the broader networks of meaning. In Diniwiddie, as in Kingsborough, the network of meaning narrows to the antebellum past, with its inflections of gentility dictating and shaping the present. The effect is *différance* and, Glasgow implies, it is as damning as it is constant. It creeps into every sphere of existence, undermining the verisimilitude of the fiction of whiteness to which the Dinwiddians cling. The devil is in the detail, and Glasgow's narrator spares none. Mrs. Peachy, once a lady and now the manager of a boarding house, wears "the look of unnatural pleasantness which becomes fixed on the features of persons who spend their lives making the best of things."[43] Negation as a means of reaffirmation that reveals that things are not as they once were. Hinting at the idea of a better past, Glasgow casts the present and Mrs. Peachy in opposition that implies irreducible *différance.*

Glasgow effects this *différance* through Mrs. Peachy without naming its quiddity, yet the overall impression is that it permeates Dinwiddie, so much so that it attains the status as an independent tradition. Like Mrs. Peachy and her mother, Virginia will continue the tradition of doing her best. And the schooling she obtains at Miss Priscilla Batte's "Academy for Young Ladies" lays a solid, if not sound, foundation for the passive turpitude of emulation that becomes Virginia's lot. That lot, Glasgow suggests, is not a matter of choice; it is part of submitting to the doctrine of genteel womanhood. It is the kind of education imparted by countless Miss Priscilla Battes across the region to "every well-born and well-bred Southern woman" with the unspoken intention of paralyzing "her reasoning faculties so completely that all danger of 'mental unsettling' or even movement was eliminated from her future," and "to solidify the forces of mind into the inherited mold of fixed beliefs." Glasgow calls Virginia "the logical result of an inordinate sense of duty, the crowning achievement of the code of beautiful behavior and of the Episcopal Church."[44] Virginia is a star pupil at Miss Batte's academy, and the education, Glasgow suggests, is responsible for the kind of white-washing that, by closing the mind to difference of context, results in *différance* in practice. The "code of beautiful behavior," the yardstick against which female whiteness is measured, practiced by Mrs. Ambler of *The Battle-Ground* and envied by her daughter Betty, only exacerbates the disjunction between the ideal and reality. The rhetoric is the more invidious, Glasgow implies, because it is so ubiquitous as to render it a force of nature against which Virginia and her kind are powerless. On their way from the market, Virginia and her mother witness a scene of hustle and bustle of urban life (as urban as Dinwiddie with its twenty-one thousand inhabitants can offer). In the center stands "an overladen mule with a sore shoulder," yet neither Virginia nor her mother notices the suffering animal. Their blindness is not the result of an insensibility to suffering, but the consequence of an entrenched moral incapability "of looking an unpleasant fact in the face if there was an honorable manner of avoiding it." A few years later, James Branch Cabell would give this particularly Southern tendency to gaze-averting the gloss of a coping mechanism. Life can be very pleasant, asserts Robert Etheridge Townsend in *The Cords of Vanity*, "if you keep away from ugly things and fussy people." This ability to transform sight perception to fit a desired mold is also the special brand of the "Pendleton idealism" that, in Virginia and her mother, has finally achieved "absolute triumph over actuality."[45] Theirs is the fiction of verisimilitude gone bad.

Glasgow's detailed sketch of Dinwiddie—its sensibility and inertia—is essential to understanding the plight of Virginia. The world she inhabits is one of cross purposes marked by a refusal to acknowledge actuality in the mistaken belief that it will keep ideals alive. In the absence of plantations and their head honchos, the gentlemen planters, this world pivots on the cult of Southern genteel femininity. As so much in Dinwiddie, her stature has shrunk in size that corresponds with the reduced circumstances of the former elite. With the shrinkage came the shift of emphasis on the saintliness of the Marian ideal, with an inexhaustible supply of patience and an astonishing proclivity for self-effacement. Her domain has also diminished to that of "the perfect wife as man had invented her, and as he still believed that he cherished her."[46] This is the ideal that Virginia inherits from her mother and which she feels duty-bound to replicate. So strong is its influence that even long after her parents departed Dinwiddie for the paradise of the Scriptures, Virginia is unable to stray from the path they had plotted for her out of the remnants of tradition. Glasgow's Virginia, more so than any other of her protagonists, is a helpless victim because she is incapable of rebellion against tradition. Her very name carries connotations of saintliness and purity and, with a rector for a father and a martyr to tradition for a mother, there is no escape from the inflexibility of genteel beliefs and their crippling effect on her subjectivity which eventually lead to loss of self.

Virginia's mother could be an object lesson to her, Glasgow suggests, if it were not for the "Pendleton idealism" that prevents her from seeing what is. Mrs. Pendleton who, like her voice "was meant to distract attention rather than impart information," mastered the art of martyrdom out of necessity and turned it into a veritable genteel virtue. Since the end of the war, she has struggled relentlessly to keep "an open house on starvation fare," stealing fitful hours of sleep at night for fear of not rising in time to "scrub the floors and furniture" before her neighbors stirred. This is her one terror and failing, of which her husband remains oblivious, and which she calls "false pride;" the fear of being seen as she is, "on her knees in her old black calico dress before she had gone upstairs again, washed her hands with cornmeal, powdered her face with pink flannel starchback, and descended in her gown of black cashmere or lawn, with a net scarf tied daintily around her thin throat, and a pair of exquisitely darned lace ruffles hiding her wrists." It is a desperate and pitiful attempt at subterfuge bent on keeping up appearances, an extreme and less comical version of Hyacinth Bucket, desperate to impress if not for her own sake then for that of her husband and daughter with whom she "could not bear to associate the virtue of humility."[47] The subterfuge is in vain because Virginia's selflessness and humility exceed her mother's and manifest in a disregard for keeping up appearances, which becomes one of the causes of Oliver's resentment.

Keeping up appearances with a convenient resignation is the driving force behind the Pendletons' familial idyll. The Pendletons' matrimonial relations rely on misapprehension for the mutual felicity of all parties involved. Glasgow's subtle but acute sense of irony comes into full force in renditions of the Pendletons' marital bliss. And so, the rector loves "his wife as much as a man can love a wife who has sacrificed herself to him wisely and unwisely for nearly thirty years"—a lukewarm affection that carries traces of willful misconception. His wife's sacrifices, big and small, do not go unnoticed, yet the rector has grown so accustomed to seeing his wife "suffer with a smile that he had drifted at last into the belief that it was the only activity she really enjoyed." A remarkable example of convenient reasoning that takes its cue from the Marian ideal that demands a woman put her husband's needs above her own. Were he aware of his wife's "false pride," he might perhaps reconsider the wisdom of allowing her "the privilege of working herself to death for his sake when the opportunity offered." Such musings reveal, Glasgow suggests, the pathology of pedestalization that solidifies the disjunction between ideality and actuality, leaving difference in its wake. And Mrs. Pendlenton is as culpable in cultivating misconception as her husband. In the early days of their marriage Mrs. Pendleton convinced herself that whenever her husband was alone, his "thoughts naturally deflected into spiritual paths." Despite his best efforts to live up to her "exalted idea of his character," he finds the feat outstrips his ability. Any attempt to "disabuse his wife's imagination of the mistaken belief in his divinity" meets with abject failure, for Mrs. Pendleton is possessed of a remarkable quality, not unlike the rector, that enables her to "believe in an illusion all the more intensely because it had vanished." The belief is so intense and unshakable that it leads to a triumph "not only over circumstances, but over truth itself."[48] Misconception breeds misconception, until it turns the Pendleton household into a microcosm of well-intentioned deception. It is an endless cycle of substitution of what is imagined for what is that has its roots in the very conception of the ideals of Southern gentility. Glasgow uses the little deceptions, so innocuous on the surface, to amplify the travesty of irremediable determination to replicate ideals in actuality. It is a tragic malady as virulent in Dinwiddie as it is in Kingsborough, and its symptom is difference, against which remedy is powerless. Faced with the rigidity of the ideal, even the selfless and perpetually suffering Mrs. Pendleton does not escape unscathed. Her selflessness and sacrifice produce an overflow that turns virtue into a flaw and leads Mrs. Peachy to diagnose her earthly failing as being "too unselfish."[49] The fact that the flaw cannot compete with the seven deadly sins when it comes to grievousness only serves to highlight the tragi-comedy of Mrs. Pendleton's predicament, which, in surpassing the Marian paradigm of femininity, makes her its inchoate embodiment.

An ideal overdone is as bad as an ideal underdone. In an eerie echo of her mother, Virginia will face the same criticism—of being "too unselfish." Susan, her lifelong friend and a woman as emancipated as Dinwiddie would allow a woman to be, passes the judgment. Glasgow casts Susan as foil to Virginia's old-fashioned femininity early on in the novel. There is an unmistakable whiff of antiquity about Virginia, who first enters the scene wearing a "Jacqueminot rose" in her hair, parted "after an earlier fashion" before Glasgow clinches it with an unequivocal pronouncement that she "embodied the feminine ideal of the ages." No such sentimentality shrouds Susan, whom Glasgow simply describes as "the stronger of the two" who "dominated the other." But if she dominated the other, it is because, unlike Virginia, Glasgow cast her in a stronger mold, capable of freeing herself from the shackles of the feminine ideal of being "morally passive."[50] She is no shrinking violet, but a girl with the un-Marian ambition of going to college. Her industrialist father, who delights in frugality as an ascetic would in self-deprivation, thwarts this dream. And it is the last time Susan asks for permission. When she decides to marry John Henry, Virginia's cousin, she simply announces it to her father. The irony is, of course, that she earns her father's respect only when she asserts her authority and discards the passivity enshrined in the feminine ideal; only then does he realize that "there might be something better even for a woman than beauty." It is a watershed moment for Cyrus, a moment in which he glimpses a reflection of himself in his daughter. That he is able to cherish Susan's departure from the ideal of Southern genteel femininity suggests that here is a man capable of looking at ideals pragmatically without becoming enslaved to them, perhaps because of the "Scotch-Irish blood" that runs "a little muddy in his veins."[51] Cyrus's irreverence for the virtues of genteel femininity, the mixture of pity and condemnation with which he treats his own wife, puts his own gentility into question, although it spares him a life of pretense. Because neither Cyrus nor Susan suffers from the crippling inability to distinguish between ideality and reality, they avoid laboring under misapprehension. Theirs is the awareness of not being ideal that spares them the dubious glory of verisimilitude falling short of expectation.

Expectation is what defines Virginia and what lies at the heart of her failure as a genteel woman. Virginia's case is the more pitiful, for, Glasgow suggests, nothing in her life has prepared her for the opacity of expectation. From the "black silk gown" that has graced the trousseau of every Dinwiddian bride since the end of the Civil War, to her mother's sanctifying and uplifting speeches on wifely duty, Virginia is a genteel wife made to measure. Mrs. Pendleton's motherly wisdom requires her to instruct her daughter in wifely duties, the first of which is unswerving obedience to her husband to the point of self-effacement. It is a woman's role to "sacrifice herself" and to do so cheerfully because her "strength lies in her gentleness."[52] If self-immolation were required, Virginia would step in the flames as readily as she enters into matrimony. In her visions of connubial felicity, she does not stray from the path chosen for her by her mother and father. She sees herself in the bliss of absolute surrender of her will to his, the ghostly adjunct to the life force that is Oliver, her future husband. She conjures pictures of herself in "the immemorial attitude of woman," always waiting but "waiting happily" and the "thrilling expectancy" of the wait.[53] The crowning glory of her effort is the ultimate fulfilment of a woman's duty: motherhood.

Virginia's musings evoke countless Madonnas of the Renaissance masters with a beatific smile illumining their features and whose passivity and resignation speak of a certain foreknowledge and possibilities undisclosed to the viewer. Glasgow makes this connection with the sanctified ideal explicit when she describes Virginia's face possessing the look of "Madonna-like possibilities." By this time, Virginia, having had four children and buried one, has become familiar with sacrifice and suffering and ceased to "consider whether or not her clothes were becoming." In this pattern she will continue, scrimping and saving, having her gowns remade for her daughters, until her children grow up and Oliver finds fame as a playwright. Even as her children fly the nest, she is still waiting happily for Oliver to return from New York, where he oversees rehearsals of his plays, without any perceptible dent in her fortitude. She is incapable of outgrowing the saintly mold of duty that her parents fashioned for her. When Susan suggests she may try charity work, she timidly observes that not only has she "no executive ability," but also her father "used to have such a horror of women who were always running about to meetings." Just like her mother before her, Virginia clings with unyielding fidelity to ideals, although those who imparted them had long perished. Verisimilitude finally becomes reality when Virginia literally becomes indistinguishable from her mother, causing Miss Batte to exclaim upon seeing her that "Lucy Pendleton had returned to life."[54] The point is forceful: in this ghostly transference, Virginia becomes the literal embodiment of a dead ideal. This realization dawns on Virginia when Oliver deserts her for an actress he met in New York and forces her to admit that she "had outlived her usefulness."[55] The tragedy of Virginia lies in the constricting conformity to an imagined ideal of female whiteness. If she outlived her "usefulness," so did her mother before her. Much like her mother, she allowed herself to live a life of fiction based on the infallibility of a woman's duty. She cuts a pathetic figure, but not a blameless one, because, in following the path of extreme sanctity, she depedestalizes herself and desanctifies Oliver.

Oliver, like Virginia, falls victim to what Glasgow sees as an insidious power of the ideal of whiteness that lies in its overdetermination and opacity. He, like Virginia, has a fixed notion of the ideal of genteel femininity, but he is also the only man in Dinwiddie who questions the Marian ideal based on cheerful resignation and a still more cheerful desire to serve others. When he meets Virginia at the market, he wonders why women do not revolt against a life of domestic drudgery. Virginia's answer is exactly what is to be expected from a girl trained in womanly duty from infancy: she suspects they like it. Oliver's answer, however, betrays a discernment that goes to the heart of ideal cultivation: "Do they really like it? or have they been throwing dust in our eyes through the centuries." The remark marks Oliver as a man out of step with Dinwiddie. If Virginia is the embodiment of feminine gentility, Oliver is the embodiment of the conflict between ideality and actuality. Glasgow stresses that conflict by making Oliver a blood relation to both Cyrus Treadwell and Miss Priscilla Batte, who represent the progress of the industrializing South and the waning glory of the old order. Oliver does not belong to either of these worlds. An apostate when it comes to growing the Southern staple that is tobacco, he harbors equal disdain for the materialism that his uncle Cyrus represents. His only ambition is to become a dramatist, and to achieve this dream he will gladly struggle and suffer because "art can only grow out of sacrifice."[56] Oliver's idealism, because an idealist he is, Glasgow implies, consists in artistic self-fulfillment, not mere expression. Nor is he short of ideas. Oliver's trouble is that the public "don't want life on stage; they want a kind of theatrical wedding-cake," and to producing such secondary fare he will never degrade himself. Oliver inhabits a curious paradox, which allows him to reject verisimilitude in art but embrace it in life. He may scorn the backwardness of Dinwiddie with its ideal-worship, but when it comes to genteel femininity, he defines it as if it were a lesson learned by rote and proves himself as imaginative as the rector. The image is vivid only insofar as it divivifies its object. He envisions the ideal woman as "always soft, exquisite, tender, womanly to the innermost fiber of her being, and perfect in unselfishness." She should be passive to the point of incapacitation "sitting forever aloof and colorless, waiting eternally, patient, beautiful and unwearied." In this, Oliver's and Virginia's minds work in marvelous unanimity; he wants to marry a conjuration and she wants to fit the conjured image. The images only differ in one point. Like the reverend in *The Miller of Old Church*, Oliver sees the ideal woman as "an incentive," a requirement at variance with passivity and self-effacement, which rely on the erasure of individual incentive, even when incentive means nothing more than looking pretty.[57] Once again, Glasgow evokes the image of Marian perfection only to emphasize its clash with the ordinary.

Oliver, like Virginia, labors under a misconception. Such misconception is unavoidable, not only because actuality cannot live up to ideality, but because of the overdetermination of the female ideal of Southern whiteness.

Overdetermination increases the possibility of interpretability, mutation, and difference. Glasgow calls it Oliver's being betrayed by the ideal that begins his growing resentment of Virginia and the broader tradition that created her. The rebellion starts with a reimagination born out of the compositeness of the ideal of Southern whiteness, when Oliver fetches that other venerated relic of the Old South out of the garret of memory, the Southern belle. Virginia fails as an incentive on both intellectual and aesthetic levels because she lets herself "go to pieces" in dress and looks. In a perverse twist, he begins to resent both ideality and actuality: ideality because it leads to disillusionment and reality as its manifest expression. In Oliver, Glasgow presents a man who eventually turns his back on ideals—masculine, feminine, and artistic. After the failure of his first play, he does what he once vowed never to do: sells out. His later plays are resounding successes that bring him wealth, yet he always disparages and dismisses them as "trash" and "rot."[58] The plays remind him that he has turned into a travesty of his former self, for he lets compromise and passive capitulation to the common appetite of society partial to pretty fictions triumph over striving, principle, and self-denial. Oliver is a man who ends up discarding ideals, but the ultimate irony is that now he lives in actuality and peddles ideality, for which he blames Virginia, one who has always been in denial of the real. There are no winners in *Virginia*, only victims of the elusive fiction of Southern whiteness who, in quest for the perfection of ideal, produce difference.

NINE

"THERE AIN'T NO GOING BACK"
The Work of Charles Waddell Chesnutt

Difference, change, metamorphosis, and transformation endure and become more pronounced in contexts such as the post-Reconstruction South, in which attempts to cultivate ideological stasis are based on sustaining a sense of historic continuity. And, the stronger the insistence on sameness, the more acute and visible the transformation. Difference is ever present and transformation is inescapable in Ellen Glasgow's *The Voice of the People* and *Virginia*, in which she destroys the impossible dream of resurrecting the paradigm of Southern whiteness by casting her characters as collateral damage of living the ideal. Glasgow's is a vision of a utopian world bordering on dystopia, driven by an illusion of gentility. Charles Waddell Chesnutt shares this image in *The Colonel's Dream*: a dream of what has been and cannot be revived, and a utopian vision of what could be rendered out of place.[1]

The novel appeared in print in 1905 and, despite one critic's call to encourage Chesnutt "in his literary work" because it ranked "among the best of its kind issued from the American press," it would be Chesnutt's last attempt to publish during his lifetime.[2] Before he embarked on his literary career, Chesnutt had set himself the noble task of educating white readers. And, according to a reviewer for the *Los Angeles Herald*, he partly succeeded. In tackling the question of race in the South and "avoiding any intemperate or acrimonious reflection upon the past or present condition of affairs," he set an example that "might well be followed by his white brethren who have occasion to exploit the same field." The critics focused on Chesnutt's critique of the social stagnation of the South. He received praise for the condemnation of "the peonage system" and for setting "forth vividly some of the reasons why the South has not progressed more rapidly than it has along the path of industrial development." Another reviewer openly named one of the reasons, and it was not flattering to either the South or Southerners. Chesnutt, he wrote, found "the white Southerner an irredeemable loafer, with all a loafer's lethargic opposition to improvements." The picture of the South, he added, that emerged from the pages of the novel was "that of increasing degeneracy and racial hatred." A Southern reviewer, predictably, took exception to Chesnutt's view of the South, particularly "its laziness, slowness, its narrowness and lack of progressiveness." Though true of the small town, he conceded reluctantly, it did not reflect "the commendable energy" of the New South— and its "larger cities"—that was "bidding fair to rise again to its former rank as the most prosperous section of the land."[3] A lesson in sectional difference rather than critique that shows the education of white readers did not run smoothly and, certainly, not without ruffling a few feathers.

This kind of defense sounds a death knell for the very progressiveness it avows. But, despite the odd accusation of prejudice, the novel was considered "very good" and ranked as "exceptional among the novels of the South." Chesnutt received praise for his novelty of approach, for presenting "a view of some of the South's problems from an angle different from any yet taken by a novelist."[4] The clue to this new angle lay in the titular "dream." While other novelists, Page, Glasgow, and Corra Harris to name a few, had all presented narratives of loss that was mourned, irrecuperable, stultifying in its effect— but real—Chesnutt's choice of "dream" called into question the quiddity of that loss and stopped short of declaring it a figment of historically cultural consciousness. At the center of this positivist study stands repetition, a literal attempt at reliving a dream, an ultimately impossible and doomed enterprise.

The dream unfolds and unravels in nineteenth-century Clarendon, North Carolina. For its mastermind, Chesnutt chooses Colonel Henry French, who struggles—and fails—to regain a foothold in the circuit of inheritance. Descended from a line of planters and born on the right side of the blanket, Henry is not a typical Chesnutt hero, a fact that perhaps spared Chesnutt from accusations of racial if not regional bias. Henry's story is not much different from the narratives of Page's or Glasgow's protagonists. He distinguishes himself on the battlefields of the Civil War, which earns him "the honor of colonelcy." After the conflict which brought "ruin to his fortunes" and led to the by-now familiar sale of the familial "mansion," Henry leaves Clarendon for New York, where he enters "his uncle's office as a clerk." Thanks to his diligence and capability, he first becomes a partner and then, upon his uncle's death, succeeds him as the head of the company. Wilson notes that in creating Henry, Chesnutt crafts "a hybrid," a man who unites a Southern aristocratic pedigree with business acumen typically associated with the North. But Chesnutt merges the two seemingly antagonistic value systems of Northern industry and Southern gentility to mark Henry as inherently transgressive. Having evaluated the company's market position, Henry and his partner decide to sell the business to "the recently organized bagging trust," a move that will make the two men "richer than they could have hoped to be after ten years of business stress and struggle."[5] When Henry, who has been awaiting the news as immovable as "a wax figure," hears of the successful completion of the transaction, he is overwhelmed and faints. In this pivotal and symbolic moment, Chesnutt uses the waxy pallor of Henry's face to mark an excess of appearance and symptom of his monetary success. The metaphorically and literally whitened Henry is now a symbol of Northern capitalism, but the vampiric stillness and whiteness of his countenance that lead to the loss of consciousness signify a conflict occasioned by the amalgamation of two antagonistic whitenesses: the Northern one equated with the accumulation of capital and the Southern vested in genteel heritage. Such conflict, Žižek observes, demonstrates itself in external ugliness that is the sign of existence exceeding representation.[6] Since the ghostly excess of capitalism Henry embodies cannot be represented—let alone reconciled with the Southern notion of hereditary gentility—it manifests in the paradoxical oversaturation of a lack of color and culminates in the temporary suspension of signification that is his weakness. To externalize his mutability, Chesnutt transforms Henry into a wax figure.

Chesnutt casts Henry's weakness as a symptom of his mutated gentility and a harbinger of both the success and failure that will turn him into a pariah and monster. Thanks to the lucrative deal brought about by years of hard work, Henry intends to "take a long rest, and then travel for a year or two, and after that settle down and take life comfortably." In other words, his capital will now endow the life of a gentleman. Spurred partly by the benefits of the salubrious Southern climate to his son's health and partly by "a twinge of something like remorse" at not having "set foot within its borders" for over twenty years, Henry travels to Clarendon.[7] Upon his arrival, he observes the changes that time has wrought upon the place: "the once white weatherboarding and Venetian blinds" adorning the house that "the colonel's grandfather had built" to serve "as a town residence" have been reduced to a "gray monotone" by "the paintless years." The outward decrepitude of the scene is comparable to the shabbiness of Glasgow's Kingsborough or Dinwiddie. But, despite the deterioration, Henry muses, the house still stands as a metonymy for "other things Southern" that "live long and die hard."⁸ Chesnutt tempers this observation of the endurance of the Southern tradition through Henry's acceptance of change, which testifies to his altered sensibility, the result of the lessening of family ties occasioned by a long absence from the region. Chesnutt exploits Henry's precarious position as a self-made man who still feels the pull of tradition to comment on the anachronistic Southern view of the genteel legacy.

Henry's progressiveness strikes a discordant note with the fidelity to tradition championed in the region, prompting him to reflect that the old aristocratic system "carried the seeds of decay within itself and was doomed to perish." The institution of "aristocracy," Henry muses, "is quite endurable, for the aristocrat," but because, like capitalism, it rests on the exploitation of others, it is irreconcilable with the ethereal attributes of whiteness; it carries within itself its own antagonism, which precludes the attainment of whiteness proper and renders all aspirants monstrous simulacra. In Henry, Chesnutt carves the image of an alternative gentleman devoid of the spurious conviction of social entitlement. Henry deems "himself a gentleman, and the descendant of a long line of gentlemen," but he does not subscribe to the creed that "blood alone entitled him to any social privileges."⁹ It is an open declaration of rebellion against the Southern conception of whiteness as hereditary privilege that stresses Henry's ontological instability. His qualification of the term gentleman both includes him in the circuit of heredity and questions the validity of such designations. This questioning of the *status quo* is present in Chesnutt's *The Marrow of Tradition, The House behind the Cedars*, and *Mandy Oxendine*, but never in such an overt and direct manner. Choosing a Southern gentleman as his medium allows Chesnutt to be more outspoken in his condemnation of hereditary gentility. Henry's verdict on aristocracy is uncompromising when it comes: it should "scarcely be boasted of" if it is not supported by an excellence "born of personal effort," and any pride worthy of cultivating is "that of achievement."¹⁰ This is a direct and bold statement that privileges meritocracy over a hereditarily predetermined right to virtue that places Henry in opposition to its Southern archetype.

To add objectivity to Henry's tacit rebellion against the model of Southern gentility, Chesnutt creates a backdrop of an historic relationship and chooses a former family slave, Peter French, as his mouthpiece. The two men meet at a graveyard when Henry visits family graves and, initially, they do not recognize each other. Peter, however, encouraged by the willing audience, launches into a tale of the French family history. He tends the plot "jes' lak," he supposes, "Mars Henry'd 'a' had it done ef he'd 'a' lived hyuh in de ole home, stidder 'way off yandah in de Norf, whar he so busy makin' money dat he done fergot all 'bout his own folks." Moving to the North in search of fortune is bad enough because it is a betrayal of the region, but forgetting the past is by far the greater offence. Chesnutt turns Peter into an example of the ubiquity of the backward view, which, like a malady, permeates all spheres of Southern society. The freshly arrived Henry catches the bug. Peter's chastisement leads to a reflection upon his literal and metaphorical detachment from the site of origin. The time "when he had thought of Confederacy as his country" seems "far away," while the only family heirloom, "his grandfather's sword, had been for years stored away in a dark closet" instead of being "displayed upon the drawing-room wall" as "his father had kept it."[11] Such blatant disregard for family mementoes bespeaks Henry's departure from his forefathers' legacy, the legacy that now faces him in the person of Peter, the only other familial connection linking Henry to his past. The pull of the past reasserts itself, and the encounter with Peter touches "a tender cord in the colonel's nature, already tuned to sympathy with the dead past of which Peter seemed the only survival." But it is not yet the pull of nostalgia, but rather a pang of conscience prompting guilt at the neglect of the old values that Peter and the sword represent. Chesnutt makes Peter, who is capable of "a touching loyalty to a family from which he could no longer expect anything in return," a foil to Henry's transparent lack of sentiment.[12]

Sentiments of the wrong kind may stand in the way of progress and enlightenment. Sentiment keeps Peter rooted to the spot, and Chesnutt uses him as a device through which Henry re-enters the circuit of inheritance. Following the meeting, Peter is unlawfully arrested on charges of vagrancy, and the next day Henry happens to pass by the courthouse where the hearing takes place. Peter is to be sentenced to two years of forced labor to redeem the fine levied on him for the alleged offence. Outraged, Henry intervenes, pays the fine, and departs "with his purchase—a purchase which his father had made, upon terms not very different, fifty years before." Chesnutt exploits the pathos and contradiction of the purchase to emphasize the instability of Henry's position as a gentleman suddenly caught up in a discourse that forces him into conformity with the pre–Civil War realities of the slave market. Henry's historically blighted positioning allows Chesnutt to cast him as both victim and indictment of the heritage that bred him. Henry performs a seemingly selfless gesture, which ensures Peter's freedom but, in doing so, both replicates the discourse of the father and departs from it: his father, who owned Peter, "had given him" to Henry "as his own boy," whereas Henry pays the fine out of charity.[13] The outcome may be similar since the judge sells Peter "for life," but Henry's motivation for the transaction is different from his father's, who, Peter asserts, "wuz a monstus keerful man," and to whom Peter "wuz wuth five hundred dollahs."[14] It may be ungentlemanly to talk money, but Peter's price tag is Chesnutt's deliberate and overt allusion to the inherent instability of the antebellum standard of whiteness which, though driven by material concerns, advocates a dissociation from them. Henry's abortive replication of his father's whiteness renders it intrinsically untenable by revealing the innate disintegration of the wholeness of gentility prefigured in the construct of the gentleman planter. It is a doubling in which Chesnutt uses Henry's difference; it consists in his departure from the standard of gentility practiced by his father to reveal the corruption of its organic wholeness, where the divine attributes of whiteness clash with its earthlier concerns.

Throughout the narrative, Chesnutt stresses Henry's difference and the in-betweenness that will culminate in the failure of his dream. The portrait he paints is that of contradiction, of the new vying for primacy of place with the old. Henry is a man of altered sensibility who does not actively endorse the antebellum model of gentility and outwardly condemns Clarendon's "quixotic devotion to lost causes and vanished ideals," but he also concedes that in "the old town the ideas of race and blood attained a new and larger perspective." He believes in "the rights of man" and the extension of "the doctrine to include all who bore the human form," but his conviction of being "an equally pronounced aristocrat" somewhat undermines the belief. A conflict of sentiments reifies Henry's transgressive positioning between the conservatism of the South and the progressiveness of the North. Wilson considers such contradictions to be symptomatic of Henry's and the South's conceptual inflexibility, which translates into an inability to find a compromise between tradition and progress.[15] But the opposite is equally true. In Henry's case, such inconsistencies are suggestive precisely because of a tenuous compromise, or amalgamation, of these antagonistic sensibilities, through which Chesnutt reinforces the undecidability of his gentility. An aristocratic democrat, subscribing to his own idea of humanism, Henry is indeed an anomaly, and this altered sensibility—combined with an awareness of the impossibility of the revivification of the "vanished ideals"—renders his subsequent endeavors doubly monstrous.

Upon his arrival in Clarendon, Henry renews an old acquaintance with the Treadwells—remnants of the aristocratic South and symbols of the "vanished ideals"—whose name carries not only connotations, but also the injunction of decorum. The growing intimacy between Henry and the Treadwell ladies, which culminates in his engagement to Laura, is responsible for his increasing attachment to Clarendon and the romanticizing of his youth spent there. Succumbing to the quixotism that he so condemns, Henry purchases his grandfather's town house from Nichols, "a keen-eyed mulatto," who, like Henry, "was a man of thrift and good sense." Chesnutt has Henry revert to the type of gentleman immortalized by Page in the characters of Gordon Keith or Jacquelin Gray, whose gentility cannot signify without the monumental space of the plantation house. To reclaim this space is to reclaim one's hereditary right to be a gentleman. The irony is, of course, that to reclaim means to repeat, to cover over the fissure, to project the timelessness and immutability upon which the ideal of gentility depends. Discussing repetition in his seminal work *Repetition: An Essay in Experimental Psychology*, Søren Kierkegaard notes its problematic nature, which goes against the grain of what the term denotes. Repetition conveys pastness, a *fait accompli*, Kierkegaard writes, but "the fact that it has been" is what "gives to repetition the character of novelty."[16] Chesnutt is fully aware that repetition does not ultimately deliver what it says on the tin and, instead of linking the past and the present, it irrevocably divides them. What begins for Henry as an indulgence born out of nostalgia soon transforms into a quest for repetition. Yet, rather than establish a link connecting him to his past, Henry's ancestral home and its subsequent renovation serve to emphasize his discontinuity. He spares no expense to restore "the interior as he remembered it in his childhood" and even manages "to recover several of the pieces" of furniture that "had been sold and scattered." What cannot be recovered Henry has "reproduced from their description." Chesnutt casts the restoration of the house as symbolic of Henry's attempt to piece together not only what would have constituted his inheritance, but also what represents the tangible effects of his gentility. The effort, however, is counterproductive, for repetition, Chesnutt suggests, ushers in mutation in place of sameness. The traces of mutation are visible everywhere, in "some modern additions" and "a few choice books and pictures—for, the colonel had not attempted to conform his own tastes and habits to those of his father."[17] The devil is in the detail, and these seemingly innocuous touches expose Henry's non-conformity because they signal the individuality of his creation.

Chesnutt exploits detail to accentuate the point that repetition may only be a faux-repetition. He has Henry crown his attempts at restoration of his gentility with "an old-time party, with old-time costumes—any period between 1830 and 1860 permissible." Complete with "old-time entertainment," the ball is intended to mark a revival of the old traditions, but the only thing it succeeds in reviving is the unbridgeable gap separating Clarendon's self-designated finest and their antecedents. Aspiring young ladies need to be taught "beforehand how to dance" a minuet. At the same time, "making and altering men's garments" generates enough profit for Archie Christmas—"the mulatto tailor" —to support himself "for another twelve months."[18] Chesnutt presents the scene as a parody of gentility, an image devoid of substance. Speaking of the dissonance between the real and the image, Žižek concludes that it leads to the emergence of "representation without existence." Chesnutt recreates this dynamic through the temporarily resurrected splendor of the costumes, which he pits against the monstrous lack of form and the requisites of whiteness that are its constituents in the ordinary. The conclusion is self-evident: for the inhabitants of Clarendon, as for Henry, the life of plantation gentility is a distant memory. Those with "any claims to gentility" have lost their estates to William Fetters, a not inaptly named local entrepreneur who has risen from obscurity to prominence and now runs his plantation "with convict labor."[19] Unsupported by the possession of land and its attendant fiscal advantages, such projections of gentility are representations without the substance to support them. Chesnutt turns the ball into a display of mutilated whiteness where excess and lack become interchangeable and create a monstrous distortion.[20]

The ball is not without symbolic significance in that it marks Henry's return to Clarendon and the recovery of his inheritance. But the artificiality of preparations that precede it foreshadows a partial realization of Henry's dream. His entrepreneurial spirit awakens—and, with it, another dream of creating a fairer society. In an effort to provide employment for the poorest of the town, he plans "to build a new and larger cotton mill" that will "shake up this lethargic community," teaching it the habits of "industry, efficiency and thrift." To erect this new edifice, Henry employs both black and white laborers, paying all "a dollar and a half a day."[21] His other projects include a library, or rather two libraries, since, as his fiancée points out, "the white people wouldn't wish to handle the same books" as the colored population, together with support for the local schools, both for white and colored citizens. Truly admirable examples of striving and sacrifice *pro bono publico* which only deepen the gulf between Henry and the Clarendon standard of gentility. Chesnutt casts Henry as a promethean figure who, despite a fondness for the past, is capable of bringing light to the inhabitants of Clarendon. But the Clarendon he inhabits, the Clarendon that Chesnutt sees as emblematic of the South at large, is not ready to accept the gift. The obstacle is of its own fashioning and, at its heart, lies the essential irreconcilability of progress versus stagnation, not unlike that which plagues Glasgow's Dinwiddie. To emphasize Henry's predicament as a man caught in the grip of this irreconcilability, Chesnutt renders him placeless. His life in New York and "the Clarendon of the present" are "mere transitory embodiments." Henry lives "in the Clarendon yet to be, a Clarendon rescued from Fetters, purified," and "rehabilitated." This is a quest for the perfection of a new Clarendon, free not just from Fetters but also the fetters of what Nietzsche terms a "slave morality" that demands obedience to certain codes of behavior.[22] In Chesnutt's Clarendon, this slave morality translates into the blind adherence to outdated models of gentility. The rules are rigid and disobedience alienates, which Chesnutt demonstrates through Henry's rapid descent from the toast of the town to social pariah.

Henry's transformation also exposes the malleability of the monstrous and emphasizes its instability as an unequivocal category. The category of the monstrous, Chesnutt implies, is fluid and capable of being remade as the zeitgeist demands. Owing to this fluidity, Henry's philanthropic qualities—emblematic of spiritual whiteness—may be *mis*constructed into manifestations of evil that turn him into "an enemy of his race."[23] This is a *mis*construction, however, because it reveals the moral passivity and lethargy that destroy the nobler impulses associated with whiteness, such as courage, integrity, and the struggle for self-improvement. It is necessary for the inhabitants of Clarendon, Chesnutt suggests, to *mis*construct Henry because not to do so would amount to admitting that they are already *mis*constructed. Chesnutt treats Henry's growing isolation as a symbol of the South's fear of confronting and addressing its own ailments. The *Louisville Courier-Journal's* critic's comment begging that Henry "stays where he belongs"—that is, in the North—reveals just how reluctant the South was to review, let alone alter, its sensibility.[24]

Chesnutt may as well have been tilting at the windmills. And so, Henry's intervention to bring to justice the perpetrators of the unlawful lynching of Bud Johnson fails because those who could help "became increasingly difficult to find as it became known that he was seeking them." His ostracism is complete when, following the accidental deaths of his son and of Peter, who rushed to his rescue, Henry buries them both in the family plot. Although the funeral service goes without a hitch and is attended by "the more refined and cultured of the townspeople" who wanted to pay "tribute of respect and appreciation" for Peter's "heroic deed," his coffin is exhumed and deposited on Henry's porch by those who "dident tend yore nigger funarl." Chesnutt lets the note speak for itself. Its orthography indicates that its authors stand beyond the pale of whiteness, whether it be constructed as a hereditary right or result of personal achievement. He saves his critique for the supposedly "better" half of Clarendon "who reprobated the action in silence."[25] The lack of response from the genteel part of the town merits condemnation, for it implicates them in this profane act by betraying a cowardly reluctance to confront the mob. If Chesnutt's aim in writing novels is to educate his readers, he approaches the task in the spirit of true didacticism, teaching by example. Henry, the white gentleman, learns his lesson the hard way. The silence of the elite is the ultimate betrayal, all the more bitter because delivered by those of his own class, and leads him to the realization that "the best people" are nothing more than "an abstraction," as is the whiteness they project. Like the costumes donned for the ball, it remains a veneer that inadequately masks the caricatured ideal. Henry's dream fails because, as his fiancée observes, it was built upon, and attempted to revive, another dream "of the old and happy past" that cannot be resurrected and of which she was a part and which only endures because of the supra-temporality of all abstraction.[26]

The supra-temporality of abstraction creates a dissonance not just between the ideal and actuality, but also between Henry's perception of reality and actuality. Before the exhumation of Peter breaks the spell, Henry is as prone to building fantasies of gentility, as are Glasgow's Dinwiddians. In a perverse way, the success of a fantasy depends on the lack that prefigures it and that the desiring subject seeks to overcome. The more visible the evidence of this lack, the more convincing and alluring the fantasy becomes, which is why, upon his first visit to the Treadwells, Henry begins to build a picture of their gentility and continuing prosperity despite evidence to the contrary. He notices the softness and smoothness of the napkins, but remains oblivious to their having "been carefully darned in many places." He is struck by the fragility of the family silver "worn very thin," yet considers it "charming" and symbolic of "the simple dignity of the past." Even Laura fails to break the illusion, though, following Mrs. Treadwell's assurances of their material stability, she points to the "parlor carpet" that "has been down for twenty-five years," telling him candidly that they "are not well off." The "rentable property," of which Mrs. Treadwell boasts, comprises "three ramshackle cabins" that fetch "four dollars a month each."[27] Yet, so strong is the fantasy Henry has conjured that, despite Laura's frank admission to their passing for gentility, he does not desist from constructing their and Laura's ideality, and remains stubbornly unmindful of the contradictions inherent in that image.

And it is an image with many flaws. Mrs. Treadwell had received the kind of education befitting the "daughter of a wealthy planter," but Laura, having "spent her youth in a transition period," enjoyed no such privileges. Through no fault of her own, Laura's gentility is a diluted version of the standard her mother represents and derives from "duty well performed" that "has no root in anything corruptible." Her unswerving devotion to her family leads her "to give the barber's daughter music lessons—for money," the one thing unmentionable in genteel circles that decides her deviation from the standard of the Southern lady. Chesnutt casts Laura as the victim of the genteel ethos, which forces her to live a life of pretense; and he chooses Henry, another victim, to voice Laura's in-betweenness. Henry praises Laura's "self-sacrifice and devotion to duty" and elevates her to the status of "a queen among women" and "the embodiment of all that is best" of his "memories of the Old South."[28] Chesnutt has Henry reconstruct Laura's gentility only to reveal its incompleteness. Chesnutt compounds this effect of incompleteness through allusions to the Old South and memories. The emphasis on the spiritual aspects of whiteness is essential to confirming their very absence among the Clarendon's pseudo-elite whose gentility rests on deception. The Treadwells "never speak about the money" Laura earns "at the house," and although Mrs. Treadwell knows Laura teaches for recompense, she "feigns" that she does "it of mere kindness." The Treadwells' friends "are not supposed to know it" and, if they do, "they are kind and never speak of it."[29] This kind of deception, Chesnutt implies, is practiced on an almost industrial scale, not just in Clarendon but in the region. It renders the Clarendon elite a monstrous aberration, for it insists on the projection of gentility in which the honesty and truth associated with the antebellum ideal, so cherished by Henry and espoused by Laura, become obsolete. The irony is that what transforms Henry into an outcast is precisely his adherence to the loftier sentiments of the antebellum code of conduct.

Chesnutt's critique of Southern whiteness does not end with his placing it beyond the reach of Clarendon gentry; in the character of Malcolm Dudley, he casts doubt over its very existence. Dudley, whose name is another reminder of the South's love for aristocratic descent, managed the Mink Run plantation for his uncle Ralph Dudley before the outbreak of the Civil War, and became romantically involved with one of his slaves, Viney. When he falls on hard times during the war, he forsakes Viney and, to augment his fortune, proposes to a rich widow and is accepted. Viney visits the widow and, presumably, informs her of Malcolm's "indiscretion," after which the lady promptly breaks off the engagement. In a fit of anger, Malcolm has the overseer whip Viney; the brutality of the act brings on a stroke. Dr. Price, summoned to attend Viney, does not conceal his contempt for Malcolm: "By

God, Dudley, I wouldn't have thought this of you!" His dishonorable conduct and brutality toward Viney turn Malcolm into the caricature of a gentleman, a status that Chesnutt seals by stressing Dudley's lack of moral courage. He apologizes to Viney, assuring her that the overseer "went further than" was his intention, but he is incapable of accepting responsibility for his action.[30]

This is but a prelude to a tale of greed and just punishment. Before the whipping, and unbeknownst to Malcolm, Ralph returns to the plantation to bury fifty thousand dollars, and Viney is the only witness to the whereabouts of the treasure. Ralph leaves a letter for Malcolm informing him that Viney will point the location to him. Ironically, as the result of the punishment Viney loses the ability to speak and is unable to direct Malcolm to the money. Eventually, Malcolm's obsession with finding the treasure leaves him mentally unstable and turns the plantation into a mining ground where "no crack or cranny had been left unexplored," all to no avail. Malcolm's mental instability bespeaks a greed that, Chesnutt suggests, has always been present, and that overrides whatever morals he may have possessed. It is a greed that is indelibly etched in his face, which, though possessing "a highbred and strongly marked type, emphasized by age," has "the hawk-like contour, that is supposed to betoken extreme acquisitiveness."[31] Like Page and Glasgow, Chesnutt shares an obsession with outward expressions of inner monstrosity. The implication is that Malcolm's gentility is as distorted as his "hawk-like" profile. His face represents a collage of conflicting values that indicate that even before the war whiteness was in short supply. The device of visible exaggeration that Chesnutt uses, although limiting insofar as it narrows the field of interpretation, is emblematic of the inherent instability of hereditary whiteness that also permeates Page's *John Marvel Assistant* or Glasgow's *The Voice of the People*. In visibly blighting its aspirants, such malformations *demonstrate* that Southern whiteness is subject to, and subjected to, incessant reinterpretations, but always beyond attainment. The quest for it proves as elusive as Malcolm's search for the hoard, which Ralph had removed from the plantation, forgetting in his haste to destroy the note. While its virtues grow in the recollecting, as Henry discovers, its value remains within the realm of abstraction.

Chesnutt understood the simultaneous allure and deceptive innocence of the ploy of recollection early on in his career when he embarked on debunking the myth of antebellum gentility by conjuring the raconteur *par excellence* in the character of Uncle Julius McAdoo. Chesnutt was not a complete novice in the literary world, having had stories published in magazines in 1887 and 1893, but it was not until the publication of the collection titled *The Conjure*

Woman and Other Conjure Tales in 1899 that he gained a reputation as an author.[32] Critics were in raptures; even the dialect, which was "no easy reading," could not dampen their enthusiasm. The stories were valuable additions to American literature and proof positive of "the fertility of Southern literary field." Chesnutt's exploitation of his subject "with a measure of skill and appreciation," "mysticism," and "description" were not only worthy of praise but also secured him "a position in the front rank of the writers of the 'New South' in literature." The stories were "curious," "interesting," "vigorous, vivid, and strikingly dramatic," and reflective of Chesnutt's acquaintance with the "negro superstitions and dialect."[33] Such focus on the entertainment value of the stories undoubtedly bolstered sales, but failed to address the bigger issue that lurked beneath the surface of the mysticism and superstition—the misconception that is Southern whiteness. Things may not go bump in the night in any of the stories, and yet they are populated by ghosts.

Uncle Julius McAdoo, who does the recollecting, is both a ghost and a medium through whom other ghosts come to life. Two Northerners, John and Annie, supply his willing audience. John is a Northern entrepreneur who, led by concerns for his wife's health, relocates to the South, where, after the war, "land could be bought for a mere song." He acquires the former McAdoo plantation with the intention of growing grapes. Richard H. Brodhead observes that Chesnutt's stereotypical characterization of John and Uncle Julius serves to undermine the popular assumption that short stories and stereotype are inseparable.[34] This surface conventionality enables Chesnutt to dispel another stereotype, that of the gentleman planter, and expose it as a monstrous misconstruction.

In "The Goophered Grapevine," Chesnutt portrays Uncle Julius's former owner, "ole Mars Dugal' McAdoo" as the antithesis of the ideal of Southern gentility. Beneath his veneer of benevolence lies avarice worthy of a carpetbagger: "it ha' ter be a mighty rainy day when he couldn' fine sump'n fer his niggers to do, en it ha' ter be a mighty little hole he couldn' crawl thoo, en ha' ter be a monst'us cloudy night when a dollar git by him in de dahkness." Uncle Julius's deceptively innocuous misapplication of the adjective "monst'us" allows Chesnutt to transform Mars Dugal's seemingly positive thrift into excess. In this parody of the monstrous, the monster is craftily implicated by circumstantial evidence. When his prized "scuppernon's" grapes begin to disappear, Mars Dugal seeks the help of a local conjure woman, Aunt Peggy.[35] Aunt Peggy prepares a "goopher," which she buries "under de root uv a red oak tree," and, for good measure, spreads the news among the slaves that "a nigger w'at eat dem grapes 'ud be sho ter die inside'n twel' mont's." Thenceforth the grapes are undisturbed, until a new addition to the plantation, Henry, avails himself of some. Learning of the curse, Henry is so overcome with fear about his fate that the overseer takes him to Aunt Peggy, who concocts an antidote. As part of the remedy, every spring, Henry must anoint his head with "de sap whar it ooze out'n de cut een's er de vimes." And so, his life begins to follow the cycle of the grapevine, when bouts of "rheumatiz" in autumn invariably follow spring rejuvenation. It is not long before Mars Dugal sniffs out a business opportunity in Henry. He waits until spring and sells him "fer fifteen huder' dollars." When he meets Henry's new owner again it is autumn, and Henry has reverted to being an old man. Seemingly perturbed, Mars Dugal offers to buy Henry back "fer five hund'ed dollars."[36] Such transactions are repeated over several years, until "Mars Dugal made 'nuff money off'n Henry to buy anudder plantation."[37] Like other gentlemen before him, Mars Dugal repeats the ideal of a landed aristocrat, except the ideal is its own antithesis. It thrives on avarice and duplicity; it is not even a ghost of the antebellum ideal of gentility that supposedly celebrates the love of truth, honesty, and honor. In Uncle Julius's simple narrative of revival as a natural phenomenon, Chesnutt refuses to revive the spirit of Southern whiteness. His method is effective because, in place of militant criticism, it offers a gradual unravelling of the premises of Southern gentility, building a picture of vice rather than virtue.

The vices in "The Goohphered Grapevine" include dubious industriousness and intentional deception worthy of a scoundrel. In "Sis Becky's Pickaninny," the proclivity for gambling and moral cowardice betoken an absence of honor, betraying the gentility of "Kunnel Pen'leton" as a mere sham. Having squandered his fortune on "hosses" with which he "nebber hab no luck," the "kunnel" decides to purchase a winning horse from another gentleman. At "a thousan' dollahs," the price is too high for the "kunnel's" purse, who "owed ez much ez he could borry a'ready on de skyo'ity he could gib."[38] His gentility is therefore a mere husk, devoid of kernel. The note he offers to the owner of the horse is promptly declined, suggesting that this gentleman's honor and word are no longer acceptable currency. Eventually, the "gentlemen" reach an agreement, and Becky, a slave, is to be traded for the horse. The owner of the horse, however, refuses to take Becky's little son, despite the "kunnel's" willingness to add him gratis to the bargain. As sacrifices go, this is, indeed, a feeble attempt brought about by guilt and the "kunnel's" awareness of the moral ugliness of his conduct. He lies to Becky, telling her that her absence will only be temporary, simply because he lacks courage and integrity. Chesnutt turns Becky's departure into proof positive of the "kunnel's" shortcomings. The lie is essential because acknowledging the truth would be analogous to admitting to a lack of gentility. Uncle Julius, however, in his deceptively naïve simplicity, calls him "a kin'-hea'ted man."[39] This cutting irony that enables Chesnutt to pass judgment through understatement is possible because of Uncle Julius's stereotypical characterization as a black man of limited intellect.

Uncle Julius is anything but a man of narrow horizons, but Chesnutt mines his preordained limitations of judgment to foreground the limitations of Southern gentility. He challenges the readers to imagine for themselves a scenario without Uncle Julius's conciliatory and mitigating embellishments. This is what happens in "Mars Jeems's Nightmare," in which Chesnutt adds a pinch of realism to his tales of conjure, combining an eye witness account with Uncle Julius's reminiscence. In this tale, the notion of hereditary whiteness is turned into hereditary monstrosity, and its intrinsic distortion spills onto the outside. The eye witness is John who, when out driving with his wife, passes a gentleman whipping "a high-spirited" horse that possessed "the marks of good temper and good breeding." Judging by his behavior, John finds the gentleman "deficient in both." Now Uncle Julius steps in to enlighten the ignorant Northerners. The gentleman's name is McLean, and he descends from a long line of planters who "had a big plantation en a heap er niggers." The apple does not fall far from the tree. McLean's grandfather was the Mars Jeems of the story's title. Mars Jeems, a far cry from the beneficent master, "wuz a ha'd man en monst'us stric wid his han's."[40] Chesnutt charges Uncle Julius's innocent statement with irony that allows his words to be *mis*constructed to unveil the true nature of Mars Jeems's monstrosity—overzealous management—without the necessity for explicitness. Mars Jeems eventually changes his ways after, in a reversal helped by a pinch of conjuring, he is transformed into a slave and delivered to his own plantation by Mars Dunkin as payment for a bet made while the two men "wuz playin' kya'ds te'gedder."[41] Under the guise of the improbability of the conjure tale that makes such metamorphoses permissible, Chesnutt responds to and challenges the accepted fiction of Southern gentility. Through Uncle Julius's seeming acquiescence to the perpetuation of the myth of antebellum whiteness, Chesnutt re-articulates the truth of its imagined perfection and unmasks it as a monstrous lie.

Uncle Julius's stock conventionality enables him to voice this lie: "dey's so many things a body knows is lies dat dey ain' no use gwine roun' findin' fault wid tales." Through the simple wisdom of Uncle Julius's words, Chesnutt moves beyond mere "findin' fault" to express the indispensability of the lie in sustaining the re-interpretability of the fiction of whiteness that establishes its status as a discourse of monstrous distortions. Like Chesnutt, Alice Dunbar-Nelson understands and exposes the insidious nature of the fiction of imagined perfection of whiteness that titillates with gold but delivers dross. Both Chesnutt and Dunbar-Nelson offer an alternative view of Southern whiteness based on meritocracy not birth. The difference lies in the manner of exposition. Chesnutt's preferred method is irony and understatement, while Dunbar-Nelson follows the path of full disclosure. The lie that is gentility manifests belatedly to Victor Grabért, the hero of "The Stones of the Village," who becomes aware of his own monstrosity only after reaching the pinnacle of gentility. A landed aristocrat through marriage, and eventually a judge, Victor's reconstruction of himself as a gentleman is so brittle that it crumbles when faced with opposition from a black lawyer, Pavageau. The two battle it out in court and, although Victor wins, he realizes he is no victor at all. His victory does not rest on merit, but is a fluke, the result of the prejudice of "the judge, the jury," and "the people" against the black lawyer.[42] The congratulations he receives sicken him, for he is aware that, by virtue of ability, they belong to the black lawyer whom Victor secretly "respected" and "admired."[43] In Pavageau, Dunbar-Nelson constructs a foil to Victor, a nemesis whose integrity forces Victor to acknowledge that his whiteness is a lie, not because of the lack of aristocratic descent, but the lack of honor and truthfulness.

Victor compromises both when he decides to pass for white, a secret Pavageau knows but never betrays despite Victor's outward hostility toward him. The knowledge of Pavageau's moral superiority spells defeat for Victor and leaves him wallowing "in a self-abasement at his position."[44] And the position is precarious. In the eyes of the observers, Victor's courtroom victories over Pavageau both validate his career and gentility; privately, they foster the growing awareness of his own inadequacy. Thanks to the outward trappings of gentility, Dunbar-Nelson suggests, Victor personifies the illusion of its attainability. But it is only an illusion that cannot prevent the metaphorical blackness of his own creation from spilling out. Victor pays the ultimate price and dies in the grip of hallucinations. His death symbolizes the perpetuation of the lie and, in an ironic twist, marks self-sacrifice on Victor's part and points a way to redemption. Victor resists the temptation to reveal the truth of his past for fear that it will taint his wife and son's whiteness. In a contradictory fashion characteristic of whiteness, Victor's refusal to reveal the secret of his origins is both an act of courage and cowardice.

Courage, honor, and integrity feature at the top of Dunbar-Nelson's attributes of whiteness, the loss of which results in the monstrous distortion that Victor becomes. In "La Juanita," she makes it a matter of nationality. The story unfolds in Mandeville, located in the vicinity of New Orleans, where whiteness is synonymous with Spanish and French descent. Juanita Alvarez, the "half-Spanish" and "half-French" heroine, unites the two heritages and becomes its embodiment in the eyes of Mandeville.[45] But filial disobedience mars Juanita's hereditary perfection. She defies not only her Grandpère Colomes by insisting on going to "meet her Mercer," but also the ideal of Mandevillian whiteness, for Mercer is "un Americain, pah!" Stunned by such an ostentatious betrayal of what they hold sacred, all of Mandeville "sighed sadly and shook its head."[46] The disdain for all things American is something of a family tradition. Grandpère Colomes's family "had held itself proudly aloof from 'those Americain' from time immemorial," until his granddaughter demeaned "herself by walking upon the pier with" one of them. In this transference of monstrosity, Juanita becomes tainted by association. Even when Mercer distinguishes himself through a display of extraordinary bravery during a regatta, leading all the boats to safety amid a raging storm, Grandpère Colomes only grudgingly allows that "some time dose Americain can mos' be like one Frenchman." With these words, Grandpère Colomes seals Mercer's status as an almost, but not quite adequate, imitation of a Frenchman. Locating her narratives in New Orleans, where the conviction that "a Louisianian—is a Louisianian" and not an "Americain" or a Southerner obtains, Dunbar-Nelson emphasizes the multiplicity and permeability of whiteness and monstrosity.[47] No more can regional affiliation erase the loss of integrity that blights Victor's whiteness or filial disobedience that tarnishes Juanita's, than Mercer's courage can expunge the imperfection of his "Americain" origin and lead to the attainment of the Louisianian variety of whiteness. What the diegesis of Southern whiteness perpetuates are degrees of monstrosity grounded in the myth of flawless gentility.

EPILOGUE
Southern Heroes and Symbols

Whiteness confounds. It plays with the multivalence of its significations, all the while dangling the carrot of attaining its perfection on an infinitely extending stick. Like the monument to the Confederate soldier in Corra Harris's *Recording Angel*, which "was of extremely short stature" because the "Daughters of Confederacy" who commissioned the statue "had not been able to afford the price demanded and the skinflint sculptor shortened the legs," it works in theory but not in practice. But, the astute Harris adds, "hero worship requires" that "if you raise a statue to the memory of a man, even if he is not over five feet in height, that the thing shall be at least ten to produce the proper effect."[1] The ideal dwarfs the subject as it grows in the telling; there is no catching up. What plagues the aspiring gentlemen and ladies peopling the pages of Page's, Glasgow's, Chesnutt's, and Dunbar-Nelson's works is an awareness of the antebellum ideal of Southern whiteness against which their reconstructions of it are pitted in a repetitive cycle of comparison and found incomplete. The pursuit of the wholeness of the ideal whiteness resembles Žižek's interpretation of *jouissance*: an idealized state of unity and perfect harmony that deconstructs the subject by pointing to his disunity and disharmony.

This illusion of completeness that the possibility of *jouissance* furnishes is indispensable to the functioning of ideology—and the rhetoric of whiteness is no exception.[2] The possibility of achieving *jouissance*, or ideal whiteness in which the biblical and antebellum attributes unite, creates an irreconcilable tension that juxtaposes the symbolism of the paradigm and its reconstruction, and condemns it as lacking. This conundrum is manifest in Melville's *Moby-Dick*, in which, musing upon "the mystic sign" of whiteness, he concludes "that by its indefiniteness it shadows forth the heartless voids and immensities of the universe, and thus stabs us from behind with the thought of annihilation, when beholding the white depths of the milky way."[3] For Melville, the mysticism of whiteness presupposes failure without which the promise of its ideal could not manifest itself; and without which its pursuit could not be initiated.

The quest to fathom the meaning of "the mystic sign" confounds the subject, just as it perplexed Ahab. The interpretations of Ahab's obsession with the whale have varied, ranging from comparisons with civilization and its need to impose meaning, through manifestations of self-delusion and struggle against the darker impulses of nature, to allegorical readings of man's hubris.[4] The fluidity with which the tale lends itself to reinterpretation has its roots in Melville's indebtedness to the practice of puritan typology, with its incessant need to create and search for time-defying connections to write its practitioners into God's providential narrative.[5] And, as Leslie Fiedler observes, Melville proves himself incapable of meeting the Old Testament challenge. At the heart of the challenge, according to Erich Auerbach, lies the proposition of the undeniable veracity of the biblical narrative. What mitigates this veracity, however, is the darkness and incompleteness of the knowledge that God is, but he is nowhere to be seen. The tension this dogma creates between truth and obscurity, or obscurity as truth, lends itself, Auerbach writes, to constant reinterpretability, which contributes to the emergence of the puritan sensibility of regarding the world not as a reality but as a puzzle in need of constant resolution.[6] This mode of perception determines American sensibility and creates the kind of conceptual environment prone to a fusion of symbolism and allegory, which is evident in *Moby-Dick*.[7]

In the kaleidoscopic sequence of allegories that unfolds in the novel, the connection between the symbol and its meaning is kept obscure, lurking in the text but never made explicit. Such obscurity invests the interpretative process itself with an allegorical significance redolent of Adam's transgression and transforms it into the symbol of the temptation of knowledge, of comprehending the one, inalienable truth that constitutes God's prerogative and cannot be fathomed. Although the kind of typology practiced by Melville is associated with the North, the region which, unlike the South, was supposedly peopled by "religious zealots and revolutionists," the postbellum South cultivated its own brand of symbolism vested in the concepts of the Old South and its genteel ways.[8] In this mythical land of plenty, the Southern gentleman and lady ruled benevolently over their inferiors, providing standards for emulation in the postbellum era, which proved to be rather malleable in their rigidity. The whiteness that Page's, Glasgow's, Chesnutt's, and Dunbar-Nelson's protagonists reconstruct is as multivalent and elusive as Melville's, and equally dependent on symbols. What distinguishes the symbolism of Southern whiteness from Melville's, however, is its blend of secularism and finiteness.

The Southern symbolism practiced by these authors operates through discreet associations grounded in hypersensitivity to class and race, rather than the hermeneutic overdetermination characteristic of Melville. Though the link between the symbol and its meaning may only be read by a select few, it invariably conjures the glory of the antebellum archetype of whiteness. Ironically, the symbols through which it is evoked are both reificatory and deny legitimacy to reconstructions of whiteness. The iconic image of the plantation house, which, though an enduring monument to tradition, is also symbolic of the impossibility of its resurrection. Inhabited equally by the dead and the living, the plantation house is both indispensable to projections of whiteness and a reminder of their imperfection. Though perhaps admitted reluctantly, this power of the plantation house to unmake whiteness, while remaining a continuing emblem of gentility is evident in Page's *Red Rock* and *Gordon Keith*, and Glasgow's *The Deliverance* and *The Voice of the People*. The "paintless house with its rotting portico" greets Colonel French upon his return to Clarendon in Chesnutt's *The Colonel's Dream*, and haunts Faulkner's *The Sound and the Fury*, bearing witness to the Compsons' decline.[9] Another such symbol is the Confederate button with which Blair in *Red Rock* adorns her blouse, the significance of which is lost upon Ruth, who represents Northern sensibility.

At times, the symbol becomes an instrument of critique, as it does in Glasgow's *The Voice of the People*. In Mrs. Dudley Webb's grim persistence in wearing black ornamented with the immortal Confederate button, Glasgow transforms the fidelity to the Southern tradition into the folly of allowing the past to bear an injudicious influence upon the present. In *The Sound and the Fury*, Faulkner undertakes a more overt critique of such nostalgic impulses when he has the disillusioned Jason Compson present his son, Quentin, with his grandfather's watch, declaring that it will enable him "to gain the reducto absurdum of all human experience which can fit your individual needs no better than it fitted his or his father's."[10] Time transforms such symbols of inheritance into empty signifiers, which, in their very materiality, are invested with a trace of the ideal, but are never reducible to it. Faulkner both emphasizes the futility of recreating the past and renders it a chronic Southern malady.

Curiously, when it comes to reconstructing tradition, both Page and Glasgow perform a reversal of gender roles. It is women who, adorned with military relics, continue the battlefield heroism, albeit in a less militant form; while men are emasculated. General Legaie and Dr. Cary in *Red Rock* parade in shirts made by ladies from their undergarments. Through these new garments, a continuity with the antebellum tradition is re-established, and the men perform gentility almost, but not quite, in drag. The heroes of the drama are not the male performers, but the female orchestrators.

In the discourse of reconstructions of whiteness, this interdependence of male and female characters seems a particularly Southern trend. The American hero has always ridden the plains of literary fiction as a lonely man, a man free of the fetters of history, ancestry or familial and racial affinities.[11] He is a Natty Bumppo type who, accompanied by a suitably inferior Chingachgook with whom he enjoys a unique bond, is always in search of the unspoiled American wilderness. Spurred by a dual vision of pristine virginity and conquest, he is a man who, like Huck Finn, feels the compulsion to "light out for the Territory ahead of the rest" to seek "the orgastic future," in which Fitzgerald's Gatsby believed. It is the repetition of an age-old American Dream, in which each of these heroes replicates the flight from the corruption of the Old World to the unspoiled innocence of the one that once motivated the puritan settlers.[12] No such flight from society or Old-World corruption characterizes Page's, Glasgow's, and Chesnutt's heroes, who are never free from tradition, history, or women. They are firmly embedded in the *patria* of plantation and region to which they are bound by the ties of history and heritage. Unlike Natty Bumppo or Huck, they are dependent on ladies who elevate them spiritually and inspire heroic deeds. This dependence is indebted to the traditions of courtly love, with perfect knights of impeccable manners, an endless supply of courage and honor, and ladies beyond attainment and reproach.

The South prided itself upon the cultivation of tradition that was as "nearly a copy of that in England" as "the conditions of the new land admitted," and adopted the chivalric model with alacrity.[13] The echoes of chivalry sound in Jacquelin's chaste admiration for Blair in *Red Rock*, and George Tryon's initial courtship of Rowena in Chesnutt's *The House behind the Cedars* which, ironically, begins at a re-enactment of a medieval joust when he chooses her as "the Queen of Love and Beauty." Its caricatured version appears in Glasgow's portrayal of Miss Angela in *The Miller of Old Church*, in which the worship of the feminine ideal literally destroys two generations of Jonathan Gays, while the lady serenely continues to inspire devotion. Miss Angela, whose failing health never succeeds in failing her, anticipates the irascible and hypochondriac Mrs. Compson of Faulkner's *The Sound and the Fury*, who, in upholding the tradition of female frailty, "kept herself sick all the time." This veiled critique of the cult of womanhood reaches its climax in *The Sound and the Fury*, when Jason Compson declares that "men invented virginity not women."[14] The ability to venerate femininity becomes the mark of a gentleman along with courage, loyalty, and honor. Unsurprisingly, all Page's gentlemen, including the reformed wastrel Henry Glave, are abundantly endowed with these qualities; while in Chesnutt's George Tryon, Major Carteret, and Tom Delamere as well as Glasgow's two Jonathan Gays, these values only resonate with a faint echo that, on occasion, might produce an uneasy pang of conscience.

Unlike the American hero who is unencumbered by tradition, the Southern hero is not only unmanned by the lady, but also burdened with history and tradition. The true Southern hero never loses awareness of an historical heritage that invariably links him to the aristocracy of the Old World, meticulously dusting royal grants that still tie him to England. It is this model of aristocracy that inspires Sutpen's plan in *Absalom, Absalom!* to accomplish which he requires "money, a house, a plantation, slaves, a family—incidentally of course, a wife." And although he acquires all, he can only pass for a gentleman because he is "underbred."[15] Land and wealth, if not sanctified by appropriate heritage, cannot furnish a claim to whiteness. The hereditary aspect of Southern whiteness that Sutpen lacks is apotheosized in the landed aristocrat and, in order to effect it, he is placed in opposition to a representative of off whiteness—the likes of Glasgow's irascible Major Lightfoot or Page's Squire Rawson, who still perch comfortably above "southern bullies" and "white trash."[16] This pairing of the supposedly purebred aristocrat and his less cultivated counterpart comes closest to resembling the inter-male relationships between Huck and Jim, or Natty Bumppo and Chingachgook. Accordingly, Page juxtaposes Gordon Keith and General Keith's gentility with Squire Rawson's blunt pragmatism in *Gordon Keith*; while in *Red Rock*, Andy Stamper, a white farmer, acts as a catalyst that provokes the assumption that the qualities of courage, loyalty, and honor, which he as a Southerner espouses, are amplified in his aristocratic neighbors—Dr. Cary and Jacquelin Gray. Glasgow recreates this dyad in the pairing of Governor Ambler and Major Lightfoot. This union permits Page and Glasgow to enunciate the plight of the postbellum aristocrat as a man out of step with his time, an Adam whose memory of paradise keeps him anchored in place, though he realizes that re-entry is impossible. Gordon Keith, despite his sojourns in New York and Appalachia, always remains an outsider, even after his return to the South; Jacquelin, swindled out of his birthright, becomes alienated from his ancestors; while Chesnutt's Colonel French experiences metaphorical and physical isolation only when he returns to his hometown.

A variation of the theme of individual isolation stands at the center of American identity. In place of an unconquered but beckoning frontier, Page, Glasgow, and Chesnutt evoke the charmed world of an antebellum genteel fairy tale to portray this sense of individual isolation.[17] What alienates Gordon Keith, Colonel French, or Dr. Cary is an insistence upon the revivification of antebellum whiteness in the "spoilt" territory of the post-Reconstruction South. The idea of quest remains, but what distinguishes the Southern hero from the American one is that his quest is spurred not by a desire for an innocent, unencumbered future such as that which impels Huck and his ilk to depart for the wilderness; rather it consists in a futile restoration of an imagined past that results in maimed whiteness. For the Southern hero, the dream is no less elusive because it has already been lived, the awareness of which returns with mocking clarity to plague him and his gentility. The alienation of these characters is therefore twofold, for in replicating the antebellum paradigms of whiteness they become isolated in the present; while by virtue of the incompleteness of such reconstructions, they are also alienated from the ideals of whiteness.

Faulkner formulates this sense of alienation as a matter of heritage in *Absalom, Absalom!* where Quentin Compson, though "still too young to deserve yet to be a ghost," is nonetheless already a specter by virtue of being born "in the deep South," which "was peopled with garrulous outraged baffled ghosts."[18] Faulkner verbalizes what Glasgow, Chesnutt, and Page imply: that the preservation of tradition is both an inextricable part of the Southern sensibility and impossible. Even in Page's sentimentalized account of the continuity of antebellum gentility, which pits the helpless and sometimes hapless aristocrat against the iniquity of the former overseers or rapacity of carpetbaggers, reconstructions of whiteness are inevitably reduced to ghostly palimpsests. Glasgow anticipates Faulkner in that she dispenses with sentimentalist and pseudo-realistic portrayals of the aristocratic plight, but she cannot liberate herself completely from the allure of aristocratic breeding. What emerges therefore is a curious mixture of admiration and irony exemplified in the portrayal of Mrs. Lightfoot in *The Battle-Ground*, who, through the tears shed over "Thaddeus of Warsaw," is included in the universal body aristocratic.[19] Glasgow's compulsion to critique such outdated sentiments is always mediated by the need to guard them. Although she permits Nicholas Burr in *The Voice of the People* to rise from the obscurity of peanut farming to the governorship of Virginia, she annihilates him at the pinnacle of his career. In a sense, Nicholas is a blueprint for Faulkner's Sutpen or Fitzgerald's Gatsby, whose acquired gentility dissolves in the end to oust the parvenu from the ranks of aristocracy or "old money." The same protective impulse guides Page in *John Marvel*, perhaps his most realistically painted plight of the Southern aristocrat. Although Henry Glave's whiteness is undermined from within through his disregard for *noblesse oblige*, he perceives the error of his ways, reforms, and prospers—while Wolffert's populist notions lead to a tragic end like Burr's. Marvel alone escapes critique because he remains in his place among his working-class parishioners and, thus maintaining the *status quo*, presents no threat.

This tendency to see the Southern aristocrat triumphant, evident in Page and Glasgow's works, owes something to their own heritage. Hailing from Virginian aristocratic stock, both writers find it hard to bury the myth of antebellum innocence and gentility. Indeed, Glasgow confesses that she "had been born with an intimate feeling for the spirit of the past, and the lingering poetry of time and place;" and growing up "in the South there was not only adolescence to outgrow, there was an insidious sentimental tradition to live down."[20] The individual social positions of these writers bear upon the objectivity of their critique of Southern aristocracy, adulterating it with a modified version of social determinism. The aristocrats in *The Voice of the People*, *The Deliverance*, and *John Marvel*, are certainly not the fittest, yet they survive; while self-made men like Burr, or reformers like Wolffert, perish. In *The Voice of the People*, Dudley Webb succeeds as governor; in *The Deliverance*, Christopher is miraculously restored to his ancestral home, and even Henry Glave in *John Marvel*, after a period of repentance and struggle, marries a lady and heiress. The extent to which the individual reluctance to de-sentimentalize the story of Southern aristocracy is influenced by public demand can never be accurately divined. The fascination with all things Southern and the appetite for Southern fiction continued to grow above and below the Mason-Dixon line after the last sounds of guns had died out at Appomattox. In order to accommodate affection for the genteel values and respond to a popular demand for the image of antebellum pastoral, both Glasgow and Page vacillate between realism and sentimentalism in their versions of the myth, which permit only a veiled critique.

A similarly tempered critique is evident in Chesnutt's work, although it is safe to assume that affection for aristocratic values was not his primary concern. The son of "free Negroes from North Carolina" who was, by his own admission, "as white as any" white man, Chesnutt's heritage marked him as an antithesis of the values that Page and Glasgow espouse. His motives for keeping a journal are rather complex; the lofty notion of elevating and educating the whites contrasts sharply with the candid admission of wanting "fame," "money," and social mobility for his children.[21] Unsurprisingly, like Chesnutt, many of his protagonists set out to live the American Dream, earning the privilege with hard work and diligence. Dr. Miller in *The Marrow of Tradition* is a gentleman in all but name, while John Walden in *The House behind the Cedars* is worthier of the appellation than George Tryon. Compared to Janet Miller's and Rowena Walden's flawless characters, the preordained ladies like Polly Ochiltree or Olivia Carteret seem like ogres. Through the success and social mobility of these men, which in the case of Walden is accomplished by passing the color line, Chesnutt demonstrates that whiteness need not be circumscribed by outdated notions of heredity. His critique of the rhetoric of hereditary whiteness in *Mandy Oxendine, The Marrow of Tradition, The House behind the Cedars,* and *The Colonel's Dream* is conveyed from the perspective of a genteel mind, even if this gentility is acquired through education. Key to social mobility is, in part, Chesnutt's heroes' ability to assimilate, not necessarily when it comes to color, but achievement.[22] Therein lies Chesnutt's dual didactic message, in demonstrating the imperfect gentility of the whites and proving that whiteness can transcend the color line. In order to render such a revolutionary idea more palatable to his contemporaneous audience, Chesnutt's realism at times suffers from maudlin sentimentality of which Page would have been proud, particularly in his portrayal of the virtuous Rowena. Only when he speaks through Uncle Julius does Chesnutt abandon sentimentalism and, through a curious combination of folk tale, realism, and irony undermines the myth of antebellum whiteness.

Unlike Chesnutt, though she shares a similar heritage, Dunbar-Nelson's characters rarely live to reap the benefits of upward mobility.[23] Placing her characters beyond the pale of whiteness enables her to critique not only the arbitrariness of its rhetoric that maims those who dare to aspire, like Victor Grabért, but also to explore the duality inherent in the concept of Creole.[24] Dunbar-Nelson's preoccupation with the ambiguity of Creole serves a dual purpose in that it constitutes an indictment of blood classifications and reifies her regional affiliation with Louisiana. Her concern with the blood designations mirrors that of another fellow Louisianian, George Washington Cable, whose *The Grandissimes* tells a story of two Honoré Grandissmes who, despite sharing a father and a name, embody the disparate meanings of Creole: a person of pure Latin descent and a person with a drop of black blood.

This burden of blood that haunts her stories is not unique to Dunbar-Nelson; nor can Page, Glasgow, Chesnutt, and Faulkner put its unquiet spirit to rest, for it is intertwined with the past and heritage, for in the South, "blood is blood and you can't get around it." Blood is a metonymy that stands for continuity, history, past, and, simultaneously, connotes a living force that secures their renewal. This preoccupation with the past, lived and *re*-lived inflects the works of these authors with a gothicism manifest as a haunting presence. What these Southern writers share is not only an awareness of the past as past, but also its continuing influence upon the present, which indiscriminately blights both reconstructions of and aspirations to Southern whiteness. Their protagonists choose to "live among defeated grandfathers" and "bullets in the dining room table and such" to remind them "never to forget."[25] Surrounded by monuments of the past, whether inherited or acquired, their heroes and heroines are both compelled to attempt and fail to replicate the gentility of the antebellum antecedents. Theirs is a Faustian bargain sealed in blood, which condemns the preordained aristocrat and the upstart alike, and transforms each reconstruction of whiteness into a site of mutation, while whiteness proper remains a promise beyond attainment.

NOTES

INTRODUCTION

1. *Hart of Dixie*, directed by Lila Gerstein (2011–2015, CW). For the symbolism of the hart (stag, fawn) see, James MacKillop, *A Dictionary of Celtic Mythology* (Oxford: Oxford University Press, 2016); J. A. Coleman, *The Dictionary of Mythology: An A-Z of Themes, Legends and Heroes* (London: Arcturus, 2018). John Gage's *Colour and Culture: Practice and Meaning from Antiquity to Abstraction*, new ed. (London, Thames & Hudson, 1995) delves into the symbolism of the color white.

2. *The Birth of a Nation*, directed by D. W. Griffith (1915; Epoch Producing Corporation); *The Help*, directed by Tate Taylor (2011; Walt Disney Studios Motion Pictures); *Gone with the Wind*, directed by Victor Fleming (1939; Loew's Inc.); *Song of the South*, directed by Harve Foster and Wilfred Jackson (1946; RKO Radio Pictures).

3. See, for example, Toni Morrison, *Playing in the Dark: Whiteness and the Literary Imagination* (London: Pan Books, 1993); Stephanie Li, *Playing in the White: Black Writers, White Subjects* (New York: Oxford University Press, 2015); Susan Gillman, *Blood Talk: American Race Melodrama and the Culture of the Occult* (Chicago: The University of Chicago Press, 2003); Mark Twain, *Pudd'nhead Wilson*, ed. Malcolm Bradbury, Penguin Classics (Harmondsworth, UK: Penguin, 1969), 103.

4. William Shakespeare, *The New Penguin Shakespeare: Macbeth*, ed. G. K. Hunter (London: Penguin, 1967), 1.3.141–42.

5. For discussions of the instability and arbitrariness of color classifications, see Edward Marguia and Tyrone Forman, "Shades of Whiteness: The Mexican American Experience in Relation to Anglos and Blacks," in *White Out: The Continuing Significance of Racism*, ed. Ashley Doane and Eduardo Bonilla-Silva (London: Routledge, 2003), 65; Richard Dyer, *White* (London: Routledge, 1997), 25; Felipe Smith, *American Body Politics: Gender, and Black Literary Renaissance* (Athens: The University of Georgia Press, 1998), 45; Theodore W. Allen, *The Invention of the White Race*, 2 vols. (London: Verso, 1995–97), 1.27–28. Each volume contains a subtitle: *Racial Oppression and Social Control* and *The Origin of Racial Oppression in Anglo-America*, respectively.

6. Jessica Adams, "Local Color: The Southern Plantation in Popular Culture," *Cultural Critique* 42 (1999): 164, http://www.jstor.org/stable/1354595. For the concept of context, see Jacques Derrida, "Afterward: Toward an Ethic of Discussion," in *Limited Inc*, trans. Samuel Weber and Jeffrey Mehlman (Evanston, IL: Northwestern University Press, 1988), 136; Jacques Derrida, *Of Grammatology*, trans. Gayatri Chakravorty Spivak (Baltimore, MD: The Johns Hopkins University Press, 1976), 158; Jacques Derrida, "Living On," in *Deconstruction and Criticism*, trans. James Hulbert (London: Continuum,

2004), 67; Ross Chambers offers a discussion of contextual marking and stereotyping in "The Unexamined," in *Whiteness: A Critical Reader*, ed. Mike Hill (New York: New York University Press, 1997), 187–203. The volume is cited in the bibliography. Susan-Mary Grant's *The War for a Nation: The American Civil War* (London: Routledge, 2006) and *North over South: Northern Nationalism and American Identity in the Antebellum Era* (Lawrence, KA: University of Kansas Press, 2000) delineate perspicuously the complexity of Northern and Southern attitudes toward slavery. For a discussion of socioeconomic conditions prevalent in the South, see Allen, *Invention*, 2.174; see also Grant, *War for a Nation*, 23, for a discussion of the interdependence of slavery and Southern representation in Congress.

7. John C. Calhoun, *Speeches of Mr. Calhuon of S. Carolina, on the bill for the Admission of Michigan: delivered in the Senate of the United States, January, 1837* (Washington, DC: Duff Green, 1837), 6.

8. Judith Butler deems violence the most effective and direct route to nullifying the body of the Other, *Subjects of Desire: Hegelian Reflections in Twentieth-Century France* (New York: Columbia University Press, 1987), 52. For the spurious sense of collective whiteness, see David R. Roediger, *The Wages of Whiteness: Race and the Making of the American Working Class* (London: Verso, 1991), 107. Ralph Ellison discusses the spectacle as a cathartic experience in "Change the Joke and Slip the Yoke," in *Shadow and Act* (New York: Vintage International, 1995), 49. For linguistic re-appropriations of terms such as "coon," "Mose," and "buck," see David R. Roediger, *Towards the Abolition of Whiteness* (London: Verso, 1994), 66; and Roediger, *Wages*, 98–99. For definitions of "Mose," see also Alexander Saxton, "Blackface Minstrelsy and Jacksonian Ideology," *American Quarterly* 27, no. 1 (1975): 9, doi: 10.2307/2711892. Roediger also discusses the terms "hands" or "helpers" as substitute words used by white workers in an attempt to dissociate themselves from the stigma of servitude. But history and etymology suggest otherwise. In the seventeenth century, "hand" was used to denote a "manual worker," while an earlier example "*handþegn* manservant," which derives from Old English, suggests that derivatives of the term would have been in circulation for a considerable time before slavery was institutionalized in the United States, in *Oxford Dictionary of English Etymology*, ed. C. T. Onions (London: Oxford University Press, 1969), 425–26. However, the most compelling counterargument to Roediger's theory can be found in Charles Waddell Chesnutt's collection of stories, *The Conjure Woman and Other Conjure Tales*. Here, Chesnutt recreates the black vernacular speech of the nineteenth century, and the narrator of the stories, Uncle Julius, who is a former slave, frequently uses the term "han's" to refer to other slaves. I discuss the stories from that collection in the last chapter. Similarly, in her autobiography, Ellen Glasgow recalls that her mammy "would make one of the colored 'hands' harness a horse to an old wagon," and they would pretend to be gypsies, in *The Woman Within* (New York: Hill and Wang, 1980), 33. Both Chesnutt's and Glasgow's use of the term and its etymology suggest that it would have been employed to denote manual workers regardless of skin color. Peter Kolchin offers a critique of Roediger's discussion of those terms in "Whiteness Studies: The New History of Race in America," *The Journal of American History* 89, no.1 (2002): 156, http://www.jstor.org

/stable/2700788. Grace Elizabeth Hale offers a detailed description of nineteenth-century advertisements relying on black-figure imagery in *Making Whiteness: The Culture of Segregation in the South, 1890-1940* (New York: Vintage Books, 1999), 138-68. bell hooks notes the parallel between "domination and castration" as one of the "gendered metaphors for colonization," in *Yearning: Race, Gender, and Cultural Politics* (London: Turnaround, 1991), 57.

9. Allen, *Invention*, 2.120, 1.72-75, 2.20, 1.74, 2.183, 1.84-85, 1.153, 1.138. Nancy Isenberg proves that disenfranchisement in the Southern colonies was first and foremost a class phenomenon, adopted from the fatherland, in *White Trash: The 400-Year Untold History of Class in America* (London: Atlantic Books, 2017), 20-21; cited in Allen, *Invention*, 2.256; Glasgow, *Woman Within*, 52.

10. Mike Hill, "Introduction: Vipers in Shangri-La," in *Whiteness: A Critical Reader*, 3; Benjamin Franklin, "Observations Concerning the Increase of Mankind and the Peopling of Countries (1751)," in *The Autobiography and Other Writings*, ed. Peter Shaw (New York: Bantam, 1982), 226. Johan Gottlieb Fichte sings the praises of Anglo-Saxon superiority in his *Addresses to the German Nation*, ed. Gregory Moore (Cambridge: Cambridge University Press, 2008); Herman Melville, *Moby-Dick* (1851), ed. Harrison Hayford and Hershel Parker (New York: Norton, 1967), 169.

11. Valerie Melissa Babb, *Whiteness Visible: The Meaning of Whiteness in American Literature and Culture* (New York: New York University Press, 1998), 9-10; Rebecca Aanerud, "Fictions of Whiteness: Speaking the Names of Whiteness in U.S. Literature," in *Displacing Whiteness: Essays in Social and Cultural Criticism*, ed. Ruth Frankenberg (Durham, NC: Duke University Press, 1997), 37; Henry A. Giroux, "Racial Politics and the Pedagogy of Whiteness," in *Whiteness: A Critical Reader*, 311-12; Giroux, "Racial Politics," in *Whiteness: A Critical Reader*, 295. For discussions of whiteness and race, see also Maurice Berger, *White Lies: Race and the Myths of Whiteness* (New York: Farrar, Strauss and Giroux, 1999) and Angelo Rich Robinson, "Race, Place and Space: Remaking Whiteness in the Post-Reconstruction South," *Southern Literary Journal* 35, no. 1 (2002): 97-107, http://www.jstor.org/stable/20078351; Babb, *Whiteness*, 9; Butler, *Subjects of Desire*, 67. For a psychoanalytic dissection of whiteness with a Lacanian twist, see Kalpana Sheshadri-Crooks, *Desiring Whiteness: A Lacanian Analysis of Race* (London: Routledge, 2000). Ruth Frankenberg offers an interesting discussion of the heterogeneity of whiteness in *White Women, Race Matters: The Social Construction of Whiteness* (Minneapolis: University of Minnesota Press, 1994). For the social construction of gender roles, see Judith Lorber, "The Social Construction of Gender," in *Race, Class, and Gender in the United States*, ed. Paula S. Rothenberg, 5th ed. (New York: Worth Publishers, 2001), 52.

12. Alexandre Kojève, *Introduction to the Reading of Hegel*, ed. Allan Bloom, trans. James H. Nicholls, Jr. (New York: Basic Books, 1969), 43. For more on detotalizing history, see Jacques Derrida, *Positions*, trans. Alan Bass (Chicago: The University of Chicago Press, 1981). The very concept of the whole or totality, as Robert Young demonstrates, engenders its own antagonism in that its constitutive elements can only furnish partial meanings precisely because the totality itself only exists as a concept, *White Mythologies: Writing History and the West* (London: Routledge, 1995), 61.

13. Marguia and Forman use the term "shades of whiteness" in their discussion of preconceived notions of whiteness that lead to the emergence of hegemonic whiteness, in "Shades of Whiteness," in *White Out*, 65; Kolchin, "Whiteness Studies," 163.

14. Franklin, *Autobiography*, 122. For linguistic shellacking and stereotyping, see John Hartigan, Jr.'s fascinating discussion of the application of the terms "mean whites," "clayeaters," and "sandhillers," in *Odd Tribes: Toward a Cultural Analysis of White People* (Durham, NC: Duke University Press, 2005), 61. Isenberg offers a splendid historical study of the etymology and usage of the terms "cracker" and its Northern equivalent "squatter," "sandhiller" and "piney," in *White Trash*, 105–34. John A. Burrison presents an alternative definition, which proposes that the term "cracker" derives from Gaelic "craic" which was in circulation in Elizabethan England. In the United States, the term was applied to cowboys of Florida and Georgia who used bullwhips with a cracker tip to herd cattle; while African Americans employed the term to poor white Southerners, in "Crackers," in the *New Georgia Encyclopedia*, last modified August 6, 2013, accessed 3 June 2019, http:// www.georgiaencyclopedia.org/articles/arts-culture/crackers. Roediger's discussion of the moniker "redneck" cites a study conducted by Billy Bowles and Remer Tyson concerning its etymology, in *Towards*, 136–37. For the treatment accorded white Appalachians, see Suzanne W. Jones, "City Folks in Hoot Owl Holler: Narrative Strategy in Lee Smith's *Oral History*," *Southern Literary Journal* 20, no. 1 (1987): 101, https://www.jstor.org/stable/20077851.

15. Dyer, *White*, 17; Babb, *Whiteness*, 68, 76. Sir Walter Scott, *Ivanhoe*, ed. A. N. Wilson (Harmondsworth, UK: Penguin, 1982). Jacques Derrida observes of identity that it "is never given, received or attained, only the indeterminable and indefinitely phantasmatic process of identification endures," in *Monolingualism of the Other, or, the Prosthesis of Origin*, trans. Patrick Mensah (Stanford, CA: Stanford University Press, 1998), 28. For the formation of identity as a process of negation, see Jacques Lacan, *Écrits: A Selection*, trans. Alan Sheridan (London: Routledge, 2009), 183.

16. Erich Auerbach, *Mimesis: The Representation of Reality in Western Literature*, trans. Willard R. Trask (Princeton, NJ: Princeton University Press, 1991), 139.

17. Dyer, *White*, 16. For my formulation of the concept of truth, I am indebted to Jacques Derrida, *Dissemination*, trans. Barbara Johnson (London: Continuum, 2011), 206.

18. For the ideas of Christian asceticism, the renunciation of sin, and the legalization of the carnivalesque, see Mikhail Bakhtin, *Rabelais and His World*, in *The Bakhtin Reader: Selected Writings of Bakhtin, Medvedev, Voloshinov*, ed. Pam Morris, trans. H. Iswolsky (London: Arnold Hodder, 2002), 208. The volume is cited in the bibliography. Michael Omi and Howard Winant suggest that a similar logic guided and formed the colonizers' perceptions and subsequent treatment of native peoples. "Racial Formations," in *Race, Class*, 12. Eric Lott sees otherness as a "moral and psychological" phenomenon stemming from the recognition of "the 'dark' side of the white Western self," in "The Whiteness of Film Noir," in *Whiteness: A Critical Reader*, 82.

19. Frederick Turner, "Cultivating the American Garden," in *The Ecocriticism Reader: Landmarks in Literary Ecology*, ed. Cheryll Glotfelty and Harold Fromm (Athens: University of Georgia Press, 1996), 48. In all subsequent quotations from essays in this col-

lection, the collection will be referenced as *Ecocriticism*. The volume is cited in the bibliography. For readings on environment and literature, see Laurence Coupe, ed., *The Green Studies Reader: From Romanticism to Ecocriticism* (London: Routledge, 2000); Lindsay Claire Smith, *Indians, Environment and Identity on the Borders of American Literature: From Faulkner and Morrison to Walker and Silko* (New York: Palgrave Macmillan, 2008). For an account of Southern belles and cavaliers, see Ritchie Devon Watson Jr., *Normans and Saxons: Southern Race Mythology and the Intellectual History of the American Civil War* (Baton Rouge: Louisiana State University Press, 2008), and Smith, *American Body Politics*.

20. Allen Tate, "Religion and the Old South," in *Collected Essays* (Denver, CO: Alan Swallow, 1959); Patrick D. Murphy, *Further Afield in the Study of Nature-Oriented Literature* (Charlottesville, VA: The University Press of Virginia, 2000); David Landis Barnhill, "Introduction," in *At Home on the Earth: Becoming Native to Our Place: A Multicultural Anthology* (Berkeley: University of California Press, 1999); Allen, *Invention*, 2.174. Allen observes that before Virginia was settled, "a distinction was made between those who invested money but stayed in England, and those who went to Virginia as colonists. The former were called 'Adventurers,' the latter were called 'Planters.'" Allen continues that "these Adventurers and Planters would then be free and independent Virginia landowners," in *Invention*, 2.53–54. The status of planter as the apotheosis of Southern society was confirmed in England, and the emerging planter class consisted of those who were already socially privileged. Richard Gray concurs with Allen, noting that "the colonization of Virginia was primarily a business enterprise, financed by merchants and nobles who wanted a good return on their investment," in *Writing the South: Ideas of an American Region* (Baton Rouge: Louisiana State University Press, 1997), 1.

21. Ralph Waldo Emerson, cited in Watson, *Normans and Saxons*, 133; Aristotle, *The Politics*, trans. T. A. Sinclair, rev. by Trevor J. Saunders (London: Penguin, 1992), 410; Vitruvius Pollio, *The Ten Books on Architecture*, trans. Richard Schofield, intro. Robert Tavernor (London: Penguin, 2009), 168–69; "Cuba: The March of Empire and the Course of Trade," *DeBow's Review* 30, no. 1 (1861): 41, http://quod.lib.umich.edu/m/moajrnl/acg1336.1-30.001/30.

22. J. Quitman Moore, "Feudalism in America," *DeBow's Review* 28, no. 6 (1860): 619, http://quod.lib.umich.edu/m/moajrnl/acg1336.1-28.006/619; Thomas Nelson Page, *The Old South: Essays Social and Political* (1892; New York: Cosimo, 2008), 8. Facsimile of the first edition; Isenberg, *White Trash*, 24–28; Page, *Old South*, 5.

23. See, for example, Ernst Robert Curtius, *European Literature and the Latin Middle Ages*, intro. Colin Burrow (Princeton, NJ: Princeton University Press, 2013); Ezra Pound, *The Spirit of Romance*, intro. Richard Sieburth (New York: New Directions, 2005).

24. Page, *Old South*, 6–7.

25. John Winthrop, "A Modell of Christian Charity" (1630), in *Early American Writing*, ed. Giles Gunn (Harmondsworth, UK: Penguin, 1994), 107. For historical context, see Daniel T. Rodgers, *As a City on a Hill: The Story of America's Most Famous Lay Sermon* (Princeton, NJ: Princeton University Press, 2018).

26. A. Clarkson, "The Basis of Northern Hostility to the South," *DeBow's Review* 28, no. 1

(1860): 10–11, https://quod.lib.umich.edu/m/moajrnl/acg1336.1-28.001/11; Watson, *Normans and Saxons*, 173; Clarkson, "The Basis," 11; J. T. Wiswall, "Causes of Aristocracy," *DeBow's Review* 28, no. 5 (1860): 565, http://quod.lib.umich.edu/m/moajrnl/acg1336.1-28.005/555.

27. The term "universal Yankee" was coined by Robert Walsh, a journalist from Philadelphia, in 1822 and, by 1860, was in wide circulation in the North; in Watson, *Normans and Saxons*, 125–26. For the similarity between the function of mask and the myth, see Roman Jakobson, "Dear Claude, Cher Maître," in *On Signs*, ed. Marshall Blonsky (Oxford: Blackwell, 1985), 185.

28. Hale, *Making*, 3. For accounts of the Old South, see Hale, Saxton, Roediger, and Tara MacPherson, *Reconstructing Dixie: Race, Gender, and Nostalgia in the Imagined Old South* (Durham, NC: Duke University Press, 2003).

29. Richard Gray, *Southern Aberrations* (Baton Rouge: Louisiana State University Press, 2000), 61. See also Donna Campbell, "Realism and Regionalism"; and Lori Robinson, "Region and Race: National Identity and the Southern Past"; and Stephanie Foote, "The Cultural Work of Southern Regionalism," in *A Companion to the Regional Literatures of America*, ed. Charles L. Crow (Oxford: Blackwell, 2003). The volume is cited in the bibliography. Bill Hardwig's examination of inter-regional relations in *Upon Provincialism: Southern Literature and National Periodical Culture, 1870-1900* (Charlottesville, VA: University of Virginia Press, 2013) also merits close scrutiny.

30. Ellen Glasgow, *A Certain Measure: An Interpretation of Prose Fiction* (New York: Harcourt, Brace and Company, 1938), 195.

31. See Hardwig, *Upon Provincialism*, 12–13; Hamlin Garland, *Crumbling Idols*, ed. Jane Johnson (Cambridge, MA: Belknap Press of Harvard University Press, 1960), 51–52.

32. Tate, "The New Provincialism," in *Collected Essays*, 286; Tate, "The New Provincialism," in *Collected Essays*, 292; Sarah E. Gardner, *Blood and Irony: Southern White Women's Narratives of the Civil War, 1861-1937* (Chapel Hill: The University of North Carolina Press, 2004), Kindle edition, loc.1132, 1534, 1660.

33. Thomas Nelson Page, *Red Rock: A Chronicle of Reconstruction* (New York: Grosset & Dunlap, 1904); Thomas Nelson Page, *Gordon Keith* (New York: Charles Scribner's Sons, 1910); Ellen Glasgow, *The Voice of the People* (New York: Doubleday, Page & Co., 1900); Ellen Glasgow, *The Battle-Ground* (New York: Doubleday, Page & Co., 1902); Eric Hobsbawm, "Introduction," in *The Invention of Tradition*, ed. Eric Hobsbawm and Terence Ranger (Cambridge: Cambridge University Press, 1992), 2.

34. See Mark Twain, *Life on the Mississippi*, intro. Petr Barta (London: Wordsworth, 2012); Mark Twain, *The Adventures of Huckleberry Finn*, ed. Jane Ogborn (Cambridge: Cambridge University Press, 1995). For more on the influence of Scott on Page, Glasgow, and Chesnutt, see also Izabela Hopkins, "Beyond Coincidence: Scottish Inflections in Thomas Nelson Page's *Gordon Keith* and *Red Rock: A Chronicle of Reconstruction*," *South Central Review* 33, no. 3 (2016): 53-68.; Sir Walter Scott, *Waverley; or 'Tis Sixty Years Since*, ed. Claire Lamont (Oxford: Oxford University Press, 1998), 41. For a refreshing critique of the privileging of things European in nineteenth-century American art, see B. "A Plea for Art," *Southern Literary Messenger; devoted to every department of literature and the fine arts* 15, no. 10 (Oct. 1849): 624–26, http://quod.lib.umich.edu/m/moajrnl/acf2679.0015.010/628.

35. Charles Waddell Chesnutt, *The House behind the Cedars* (Boston, MA: Houghton, Mifflin and Co., 1900; repr., Mineola, NY: Dover Publications Inc., 2007).

36. See John Pendleton Kennedy, *The Swallow Barn; or, the Sojourn in the Old Dominion, Horseshoe Robinson: A Tale of the Tory Ascendancy*, and William Gilmore Simms, *Guy Rivers: A Tale of Georgia*.

37. Ellen Glasgow, *The Deliverance: A Romance of the Virginia Tobacco Fields* (Doubleday, Page & Co., 1904); Thomas Nelson Page, *In Ole Virginia; Or, Marse Chan and Other Stories, Southern Classics Series*, intr. Clyde N. Wilson (1887; repr., Nashville: J.S. Sanders and Company, 1991). The technique is a borrowing from Scott, although Lori Robinson sees it as a characteristic of regional writing. "Region and Race," in *Companion*, 64.

38. For a discussion of Scott's influence on the historical novel, see Georg Lukács, *The Historical Novel*, trans. Hannah and Stanley Mitchell (Harmondsworth, UK: Penguin, 1969); George Dekker, *The American Historical Romance* (Cambridge: Cambridge University Press, 1987). The technique may be seen in practice in such Scott's novels as *Waverley*; or *'Tis Sixty Years Since* or *Rob Roy*.

39. Alice Dunbar-Nelson, "The Stones of the Village," in *Laughing to Stop Myself Crying* (London: The X Press, 2000). According to Gloria T. Hull, the story remained in manuscript and, in 1900, Dunbar-Nelson's proposition to Bliss Perry at the *Atlantic Monthly* to expand it into a novel was rejected. In "Introduction," *The Works of Alice Dunbar-Nelson*, ed. Gloria T. Hull, vol. 2 (New York: Oxford University Press, 1988), xxxvi. Page references to all Dunbar-Nelson stories are to the 2000 reprint.

CHAPTER 1

1. Hobsbawm, "Introduction," 7–9; Michel De Certeau, "Practices of Space," trans. Richard Miller and Edward Schneider, in *On Signs*, ed. Marshall Blonsky (Oxford: Blackwell, 1985), 131; Allen, *Invention*, 2.174; Allen, *Invention*, 2.53–54; Gray, *Writing the South*, 1 (see intr., n. 20).

2. Murphy, *Further Afield*, 14. For accounts of founding the colony, see Allen's *Invention*, 2 vols.; Gray, *Writing the South*; and Watson, *Normans and Saxons*.

3. See Hale, *Making*, 3–4; Certeau, "Practices of Space," 127. For discussions of the concept of the idyllic Old South, see Saxton, Roediger, and Hale.

4. Page, *Old South*, 5.

5. "The South's Dire Need," report from Thomas Nelson Page's address to the Society of Virginia Alumni, *Louisville Courier Journal* (Louisville, KY), April 14, 1891, morning edition, 1, https://www.newspapers.com/image/32460948; "Thomas Nelson Page," review of the Plantation Edition of Thomas Nelson Page's works, *New York Times*, January 19, 1907, 27, https://www.newspapers.com/image/20611363. See, for example, Sarah E. Gardner, "The Plantation School: Dissenters and Countermyths," 267; and Lucinda Hardiwck MacKethan, *The Dream of Arcady: Place and Time in Southern Literature* (Baton Rouge: Louisiana State University Press, 1980), 17.

6. Richard Channing Moore Page, "Virginia Heraldry: The Great Clan of Page," *Baltimore Sun* (Baltimore, MD), January 27, 1907, morning edition, 17, https://www.newspapers.com/image/214436858; Moore Page, "Virginia Heraldry," 17; Dexter Marshall,

"Descendants of the Signers of '76 Prominent in the History of the Nation," *Indianapolis Star* (Indianapolis, IN), June 30, 1907, magazine section, 3, https://www.newspapers.com/image/118563922. See also Lucinda H. MacKethan, "Plantation Fiction, 1865-1900," in *The History of Southern Literature*, ed. Louis D. Rubin, Jr. et al. (Baton Rouge: Louisiana State University Press, 1985), 212

7. Marshall, "Descendants," 3; Clyde N. Wilson, "Introduction," xii.
8. Page, "Marse Chan," 1, 4; Hardwig, *Upon Provincialism*, 28.
9. Page, "Marse Chan," 6.
10. Page, "Unc' Edinburg's Drowndin'," 40.
11. Ibid.; Ibid., 53; Page, "Meh Lady," 81.
12. Page, "Meh Lady," 82; Thomas Nelson Page, "Bred in the Bone" (New York: Charles Scribner's Sons, 1891).
13. Page, "Meh Lady," 93.
14. Ibid.; Hardwig, *Upon Provincialism*, 29.
15. Review of Thomas Nelson Page's *In Ole Virginia*, *Boston Post* (Boston, MA), May 30, 1887, morning edition, 4, https://www.newspapers.com/image/67555878.
16. "Books and Authors," review of Thomas Nelson Page's *In Ole Virginia*, *Atlanta Constitution* (Atlanta, Georgia), June 5, 1887, 14, https://www.newspapers.com/image/26949042; Samuel M. Smith, "The New and the Old South: A Review of Page's Popular Book 'In Ole Virginia,'" *Weekly State Chronicle* (Raleigh, NC), October 27, 1887, 1, https://www.newspapers.com/image/56761211; "New Publications," *Baltimore Sun* (Baltimore, MD), June 21, 1887, supplement section, 5, https://www.newspapers.com/image/214376739.
17. "Thomas Nelson Page Will Raise Mules," *Louisville Courier-Journal* (Louisville, KY), April 8, 1907, morning edition, 1, https://www.newspapers.com/image/119174431.
18. William Morton Payne, review of Thomas Nelson Page's *On Newfound River*, *The Dial: A Monthly Journal of Current Literature* XII, 1891, 278, http://www.hathitrust.prg; "Talk about New Books," review of Thomas Nelson Page's *On Newfound River*, *Catholic World* 54, no. 319 (October 1891): 138, http://www.internetarchive.org; review of Thomas Nelson Page's *On Newfound River*, *Chicago Daily Tribune*, June 6, 1891, 12, https://www.newspapers.com/image/28513424; "A Charming Love Story," review of Thomas Nelson Page's *On Newfound River*, *Harrisburg Telegraph* (Harrisburg, PA), July 11, 1891, evening edition, 2; "In the World of Books," review of Thomas Nelson Page's *On Newfound River*, *Pinehurst Outlook* (Pinehurst, NC), February 16, 1907, 6, https://www.newspapers.com/image/67842329; review of Thomas Nelson Page's *On Newfound River*, *Brooklyn Daily Eagle* (Brooklyn, New York), June 14, 1891, 16, https://www.newspapers.com/image/50449103.
19. Thomas Nelson Page, *On Newfound River* (New York: Charles Scribner's Sons, 1891), 2.
20. Ibid., 3.
21. Ibid., 3, 4.
22. Henri Lefebvre, *The Production of Space*, trans. Donald Nicholson-Smith (Oxford: Blackwell, 1991), 220; Page, *On Newfound*, 4, 96.
23. Page, *On Newfound*, 6, 42, 32, 36-38.
24. Ibid., 154-55.

25. For discussions of such labels as white trash, hillbillies, and rednecks, see, for example, John Hartigan, Jr., "Who Are These White People?: 'Rednecks,' 'Hillbillies,' and 'White Trash' as White Racial Subjects," in *White Out*, 95; John Hartigan, Jr., *Odd Tribes*; David R. Roediger, *Towards the Abolition of Whiteness*.

26. Page, *On Newfound*, 156–57.

27. Ibid., 158, 200, 9.

28. Ibid., 212.

29. Ibid., 234.

30. "New Books," review of Thomas Nelson Page's *Gordon Keith*, *Minneapolis Journal* (Minneapolis, MN), July 1, 1903, evening edition, 4, https://www.newspapers.com/image/76297378.

31. "Recent Fiction," review of Thomas Nelson Page's *Gordon Keith*, *The Dial: A Semi-Monthly Journal of Literary Criticism, Discussion, and Information* XXXV (July–December 1903): 66–67, http://www.internetarchive.org; Jeannette L. Gilder, "Page's 'Gordon Keith,'" *Chicago Daily Tribune*, May 23, 1903, 9, https://www.newspapers.com/image/28621852; "Thomas Page's 'Gordon Keith,'" *Louisville Courier-Journal* (Louisville, KY), June 6, 1903, morning edition, 5, https://www.newspapers.com/image/118985395; "Latest Work of Mr. Page," review of Thomas Nelson Page's *Gordon Keith*, *Washington Times*, July 19, 1903, 13, https://www.newspapers.com/image/80644350.

32. *Brewer's Dictionary of Names*, ed. Adrian Room (Oxford: Helicon, 1997), gives the following definitions of Gordon and Keith: Gordon—"the name comes from the Scottish surname, which is itself from the village of *Gordon* near Kelso, not far from the English border. Its own name is said to mean 'spacious fort'" (213). Keith "derives from a Scottish surname, itself from the Celtic name of a place in East Lothian meaning 'wood'"(281). Curiously, in her "Introduction" to Sir Walter Scott's *Waverley; or, 'Tis Sixty Years Since*, Claire Lamont observes that Scott spent his childhood "partly in Edinburgh and partly in the Borders near Kelso" (vii). In naming his protagonist Gordon, Page introduces a subtle allusion to Scott.

33. See, for example, the Scottish ballad "The Elfin Knight," in David Buchan, ed., *A Scottish Ballad Book* (London: Routledge, 1973), 137. In what appears to be a modern English version of the ballad published in *The Faber Book of Ballads*, ed. Matthew Hodgart (London: Faber & Faber, 1965), "the elfin knight" is transformed into "the elphin knight" (26–28). The latter example suggests that the two variations of the word could have been used interchangeably or, at the very least, that the spelling of "elfin" changed over time to "elphin." What matters is that both variations evoke supernatural, magical connotations: "elfin," orthographically, and "elphin," phonetically. The historical Elphin was the King of Pictland and ruled from 775–880, in James E. Fraser, *From Caledonia to Pictland: Scotland to 795* (Edinburgh: Edinburgh University Press, 2009), 273. Elphinstone was the name of William, the Bishop of Aberdeen and founder of the University of Aberdeen in 1495, see Leslie Macfarlane's *William Elphinstone and The Kingdom of Scotland 1431–1514: The Struggle for Order*, (Aberdeen: Aberdeen University Press, 1995). Another famous bearer of the name was George Keith Elphinstone, Viscount Keith and "Baron Keith of Stonehaven Marischal," in *Burke's Peerage*, 2002–2012 Burke's Peerage

(UK) Limited, http://www.burkespeerage.com. Alexander Allardyce's *Memoir of the Honourable George Keith Elphinstone Viscount Keith, Admiral of the Red* (Edinburgh: William Blackwood and Sons, 1882), though dated, is a valuable source of information on the Keith Elphinstone family. See also Juliet Gardiner and Neil Wenborn, eds., *The History Today Companion to British History* (London: Collins & Brown, 1995).

34. Scott, *Waverley*, 34–35; Page, *Gordon Keith*, 4.

35. Page, *Gordon Keith*, 4.

36. Julius Evola, *Meditations on the Peaks: Mountain Climbing as Metaphor for Spiritual Quest*, trans. Guido Stucco (Rochester, VT: Inner Traditions, 1998), 12; Certeau, "Practices of Space," 123. For Mount Olympus and Greek gods, see Bergen Evans, *Dictionary of Mythology: Mainly Classical* (London: Franklin Watts, 1971). For a puritan interpretation of the biblical narrative of the mountain, see Winthrop, "The Modell of Christian Charity," (see intr. n. 25). In the sermon, Winthrop paraphrases Matthew, who proclaims: "Ye are the light of the world. A city that is set on a hill cannot be hid," King James Bible, Authorized Version, Matthew 5:14.

37. Page, *Gordon Keith*, 5.

38. Ibid., 5–6, 5.

39. Lefebvre, *Production*, 115; Page, *Gordon Keith*, 28; William Faulkner, *Requiem for a Nun* (London: Chatto & Windus, 1965), 85.

40. Adams notes the notion of continuity between history and the present that is encoded in the construct of the plantation house: "Plantation houses satisfy some desire for connection with history; as these sites contextualize the present within a history that is tangible, they convey a sense of collective identity, of a heritage that Americans share," "Local Color," 164; Page, *Gordon Keith*, 28; Werner Sollors, *Neither Black Nor White: Thematic Explorations of Interracial Literature* (New York: Oxford University Press, 1997), 247.

41. Page, *Gordon Keith*, 33.

42. Ibid., 54, 55, 54; Gavin Jones, *Strange Talk: The Politics of Dialect Literature in Gilded Age America* (Berkeley: University of California Press, 1999), 39; Page, *Gordon Keith*, 54, 55.

43. Page, *Gordon Keith*, 93. The line in question seems to be a paraphrase of Emily Dickinson's Poem No. 80, composed in 1859 and published in 1891, where it reads: "*Italy* stands the other side!," in *The Complete Poems of Emily Dickinson*, ed. Thomas H. Johnson (London: Faber and Faber, 1975), 42.

44. For Shelley and Byron's expedition to Italy, see, for example, Benjamin Colbert, *Shelley's Eye: Travel Writing and Aesthetic Vision* (London: Routledge, 2016).

45. Page, *Gordon Keith*, 93, 171.

46. For a discussion of stereotypical traits attributed to the North, see MacKethan, *Dream of Arcady*, 47.

47. Page, *Gordon Keith*, 80; Dickinson, Poem No. 80, 42. Helen Barolini suggests that Dickinson may be invoking Hannibal's rallying cry to his soldiers before crossing into Italy, in *Their Other Side: Six American Women and the Lure of Italy* (New York: Fordham

University Press, 2010), 75. Page's citation of the line adds a tint of ambition for more than classical learning to Gordon's striving.

48. Page, *Gordon Keith*, 71.
49. Ibid., 215, 307.
50. Ibid., 102, 104, 105.
51. Ibid., 35, 106.
52. Ibid., 515.
53. Ibid., 515, 515–16.
54. Ibid., 545.
55. Evola, *Meditations*, 15; Certeau, "Practices of Space," 141.

CHAPTER 2

1. Glasgow, *Certain Measure*, 3, 4, 165.
2. Glasgow, *Woman Within*, 15; Glasgow, *Certain Measure*, 12, 67, 12.
3. Glasgow, *Certain Measure*, 28, 67.
4. Frederick P. W. McDowell, *Ellen Glasgow and the Ironic Art of Fiction* (Madison: University of Wisconsin Press, 1963), 20, 22; R. H. W. Dillard, "On Ellen Glasgow's *The Battle-Ground*," *Classics of Civil War Fictions*, ed. David Madden and Peggy Bach (Jackson: University of Mississippi Press, 1991), 67; William Dean Howells, *Criticism and Fiction* (New York: Harper and Brothers, 1892), 73; see also William Dean Howells, "Editor's Study," *Harper's New Monthly Magazine* (November 1889): 966; Glasgow, *Certain Measure*, 14, 139, 14.
5. Gray, *Southern Aberrations*, 72; Glasgow, *Deliverance*, 479, 478; Glasgow, *Certain Measure*, 27;
6. Glasgow, *Certain Measure*, 157; Glasgow, *Deliverance*, 59, 359; McDowell, *Ellen Glasgow*, 93.
7. Glasgow, *Certain Measure*, 42.
8. Glasgow, *Deliverance*, 4, 6; Neil Evernden, "Beyond Ecology: Self, Place, and the Pathetic Fallacy," in *Ecocriticism*, 103.
9. Glasgow, *Deliverance*, 12, 8.
10. Glasgow, *Deliverance*, 12; Page, *Red Rock*, 253; Glasgow, *Deliverance*, 7.
11. McDowell, *Ellen Glasgow*, 92.
12. Glasgow, *Deliverance*, 25.
13. Ibid., 16; Murphy, "Anotherness" 46, 40.
14. Glasgow, *Deliverance*, 28, 36; Valentin Nikolaevich Vološinov, *Freudianism: A Marxist Critique*, trans. I. R. Titunik (New York: Academic Press, 1976), 45.
15. For a discussion of mimicry in contexts marred by colonialism, see Homi K. Bhabha's seminal essay "Of Mimicry and Man: The Ambivalence of Colonial Discourse," in *The Location of Culture* (London: Routledge, 1994), 85–92; Glasgow, *Deliverance*, 37, 44.
16. Glasgow, *Deliverance*, 44, 39, 15.
17. Ibid., 133; Sollors, *Neither Black Nor White*, 247.
18. Glasgow, *Deliverance*, 407.
19. Ibid., 144–45.

20. Ibid., 343, 418, 413.

21. Ibid., 70; Chad T. May, "'The Horrors of My Tale:' Trauma, the Historical Imagination, and Sir Walter Scott," *Pacific Coast Philology*, 40, no. 1 (2005): 99, http://www.jstor.org/stable/25474171.

22. Glasgow, *Deliverance*, 533.

23. Ibid., 74, 69.

24. Ibid., 71.

25. Ibid., 72-73.

26. Ibid., 159.

27. Ibid., 159, 198, 74, 269.

28. Ibid., 245, 431.

29. Ibid., 450, 487.

30. Ibid., 486; for a discussion of simulacrum, see Frederic Jameson, *Postmodernism, or, the Cultural Logic of Late Capitalism* (Durham, NC: Duke University Press, 1991); Jean Baudrillard, "Simulacra and Simulations," *Literary Theory: An Anthology*, 2nd ed., ed. Julie Rivkin and Michael Ryan (Oxford: Blackwell Publishing, 2004), 365-77.

31. Glasgow, *Deliverance*, 202-3, 419.

32. Ibid., 421.

33. Ibid., 421, 172.

34. King James Bible, Authorized Version, Job. 1.2, where it reads: "the Lord gave, and the Lord hath taken away." Colin Dayan uses the phrase to discuss the power of the law to make and unmake persons, observing: "The law giveth and the law taketh away," *The Law Is a White Dog: How Legal Rituals Make and Unmake Persons* (Princeton, NJ: Princeton University Press, 2011), 42.

35. Barnhill terms it "living with the land and its processes," in "Introduction," in *At Home on the Earth: Becoming Native to Our Place: A Multicultural Anthology*, ed. David Landis Barnhill (Berkeley: University of California Press, 1999), 5

36. Glasgow, *The Deliverance*, 182.

37. *New York Evening Post* (New York), January 4, 1904, 4, http://newspapers.com; William Morton Payne, review of Ellen Glasgow's *The Deliverance: A Romance of the Virginia Tobacco Fields*, *The Dial: A Semi-monthly Journal of Criticism, Discussion, and Information* XXXVI 1904, 118-19, http://www.hathitrust.org.

38. "A New Field in Southern Fiction," review of Ellen Glasgow's *The Deliverance: A Romance of the Virginia Tobacco Fields*, *New York Post* (New York), January 23, 1904, Saturday supplement, 7, http://www.newspapers.com.

CHAPTER 3

1. Charles W. Chesnutt, *The Journals of Charles W. Chesnutt*, ed. Richard Brodhead (Durham, NC: Duke University Press, 1993), 78.

2. Ibid., 108. For details of Chesnutt's origins and early life, see William L. Andrews, *The Literary Career of Charles W. Chesnutt* (Baton Rouge: Louisiana State University Press, 1980); and Frances Richardson Keller, *An American Crusade: The Life of Charles*

Waddell Chesnutt (Provo, UT: Brigham Young University Press, 1978); and Richard Brodhead, "Introduction."

3. Chesnutt, *Journals*, 139, 157.

4. William L. Andrews, "Foreword," in *Mandy Oxendine*, ed. Charles Hackenberry (Chicago: University of Illinois Press, 1997), xiv.

5. "New Publications," review of Charles Waddell Chesnutt's *The Conjure Woman and Other Conjure Tales, Baltimore Sun* (Baltimore, MD), April 15, 1899, morning edition, 7, https://www.newspapers.com/image/214446139.

6. Andrews gives both 1896 and early 1897 as equally probable dates. He also suggests that Chesnutt may have begun work on the novel around 1894, although it is possible that the story already existed in a draft form. What he states with certainty, however, is that *Mandy Oxendine* is Chesnutt's "earliest extant novel." "Foreword," in *Mandy Oxendine*, xv.

7. Houghton Mifflin to Chesnutt, March 26, 1897, Chesnutt Collection, cited in Charles Hackenberry, "Introduction," xv; Andrews, "Foreword," ix–x; Matthew Wilson, *Whiteness in the Novels of Charles W. Chesnutt* (Jackson: The University Press of Mississippi, 2004), 50. For Chesnutt and race, see Dean McWilliams *Charles W. Chesnutt and the Fictions of Race* (Athens: University of Georgia Press, 2006).

8. Hackenberry, "Introduction," xix–xx.

9. Ibid., xviii.

10. Chesnutt, *Mandy Oxendine*, 3, 9, 3.

11. Ibid., 4.

12. Ibid., 6.

13. Ibid., 7.

14. Ibid., 9–10.

15. Ibid., 28, 29.

16. Ibid., 24, 31.

17. Ibid., 23.

18. Ibid., 65. Flora McDonald, born in 1722, earned fame by aiding Bonnie Prince Charles in his escape after the Battle of Culloden in 1745. She subsequently stood trial in London and was imprisoned. She later emigrated to North Carolina with her husband, Allan MacDonald, who supported the Loyalist cause in the War of Independence. After the war, the family returned to Scotland, where she died in 1790. See Alexander MacGregor, *The Life of Flora MacDonald and her Adventures with Prince Charles* (Inverness: A&W MacKenzie, 1882).

19. Chesnutt, *Mandy Oxendine*, 12.

20. Ibid., 54.

21. Ibid., 61, 64. Chesnutt recycles the name Ochiltree in *The House behind the Cedars*, where the bearer is Aunt Polly, also a person of dubious morality who meets a tragic death.

22. Chesnutt, *Mandy Oxendine*, 103, 110, 46.

23. "The Year's Most Notable Book," review of Charles Waddell Chesnutt's *The House behind the Cedars, Pittsburgh Post* (Pittsburgh, PA), December 2, 1900, morning edition, 4, https://www.newspapers.com/image/86547774.

24. "One of the Books of the Season," review of Charles Waddell Chesnutt's *The House behind the Cedars*, *New York Times*, December 22, 1900, 23, https://www.newspapers.com/image/20521392; "An Issue in the Race Problem," review of Charles Waddell Chesnutt's *The House behind the Cedars*, *Detroit Free Press* (Detroit, MI), November 17, 1900, 11, https://www.newspapers.com/image/119477558; "Books and Authors," review of Charles Waddell Chesnutt's *The House behind the Cedars*, *Richmond Times* (Richmond, VA), December 9, 1900, 16, https://www.newspapers.com/image/79926299.

25. Chesnutt, *House*, 1.

26. Ibid., 13, 23.

27. Ibid., 116, 117; W. E. B. du Bois, *The Souls of Black Folk: Essays and Sketches* (Chicago: A.C. McClurg & Co., 1903), 94. The sentence reads: "Race-prejudices, which keep brown and black men in their 'places', we are coming to regard as useful allies with such a theory, no matter how much they may dull the ambition and sicken the hearts of struggling human beings."

28. Chesnutt, *House*, 117. I base my thinking here on Theodor W. Adorno and Max Horkheimer, "The Logic of Domination," in *Green Studies Reader*, 79. Adorno and Horkheimer recount the paradigm of Odysseus's encounter with the sirens when he instructs his crewmen to put wax in their ears, and tie him to the mast to resist the deadly song. They conclude that Odysseus's command transforms him into the bondsman, at the mercy of his crew, simply because his orders preclude them from hearing his pleas.

29. Chesnutt, *House*, 30, 31.

30. Peter Schmidt, "Walter Scott, Postcolonial Theory, and New South Literature," *Mississippi Quarterly* 56 (2003): 545, http://www.jstor.org/stable/26476805.

31. Allen notes: "In 1662, the Virginia Assembly discarded English common law of descent through the father, and instituted the principle of *patris sequitur ventrem*, according to which the child was declared "bond or free according to the condition of the mother." That law was specifically aimed at giving the plantation bourgeoisie a predefined supply of self-perpetuating unpaid labor, in *Invention*, 2.134. Smith observes of these early statutes that they "sited female bodies as the theoretical and functional dividing points of slave and free status, and, by extension, effected the division of the races based on 'the condition of the mother,'" in *Body Politics*, 10.

32. Chesnutt, *House*, 90; M. Gulia Fabi, *Passing and the Rise of the African American Novel* (Chicago: University of Illinois Press, 2004), 76. For discussions of the concept of passing, see also Elaine K. Ginsberg ed., *Passing and the Fictions of Identity* (Durham, NC: Duke University Press, 1996); and Sollors, *Neither Black Nor White*.

33. David Baldwin offers a detailed account of the turbulent relations between Edward IV, his brother George Duke of Clarence, and Warwick the Kingmaker (Richard Neville, 16th Earl of Warwick and 6th Earl of Salisbury) in *Richard III* (Stroud: Amberley, 2012).

34. Chesnutt, *House*, 56, 56–57, 44.

35. "An Unfortunate Heroine," review of Charles Waddell Chesnutt's *The House behind the Cedars*, *New York Times*, December 15, 1900, 39, https://www.newspapers.com/image/20515568.

36. Chesnutt, *House*, 57, 73, 90–91; Dayan, *Law*, 16; Chesnutt, *House*, 103.

37. Chesnutt, *House*, 103–4, 128.

38. Dayan, "Preface," *Law*, xii. Among those disabled by law, she includes "slaves, animals, criminals, and detainees"; Chesnutt, *House*, 130, 197.

39. Chesnutt, *House*, 189, 190.

40. Gloria T. Hull, ed., *Give Us Each Day: The Diary of Alice Dunbar-Nelson* (New York: Norton & Company), 13–33. See also Hull's short biography of Alice Dunbar-Nelson, titled "Alice Dunbar-Nelson 1875–1935," in *The Heath Anthology of American Literature*, vol. 2, 4th ed., ed. Paul Lauter et al. (New York: Houghton Mifflin Company, 2002), 199–205.

41. Hull, *Give Us Each Day*, 19.

42. "Topics of the Week," review of Alice Dunbar-Nelson's *The Goodness of St. Rocque*, *New York Times*, August 26, 1899, Saturday supplement, 13, https://www.newspapers.com/image/20317911; "Literary Notes," review of Alice Dunbar-Nelson's *The Goodness of St. Rocque*, *Washington Times*, September 3, 1899, 16, https://www.newspapers.com/image/80854606; "Few Notes on Literary Topics," review of Alice Dunbar-Nelson's *The Goodness of St Rocque*, *Oakland Tribune* (Oakland, CA) December 6, 1899, evening edition, 3, https://www.newspapers.com/image/71559927.

43. Hull, *Give Us Each Day*, 87. Dunbar-Nelson made the entry on October 1, 1921. The audience took place on Wednesday, September 28, 1921; one of the delegates was James Weldon Johnson.

44. Toni Morrison cited in Isenberg, *White Trash*, 302.

45. Alice Moore Dunbar-Nelson, "In Our Neighborhood" (1895; repr., in *Laughing to Stop Myself Crying*). In her "Introduction," Yvette Richards praises the collection as "a compilation of the best [stories] from *Violets and Other Tales* and *The Goodness of St. Roque*." The stories from this compilation are referenced individually in the bibliography. See also the author's "Introduction" and "Preface" by Sylvanie F. Williams to the 1895 edition of *Violets and Other Tales* (Charleston, SC: BiblioBazaar, 2008).

46. Pierre Macherey, *A Theory of Literary Production*, trans. Geoffrey Wall (London: Routledge, 1978), 82. Macherey notes that "meaning is in the *relation* between the implicit and the explicit," 87. Explicit, in this instance, is the nonwhiteness of the neighborhood measured against the presupposed, but kept implicit, standards represented by the Avenue.

47. Dunbar-Nelson, "In Our Neighborhood," 123, 124.

48. Dunbar-Nelson, "Tony's Wife" in *Laughing to Stop Myself Crying* (Cambridge, MA: John Wilson and Son, 1899; repr., London: The X Press, 2000), 26–27.

49. Ibid., 26.

50. Glasgow, *Certain Measure*, 121.

CHAPTER 4

1. Jacques Derrida, *Spectres of Marx: The State of National Debt, the Work of Mourning and the New International*, "Editor's Introduction" by Bernard Magnus and Stephen Cullenberg, trans. Peggy Kamuf (New York: Routledge, 2006), 24.

2. James Branch Cabell, *The High Place: A Comedy of Disenchantment* (New York: Robert McBride & Company, 1923), 164–65.

3. James Branch Cabell, *Let Me Lie: Being in the Main an Ethnological Account of the Remarkable Commonwealth of Virginia and the Making of its History* (Charlottesville: University of Virginia Press, 1947), 153–54.

4. "Books of the Week," review of Thomas Nelson Page's *Red Rock*, *Chicago Daily Tribune*, October 29, 1898, 7, https://www.newspapers.com/image/28486297.

5. "Literary Notes," review of Thomas Nelson Page's *Red Rock*, *Scranton Republican* (Scranton, PA), November 12, 1898, morning edition, 6, https://www.newspapers.com/image/48210721; "The Lady and the Carpet-Bagger," review of Thomas Nelson Page's *Red Rock*, *Baltimore Sun* (Baltimore, MD) November 21, 1898, morning edition, 8, https://www.newspapers.com/image/214556038.

6. Gardner, "The Plantation School," 269; Page, "Preface," in *Red Rock*, vii.

7. Page, *Red Rock*, 1, 27.

8. Ibid., 29.

9. Sir Walter Scott, "Introduction," *The Fair Maid of Perth or St. Valentine's Day* (New York: John B. Alden, 1885), xii–xiii; Scott, *Waverley*, 16.

10. Page, *Red Rock*, 2.

11. Page, *Red Rock*, 1; Lefebvre, *Production*, 118.

12. Page, *Red Rock*, 29; Page, 'Preface,' in *Red Rock*, vii; Page, *Red Rock*, 29; Page, 'Preface', in *Red Rock*, x.

13. Page, *Red Rock*, 12, 48, 47.

14. Ibid., 48.

15. Ibid., 252.

16. Cabell, *High Place*, 165.

17. Page, *Red Rock*, 262.

18. Avital Ronell offers an interesting discussion of the telephone as a metaphor for absence, which "presupposes the existence of another telephone." *The Telephone Book: Technology, Schizophrenia, Electric Speech* (Lincoln: University of Nebraska Press, 1989), 3; Derrida, *Spectres of Marx*, 45.

19. Page, *Red Rock*, 59.

20. Ibid., 228.

21. Ibid., 221, 222; MacKethan, *Dream of Arcady*, 49.

22. Page, *Red Rock*, 283, 282.

23. Ibid., 331–32.

24. Ibid., 564, 100, 564, 518; Frantz Fanon, *Black Skin, White Masks*, trans. Charles Lam Markmann (New York: Grove Press, 1967), 34. For readings of the vampire, see for example, Ken Gelder's *Reading the Vampire* (London: Routledge, 1994). For a comparison between the vampire and capitalism, see Karl Marx, "The Working Day," in *Capital: A Critique of Political Economy*, ed. Frederick Engels, trans. Samuel Moore and Edward Aveling, vol. 1 (London: Lawrence & Wishart, 1970), 233. Another characterization of a carpetbagger is given by Al Turley, a local farmer, who escorts the newly arrived Mrs. Welch to Red Rock: "some says it's the Yankee carpet-baggers steals all the money " (326).

25. Page, *Red Rock*, 287.
26. Derrida, *Spectres of Marx*, 81.
27. Dyer, *White*, 17 (see intr. no. 15); Smith, *American Body Politics*, 11. Isenberg offers a valuable and detailed study of the settlement of the colonies in "Taking Out the Trash," in *White Trash*, 17–42; George Alsop, *A Character of the Province of Maryland* (London, 1666), cited in Isenberg, *White Trash*, 36; Smith, *American Body Politics*, 11, 129. Martha Hodes notes that in the antebellum South, "communities were likely to consider poorer white women to be the depraved agents of illicit liaisons, including liaisons with black men. Thus could white ideology about lower-class female sexuality overshadow ideas about the dangers of black male sexuality," cited in Smith, *American Body Politics*, 129. Hodes demonstrates that illicit sexuality and skin color need not walk hand in hand.
28. Klaus Theweleit, *Male Fantasies: Male Bodies: Psychoanalyzing the White Terror*, vol. 2, trans. Erica Carter and Chris Turner (Minneapolis: University of Minnesota Press, 1992), 28.
29. *A Dictionary of First Names*, 2nd ed., ed. Patrick Hanks, Kate Hardcastle, and Flavia Hodges (Oxford: Oxford University Press, 2006), defines Blair as: "Transferred use of the Scottish surname, in origin a local name from any of various places named with Gaelic *blàr* 'plain field.' Outside Scotland, where it is a male name, it is found chiefly in North America, where it is also popular for girls." Considering its etymology, Blair's name provides another possible link with Sir Walter Scott's *The Fair Maid of Perth*, in which one of the protagonists, Father Clement Blair—an advocate of reform in the Catholic Church—is forced to flee Perth to avoid persecution. Blair, therefore, connotes non-conformity. Full publication details are given in the bibliography. Jacquelin appears to be a variety of Jacqueline, which derives from "the French male name *Jacques*, itself corresponding to English James and Jacob." The name Jacob is Hebrew in origin and denotes "may God protect," *Brewer's Dictionary of First Names*, 265–66. The link to Jacob renders Jacquelin both the protector of Blair and, later, the Grays' gentility, reaffirming the divinely sanctioned nature of the Grays' whiteness.
30. Page, *Red Rock*, 10.
31. Ibid., 82; Theweleit, *Male Fantasies*, 223.
32. Theweleit, *Male Fantasies*, 103.
33. Clarkson, "The Basis," 13. General Middleton is one of the heroes of the tale with which Fergus MacIvor—one of the protagonists of *Waverley*—regales Waverley. Despite his demotion and relocation to the South, Page's Middleton is possessed of a loyalty and honor that distinguish him among his compatriots; Page, *Red Rock*, 128.
34. Theweleit, *Male Fantasies*, 59.
35. Page, *Red Rock*, 144–45, 85.
36. Ibid., 158.
37. Ibid.
38. Ibid., 157, 346.
39. Ibid., 305, 184, 184.
40. Fanon, *Black Skin*, 191.
41. Toni Morrison sees the function of "the Africanist character" in American

literature "as surrogate and enabler," in *Playing in the Dark,* 51. I propose that, similarly, in reconstructions of male whiteness, the female characters perform the function of "enablers" and disablers.

42. Page, *Red Rock,* 83; in Derrida's *Of Grammatology,* the sentence reads: "The supplement transgresses and at the same time respects the interdict," 155.

43. Page, *Red Rock,* 93.

CHAPTER 5

1. For the etymology of the phrase "tar with the same brush" see *The Oxford Dictionary of Word Histories,* ed. Glynis Chantrell (Oxford: Oxford University Press, 2002), 503; for its application to the one-drop rule, see *Brewer's Dictionary of Phrase and Fable,* ed. Ivor H. Evans, 14th ed. (London: Cassell Publishers, 1989), 1082; Fanon, *Black Skin,* 191.

2. "Ellen Glasgow's New Novel Describes Ante-Bellum Days and War Time Scenes," review of Ellen Glasgow's *The Battle-Ground, Brooklyn Daily Eagle* (Brooklyn, NY), March 8, 1902, 10, https://www.newspapers.com/image/50417046; Glasgow, *Certain Measure,* 4; Glasgow, *Battle-Ground,* 61.

3. McDowell, *Ellen Glasgow,* 62. In her autobiography, Glasgow gives 1850 as the beginning of the narrative, in *Woman Within,* 286. In *Certain Measure,* she gives the chronology and time-span of all the novels of the Commonwealth and the City (3–4).

4. Lukács, *Historical Novel,* 15, 38.

5. Glasgow, *Woman Within,* 24; Glasgow, *Certain Measure,* 19, 84. *Surry of Eagle's Nest; or the Memoirs of a Staff Officer Serving in Virginia* is a novel by John Esten Cooke, first published in 1866. One of a trilogy, it is a paean to the valor of Southern soldiers, where fictional and historical figures comingle happily in the joint effort to save the Confederacy.

6. Gray, *Southern Aberrations,* 69; Glasgow, *Battle-Ground,* 30, 31.

7. Glasgow, *Battle-Ground,* 504; Dillard, "On Ellen Glasgow's *The Battle-Ground,*" 74.

8. Glasgow, *Battle-Ground,* 52, 51; Butler, *Subjects of Desire,* 37; Glasgow, *Battle-Ground,* 51.

9. Glasgow, *Battle-Ground,* 52. Like Aunt Lydia, Page's Aunt Thomasia deems bonnets outward markers of genteel deportment since "nothing characterizes a woman more than her bonnet" (*Red Rock,* 304).

10. Glasgow, *Battle-Ground,* 53.

11. Ibid., 95.

12. Ibid., 95; Ellen Glasgow, *The Sheltered Life* (Toronto: Aegitas, 2015), Kindle Edition, loc. 3964, loc. 5165.

13. Michel Foucault, *Language, Counter-Memory, Practice: Selected Essays and Interviews,* ed. Donald F. Bouchard, trans. Donald F. Bouchard and Sherry Simon (Oxford: Blackwell, 1977), 154; Glasgow, *Certain Measure,* 5.

14. Twain, *Pudd'nhead Wilson,* 87; Glasgow, *Battle-Ground,* 24.

15. Glasgow, *Battle-Ground,* 24; see Isenberg, *White Trash,* 73; Glasgow, *Battle-Ground,* 70.

16. Glasgow, *Battle-Ground,* 78.

17. Ibid., 119, 82, 49.
18. Ibid., 69, 48; Smith, *American Body Politics*, 116.
19. Glasgow, *Battle-Ground*, 45; McDowell, *Ellen Glasgow*, 116; Glasgow, *Battle-Ground*, 451, 431.
20. Glasgow, *Battle-Ground*, 199, 75, 75–76.
21. Ibid., 44.
22. Clarkson, "Basis," 13–14; Glasgow, *Battle-Ground*, 44.
23. Glasgow, *Battle-Ground*, 206.
24. Ibid., 132, 206, 212.
25. Ibid., 198; Derrida, *Spectres of Marx*, 24.
26. Glasgow, *Battle-Ground*, 234–35; Flannery O'Conner, "Revelation," in *The Secret Self: Short Stories by Women*, ed. Hermione Lee (London: J.M. Dent & Sons, 1989), 207–8; Glasgow, *Battle-Ground*, 241.
27. Glasgow, *Battle-Ground*, 169–70, 511–12.
28. "Ellen Glasgow's New Novel," March 8, 1902, 10; M. D. McLean, "Books: New Work of Fiction Coming from Miss Glasgow," review of Ellen Glasgow's *The Battle-Ground*, *Boston Post* (Boston, MA), January 26, 1902, 18, https://www.newspapers.com/image/68955049; M. D. McLean, "Books: *The Battle-Ground* by Miss Ellen Glasgow," review of Ellen Glasgow's *The Battle-Ground*, *Boston Post* (Boston, MA), May 25, 1902, 18, https://www.newspapers.com/image/72034679; "The Miller of Old Church," review of Ellen Glasgow's *The Miller of Old Church*, *San Francisco Call* (San Francisco, CA), August 6, 1911, 27, https://www.newspapers.com/image/82707277.
29. "Miss Glasgow's Strongest Book," review of Ellen Glasgow's *The Miller of Old Church*, *New York Times*, July 2, 1911, 51, https://www.newspapers.com/image/20667267; "Strong American Novels," review of Ellen Glasgow's *The Miller of Old Church*, *Brooklyn Daily Eagle* (Brooklyn, NY), June 10, 1911, 5, https://www.newspapers.com/image/53895257; Elia W. Peattie, "Among the New Books," review of Ellen Glasgow's *The Miller of Old Church*, *Chicago Daily Tribune* (Chicago, IL), June 24, 1911, 9, https://www.newspapers.com/image/28584140; Glasgow, *Certain Measure*, 129, 127, 4.
30. "The Miller of Old Church," August 6, 1911, 27.
31. Glasgow, *Miller*, 164; Foucault, *Language*, 164; Glasgow, *Miller*, 48, 164, 110.
32. Glasgow, *Miller*, 207, 138, 136–37.
33. Ibid., 64.
34. Ibid., 326.
35. Ibid., 132, 130, 131, 132.
36. Ibid., 134.
37. Thomas Jefferson, *Notes on the State of Virginia*, A New Edition (Richmond: J.W. Randolph, 1853), 150.
38. Glasgow, *Miller*, 38, 21, 23, 21.
39. Ibid., 151, 294, 329.
40. Leslie A. Fiedler, *Love and Death in the American Novel*, 1st Dalkey Archive ed. (Champaign, IL: Dalkey Archive Press, 2003), 52.
41. Derrida asserts that "the commodity is a 'thing' without phenomenon" that

acquires corporeality through the appropriation of the use-value and transcends it. This transcendence "renders the non-sensuous sensuous," in that it grants a visibility to the phantom of commodity that haunts the use-value (*Spectres of Marx*, 189).

42. Glasgow, *Miller*, 70, 193, 97, 98.

43. Ibid., 73.

44. Ibid., 80, 72, 426.

45. McDowell talks of tyranny masquerading as passivity in his evaluation of Mrs. Lightfoot in *The Battle-Ground*, in *Ellen Glasgow*, 64; see also McDowell's characterization of Miss Angela, in *Ellen Glasgow*, 99.

46. Glasgow, *Miller*, 77, 195.

47. Glasgow, *Miller*, 194, 192.

48. "Strong American Novels," June 10, 1911, 5; Glasgow, *Miller*, 195, 327.

49. I owe my formulation to Klaus Theweleit, who suggests that "the focus of repression in the soldier male is the 'desire to desire,'" the eradication of "everything that constitutes enjoyment and pleasure" (*Male Fantasies*, 7). Miss Angela subverts this paradigm because her status depends on fueling desire but deferring its fulfillment.

50. Glasgow, *Miller*, 175.

51. Ibid., 423.

52. Ibid., 426.

CHAPTER 6

1. Glasgow, *Certain Measure*, 50.

2. Gardner, in *Blood and Irony*, offers an invaluable historical account of the origin of the United Daughters of Confederacy and their activities devoted to the promotion of the Old South.

3. Glasgow, *Certain Measure*, 12, 89.

4. This paradigm may be extended to the conception of the South as a region dominated by vast plantations whose owners invariably are presented as scions of English or Scottish nobility. The accounts of the settlement of Virginia, as Isenberg demonstrates, prove the opposite. By 1770, a land-owning oligarchy had emerged in Virginia constituting less than 10 percent of the white population, to whom belonged "over half the land in the colony. More than half of white men held no land at all, working as tenants or hired laborers, or contracted as servants" (*White Trash*, 85).

5. Glasgow, *Certain Measure*, 142–43; James Branch Cabell, *Jurgen: A Comedy of Justice* (Harmondsworth, UK: Penguin, 1940), 234; Cabell, *High Place*, 312; Charles Waddell Chesnutt, *The Marrow of Tradition* (Boston, MA: Houghton, Mifflin and Company, 1901; repr., Boston, MA: Bedford, 2002). Citations refer to the Bedford reprint.

6. For a detailed account of the riot, see Nancy Bentley and Sandra Gunning, "Introduction: Cultural and Historical Background" (*Marrow*, 4) on which this summary is based. For Wilmington black tradesmen, see Wilson, *Whiteness*, 102.

7. "With ye Books," review of Charles Waddell Chesnutt's *The Marrow of Tradition*, *Washington Evening Star* (Washington, DC), November 9, 1901, 28, https://www.newspapers.com/image/207674545.

8. "Raking a Libeller," review of Charles Waddell Chesnutt's *The Marrow of Tradition, Richmond Dispatch* (Richmond, VA), December 15, 1901, 4, https://www.newspapers.com/image/92976317.

9. Review of Charles Waddell Chesnutt's *The Marrow of Tradition, Detroit Free Press* (Detroit, MI), November 16, 1901, 9, https://www.newspapers.com/image/119582461; "Literary Notes from Many Fields," review of Charles Waddell Chesnutt's *The Marrow of Tradition, Oakland Tribune* (Oakland, CA), November 9, 1901, evening edition, 12, https://www.newspapers.com/image/72362061. For other reviews comparing the novel with Harriet Beecher-Stowe's work see, for example, "Book Reviews," review of Charles Waddell Chesnutt's *The Marrow of Tradition, Lincoln Courier* (Lincoln, NE), December 28, 1901, 10, https://www.newspapers.com/image/46354628; "Late Books and Magazines," review of Charles Waddell Chesnutt's *The Marrow of Tradition, Davenport Daily Republican* (Davenport, IA), November 10, 1901, 4, https://www.newspapers.com/image/37250110.

10. "Late Books and Magazines," November 10, 1901, 4; "Book Reviews," December 28, 1901, 10.

11. "Book Reviews," December 28, 1901, 10; Chesnutt, *Journals*, 62.

12. Wilson, *Whiteness*, 99, 112.

13. Stephen P. Knadler, "Untragic Mulatto: Charles Chesnutt and the Discourse of Whiteness," *American Literary History* 8, no. 3 (1996): 429, http://www.jstor.org/stable/490151; Wilson, "Introduction," in *Whiteness*, xiv–xv.

14. Fanon, *Black Skin*, 139.

15. Knadler observes that Chesnutt "asks them [his readers] to see race itself as a matter of positionality," in "Untragic Mulatto," 435. I suggest that Chesnutt also sees whiteness as a question of positionality.

16. Chesnutt, *The Marrow*, 44.

17. Ibid.

18. Ibid., 64, 89.

19. Ibid., 64.

20. Ibid., 63, 98, 65, 64.

21. Thomas Jefferson to William Writ, August 5, 1815, *PTJ-R*, 8:642–43, cited in Isenberg, *White Trash*, 103. See also "Thomas Jefferson's Rubbish: A Curious Topography of Class", in Isenberg, *White Trash*, 13.

22. Chesnutt, *Marrow*, 140.

23. Ibid., 98.

24. Theweleit, *Male Fantasies*, 4; Chesnutt, *Marrow*, 175.

25. Chesnutt, *Marrow*, 199.

26. Theweleit, *Male Fantasies*, 20.

27. Chesnutt, *Marrow*, 239, 241.

28. Chesnutt, *Marrow*, 53, 143.

29. Chesnutt, *Marrow*, 119. In "Segregation as Culture: Etiquette, Spectacle, and Fiction," Nancy Bentley and Sandra Gunning explain the origin of the cakewalk: "In its early plantation origins, the stylized dancing and strutting that came to be called the

cakewalk was a vital part of the community life of enslaved Africans. The celebratory dancing probably drew upon rites that originated in African homelands, but descendants introduced innovations that included moves—exaggerated or grotesque stepping—enacting a disguised mockery of white owners. . . . Even with its coded criticism, however, the cakewalk was seized upon by white performers in blackface and turned into the centerpiece of countless racist minstrel shows during this period [the latter part of the nineteenth century]" (*Marrow*, 426).

30. Ibid., 144, 145.
31. Ibid., 105, 61.
32. Ibid., 54, 53.
33. "Last Name: Ochiltree," The Internet Surname Database, accessed September 4, 2019, http://www.surnamedb.com/Surname/Ochiltree.
34. Chesnutt, *Marrow*, 129.
35. Ibid., 202, 208.
36. Ibid., 245, 246.
37. Knadler, "Untragic Mulatto," 441.
38. Dunbar-Nelson, "Stones," 76–77.
39. Ibid., 97, 112, 104.
40. Dunbar-Nelson, "Little Miss Sophie" (Cambridge, MA: John Wilson and Son, 1899; repr., in *Laughing to Stop Myself Crying*, London: The X Press, 2000), 141.
41. Jones notes that "during the post-Civil War years," the term Creole, "instead of signifying only a line of pure Latin descent, . . . had somehow come to signify a person of mixed blood", *Strange Talk*, 116; Dunbar-Nelson, "Little Miss Sophie," 141.
42. Theweleit, *Male Fantasies*, 422; Daniel Robinson Hundley, *Social Relations in Our Southern States* (New York: Henry B. Price, 1860), 23.

CHAPTER 7

1. Jane Gaines, in "The Birth of a Nation and within Our Gates," explains that "the lives of very few families approximated the mythologised lives of the southern planter class," in *Dixie Debates: Perspectives on Southern Cultures*, ed. Richard H. King and Helen Taylor (Pluto Press, 1996), 184; Isenberg, *White Trash*, 85 (see chap. 6, n. 281).
2. Dyer, *White*, 16-17 (see intr. no. 15; and intr. no. 17).
3. Thomas Nelson Page, *John Marvel Assistant* (New York: Charles Scribner's Sons, 1910); "Socialism or What? Mr. Page's New Novel," review of Thomas Nelson Page's *John Marvel Assistant*, *Louisville Courier-Journal* (Louisville, KY), November 13, 1909, morning edition, 5, https://www.newspapers.com/image/119524016; review of Thomas Nelson Page's *John Marvel Assistant*, *Houston Post* (Houston, TX), November 14, 1909, morning edition, 28, https://www.newspapers.com/image/95170743.
4. "Novels New This Week," review of Thomas Nelson Page's *John Marvel Assistant*, *Detroit Free Press* (Detroit, MI), November 6, 1909, 6, https://www.newspapers.com/image/118642560; "New Volumes for Winter Evenings," review of Thomas Nelson Page's *John Marvel Assistant*, *San Francisco Call* (San Francisco, CA), November 21, 1909, 7,

https://www.newspapers.com/image/87853181; "Current Fiction," review of Thomas Nelson Page's *John Marvel Assistant, Des Moines Register* (Des Moines, IA), January 1, 1910, morning edition, 6, https://www.newspapers.com/image/128428815.

5. Review of *John Marvel Assistant*, November 14, 1909, 28.

6. Jacques Lacan, "The Circuit," in *The Seminar of Jacques Lacan: Book II: The Ego in Freud's Theory and in the Technique of Psychoanalysis 1954–1955*, ed. Jacques-Alain Miller, trans. Sylvana Tomaselli (New York: Norton, 1988), 89.

7. Elizabeth Young, *Black Frankenstein: The Making of an American Metaphor* (New York: New York University Press, 2008), 160. For discussions of the concept of the monster, see also Marie-Helene Huet, "Monstrosity and Representation," *Representations* 4 (1983): 74, doi:10.2307/2928548; Anthony Mellors and Fiona Robertson, eds., *Stephen Crane: The Red Badge of Courage and Other Stories* (Oxford: Oxford University Press, 2008); David Punter, *Gothic Pathologies: The Text, the Body and the Law* (Basingstoke: Macmillan, 1998).

8. Chris Baldick, *In Frankenstein's Shadow: Myth, Monstrosity, and Nineteenth-Century Writing* (Oxford: Oxford University Press, 1992), 45; Baldick, *In Frankenstein's Shadow*, 13. Young makes a similar point, calling monstrosity the "revolt against a creator," in *Black Frankenstein*, 14. Bill Brown sees the essence of monstrosity as "the result of like not proceeding from like," in *The Material Unconscious: American Amusement, Stephen Crane, and the Economics of Play* (Cambridge: Harvard University Press, 1996), 200.

9. Page, *John Marvel*, 1, 3, 2, 4, 2.

10. Ibid., 3; Ulrich Hegner, "Hans Holbein der Jüngere," *The Westminster Review* VIII (1827): 249; Page, *John Marvel*, 4.

11. Page, *John Marvel*, 4, 16.

12. Ibid., 26, 38, 39, 42; Judith Halberstam, *Skin Shows: Gothic Horror and the Technology of Monsters* (Durham NC: Duke University Press, 1995), 141; Mary Shelley, "Author's Introduction to the Standard Novels Edition" (1831), in *Frankenstein or The Modern Prometheus* (1818), ed. Marilyn Butler (Oxford: Oxford University Press, 1998), 197.

13. Slavoj Žižek, *The Plague of Fantasies* (London: Verso, 1998), 20, 28–29; Robert Penn Warren, *All the King's Men* (New York: Harcourt Brace and Company, 1946).

14. See Isenberg, *White Trash*, 10–14, 17–42.

15. For example, consider the works of Page, Glasgow, and Chesnutt discussed here. Other writes not averse to including high-ranking military and judicial officials include, for instance, Mary Johnston, John Pendleton Kennedy, John Esten Cooke, Corra Harris, William Gilmore Simms, James Lane Allen. The titles are listed in the bibliography.

16. Page, *John Marvel*, 11, 12, 26, 138, 4.

17. Ibid., 5, 7.

18. Ibid., 6.

19. Ibid., 5, 9.

20. Ibid., 7, 17; Page, *Old South*, 43; Ronell, *Telephone Book*, 194.

21. Page, *John Marvel*, 44, 45–46; Page, *Old South*, 46.

22. Page, *John Marvel*, 49.

23. Ibid., 49, 95.
24. Ibid., 312, 354; Page, *Old South*, 46; S. Allen Weiss, "Ten Theses on Monsters and Monstrosity," *TDR (1998-)* 48 no. 1 (2004): 125, http://www.jstor.org/stable/4488535; "Novels New This Week," November 6, 1909, 6.
25. Page, *John Marvel*, 203, 204.
26. Ibid., 207, 310, 206.
27. Ibid., 215; Derrida, *Spectres of Marx*, 41.
28. Page, *John Marvel*, 217, 199.
29. Jacques Lacan, *The Four Fundamental Concepts of Psychoanalysis, Book XI*, ed. Jacques-Alain Miller, trans. Alan Sheridan (New York: Norton, 1998) 267-70. Žižek says of the concept of *objet petit a* that it "emerges as being lost" (*Plague*, 13).
30. Page, *John Marvel*, 200, 215.
31. Ibid., 443, 552, 553.
32. My reasoning here is informed by Robert Young's *White Mythologies*. Although Young does not discuss whiteness *per se*, he sets out to debunk the concept of history as an unshakable totality. The supposition is untenable because, he suggests, it masks the existence of distinct histories that make up that totality. History may only be accessed at the level of individual histories, but is irreducible to them. Perceived as a totality, history, or any other conceptual truth, encodes its own negation because "each element cannot express the whole because the whole is only accessible as a concept, which is precisely not expressed at all", 61.

CHAPTER 8

1. John Esten Cooke, *Virginia: A History of the People*, 9th ed. (Boston: Hougthon, Mifflin and Company, 1887), 498.
2. Glasgow, *Certain Measure*, 3; McDowell, *Ellen Glasgow*, 54, 53; Glasgow, *Voice*, 13.
3. Glasgow, *Voice*, 197, 13, 299.
4. Incidentally, the Basset Hound is descended from the Bloodhound, a breed renowned for its unparalleled sense of smell, which furnishes a direct link between the judge's surname and the idea of not only being pure bred but also having the ability to scent "good blood." See *The Kennel Club's Illustrated Breed Standards*, new ed. (London: Ebury Press, 2003).
5. Glasgow, *Voice*, 9, 8, 4, 5.
6. Ibid., 120. McDowell calls Mrs. Webb "a symbol of the aristocratic South in eclipse" (*Ellen Glasgow*, 57).
7. Ernst H. Kantorowicz, *The King's Two Bodies: A Study in Mediaeval Theology* (1957) (Princeton, NJ: Princeton University Press, 1997), 199, 20-21, 316.
8. The name Dudley furnishes a direct link to English aristocracy. Its most famous bearers were Lord Guildford Dudley, executed in 1554 for an attempt to usurp the crown from Mary Tudor in 1553, and Robert Dudley, Earl of Leicester, and the favorite courtier of Elizabeth I, in *Oxford Dictionary of National Biography*, ed. H. C. G Matthew and Brian Harrison, vol. 17 (Oxford: Oxford University Press, 2004), 69, 92-112. Hence, in order to preserve the aristocratic connection, Mrs. Webb's father only consents to the

marriage on the condition that she "should drop the name of Jane and be known as Dudley in her husband's household" (Glasgow, *Voice*, 112).

9. Glasgow, *Voice*, 112, 114, 113.

10. Friedrich Nietzsche, "Preface," in *Beyond Good and Evil: Prelude to a Philosophy of the Future*, intr. Robert C. Holub, trans. and ed. Marion Faber, *Oxford World's Classics* (Oxford: Oxford University Press, 1998), 3; Glasgow, *Voice*, 115.

11. Glasgow, *Voice*, 350, 121.

12. Ibid., 117.

13. Ibid., 18, 19, 119.

14. Ibid., 7.

15. Ibid., 55.

16. Ibid., 68, 260.

17. Ibid., 225. Eugenia is a feminine version of Eugene, which derives from "the Greek name *Eugenios* (from *eugenēs* 'well-born, noble')," in Hanks, Hardcastle, Hodges, eds., *Dictionary*, 94; Glasgow, *Voice*, 48.

18. Glasgow, *Voice*, 30, 62, 100, 70.

19. Ibid., 223, 174.

20. Linda Brigham writes of aristocracy that its essence is "hereditary" and "not a product of learned manners," "Aristocratic Monstrosity and Sublime Femininity in De 'Montfort,'" *Studies in English Literature, 1500—1900* 43, no. 3 (Summer 2003): 702, https://www.jstor.org/stable/4625091.

21. Glasgow, *Voice*, 131, 165; McDowell, *Ellen Glasgow*, 56.

22. Glasgow, *Voice*, 5, 7, 46.

23. Ibid., 201.

24. Ibid., 86; Erskine Caldwell, *Tobacco Road* (New York: Gorsset & Dunlap, 1948).

25. Glasgow, *Voice*, 97, 212, 185, 303, 156.

26. Ibid., 244; Nietzsche, *Beyond Good*, 53.

27. Glasgow, *Voice*, 244.

28. Sir Thomas Browne, *The Major Works*, ed. C. A. Patrides (London: Penguin, 1977), 134; Glasgow, *Voice*, 255–56. For discussions of ugliness and evil, see for example, Baldick's *In Frankenstein's Shadow*, Halberstam's *Skin Shows*, Young's *Black Frankenstein*, or Denise Gigante, "Facing the Ugly: The Case of 'Frankenstein,'" *ELH* 67 no. 2 (200): 576, http://www.jstor.org/stable/30031925.

29. Oscar Wilde, *The Picture of Dorian Gray* (Harmondsworth, UK: Penguin, 1983), 159; Glasgow, *Voice*, 253.

30. Glasgow, *Voice*, 260-61; see McDowell, *Ellen Glasgow*, 22; Glasgow, *Voice*, 310.

31. Glasgow, *Voice*, 319–20, 395, 394.

32. Ibid., 443.

33. "Books of the Week: Southern Life Since the War," review of Ellen Glasgow's *The Voice of the People*, *Chicago Daily Tribune* (Chicago, IL), April 14, 1900, 10, https://www.newspapers.com/image/28494088; B. G. Lathrop, "Book Reviews," review of Ellen Glasgow's *The Voice of the People*, *San Francisco Call* (San Francisco, CA), July 29,

1900, 12, https://www.newspapers.com/image/78272925; "In Bookland," review of Ellen Glasgow's *The Voice of the People*, *Brooklyn Daily Eagle* (Brooklyn, NY), April 7, 1900, 11, https://www.newspapers.com/image/50386757.

34. "Books of the Week: Southern Life Since the War," April 14, 1900, 10; "Trio of Southern Writers," review of Ellen Glasgow's *The Voice of the People*, *Virginian-Pilot* (Norfolk, VA), July 6, 1900, 8, https://www.newspapers.com/image/68118508; "New Books," review of Ellen Glasgow's *The Voice of the People*, *Brooklyn Daily Eagle* (Brooklyn, NY), August 30, 1902, 8, https://www.newspapers.com/image/50414749; "Book Reviews," July 29, 1900, 12.

35. Ellen Glasgow, *Virginia* (Toronto: The Musson Book Company Limited, 1919).

36. Glasgow, *Certain Measure*, 78 ; "Talented Virginia Authoress Talks of Her Work," interview with Ellen Glasgow, *Charlotte Observer* (Charlotte, NC), April 20, 1913, 21, https://www.newspapers.com/image/73521839; "Concerning Books and Their Authors," review of Ellen Glasgow's *Virginia*, *Houston Post* (Houston, TX), February 23, 1913, morning edition, 43, https://www.newspapers.com/image/94995708; "New Publications: The Times-Democrat's Review of the Latest Books," review of Ellen Glasgow's *Virginia*, *Times-Democrat* (New Orleans, LA) July 27, 1913, 43, https://www.newspapers.com/image/183521084; "The Book Shelf," review of Ellen Glasgow's *Virginia*, *Vancouver Daily World* (Vancouver, British Columbia) June 28, 1913, 11, https://www.newspapers.com/image/64397609; "New woman's need for new man," review of Ellen Glasgow's *Virginia*, *Indianapolis News* (Indianapolis, IN), June 7, 1913, 14, https://www.newspapers.com/image/35189831.

37. "Her Latest Book, 'Virginia', Shatters Old Ideal of Womanhood," review of Ellen Glasgow's *Virginia*, *San Francisco Call* (San Francisco, CA), May 5, 1913, 17, https://www.newspapers.com/image/82709479; "New Publications," July 27, 1913, 43; "Her Latest Book," May 5, 1913, 17.

38. Glasgow, *Certain Measure*, 82.

39. For a discussion of perfection as monstrous, see Peggy Kamuf, "Dendritic" and Andrew Bennett "Explanations, Applications and Orientations," *Monstrism*, spec. issue of *Oxford Literary Review* 23 no. 1 (2002).

40. Glasgow, *Certain Measure*, 82; Glasgow, *Virginia*, 13, 14.

41. Glasgow, *Virginia*, 375, 39, 95.

42. Ibid., 131, 60.

43. Derrida, *Positions*, 8–9; Derrida, *Positions*, 28; Glasgow, *Virginia*, 166.

44. Glasgow, *Virginia*, 22; Glasgow, *Certain Measure*, 83.

45. Glasgow, *Virginia*, 65; James Branch Cabell, *The Cords of Vanity: A Comedy of Shirking*, intr. Wilson Follett, rev. ed. (New York: Robert M. McBride & Co., 1920), 319; Glasgow, *Virginia*, 65.

46. Glasgow, *Certain Measure*, 83.

47. Glasgow, *Virginia*, 39, 40, 146–47; *Keeping up Appearances*, dir. Harold Snoad (BBC, 1990–1995).

48. Glasgow, *Virginia*, 42, 48–49.

49. Ibid., 169.

50. Ibid., 408, 5, 6, 148.
51. Ibid., 364, 75.
52. Ibid., 196, 199.
53. Ibid., 204–05.
54. Ibid., 244, 451, 453.
55. Ibid., 522.
56. Ibid., 72, 20.
57. Ibid., 105, 160, 158, 115.
58. Ibid., 305, 235, 392, 423.

CHAPTER 9

1. Charles Waddell Chesnutt, *The Colonel's Dream, Toby Press Edition* (New York: Doubleday, Page & Company, 1905; New Milford, CT: The Toby Press, 2004). Citations refer to the 2004 edition.

2. "Afro-Americans and Fiction Writers," review of Charles Waddell Chesnutt's *The Colonel's Dream, New York Age* (New York, NY), December 14, 1905, 4, https://www.newspapers.com/image/31963734; Wilson, *Whiteness*, 148.

3. "Books of All Sorts and Kinds Now Flood the Literary Mart," review of Charles Waddell Chesnutt's *The Colonel's Dream, Los Angeles Herald* (Los Angeles, CA), November 19, 1905, Sunday supplement, 40, https://www.newspapers.com/image/76682148; "With the Books," review of Charles Waddell Chesnutt's *The Colonel's Dream, Washington Evening Star* (Washington, DC), September 16, 1905, 25, https://www.newspapers.com/image/145552936; C. W. Mason, "Books and Bookishness," review of Charles Waddell Chesnutt's *The Colonel's Dream, Brooklyn Daily Eagle* (Brooklyn, NY), September, 1905, 23, https://www.newspapers.com/image/53793835; "A Story of North and South," review of Charles Waddell Chesnutt's *The Colonel's Dream, Louisville Courier-Journal* (Louisville, KY), September 16, 1905, morning edition, 5, https://www.newspapers.com/image/119536915.

4. Mason, "Books and Bookishness," 23; "With the Books," 25; "Vexing Problems of the South as Seen by Another Novelist," review of Charles Waddell Chesnutt's *The Colonel's Dream, Minneapolis Journal* (Minneapolis, MN), November 26, 1905, editorial section, 36, https://www.newspapers.com/image/79667569.

5. Chesnutt, *Colonel's Dream*, 19, 160, 8.

6. Ibid., 9; Slavoj Žižek, "Love Thy Neighbor? No, Thanks!" in *The Psychoanalysis of Race*, ed. Christopher Lane (New York: Columbia University Press, 1998), 165. This essay is a modified version of the chapter "Love Thy Neighbor? No, Thanks!" published in *The Plague of Fantasies* the previous year.

7. Chesnutt, *Colonel's Dream*, 15, 20.
8. Ibid., 21.
9. Ibid., 32–33, 36.
10. Ibid., 36.
11. Ibid., 25, 46.

12. Ibid., 25, 64.
13. Ibid., 67, 25.
14. Ibid., 66, 27.
15. Ibid., 84, 77; Wilson, *Whiteness*, 162.
16. Chesnutt, *Colonel's Dream*, 77–78; Søren Kierkegaard, *Repetition: An Essay in Experimental Psychology*, trans. and intr. Walter Lowrie (Princeton, NJ: Princeton University Press, 1941), 34.
17. Chesnutt, *Colonel's Dream*, 89, 90.
18. Ibid., 92.
19. Žižek, "Love Thy Neighbor," 166; Chesnutt, *Colonel's Dream*, 51.
20. Žižek proposes that what "makes 'the phantom of the opera' so ugly" is "the missing nose," whereby "we have a lack that also functions as an excess" ("Love Thy Neighbor," 166).
21. Chesnutt, *Colonel's Dream*, 100, 146.
22. Ibid., 153, 112; Nietzsche, *Beyond Good*, 156.
23. Chesnutt, *Colonel's Dream*, 258.
24. "A Story of North and South," September 16, 1905, 5.
25. Chesnutt, *Colonel's Dream*, 265, 257, 268.
26. Ibid., 269, 270. Kantorowicz observes that "the most significant feature of all abstractions and personifications is their supra-temporal character, their continuity within time" (*King's*, 79).
27. Žižek, *Plague*, 13; Chesnutt, *Colonel's Dream*, 45, 50, 51.
28. Chesnutt, *Colonel's Dream*, 47, 171, 175.
29. Ibid., 171–72.
30. Ibid., 163.
31. Ibid., 166, 130.
32. Charles Waddell Chesnutt, *The Conjure Woman and Other Conjure Tales* (Boston, MA: Houghton, Mifflin and Company, 1899; repr., Durham, NC: Duke University Press, 1998). Fifth printing, edited and introduced by Richard H. Brodhead. Page references are to the 1998 reprint. The information is based on the section "Chronology of Composition" established by Brodhead, in *Conjure Woman*, 23–24; Brodhead, "Introduction," in *Conjure Woman*, 16.
33. "New Publications," review of Charles Waddell Chesnutt's *The Conjure Woman and Other Conjure Tales*, *Baltimore Sun* (Baltimore, MD), April 15, 1899, morning edition, 7; "The Darkey's Belief in Witchcraft," review of *The Conjure Woman and Other Conjure Tales*, *Brooklyn Daily Eagle* (Brooklyn, NY), April 22, 1899, 6, https://www.newspapers.com/image/50420741; "The Darkey's Belief in Witchcraft," April 22, 1899, 6; review of Charles Waddell Chesnutt's *The Conjure Woman and Other Conjure Tales*, *New York Times* (New York, NY), April 15, 1899, Saturday Review, 27, https://www.newspapers.com/image/20503000; review of Charles Waddell Chesnutt's *The Conjure Woman and Other Conjure Tales*, *Brooklyn Daily Eagle* (Brooklyn, NY), March 25, 1899, 6, https://www.newspapers.com/image/50408323.
34. Chesnutt, "The Goophered Grapevine," in *Conjure Woman*, 31; Brodhead, "Introduction," in *Conjure Woman*, 6.

35. Chesnutt, "Goopherd," 35, 39–40, 35.
36. Ibid.,37, 38, 39, 40.
37. Ibid., 41.
38. Chesnutt, "Sis Becky's Pickaninny," *Conjure Woman*, 85.
39. Ibid., 86.
40. Chesnutt, "Mars Jeems's Nightmare," in *Conjure Woman*, 57.
41. Ibid., 61.
42. Chesnutt, "The Conjurer's Revenge," in *Conjure Woman*, 79; Dunbar-Nelson, "Stones," 104.
43. Dunbar-Nelson, "Stones," 104.
44. Ibid., 111;
45. Alice Dunbar-Nelson, "La Juanita" (Cambridge, MA: John Wilson and Son, 1899; repr., in *Laughing to Stop Myself Crying*, Cambridge, London: The X Press, 2000), 215.
46. Dunbar-Nelson, "La Juanita," 215, 216.
47. Ibid., 217, 222; George Washington Cable, *The Grandissimes* (New York: Charles Scribner's Sons, 1899), 320.

EPILOGUE

1. Corra Harris, *The Recording Angel* (New York: Doubleday, Page & Company, 1912), 83.
2. Žižek, *Plague*, 49–50.
3. Melville, *Moby-Dick*, 169.
4. For readings of Ahab, see for example, Babb, *Whiteness*; Babb, *Whiteness*, 99; Harold Aspiz, "Phrenologizing the Whale," Nineteenth-*Century Fiction* 23, no. 1 (1968): 27, doi: 10.2307/2932314; Walter Allen, *Tradition and Dream: A Critical Survey of British and American Fiction from the 1920s to the Present Day* (Harmondsworth, UK: Penguin, 1971), 16; Fiedler, *Love and Death*, 385.
5. See Deborah L. Madsen, *American Exceptionalism* (Edinburgh: Edinburgh University Press, 1998), 13. Stephen Fender offers an interesting reading of the concept of American identity as a process of "movement and renewal—through a time of trial," in "The American Difference," *Modern American Culture*, ed. M. Gidley (London: Longman, 1993), 2.
6. Fiedler, *Love and Death*, 385; Auerbach, *Mimesis*, 14, 15; Fiedler, *Love and Death*, 29.
7. Allen, *Tradition and Dream*, 18.
8. Page, *Old South*, 6; see also Gray, *Southern Aberrations*, 6.
9. William Faulkner, *The Sound and the Fury*, intr. Nicholas Shakespeare (London: Everyman, 2000), 257.
10. Gray adopts a similar view in *Southern Aberrations*, 72; Faulkner, *Sound*, 64.
11. See Fiedler, *Love and Death*, 192; R. W. B. Lewis, *The American Adam: Innocence, Tragedy and Tradition in the Nineteenth Century* (Chicago: The University of Chicago Press, 1959), 5; Allen, *Tradition and Dream*, 16; Mark Twain, *The Adventures of Huckleberry Finn* (Cambridge: Cambridge University Press, 1995), 328; F. Scott Fitzgerald, *The Great Gatsby* (Harmondsworth, UK: Penguin, 1950), 171.
12. See, for example, Allen, *Tradition and Dream*, 17; Fiedler, *Love and Death*, 143.

13. For a good delineation of chivalry, see Auerbach, *Mimesis*, 137; Page, *Old South*, 110.

14. Chesnutt, *House*, 36; Faulkner, *Sound*, 224, 66.

15. William Faulkner, *Absalom, Absalom!* (London: Chatto & Windus, 1960), 263, 46.

16. An opinion advocated by Gray, *Southern Aberrations*, 12 and 69; Hundley's classification of Southern society places "southern bullies" and "white trash" at the very bottom of the social ladder (*Social Relations*, 188).

17. For isolation and American experience, see Allen, *Tradition and Dream*, 18; Gray, *Southern Aberrations*, 27.

18. Faulkner, *Absalom*, 9.

19. Glasgow, *Battle-Ground*, 199.

20. Glasgow, *Woman Within*, 104.

21. Dickson D. Bruce, Jr., *Black American Writing from the Nadir: The Evolution of a Literary Tradition 1877-1915* (Baton Rouge: Louisiana State University Press, 1989), 165; Chesnutt, *Journals*, 78, 139, 154.

22. For black writers and genteel writing, see Bruce, *Black American Writing*, 26.

23. Bruce, *Black American Writing*, 132. Thomas Richardson notes that Dunbar-Nelson was "a descendant of the proud colony of free Negroes in New Orleans which numbered no less than eighteen thousand at the beginning of the Civil War," in "Local Color in Louisiana," in *History*, 205.

24. Fabi suggests that the inclusion of racially-mixed characters in literary works was a ploy to increase readership, in *Passing*, 66.

25. Faulkner, *Sound*, 209; for the gothic, past and American fiction, see Fiedler, *Love and Death*, 137-142; Faulkner, *Absalom*, 361.

BIBLIOGRAPHY

Aanerud, Rebecca. "Fictions of Whiteness: Speaking the Names of Whiteness in U.S. Literature." In *Displacing Whiteness: Essays in Social and Cultural Criticism,* edited by Ruth Frankenberg, 35–59. Durham, NC: Duke University Press, 1997.

Adams, Jessica. "Local Color: The Southern Plantation in Popular Culture." *Cultural Critique* 42 (Spring 1999): 163–87. http://www.jstor.org/stable/1354595.

Adorno, Theodor W., and Max Horkheimer. "The Logic of Domination." Translated by John Cumming. In *The Green Studies Reader: From Romanticism to Ecocriticism,* edited by Laurence Coupe, 77–80. London: Routledge, 2000.

Allardyce, Alexander. *Memoir of the Honourable George Keith Elphinstone.* Edinburgh: William Blackwood and Sons, 1882.

Allen, James Lane. *Flute and Violin and Other Kentucky Tales and Romances.* New York: Harper and Brothers, 1891.

Allen, James Lane. *John Gray: A Kentucky Tale of the Olden Time.* Philadelphia: J.B. Lippincott Company, 1893.

———. *The Choir Invisible.* New York: The Macmillan Co., 1897.

Allen, Theodore W. *The Invention of the White Race.* 2 vols. London: Verso, 1995–97.

Allen, Walter. *Tradition and Dream: A Critical Survey of British and American Fiction from the 1920s to the Present Day.* Harmondsworth, UK: Penguin, 1971.

Andrews, William L. Foreword to *Mandy Oxendine,* edited by Charles Hackenberry, ix–x. Chicago: University of Illinois Press, 1997.

———. *The Literary Career of Charles W. Chesnutt.* Baton Rouge: Louisiana State University Press, 1980.

Aristotle. *The Politics.* Translated by T. A. Sinclair. Revised by Trevor J. Saunders. *Penguin Classics.* London: Penguin, 1992.

Aspiz, Harold. "Phrenologizing the Whale." *Nineteenth-Century Fiction* 23, no. 1 (1968): 18–27. DOI: 10.2307/2932314.

Atlanta Constitution (Atlanta, GA). "Books and Authors." Review of *In Ole Virginia,* by Thomas Nelson Page. June 5, 1887. https://www.newspapers.com/image/26949042.

Auerbach, Erich. *Mimesis: The Representation of Reality in Western Literature.* Translated by Willard R. Trask. Princeton, NJ: Princeton University Press, 1991.

B. "A Plea for Art." *Southern Literary Messenger; devoted to every department of literature and the fine arts* 15, no. 10 (Oct. 1849): 624–26. http://quod.lib.umich.edu/m/moajrnl/acf2679.0015.010/628

Babb, Valerie Melissa. *Whiteness Visible: The Meaning of Whiteness in American Literature and Culture.* New York: New York University Press, 1998.

Baldick, Chris. *In Frankenstein's Shadow: Myth, Monstrosity, and Nineteenth-Century Writing.* Oxford: Oxford University Press, 1992.

Baldwin, David. *Richard III*. Stroud: Amberley, 2012.
Baltimore Sun (Baltimore, MD). "New Publications." Review of *The Conjure Woman and Other Conjure Tales*, by Charles Waddell Chesnutt. April 15, 1899. Morning edition. https://www.newspapers.com/image/214446139.
———. "New Publications." Review of *In Ole Virginia*, by Thomas Nelson Page. June 21, 1887. Supplement. https://www.newspapers.com/image/214376739.
———. "The Lady and the Carpet-Bagger." Review of *Red Rock*, by Thomas Nelson Page. November 21, 1898. Morning edition. https://www.newspapers.com/image/214556038.
Barnhill Landis, David. Introduction to *At Home on the Earth: Becoming Native to Our Place: A Multicultural Anthology*. Edited by David Landis Barnhill, 1–18. Berkeley: University of California Press, 1999.
Barolini, Helen. *Their Other Side: Six American Women and the Lure of Italy*. New York: Fordham University Press, 2010.
Baudrillard, Jean. "Simulacra and Simulations." In *Literary Theory: An Anthology*, 2nd ed., edited by Julie Rivkin and Michael Ryan, 365–77. Oxford: Blackwell Publishing, 2004.
Bennett, Andrew. "Explanations, Applications and Orientations." *Monstrism*. Special issue. *The Oxford Literary Review* 23, no. 1 (2002): 5–31.
Berger, Maurice. *White Lies: Race and the Myths of Whiteness*. New York: Farrar, Strauss and Giroux, 1999.
Bhabha, Homi K. "Of Mimicry and Man: The Ambivalence of Colonial Discourse." In *The Location of Culture*, 85–92. London: Routledge, 1994.
Bible: Authorized Version, edited by John Stirling. Oxford: The University Press, 1960.
Boston Post (Boston, MA). Review of *In Ole Virginia*, by Thomas Nelson Page. May 30, 1887. Morning edition. https://www.newspapers.com/image/67555878.
Brigham, Linda. "Aristocratic Monstrosity and Sublime Femininity in 'De Montfort.'" *Studies in English Literature, 1500–1900* 43, no. 3 (Summer 2003): 701–18. https://www.jstor.org/stable/4625091.
Brooklyn Daily Eagle (Brooklyn, NY). "Ellen Glasgow's New Novel Describes Ante-Bellum Days and War Time Scenes." Review of *The Battle-Ground*, by Ellen Glasgow. March 8, 1902. https://www.newspapers.com/image/50417046.
———. "In Bookland." Review of *The Voice of the People*, by Ellen Glasgow. April, 7, 1900. https://www.newspapers.com/image/50386757.
———. "The Darkey's Belief in Witchcraft." Review of *The Conjure Woman and Other Conjure Tales*, by Charles Waddell Chesnutt. April 22, 1899. https://www.newspapers.com/image/50420741.
———. "New Books." Review of Ellen Glasgow's *The Voice of the People*. August 30, 1902. https://www.newspapers.com/image/50414749.
———. "Notes." Review of *On Newfound River*, by Thomas Nelson Page. June 14, 1891. https://www.newspapers.com/image/50449103.
———. Review of *The Conjure Woman and Other Conjure Tales*, by Charles Waddell Chesnutt. March 25, 1899. https://www.newspapers.com/image/50408323.
———. "Strong American Novels." Review of *The Miller of Old Church*, by Ellen Glasgow. June 10, 1911. https://www.newspapers.com/image/53895257.

Brown, Bill. *The Material Unconscious: American Amusement, Stephen Crane, and the Economics of Play*. Cambridge: Harvard University Press, 1996.
Browne, Sir Thomas. *The Major Works*. Edited by C. A. Patrides. London: Penguin, 1977.
Bruce, Dickson D Jr. *Black American Writing from the Nadir: The Evolution of a Literary Tradition 1877–1915*. Baton Rouge: Louisiana State University Press, 1989.
Buchan, David., ed. *A Scottish Ballad Book*. London: Routledge, 1973.
Burke's Peerage. 2002 –2012. Burke's Peerage (UK) Limited. http://www.burkespeerage.com.
Burrison, John A. "Crackers." *New Georgia Encyclopedia*. Last modified August 6, 2013. http://www.georgiaencyclopedia.org/articles/artsculture/crackers.
Butler, Judith P. *Subjects of Desire: Hegelian Reflections in Twentieth-Century France*. New York: Columbia University Press, 1987.
Cabell, James Branch. *The Cords of Vanity: A Comedy of Shirking*. Introduced by Wilson Follett. Revised edition. New York: Robert M. McBride & Co., 1920.
———. *The High Place: A Comedy of Disenchantment*. New York: Robert McBride & Company, 1923.
———. *Jurgen: A Comedy of Justice*. Harmondsworth, UK: Penguin, 1940.
———. *Let Me Lie: Being in the Main an Ethnological Account of the Remarkable Commonwealth of Virginia and the Making of its History*. Charlottesville, VA: University of Virginia Press, 1947.
Cable, George Washington. *The Grandissimes*. New York: Charles Scribner's Sons, 1899.
Caldwell, Erskine. *Tobacco Road*. New York: Grosset & Dunlap, 1948.
Calhoun, John C. *Speeches of Mr. Calhuon of S. Carolina, on the bill for the Admission of Michigan: delivered in the Senate of the United States, January, 1837*. Washington, DC: Duff Green, 1837.
Chantrell, Glynnis, ed. *The Oxford Dictionary of Word Histories*. Oxford: Oxford University Press, 2002.
Charlotte Observer (Charlotte, NC). "Talented Virginia Authoress Talks of Her Work." Interview with Ellen Glasgow. April 20, 1913. https://www.newspapers.com/image/73521839.
Chesnutt, Charles W. *The Colonel's Dream*. New York Doubleday, Page & Co., 1905. Reprinted with an introduction by SallyAnn H. Ferguson as the Toby Press Edition. New Milford, CT: The Toby Press, 2004. Page references are to the 2004 edition.
———. *The Conjure Woman and Other Conjure Tales*. Boston, MA: Houghton, Mifflin and Company, 1900. Fifth reprint, edited and introduced by Richard H. Brodhead. Durham, NC: Duke University Press, 1998. Page references are to the 1998 reprint.
———. *The House Behind the Cedars*. Boston, MA: Houghton, Mifflin and Co., 1900. Unabridged republication of the original text. Mineola, NY: Dover Publications Inc., 2007. Page references are to the 2007 reprint.
———. *The Journals of Charles W. Chesnutt*. Edited by Richard H.Brodhead. Durham, NC: Duke University Press, 1993.
———. *Mandy Oxendine*. Edited by Charles Hackenberry. Urbana and Chicago, IL: University of Illinois Press, 1997.

———. *The Marrow of Tradition*. Boston, MA: Houghton, Mifflin and Company, 1901. Reprinted as part of *Bedford Cultural Editions*, edited by Nancy Bentley and Sandra Gunning. Boston, MA: Bedford, 2002.

Chicago Daily Tribune (Chicago, IL). "Books of the Week." Review of *Red Rock*, by Thomas Nelson Page. October 29, 1898. https://www.newspapers.com/image/28486297.

———. "Books of the Week: Southern Life Since the War." Review of *The Voice of the People*, by Ellen Glasgow. April 14, 1900. https://www.newspapers.com/image/28494088.

———. Review of *On Newfound River*, by Thomas Nelson Page. June 6, 1891. https://www.newspapers.com/image/28513424.

Clarkson, A. "The Basis of Northern Hostility to the South." *DeBow's Review* 28, no. 1 (1860): 7–16. https://quod.lib.umich.edu/m/moajrnl/acg1336.1-28.001/11.

Colbert, Benjamin. *Shelley's Eye: Travel Writing and Aesthetic Vision*. London: Routledge, 2016.

Coleman, J. A. *The Dictionary of Mythology: An A-Z of Themes, Legends and Heroes*. London: Arcturus, 2018.

Cooke, John Esten, *Colonel Ross of Piedmont*. New York: Dillingham, 1892.

———. *Henry St. John, Gentleman*. New York: Harper and Brothers, 1859.

———. *Surry of Eagle's Nest; or the Memoirs of a Staff Officer Serving in Virginia*. New York: Bunce and Huntington, 1866.

———. *The Virginia Comedians: or Old Days in the Old Dominion*. New York: Appleton and Company, 1854.

———. *Virginia: A History of the People*. 9th ed. Boston: Houghton, Mifflin and Company, 1887.

Coupe, Laurence, ed. *The Green Studies Reader: From Romanticism to Ecocriticism*. London: Routledge, 2000.

Crow, Charles L., ed. *A Companion to the Regional Literatures of America*. Oxford: Blackwell, 2003.

"Cuba: The March of Empire and the Course of Trade." *DeBow's Review* 30, no. 1 (1861): 30–42. *Making of America Journal Articles*. http://quod.lib.umich.edu/m/moajrnl/acg1336.1-30.001/30.

Curtius, Ernst Robert. *European Literature and the Latin Middle Ages*. Introduction by Colin Burrow. Princeton: Princeton University Press, 2013.

Davenport Daily Republican (Davenport, IA). "Late Books and Magazines." Review of *The Marrow of Tradition*, by Charles Waddell Chesnutt's. November 10, 1901. https://www.newspapers.com/image/37250110.

Dayan, Colin. *The Law Is a White Dog: How Legal Rituals Make and Unmake Persons*. Princeton, NJ: Princeton University Press, 2011.

De Certeau, Michel. "Practices of Space." Translated by Richard Miller and Edward Schneider. In *On Signs*, edited by Marshall Blonsky, 122–45. Oxford: Blackwell, 1985.

Dekker, George. *The American Historical Romance*. Cambridge: Cambridge University Press, 1987.

Derrida, Jacques. "Afterward: Toward an Ethic of Discussion." *Limited Inc*. Translated

by Samuel Weber and Jeffrey Mehlman. Evanston, IL: Northwestern University Press, 1988.
———. *Dissemination*. Translated by Barbara Johnson. London: Continuum, 2011.
———. "Living On." *Deconstruction and Criticism*. Translated by James Hulbert, 62–142. London: Continuum, 2004.
———. *Monolingualism of the Other, or, the Prosthesis of Origin*. Translated by Patrick Mensah. Stanford, CA: Stanford University Press, 1998.
———. *Of Grammatology*. Translated by Gayatri Chakravorty Spivak. Baltimore, MD: The Johns Hopkins University Press, 1976.
———. *Positions*. Translated by Alan Bass. Chicago, IL: The University of Chicago Press, 1981.
———. *Spectres of Marx: The State of the Debt, the Work of Mourning and the New International*. "Editor's Introduction" by Bernard Magnus and Stephen Cullenberg. Translated by Peggy Kamuf. New York: Routledge, 2006.
Des Moines Register (Des Moines, IA). "Current Fiction." Review of *John Marvel Assistant*, by Thomas Nelson Page. January 1, 1910. Morning edition. https://www.newspapers.com/image/128428815.
Detroit Free Press (Detroit, Michigan). "Books. Novels New This Week." Review of *John Marvel Assistant*, by Thomas Nelson Page. November 6, 1909. https://www.newspapers.com/image/118642560.
———. "An Issue in the Race Problem." Review of *The House behind the Cedars*, by Charles Waddell Chesnutt. November 17, 1900. https://www.newspapers.com/image/119477558.
———. Review of *The Marrow of Tradition* by Charles Waddell Chesnutt. November 16, 1901. https://www.newspapers.com/image/119582461.
Dexter, Marshall. "Descendants of the Signers of '76 Prominent in the History of the Nation." *Indianapolis Star* (Indianapolis, IN), June 30, 1907. Magazine section. https://www.newspapers.com/image/118563922.
Dickens, Peter. *Social Darwinism: Linking Evolutionary Thought to Social Theory*. Buckingham: Open University Press, 2000.
Dillard, R. H. W. "On Ellen Glasgow's *The Battle-Ground*." In *Classics of Civil War Fictions*, edited by David Madden and Peggy Bach, 63–82. Jackson, MS: University of Mississippi Press, 1991.
Du Bois, W. E. B. *The Souls of Black Folk: Essays and Sketches*. Chicago, IL: A.C. McClurg & Co., 1903.
Dunbar-Nelson, Alice. Introduction to *Violets and Other Tales*, . 1895. Charleston, SC: BiblioBazaar, 2008.
———. "In Our Neighborhood." 1895. Reprinted with an introduction by Yvette Richards in *Laughing to Stop Myself Crying*. London: The X Press, 2000. Page references are to the 2000 reprint.
———. "La Juanita." Cambridge, MA: John Wilson and Son, 1899. Reprinted with an introduction by Yvette Richards in *Laughing to Stop Myself Crying*. London: The X Press, 2000. Page references are to the 2000 reprint.

———. "Little Miss Sophie." Cambridge, MA: John Wilson and Son, 1899. Reprinted with an introduction by Yvette Richards in *Laughing to Stop Myself Crying*. London: The X Press, 2000. Page references are to the 2000 reprint.

———. "The Stones of the Village. Reprinted with an introduction by Yvette Richards in *Laughing to Stop Myself Crying*. London: The X Press, 2000. Page references are to the 2000 reprint.

———. "Tony's Wife." Cambridge, MA: John Wilson and Son, 1899. Reprinted with an introduction by Yvette Richards in *Laughing to Stop Myself Crying*. London: The X Press, 2000. Page references are to the 2000 reprint.

Dyer, Richard. *White*. London: Routledge, 1997.

Ellison, Ralph. "Change the Joke and Slip the Yoke." In *Shadow and Act*, 45–59. New York: Vintage International, 1995.

Evans, Bergen. *Dictionary of Mythology: Mainly Classical*. London: Franklin Watts, 1971.

Evans, Ivor H., ed. *Brewer's Dictionary of Phrase and Fable*. 14th ed. London: Cassell, 1989.

Evening Post (New York, NY). Advertisement for Ellen Glasgow's *The Deliverance: A Romance of the Virginia Tobacco Fields*. January 4, 1904. https://www.news papers.com.

Evola, Julius. *Meditations on the Peaks: Mountain Climbing as Metaphor for the Spiritual Quest*. Rochester, VT: Inner Traditions, 1998.

Fabi, M. Giulia. *Passing and the Rise of the African American Novel*. Chicago, IL: University of Illinois Press, 2004.

Fanon, Frantz. *Black Skin, White Masks*. Translated by Charles Lam Markmann. New York: Grove Press, 1967.

Faulkner, William. *Absalom, Absalom!*. London: Chatto & Windus, 1960.

———. *A Requiem for a Nun*. London: Chatto & Windus, 1965.

———. *The Sound and the Fury*. London: Everyman, 1992.

Fender, Stephen. "The American Difference." In *Modern American Culture: An Introduction*. Edited by M Gidley, 1–22. London: Longman, 1993.

Fichte, Johann Gottlieb. *Addresses to the German Nation*. Edited by Gregory Moore. Cambridge: Cambridge University Press, 2008.

Fiedler, Leslie A. *Love and Death in the American Novel*. Champaign, IL: Dalkey Archive Press, 2003.

Fitzgerald, Scott F. *The Great Gatsby*. Harmondsworth, UK: Penguin, 1950.

Fleming, Victor, dir. *Gone with the Wind*. Loew's Inc., 1939.

Foster, Harve, and Wilfred Jackson, dirs. *Song of the South*. RKO Radio Pictures, 1946.

Foucault, Michel. *Language, Counter-Memory, Practice: Selected Essays and Interviews*. Translated by Donald F. Bouchard and Sherry Simon. Edited by Donald F. Bouchard. Oxford: Blackwell, 1977.

Frankenberg, Ruth. "Introduction: Local Whitenesses, Localizing Whiteness." In *Displacing Whiteness: Essays in Social and Cultural Criticism*, edited by Ruth Frankenberg, 1–34. Durham, NC: Duke University Press, 1997.

———. *White Women, Race Matters: The Social Construction of Whiteness.* Minneapolis: University of Minnesota Press, 1994.
Franklin, Benjamin. *The Autobiography and Other Writings.* Edited by Peter Shaw. New York: Bantam, 1982.
Fraser, James E. *From Caledonia to Pictland: Scotland to 795.* Edinburgh: Edinburgh University Press, 2009.
Gage, John. *Colour and Culture: Practice and Meaning from Antiquity to Abstraction.* New Edition. London: Thames & Hudson, 1995.
Gaines, Jane. "The Birth of a Nation and within Our Gates." In *Dixie Debates: Perspectives on Sothern Cultures.* Edited by Richard H. King and Helen Taylor, 177–92. New York: New York University Press, 1996.
Gardiner, Juliet, and Neil Wenborn., eds. *The History Today Companion to British History.* London: Collins & Brown, 1995.
Gardner, Sarah E. *Blood and Irony: Southern White Women's Narratives of the Civil War, 1861–1937.* Chapel Hill: The University of North Carolina Press, 2004. Kindle edition.
Garland, Hamlin. *Crumbling Idols.* Edited by Jane Johnson. Cambridge, MA: Belknap Press of Harvard University Press, 1960.
Gelder, Ken. *Reading the Vampire.* London: Routledge, 1994.
Gerstein, Lila, dir. *Hart of Dixie.* CW, 2011–2015.
Gigante, Denise. "Facing the Ugly: The Case of 'Frankenstein.'" *ELH* 67, no. 2 (2000): 565–87. http://www.jstor.org/stable/30031925.
Gilder, Jeannette L. "Page's 'Gordon Keith.'" *Chicago Daily Tribune.* May 23, 1903, 9. https://www.newspapers.com/image/28621852.
Gillman, Susan. *Blood Talk: American Race Melodrama and the Culture of the Occult.* Chicago, IL: The University of Chicago Press, 2003.
Ginsberg, Elaine K., ed., *Passing and the Fictions of Identity.* Durham, NC: Duke University Press, 1996.
Glasgow, Ellen. *The Battle-Ground.* New York: Doubleday, Page & Co., 1902.
———. *A Certain Measure: An Interpretation of Prose Fiction.* New York: Harcourt, Brace and Company, 1943.
———. *The Deliverance: A Romance of the Virginia Tobacco Fields.* New York: Doubleday, Page & Co., 1904.
———. *The Miller of Old Church.* New York: Doubleday, Page & Company, 1911.
———. *The Sheltered Life.* Toronto: Aegitas, 2015. Kindle edition.
———. *Virginia.* Toronto: The Musson Book Company Limited, 1919.
———. *The Voice of the People.* New York: Doubleday, Page & Co., 1900.
———. *The Woman Within.* New York: Hill and Wang, 1980.
Glotfelty, Cheryll, and Harold Fromm, eds. *The Ecocriticism Reader: Landmarks in Literary Ecology.* Athens, GA: The University of Georgia Press, 1996.
Grant, Susan-Mary. *North over South: Northern Nationalism and American Identity in the Antebellum Era.* Lawrence, KS: University of Kansas Press, 2000.
———. *The War for a Nation: The American Civil War.* London: Routledge, 2006.

Gray, Richard. *Southern Aberrations: Writers of the American South and the Problems of Regionalism*. Baton Rouge: Louisiana State University Press, 2000.

———. *Writing the South: Ideas of an American Region*. Baton Rouge: Louisiana State University Press, 1997.

Halberstam, Judith. *Skin Shows: Gothic Horror and the Technology of Monsters*. Durham, NC: Duke University Press, 1995.

Hale, Grace Elizabeth. *Making Whiteness: The Culture of Segregation in the South, 1890–1940*. New York: Vintage Books, 1999.

Hanks, Patrick, Kate Hardcastle, and Flavia Hodges., eds. *A Dictionary of First Names*. 2nd ed. Oxford: Oxford University Press, 2006.

Hardwig, Bill. *Upon Provincialism: Southern Literature and National Periodical Culture, 1870–1900*. Charlottesville, VA: University of Virginia Press, 2013.

Harris, Corra. *The Recording Angel*. New York: Doubleday Page & Co, 1912.

Harrisburg Telegraph (Harrisburg, PA). "A Charming Love Story." Review of *On Newfound River*, by Thomas Nelson Page. July 11, 1891. Evening edition. https://www.newspapers.com/image/44261682.

Hartigan, John, Jr. *Odd Tribes: Toward a Cultural Analysis of White People*. Durham, NC: Duke University Press, 2005.

———. "Who Are These White People?: 'Rednecks,' 'Hillbillies,' and 'White Trash' as Marked Racial Subjects." In *White Out: The Continuing Significance of Racism*, edited by Ashley W. Doane and Eduardo Bonilla-Silva, 95–113. London: Routledge, 2003.

Hegel, Georg Wilhelm Friedrich. "The Truth of Self-Certainty." *Phenomenology of Spirit*. Translated by A. V. Miller. Foreword by J. N. Finley, 104–19. Oxford: Oxford University Press, 1977.

Hegner, Ulrich. "Hans Holbein der Jüngere." *The Westminster Review* VIII (1827): 244–52. http://www.hathitrust.org.

Hill, Mike., ed. *Whiteness: A Critical Reader*. New York: New York University Press, 1997.

Hobsbawm, Eric, and Terence Ranger, eds., *The Invention of Tradition*. Cambridge: Cambridge University Press, 1992.

Hodgart, Matthew, ed. *The Faber Book of Ballads*. London: Faber & Faber, 1965.

hooks, bell. *Yearning: Race, Gender, and Cultural Politics*. London: Turnaround, 1991.

Hopkins, Izabela. "Beyond Coincidence: Scott*ish* Inflections in Thomas Nelson Page's *Gordon Keith* and *Red Rock: A Chronicle of Reconstruction*," *South Central Review* 33, no. 3 (2016): 53–68.

Houston Post (Houston, TX). "Concerning Books and Their Authors." Review of *Virginia* by Ellen Glasgow. February 23, 1913. Morning edition. https://www.newspapers.com/image/94995708.

———. Review of *John Marvel Assistant*, by Thomas Nelson Page. November 14, 1909. Morning edition. https://www.newspapers.com/image/95170743.

Howells, William Dean. *Criticism and Fiction*. New York: Harper and Brothers, 1892.

———. "Editor's Study." *Harper's New Monthly Magazine*. November 1889.

Huet, Marie-Helene. "Monstrosity and Representation." *Representations* 4 (1983): 73–87. DOI: 10.2307/2928548.

Hull, Gloria T. "Alice Dunbar-Nelson 1875–1935." In *The Heath Anthology of American Literature*, edited by Paul Lauter et al., 4th ed., Vol. 2., 199–205. New York: Houghton Mifflin Company, 2002.
———, ed. *Give Us Each Day: The Diary of Alice Dunbar-Nelson*. New York: Norton & Company, 1986.
———, ed. Introduction to *The Works of Alice Dunbar-Nelson*. Vol. 2. New York: Oxford University Press, 1988.
Hundley, Daniel Robinson. *Social Relations in Our Southern States*. New York: Henry B. Price, 1860.
Indianapolis News (Indianapolis, IN). "New woman's need for new man." Review of *Virginia*, by Ellen Glasgow. June 7, 1913. https://www.newspapers.com/image/35189831.
Isenberg, Nancy. *White Trash: The 400-Year Untold History of Class in America*. London: Atlantic Books, 2017.
Jakobson, Roman. "Dear Claude, Cher Maître." In *On Signs*, edited by Marshall Blonsky, 184–88. Oxford: Blackwell, 1985.
Jameson, Frederic. *Postmodernism, or, the Cultural Logic of Late Capitalism*. Durham NC: Duke University Press, 1991.
Jefferson, Thomas. *Notes on the State of Virginia*. A New Edition. Richmond: J.W. Randolph, 1853.
Johnson, Thomas H., ed. *The Collected Poems of Emily Dickinson*. London: Faber and Faber, 1975.
Johnston, Mary. *To Have and to Hold*. Boston: Houghton Mifflin Harcourt, 1899.
Jones, Gavin. *Strange Talk: The Politics of Dialect Literature in Gilded Age America*. Berkeley: University of California Press, 1999.
Jones, Suzanne W. "City Folks in Hoot Owl Holler: Narrative Strategy in Lee Smith's *Oral History*." *Southern Literary Journal* 20, no. 1 (1987): 101–12. https://www.jstor.org/stable/20077851.
Kamuf, Peggy, and Andrew Bennett. "Dendritic." *Monstrism*. Special issue of *The Oxford Literary Review* 23, no.1 (2002): 71–97.
Kantorowicz, Ernst H. *The King's Two Bodies: A Study in Mediaeval Theology*. Princeton, NJ: Princeton University Press, 1997. First published in 1957.
Keller Richardson, Frances. *An American Crusade: The Life of Charles Waddell Chesnutt*. Provo, UT: Brigham Young University Press, 1978.
Kennedy, John Pendleton. *Horse-Shoe Robinson. A Tale of Tory Ascendancy*. London: Bentley, 1835.
———. *Quodlibet*. Philadelphia: Lea & Blanchard, 1840.
———. *Swallow Barn, or a Sojourn in the Old Dominion*. Philadelphia: Carey & Lea, 1832.
The Kennel Club's Illustrated Breed Standards. New ed. London: Ebury Press, 2003.
Kierkegaard, Søren. *Repetition: An Essay in Experimental Psychology*. Translated and introduced by Walter Lowrie. Princeton, NJ: Princeton University Press, 1941.
Knadler, Stephen P. "Untragic Mulatto: Charles Chesnutt and the Discourse of Whiteness." *American Literary History* 8, no. 3 (1996): 426–48. http://www.jstor.org/stable/490151.

Kojève, Alexandre. *Introduction to the Reading of Hegel*. Translated by James H. Nichols, Jr. Edited by Allan Bloom. New York: Basic Books, 1969.

Kolchin, Peter. "Whiteness Studies: The New History of Race in America." *The Journal of American History* 89, no. 1 (2002): 154–73. http://www.jstor.org/stable/2700788.

Lacan, Jacques. "The Circuit." Translated by Sylvana Tomaselli. In *The Seminar of Jacques Lacan: Book II: The Ego in Freud's Theory and in the Technique of Psychoanalysis 1954–1955*, edited by Jacques-Alain Miller, 77–90. New York: Norton, 1988.

———, *Écrits: A Selection*. Translated by Alan Sheridan. London: Routledge, 2009.

———. *The Four Fundamental Concepts of Psychoanalysis, Book XI*. Translated by Alan Sheridan. Edited by Jacques-Alain Miller. New York: Norton, 1998.

———. *The Seminar of Jacques Lacan: On Feminine Sexuality: Book XX: Encore 1972–1973*. Translated by Bruce Fink. Edited by Jacques-Alain Miller. New York: Norton, 1999.

Lathrop, B. G. "Book Reviews." Review of *The Voice of the People*, by Ellen Glasgow. *San Francisco Call* (San Francisco, CA), July 29, 1900. https://www.newspapers.com/image/78272925.

Lefebvre, Henri. *The Production of Space*. Translated by Donald Nicholson-Smith. Oxford: Blackwell, 1991.

Lewis, R. W. B. *The American Adam: Innocence, Tragedy and Tradition in the Nineteenth Century*. Chicago, IL: The University of Chicago Press, 1959.

Li, Stephanie. *Playing in the White: Black Writers, White Subjects*. New York: Oxford University Press, 2015.

Lincoln Courier (Lincoln, NE). "Book Reviews." Review of *The Marrow of Tradition*, by Charles Waddell Chesnutt. December 28, 1901. https://www.newspapers.com/image/46354628.

Lorber, Judith. "The Social Construction of Gender." In *Race, Class, and Gender in the United States* 5th ed., edited by Paula S. Rothenberg, 47–57. New York: Worth Publishers, 2001.

Los Angeles Herald (Los Angeles, CA). "Books of All Sorts and Kinds Now Flood the Literary Mart." Review of *The Colonel's Dream*, by Charles Waddell Chesnutt. November 19, 1905. Sunday supplement. https://www.newspapers.com/image/76682148.

Louisville Courier-Journal (Louisville, KY). "Socialism or What? Mr. Page's New Novel." Review of *John Marvel Assistant*, by Thomas Nelson Page. November 13, 1909. Morning edition. https://www.newspapers.com/image/119524016.

———. "The South's Dire Need." Thomas Nelson Page's address to the Society of Virginia Alumni. April 14, 1891. Morning edition. https://www.newspapers.com/image/32460948.

———. "A Story of North and South." Review of *The Colonel's Dream*, by Charles Waddell Chesnutt. 16 September 16, 1905. Morning edition. https://www.newspapers.com/image/119536915.

———."Thomas Page's 'Gordon Keith.'" June 6, 1903. Morning edition. https://www.newspapers.com/image/118985395.

———. "Thomas Nelson Page Will Raise Mules." April 8, 1907. Morning edition. https://www.newspapers.com/image/119174431.

Lukács, Georg. *The Historical Novel*. Translated by Hannah and Stanley Mitchell. Harmondsworth, UK: Penguin, 1969.

Macfarlane, Leslie J. *William Elphinstone and the Kingdom of Scotland 1431–1514: The Struggle for Order*. Quincentenary Edition. Aberdeen: Aberdeen University Press, 1995.

MacGregor, Alexander. *The Life of Flora MacDonald and her Adventures with Prince Charles*. Inverness: A&W MacKenzie, 1882.

Macherey, Pierre. *A Theory of Literary Production*. Translated by Geoffrey Wall. London: Routledge, 1978.

MacKethan, Lucinda H. *The Dream of Arcady: Place and Time in Southern Literature*. Baton Rouge: Louisiana State University Press, 1980.

———. "Plantation Fiction, 1865–1900." In *The History of Southern Literature*, edited by Louis D. Rubin Jr., Blyden Jackson, Rayburn S. Moore, Lewis P. Simpson, and Thomas Daniel Young, 209–18. Baton Rouge: Louisiana State University Press, 1985.

MacKillop, James. *A Dictionary of Celtic Mythology*. Oxford: Oxford University Press, 2016.

Madsen, Deborah L. *American Exceptionalism*. Edinburgh: Edinburgh University Press, 1998.

Marguia, Edward, and Tyrone Forman. "Shades of Whiteness: The Mexican American Experience in Relation to Anglos and Blacks." In *White Out: The Continuing Significance Of Racism,* edited by Ashley W. Doane and Eduardo Bonilla-Silva, 63–79. London: Routledge, 2003.

Marx, Karl. "The Working Day." Translated by Samuel Moore and Edward Aveling. In *Capital: A Critique of Political Economy,* Vol. 1, edited by Frederick Engels, 231–302; London: Lawrence & Wishart, 1970.

Mason, C. W. "Books and Bookishness." Review of *The Colonel's Dream,* by Charles Waddell Chesnutt. *Brooklyn Daily Eagle* (Brooklyn, NY), September 21, 1905. https://www.newspapers.com/image/53793835.

May, Chad, T. "'The Horrors of My Tale:' Trauma, the Historical Imagination, and Sir Walter Scott." *Pacific Coast Philology,* 40, no. 1 (2005): 98–116. http://www.jstor.org/stable/25474171.

McDowell, Frederick P. W. *Ellen Glasgow and the Ironic Art of Fiction*. Madison: University of Wisconsin Press, 1963.

McLean, M. D. "Books: *The Battle-Ground* by Miss Ellen Glasgow." Review of *The Battle-Ground,* by Ellen Glasgow. *Boston Post* (Boston, MA), May 25, 1902. https://www.newspapers.com/image/72034679.

———. "Books: New Work of Fiction Coming from Miss Glasgow." Review of *The Battle-Ground,* by Ellen Glasgow. *Boston Post* (Boston, MA), January 26, 1902. https://www.newspapers.com/image/68955049.

McPherson, Tara. *Reconstructing Dixie: Race, Gender, and Nostalgia in the Imagined South*. Durham, NC: Duke University Press, 2003.

McWilliams, Dean. *Charles W. Chesnutt and the Fictions of Race*. Athens: University of Georgia Press, 2006.

Mellors, Anthony, and Fiona Robertson, eds. *Stephen Crane: The Red Badge of Courage and Other Stories*. Oxford: Oxford University Press, 2008.

Melville, Herman. *Moby-Dick*. Edited by Harrison Hayford and Hershel Parker. New York: Norton, 1967.

Minneapolis Journal (Minneapolis, MN). "New Books." Review of *Gordon Keith*, by Thomas Nelson Page. July 1, 1903. Evening edition. https://www.newspapers.com/image/76297378.

———. "Vexing Problems of the South as Seen by Another Novelist." Review of *The Colonel's Dream*, by Charles Waddell Chesnutt. November 26, 1905. Editorial section. https://www.newspapers.com/image/79667569.

Moore, Quitman J. "Feudalism in America." *DeBow's Review* 28, no. 6 (1860): 615–24. Making of America Journal Articles. http://quod.lib.umich.edu/m/moajrnl/acg1336.1-28.006/619.

Morris, Pam., ed. *The Bakhtin Reader: Selected Writings of Bakhtin, Medvedev, Voloshinov*. London: Arnold Hodder, 2002.

Morrison, Toni. *Playing in the Dark: Whiteness and the Literary Imagination*. London: Pan Books, 1993.

Murphy, Patrick D. "Anotherness and Inhabitation in Recent Multicultural American Literature." In *Writing the Environment: Ecocriticism and Literature*, edited by Richard Kerridge and Neil Sammells, 40–51. London: Zed Books, 1998.

———. *Further Afield in the Study of Nature-Oriented Literature*. Charlottesville: The University Press of Virginia, 2000.

New York Age (New York, NY). "Afro-Americans and Fiction Writers." Review of *The Colonel's Dream*, by Charles Waddell Chesnutt. December 14, 1905. https://www.newspapers.com/image/31963734.

New York Post (New York, NY). "A New Field in Southern Fiction." Review of *The Deliverance: A Romance of the Virginia Tobacco Fields*, by Ellen Glasgow. January 23, 1904. Saturday supplement. https://www.newspapers.com.

New York Times. "Miss Glasgow's Strongest Book." Review of *The Miller of Old Church*, by Ellen Glasgow. July 2, 1911. https://www.newspapers.com/image/20667267.

———. "One of the Books of the Season." Review of *The House behind the Cedars*, by Charles Waddell Chesnutt. December 22, 1900. https://www.newspapers.com/image/20521392.

———. Review of *The Conjure Woman and Other Conjure Tales*, by Charles Waddell Chesnutt. April 15, 1899. Saturday review. https://www.newspapers.com/image/20503000.

———. "Thomas Nelson Page." Review of Thomas Nelson Page's Plantation Edition of his works. January 19, 1907. https://www.newspapers.com/image/20611363.

———. "Topics of the Week." Review of *The Goodness of St Rocque*, by Alice Dunbar-Nelson. August 26, 1899. Saturday supplement. https://www.newspapers.com/image/20317911.

———. "An Unfortunate Heroine." Review of *The House behind the Cedars,* by Charles Waddell Chesnutt. December 15, 1900. https://www.newspapers.com/image/20515568.

Nietzsche, Friedrich. *Beyond Good and Evil: Prelude to a Philosophy of the Future.* Translated and edited by Marion Faber. "Introduction" by Robert C. Holub. *Oxford World's Classics.* Oxford: Oxford University Press, 1998.

Oakland Tribune (Oakland, CA). "Few Notes on Literary Topics." Review of *The Goodness of St Rocque,* by Alice Dunbar-Nelson. December 6, 1899. Evening edition. https://www.newspapers.com/image/71559927.

———. "Literary Notes from Many Fields." Review of *The Marrow of Tradition,* by Charles Waddell Chesnutt. November 9, 1901. Evening edition. https://www.newspapers.com/image/72362061.

O'Connor, Flannery. "Revelation." *The Secret Self: Short Stories by Women.* Edited by Hermione Lee, 205–24. London: J.M. Dent & Sons, 1989.

Omi, Michael, and Howard Winant. "Racial Formations." In *Race, Class, and Gender in the United States,* edited by Paula S. Rothenberg, 11–20. 5th ed. New York: Worth Publishers, 2001.

Oxford Dictionary of English Etymology. Edited by C. T. Onions. London: Oxford University Press, 1969.

Oxford Dictionary of National Biography. Edited by H. C. G. Matthew and Brian Harrison. Vol. 17. Oxford: Oxford University Press, 2004.

Page, Richard Channing Moore. "Virginia Heraldry: The Great Clan of Page." *Baltimore Sun* (Baltimore, MD), January 27, 1907. Morning edition. https://www.newspapers.com/image/214436858.

Page, Thomas Nelson. "Bred in the Bone." New York: Charles Scribner's Sons, 1891.

———. *Gordon Keith.* New York: Charles Scribner's Sons, 1910.

———. *In Ole Virginia; Or Marse Chan and Other Stories.* 1887. Reprinted, with an introduction by Clyde N. Wilson. Nashville, TN: J.S. Sanders and Company, 1991.

———. *John Marvel Assistant.* New York: Charles Scribner's Sons, 1910.

———. *The Old South: Essays Social and Political.* 1892. Facsimile of the first edition. New York: Cosimo, 2008.

———. *On Newfound River.* New York: Charles Scribner's Sons, 1891.

———. *Red Rock: A Chronicle of Reconstruction.* New York: Grosset & Dunlap, 1904.

Payne, William Morton. Review of *The Deliverance: A Romance of the Virginia Tobacco Fields,* by Ellen Glasgow. *The Dial: A Semi-monthly Journal of Criticism, Discussion, and Information* XXXVI (1904): 118–19. http://www.hathitrust.org.

———. Review of *On Newfound River,* by Thomas Nelson Page. *The Dial: A Monthly Journal of Current Literature* XII (1891): 278–79. http://hathitrust.org.

Peattie, Elia W. "Among the New Books." Review *The Miller of Old Church,* by Ellen Glasgow. *Chicago Daily Tribune* (Chicago, IL), June 24, 1911. https://www.newspapers.com/image/28584140.

Pinehurst Outlook (Pinehurst, NC). "In the World of Books." Review of *On Newfound River,* by Thomas Nelson Page. February 16, 1907. https://www.newspapers.com/image/67842329.

Pittsburgh Post (Pittsburgh, PA). "The Year's Most Notable Book." Review of *The House behind the Cedars,* by Charles Waddell Chesnutt. December 2, 1900. Morning edition. https://www.newspapers.com/image/86547774.

Pollio, Vitruvius. *The Ten Books on Architecture.* Translated by Richard Schofield. Introduced by Robert Tavernor. *Penguin Classics.* London: Penguin, 2009.

Pound, Ezra. *The Spirit of Romance.* Introduced by Richard Sieburth. New York: New Directions, 2005.

Punter, David. *Gothic Pathologies: The Text, the Body, and the Law.* Basingstoke: Macmillan, 1998.

Reaney, P. H, and R. M. Wilson., eds. *A Dictionary of English Surnames.* 3rd ed. Oxford University Press, 2005.

"Recent Fiction." Review of *Gordon Keith,* by Thomas Nelson Page. *The Dial: A Semi-Monthly Journal of Literary Criticism, Discussion, and Information.* XXXV (July–December 1903): 66–67. http://www.internetarchive.org.

Richardson, Thomas. "Local Color in Louisiana." In *The History of Southern Literature,* edited by Louis D. Rubin Jr., Blyden Jackson, Rayburn S. Moore, Lewis P. Simpson, and Thomas Daniel Young, 199–208. Baton Rouge: Louisiana State University Press, 1985.

Richmond Dispatch (Richmond, VA). "Raking a Libeller." Review of *The Marrow of Tradition,* by Charles Waddell Chesnutt. December 15, 1901. https://www.news papers.com/image/92976317.

Richmond Times (Richmond, VA). "Books and Authors." Review of *The House behind the Cedars,* by Charles Waddell Chesnutt. December 9, 1900. https://www.news papers.com/image/79926299.

Robinson, Angelo Rich. "Race, Place, and Space: Remaking Whiteness in the Post-Reconstruction South." *Southern Literary Journal* 35, no. 1 (2002): 97–107. http://www.jstor.org/stable/20078351.

Robinson, Lori. "Region and Race: National Identity and the Southern Past." In *A Companion to the Regional Literatures of America,* edited by Charles L. Crow, 57–73. Oxford: Blackwell, 2003.

Rodgers, Daniel T. *As a City on a Hill: The Story of America's Most Famous Lay Sermon.* Princeton, NJ: Princeton University Press, 2018.

Roediger, David R. *Towards the Abolition of Whiteness.* London: Verso, 1994.

———. *The Wages of Whiteness: Race and the Making of the American Working Class.* London: Verso, 1991.

Ronell, Avital. *The Telephone Book: Technology, Schizophrenia, Electric Speech.* Lincoln: University of Nebraska Press, 1989.

Room, Adrian, ed. *Brewer's Dictionary of Names.* Oxford: Helicon, 1997.

San Francisco Call (San Francisco, CA). "Her Latest Book, 'Virginia', Shatters Old Ideal of Womanhood." Review of *Virginia,* by Ellen Glasgow. May, 5, 1913. https://www.newspapers.com/image/82709479.

———. "The Miller of Old Church." Review of *The Miller of Old Church,* by Ellen Glasgow. August 6, 1911. https://www.newspapers.com/image/82707277.

———. "New Volumes for Winter Evenings." Review of *John Marvel Assistant*, by Thomas Nelson Page. November 21, 1909. https://www.newspapers.com/image/87853181.

Saxton, Alexander. "Blackface Minstrelsy and Jacksonian Ideology." *American Quarterly* 27, no. 1 (1975): 3–28. DOI: 10.2307/2711892.

Schmidt, Peter. "Walter Scott, Postcolonial Theory, and New South Literature." *Mississippi Quarterly* 56 (2003): 545–54. http://www.jstor.org/stable/26476805.

Scott, Sir Walter. *The Fair Maid of Perth or St. Valentine's Day*. New York: John B. Alden, 1885.

———. *Ivanhoe*. 1819. Edited by A.N. Wilson. Harmondsworth, UK: Penguin, 1982.

———. *Rob Roy*. London: J.M. Dent & Sons, 1966.

———. *Waverley; or, 'Tis Sixty Years Since*. Oxford: Oxford University Press, 1998.

Scranton Republican (Scranton, PA). "Literary Notes." Review of *Red Rock*, by Thomas Nelson Page. November 12, 1898. Morning edition. https://www.newspapers.com/image/48210721.

Shakespeare, William. *The New Penguin Shakespeare: Macbeth*. Edited by G. K. Hunter. London: Penguin, 1967.

Shelley, Mary. "Author's Introduction to the Standard Novels Edition." 1831. In *Frankenstein or the Modern Prometheus*. The 1818 text, edited by Marilyn Butler, 192–97. Oxford: Oxford University Press, 1998.

Sheridan, Alan. "Translator's Note." In *Écrits: A Selection*. Translated by Alan Sheridan, i–xiv. London: Routledge, 2009.

Sheshadri-Crooks, Kalpana. *Desiring Whiteness: A Lacanian Analysis of Race*. London: Routledge, 2000.

Simms, William Gilmore. *Guy Rivers: A Tale of Georgia*. New York: Harper & Brothers, 1834.

———. *Woodcraft; or, Hawks about the Dovecote; a Story of the South at the Close of Revolution*. New York: W.J. Widdleton, 1854.

Smith, Felipe. *American Body Politics: Race, Gender, and Black Literary Renaissance*. Athens: The University of Georgia Press, 1998.

Smith, Lindsay Claire. *Indians, Environment, and Identity on the Borders of American Literature: From Faulkner and Morrison to Walker and Silko*. New York: Palgrave Macmillan, 2008.

Smith, Samuel M. "The New and the Old South: A Review of Page's Popular Book 'In Ole Virginia.'" *Weekly State Chronicle* (Raleigh, NC). October 27, 1887. https://www.newspapers.com/image/56761211.

Snoad, Harold, dir. *Keeping up Appearances*. BBC, 1990–1995.

Sollors, Werner. *Neither Black Nor White: Thematic Explorations of Interracial Literature*. New York: Oxford University Press, 1997.

"Talk about New Books." Review of *On Newfound River*, by Thomas Nelson Page. *Catholic World* 54, no. 319 (October 1891): 134–50. http://www.internetarchive.org.

Tate, Allen. "Religion and the Old South." *Collected Essays*, 305–22. Denver: Alan Swallow, 1959.

———. "The New Provincialism." *Collected Essays*. Denver: Alan Swallow, 1959. 282–93.

Taylor, Tate, dir. *The Help*. Walt Disney Studios Motion Pictures, 2011.

Theweleit, Klaus. *Male Fantasies: Male Bodies: Psychoanalyzing the White Terror.* Translated by Erica Carter and Chris Turner. Foreword by Anson Rabinach and Jessica Benjamin. Vol. 2. Minneapolis, MN: University of Minnesota Press, 1989.

Times-Democrat (New Orleans, LA). "New Publications: The Times-Democrat's Review of the Latest Books." July 27, 1913. https://www.newspapers.com/image/183521084.

Twain, Mark. *The Adventures of Huckleberry Finn.* Edited by Jane Ogborn. Cambridge: Cambridge University Press, 1995.

———. *Life on the Mississippi.* Introduced by Petr Barta. London: Wordsworth, 2012.

———. *Pudd'nhead Wilson.* Edited by Malcolm Bradbury. Penguin Classics. Harmondsworth, UK: Penguin, 1969.

Vancouver Daily World (Vancouver, British Columbia). "The Book Shelf." Review of *Virginia*, by Ellen Glasgow. June 28, 1913. https://www.newspapers.com/image/64397609.

Virginian-Pilot (Norfolk, VA). "Trio of Southern Writers." Review of *The Voice of the People*, by Ellen Glasgow. July 6, 1900. https://www.newspapers.com/image/68118508.

Vološinov, Valentin Nikolaevich. *Freudianism: A Marxist Critique.* Translated by I. R. Titunik. New York: Academic Press, 1976.

Warren, Robert Penn. *All the King's Men.* New York: Harcourt Brace and Company, 1946.

Washington Evening Star (Washington, DC). "With the Books." Review of *The Colonel's Dream*, by Charles Waddell Chesnutt. September 16, 1905. https://www.newspapers.com/image/145552936.

———. "With ye Books." Review of *The Marrow of Tradition*, by Charles Waddell Chesnutt. November 9, 1901. https://www.newspapers.com/image/207674545.

Washington Times (Washington, DC). "Latest Work of Mr. Page." Review of Thomas Nelson Page's *Gordon Keith.* July 19, 1903. https://www.newspapers.com/image/80644350.

———. "Literary Notes." Review of *The Goodness of St Rocque*, by Alice Dunbar-Nelson. September 3, 1899. https://www.newspapers.com/image/80854606.

Watson Devon, Ritchie, Jr. *Normans and Saxons: Southern Race Mythology and the Intellectual History of the American Civil War.* Baton Rouge: Louisiana State University Press, 2008.

Weiss, Allen. S. "Ten Theses on Monsters and Monstrosity." *TDR (1988-)* 48, no.1 (2004): 124–25. http://www.jstor.org/stable/4488535.

Wilde, Oscar. *The Picture of Dorian Gray.* Harmondsworth, UK: Penguin, 1983.

Williams, Sylvanie F. "Preface." *Violets and Other Tales.* 1895. Charleston: BiblioBazaar, 2008.

Wilson, Matthew. *Whiteness in the Novels of Charles Waddell Chesnutt.* Jackson: The University Press of Mississippi, 2004.

Winthrop, John. "A Modell of Christian Charity." 1630. In *Early American Writing*, edited by Giles Gunn, 108–12. Harmondsworth, UK: Penguin, 1994.

Wiswall, J. T. "Causes of Aristocracy." *DeBow's Review* 28, no. 5 (1860): 551–66. *Making of America Journal Articles.* http://quod.lib.umich.edu/m/moajrnl/acg1336.1-28.005/555.

Young, Elizabeth. *Black Frankenstein: The Making of an American Metaphor*. New York: New York University Press, 2008.
Young, Robert. *White Mythologies: Writing History and the West*. London: Routledge, 1995.
Žižek, Slavoj. "Love Thy Neighbor? No, Thanks!." In *The Psychoanalysis of Race*, edited by Christopher Lane, 154–75. New York: Columbia University Press, 1998.
———. *The Plague of Fantasies*. London: Verso, 1997.

WEBSITES

http://www.burkespeerage.com/
http://chroniclingamerica.loc.gov/
http://www.georgiaencyclopedia.org
https://www.hathitrust.org
http://itnernetarchive.org
http://www.jstor.org
http://onlinebooks.library.upenn.edu/webbin/serial?id=thedial
https://quod.lib.umich.edu/m/moajrnl/
http://www.surnamedb.com/Surname/Ochiltree

INDEX

Aanerud, Rebecca, 207n11
Adams, Jessica, 4, 206n6, 214n40
Adorno, Theodore, 218n28
agriculture, 19. *See also* Allen, Theodore
Allardyce, Alexander, 213n33
Allen, James Lane, 227n15
Allen, Theodore, 205n5, 206n6, 207n5, 209n20, 211nn1-2, 218n31
Allen, Walter, 233n4
Alsop, George, 89, 221n27
Andrews, William L., 59, 216n2, 217n6
aristocracy, 14, 31, 44, 63, 137, 180, 199, 201
    boundaries, 66
    English, 228n8, 229n20
    heroism, 82
    homogeneity, 99
    pseudo, 160
Aristotle, 9-10
Aspiz, Harold, 233n4
Auerbach, Erich, 196, 234n13

Babb, Valerie, 6, 7, 233n4
Baldick, Chris, 140, 229n28
Baldwin, David, 218n33
Barnhill, David Landis, 216n35
Barolini, Helen, 214n47
Basset Hound, 155
Baudrillard, Jean, 216n30
Berger, Maurice, 207n11
Bhabha, Homi K., 215n15
Bible, the, 214n36, 216n34
    biblical ideals, 8, 11, 143, 156
Birth of a Nation, The, 12
blackface, 226n25
blackness, 128
    conception of, 123
    instability of, 72
    metaphorical, 89, 90, 94, 97, 100, 103, 105, 106-7, 117, 127, 192
    visibility of, 3, 4, 34, 66, 95
Bois, W.E.B. du, 66, 218n27
Brigham, Linda, 160, 229n20
Brown, Bill, 227n8. *See* monstrosity
Browne, Sir Thomas, 163
Buchan, David, 213n33
"buck," 156, 206n8
Burrison, John A. *See* "crackers"
Butler, Judith, 6, 206n8

Cabell, James Branch, 99
    Cords of Vanity, The, 170
    High Place, The, 79, 85, 120
    Jurgen, 120
    Let Me Lie, 80
Cable, George Washington, 202-3
cakewalk, 128, 225n9
Caldwell, Erskine, 3, 161
Calhoun, John C., 4
capitalism, 13, 47, 179, 180
    vampire and, 220n24
carpetbagger, 88, 92, 97, 128, 189, 220n24
Chastellux, Marquis de, 5
Chesnutt, Charles Waddell, 3
    biography, 57-59, 216n2
    Colonel's Dream, The, 177-88, 197, 202
    Conjure Woman and Other Conjure Tales, The, 15, 188-89; "The Goophered Grapevine," 189-90; "Mars Jeems's Nightmare," 191-92; "Sis Becky's Pickaninny," 190-91
    House behind the Cedars, The, 15, 59, 63, 65-71, 73, 180, 198, 202
    Journals, The, 57, 58-59, 122, 202

desire, 140

Chesnutt, Charles Waddell (*continued*)
  Mandy Oxendine, 59–65, 130, 180, 202, 217n6
  Marrow of Tradition, The, 120–32, 180, 202
chivalry, 4, 7, 8, 23, 26, 29, 89, 120, 209n23, 234n13
Clarkson, A., 10, 92, 106
"clayeaters," 208n14
context, 20, 45, 87, 156, 162, 163, 170
Cooke, John Esten, 153, 222n5, 227n15
counterhistory, 122
courtly love, 7, 89, 114, 198
"crackers," 208n14
Creole, 72, 133, 202, 203, 226n41
"Cuba: The March of Empire and the Course of Trade," 9

darkness, 51, 97, 126, 127, 129, 130, 196
Darwin, Charles, 43
Darwinism, 42, 46, 54
Dayan, Colin, 69, 70, 219n38, 216n14
De Certeau, Michel
  altitude, 33
  city, the, 20
  place, sense of, 19
  proper names, 39
Dekker, George. *See* Scott, Sir Walter: historical novel
Derrida, Jacques
  context, 205n6
  différance, 169, 170
  example, 149
  history, detotalizing of, 207n12
  identity, 208n15
  inheritance, politics of, 79
  repetition, 85
  specter, 79, 89
  supplement, 222n42
  truth, 208n17
Dexter, Marshall, 21
dialect, 22, 35, 59, 61, 189

Dickinson, Emily, 214n43, 214n47
Dillard, R.H.W., 42, 99
Donne, John, 43
Dunbar-Nelson, Alice, 3, 11–12, 15, 75, 137–38, 140, 195, 197, 202
  biography, 71–72, 219n40, 234n23
  "In Our Neighborhood," 73–74
  "La Juanita," 193
  "Little Miss Sophie," 133–34
  "Stones of the Village, The," 132–33, 192–93, 211n39
  "Tony's Wife," 74
duplex corpus Christi, 156
Dyer, Richard, 7, 8, 52, 89, 94, 138

Ellison, Ralph. *See* minstrelsy
Emerson, Ralph Waldo, 9
environment, 9, 10, 20, 33, 35, 47, 83, 164, 196, 208n19
eugenics, 62, 113, 159, 161
Evernden, Neil, 45
Evola, Julius, 33, 35, 214n36

Fabi, Giulia M., 68, 218n32, 232n24
Fanon, Frantz, 88, 95, 97, 117, 123, 197–98
fantasy, 142–43, 148, 149, 151, 186. *See* Žižek
Faulkner, William, 3
  Absalom, Absalom!, 200–201
  Requiem for a Nun, 34
  Sound and the Fury, The, 197, 199
femininity, 116, 199
  ideal of, 7, 59, 90, 92, 94, 112–13
  Northern, 10
  Southern, 93, 102–3, 106, 160, 170
Fender, Stephen, 233n5
Fichte, Johan Gottlieb. *See* heritage: Anglo-Saxon
Fiedler, Leslie A., 196
Fitzgerald, F. Scott, 198, 201
Foucault, Michel, 102, 110

Frankenberg, Ruth. *See* whiteness: heterogeneity
Franklin, Benjamin, 5, 6–7, 208n14

Gaines, Jane, 226n1. *See also* South, the: socioeconomic conditions
Gardner, Sarah E., 43, 224n2
Garland, Hamlin, 12
Gilder, Jeanette L., 31
Ginsberg, Elaine K. *See* passing
Glasgow, Ellen, 3, 5, 12, 13
  biography, 42
  Battle-Ground, The, 13, 43, 97–109, 110, 115, 119, 154, 155, 160, 170, 200
  Certain Measure, A, 12, 42, 43, 44, 74, 97, 99, 102, 110, 119, 120, 154, 166, 167, 168, 170
  Deliverance, The, 41–55, 57, 138, 140, 154, 197, 201
  Miller of Old Church, The, 59, 109–17, 119, 154, 157, 167, 175, 198
  Romance of a Plain Man, The, 98
  Sheltered Life, The, 102
  Virginia, 166–76, 177, 201
  Voice of the People, The, 13, 43, 98, 154–66, 177, 188, 197, 201
  Woman Within, 5, 42, 98, 201, 206n8
Gone with the Wind, 2
Gray, Richard, 12, 43, 99, 209n20

Halberstam, Judith, 142. *See also* monstrosity
Hale, Grace Elizabeth, 11
  black-figure imagery, 207n8
  See also South, the: Old South
"hands," 206n8
Hardwig, Bill, 12, 23, 24
Harris, Corra, 178, 195, 227n15
hart, 1, 73, 205n1
Hart of Dixie, 1–2, 3, 14
haunting, 36, 85, 93, 100, 203
Hegel, Georg, 6, 67

Help, The, 2
"helpers," 206n8
Henry VIII, 141
heritage, 26, 27, 39, 40, 43, 50, 52, 75, 120, 164
  alienation, 200
  ambiguity, 68, 70
  ambivalence, 112
  Anglo-Saxon, 5, 7, 20, 154, 207n10, 210n34
  aristocratic, 37, 74, 82, 91, 99, 123
  cultural, 120
  genteel, 9–10, 14, 41, 53, 114, 124, 179
  place and, 34–35, 46, 47, 65, 84, 198, 199
  Quaker, 7, 17, 129
  Scottish, 31, 63, 69, 217n18
hero
  American, 3, 198, 199
  Southern, 199, 200
Hill, Mike, 5
Hobsbawm, Eric, 13, 19
Hodes, Martha, 221n27
hooks, bell, 207n8
Horkheimer, Max. *See* Adorno, Theodore
Howells, Dean. *See* realism
Hull, Gloria T., 71, 72, 211n39, 219n40
Hundley, Daniel, 134, 137
hybridity, 26

identity, 6, 13, 15, 62, 200, 208n15, 214n40
  American, 200, 233n5
  Southern, 3
Isenberg, Nancy, 224n4. *See also* place: class; South, the: settlement

Jefferson, Thomas, 113, 124, 225n21
Jones, Gavin, 35. *See also* Creole
jouissance, 195

Kantorowicz, Ernst, 156, 232n26
Kennedy, John Pendleton, 14
Kierkegaard, Søren, 183

Knadler, Stephen P., 123, 131, 225n15
Kojève, Alexandre, 6, 207n12. *See also* totality

Lacan, Jacques, 139, 140, 208n28. See also *objet petit a*
land, 8, 9, 20, 26, 79, 134, 138, 199
 possession of, 9, 11, 19, 20, 26, 27, 28, 30, 43–44, 46, 65, 84, 86, 143, 184
 relationship with, 37, 54, 86, 159
Lefebvre, Henri, 27, 33, 83
local color, 12, 42, 139
Lost Cause, 13, 41, 88, 168, 210n27
Lott, Eric, 208n18
Lukács, Georg, 98

Macherey, Pierre, 73, 219n46
MacKethan, Lucinda, 87
Marguia, Edward. *See* "shades of whiteness"
masculinity, 10, 90
 masculine ideal, 7, 160, 176
May, Chad T., 50
McDowell, Frederick, 42, 45, 98, 104, 154, 224n45, 228n6
Melville, Herman, 5, 196, 197
metonymy, 33, 39, 93, 180, 203. *See also* plantation house
mimicry, 47. *See* Bhabha, Homi K.
minstrelsy, 206n8, 225n29
monster, 140, 227n7
monstrosity, 140, 142, 144, 146, 163–64, 191–92, 227n8, 230n39
 inner, 188
 permeability of, 142, 144, 193
Moore, Quitman J., 9
Morrison, Toni, 72, 221n41
 Playing in the Dark, 3
"Mose," 206n8
mountains, 35, 36, 37. *See also* Evola, Julius
Murphy, Patrick D., 9, 19, 20, 46

nature, 35, 37. *See also* mountains
Nietzsche, Friedrich, 157, 163, 185
"nigger," 3, 72, 128, 185, 189, 191
 "turn nigger," 88, 97, 128, 132
 white, 132
North, the, 4, 24, 29, 36, 41, 60, 120, 124, 196, 214n46
 concept of, 9
 South, the, comparison with, 10, 47, 83, 86, 87, 179, 182, 185
 "Yankee," 10, 168, 210n27, 220n24

objet petit a, 150, 228n29
O'Connor, Flannery, 3, 108
otherness, 22, 139, 208n18

Page, Richard Channing Moore, 21
Page, Thomas Nelson, 3, 9, 20, 74, 75, 137, 178, 195, 200, 203
 biography, 21–22
 Gordon Keith, 13, 22, 30–40, 41, 57, 80, 83, 140, 145, 150, 151, 197, 199
 In Ole Virginia, 14, 22, 23, 25, 30, 34, 35; "Marse Chan," 22–23, 24, 25; "Meh Lady," 23–24; "Unc' Edinburg's Drowndin," 23
 John Marvel, 137, 138–51, 153, 188, 201
 On Newfound River, 25–30, 31, 33, 39, 80, 86
 Red Rock, 13, 22, 30, 80–96, 97, 99, 128, 139, 145, 149, 150, 151, 156, 165, 197, 198, 199
passing, 34, 49, 57, 70, 74, 128, 218n32
past, the, 9, 11, 13, 15, 20, 50, 197–98, 200, 201, 203
Picture of Dorian Gray, The, 164
"pineys," 208n14
plantation house, 12, 26, 30, 37, 61, 71, 147
 absence of, 66, 75
 continuity, 197, 214n40
 duality of, 57

monument, 11, 16, 41, 75, 183, 197
setting, 32, 33, 83
place
  class, 28, 29, 83
  history, 34
  introduction of, 2, 14, 26, 31, 44, 65, 83, 211n37
  naming of, 31, 32, 81, 99
  participation in, 46
  sense of, 2, 21, 80
  whiteness, 6, 15
  See also De Certeau, Michel; Lefebvre, Henri
Pollio, Vitruvius, 9, 10
"poor whites," 5, 63, 121, 165, 208n14

realism, 43
"redneck," 44, 208n14, 213n25
regionalism. *See* local color
repetition, 140, 178, 183. *See also* Derrida, Jacques; Kierkegaard, Søren
Richardson, Thomas, 234n23
Robinson, Lori, 211n37
Ronell, Avital, 146, 220n18

"sandhillers," 63, 70, 71, 208n14
Schmidt, Peter, 68
Scott, Sir Walter, 4, 14, 85, 95, 98, 100, 103, 213n32
  Fair Maid of Perth, The, 82, 221n29
  historical novel, 211n38
  Ivanhoe, 67
  Waverley, 13, 32
Shakespeare, William, 4
Shelley, Mary, 142
Simms, William Gilmore, 14
simulacrum, 21, 53, 67, 216n30
slavery, 1, 3–5, 8, 9, 13, 20, 26, 206n8
  attitudes to, 205n6
  master/slave dialectic, 218n28 (*see also* Kojève, Alexandre)
Smith, Felipe, 90, 104, 218n31

social Darwinism, 54
social determinism, 42, 54, 164, 201
Sollors, Werner, 34
Song of the South, 2
South, the
  "Adventurers," 209n20
  chivalry, 8, 9–10, 20, 36 (*see also* chivalry)
  climate, 9, 10, 19, 166
  Old South, the, 11, 12, 19–20, 42, 79–80, 137, 196, 210n28
  "Planters," 209n20
  socioeconomic conditions, 4, 5, 12, 43, 122, 205n6
  settlement, 5, 9, 47, 209n20, 211n2, 224n4, 226n1
  way of life, 10, 19, 41, 119
spectrality. *See* Derrida, Jacques
"squatters," 208n14
stereotyping, 37, 38, 144, 205n6
subjectivity, 45, 164, 169
synecdoche, 74, 92, 112

Tate, Allen, 9, 12
Theweleit, Klaus, 90, 92, 125, 134, 224n49
totality, 93, 125, 207n12, 228n32. *See also* Kojève, Alexandre; Theweleit, Klaus
tradition, 2, 19, 20, 198
  continuity of, 20, 53, 82, 85
tragic mulatta, 59
truth, 8, 83, 85, 89, 110, 133–34, 196, 208n17, 228n32. *See also* Nietzsche, Friedrich
Twain, Mark, 13, 103
  Adventures of Huckleberry Finn, The, 198
  Life on the Mississippi, 13
  Pudd'nhead Wilson, 3–4, 103

United Daughters of Confederacy, 119, 120, 224n2

vampire, 220n24
Vološinov, Valentin, 47

Warren, Robert Penn, 3, 143
white mythology, 3
"white trash," 90, 199, 213n25
whiteness, 1, 10, 11, 13, 25, 75
　ambivalence, 3, 15, 90, 97, 103, 108, 114, 117, 131
　aspiration, 15, 73, 74
　blood, 8, 20, 23, 24, 30, 133–34, 138, 143, 202–3
　breeding, 8, 20, 24, 26, 30, 43, 44, 98, 99, 155, 200
　characteristics of, 8, 26
　Christianity, 7–8, 20, 89, 95, 127, 138, 148, 208n18 (see also Dyer, Richard)
　color, 1, 3, 4, 5, 7, 34, 59, 110, 120, 123, 132, 205n5,
　composite, 24, 26, 125
　continuity, 9, 13, 14
　death, 8, 70, 86, 109, 148
　definitions, 5–6, 207n11
　desire for, 6
　gentility, 20, 28, 33, 44, 62, 75, 79, 83
　heredity, 20, 41, 43, 65, 123, 139, 164, 202
　heterogeneity, 6, 138, 207n11

imitation, 3, 128
meritocracy, 15, 64, 138, 192
optics, 7
politics of, 144
privilege, 4–6, 7, 8, 121
race, 2, 3, 4, 88, 197
religion (see Christianity)
reproduction, 9, 89, 97, 110, 117, 139
"shades of," 6, 208n13
southern gentleman, 8, 13, 19, 25, 79, 90, 93, 120, 123, 126, 138, 156, 197, 199
southern lady, 8, 19, 47, 79, 90, 94, 96, 120, 123, 138, 156, 197
visibility of, 5, 73
whitenesses, 6, 179
Wilson, Matthew, 59, 122
Winthrop, John, 10, 214n36
Wiswall, J. T., 10

Young, Elizabeth, 140
Young, Robert. See totality

Žižek, Slavoj, 142, 179, 184, 195, 228n29, 232n20